TOCQUEVILLE UNVEILED

TOCQUEVILLE UNVEILED

The Historian and His Sources for
The Old Regime and the Revolution

ROBERT T. GANNETT JR.

The University of Chicago Press   Chicago & London

Robert T. Gannett Jr. is an independent scholar who has taught at the University of Chicago and the Institute for Community Empowerment.

The University of Chicago Press, Chicago 60637
The University of Chicago Press, Ltd., London
© 2003 by The University of Chicago
All rights reserved. Published 2003
Printed in the United States of America

12 11 10 09 08 07 06 05 04 03   1 2 3 4 5
ISBN: 0-226-28108-6 (cloth)

Library of Congress Cataloging-in-Publication Data

Gannett, Robert T., Jr.
Tocqueville unveiled : the historian and his sources for The Old Regime and the Revolution / Robert T. Gannett Jr.
p.   cm.
Includes bibliographical references and index.
ISBN 0-226-28108-6 (cloth : alk. paper)
1. Tocqueville, Alexis de, 1805–1859. Ancien régime et la Révolution—Sources.   I. Title.
DC138.T6344G36 2003
944.04—dc21

2002042978

To my father, and in memory of my mother

CONTENTS

Acknowledgments ix

List of Abbreviations xi

1. **Tocqueville's Historical Method**
   Continuing Themes Shaped by Discontinuous Means 1

2. **Tocqueville and Napoleon**
   Imperial History Deferred 15

3. **Tocqueville and Feudal Rights**
   A Bridge to the Old Regime 39

4. **Tocqueville's Burke**
   From Foreign Observer to Primary Protagonist 57

5. **Tocqueville and Administrative Centralization**
   Detecting Its Deep Roots in the Archives of Tours 79

6. **Tocqueville's Study of Opinion**
   Assessing Prerevolutionary "Spirit" in France 99

7. **Tocqueville's Elusive Balance**
   Art in the Service of Liberty 131

8. **Tocqueville and History**
   Telling Liberty's Revolutionary Tale 151

Appendix: Tocqueville's Endnotes for *The Old Regime* 163

Notes 167

Selected Bibliography 221

Index 231

F rançois Furet first suggested that I recount the saga of Tocqueville's shifting archival inquiries that led to *The Old Regime and the Revolution,* and he provided me with the necessary materials in Paris from 1995 to 1997 to make such a study possible. Thanks to his vision of this project, I received the opportunity of a lifetime: to retrace Tocqueville's ever discreet probes with Furet's ever unstinting advice and assistance. My gratitude to Professor Furet for envisioning this book and making my archival studies in Paris possible is equaled only by my regret that he died just as I was completing those studies.

I first read Tocqueville as a Returning Scholar at the University of Chicago in 1988 in Ralph Lerner's celebrated course. Professor Lerner's verve as a teacher and his precision as a textual scholar inspired me to seek admission to the Committee on Social Thought where, aided by his unwavering support and judicious counsel, I completed my studies, a dissertation, and this book.

In the course of this work, I have benefited from the generous assistance of many other individuals. Keith Baker provided focus and structure to my early probes of the *cahiers de doléances.* Professor Baker, Bronislaw Baczko, and Stuart Warner read my text at different stages, gave me valuable feedback, and initiated the crucial steps that led to its transformation into a book. At the University of Chicago Press, John Tryneski expressed a lively interest in my project and encouraged me to take the necessary steps to refine and strengthen my arguments. I thank Seymour Drescher and an anonymous reader of the Press who provided extensive, discerning critiques that enabled me to broaden and clarify my analysis of Tocqueville's historical method. Their efforts were certainly "worth the detour" they sent me on, stretching back in time to *Democracy in America* and forward to Tocqueville's sequel to *The Old Regime and the Revolution*. My manuscript editor, Alice Bennett, ably improved the pace and consistency of my text. Grateful for such assistance, I am solely responsible for the errors that may remain.

Central to my project were my two years of research in France. There, M. le comte Guy d'Hérouville approved my access to the Tocqueville Archives and welcomed my family and me to the Tocqueville family château in Normandy for an unforgettable luncheon in June 1997. Françoise Mélonio graciously provided me with notes and a detailed chronology describing the Archives, plus initial assistance in deciphering Tocqueville's cramped script. Roland and Marige Assathiany patiently reviewed my French transcriptions of Tocquevillian passages. They and members of the Auguste Potié and Raymond de Moustier families extended bonds of family friendship that now span several generations.

My work on this book necessitated an extended leave of absence from my job as a professional community organizer in Chicago. Throughout this time, I have benefited from the staunch support of my longtime associate Michael Smith and community leaders Joyce Zick, Joe Crutchfield, Vern and Pat Vader, Jean Mayer, and Diane Plotkin. Beyond the workplace, Peter and Joyce Barkin and my cousin, Robin Derby, and her husband, Andy Apter, each contributed valued encouragement and advice.

My greatest gratitude is to my family. My father and my mother, while she lived, were enthusiastic partners, directly or vicariously, in every stage of my endeavors, expecially the Parisian leg. My brother Bill and my sister Alden journeyed to Paris and Chicago with their families to remind me that each city's limits extended beyond the reading rooms of its libraries. My children, Jason, Kate, and Elizabeth, have grown up with their father's Tocquevillian pursuits; they have cheerfully shifted schools, sports, friends, and languages to accommodate my studies, demurring from the family program only on occasion. (But then in dramatic fashion!) Above all, my wife Joanne contributed her academic wisdom, spirit of adventure, love of France, and steady confidence in me, bringing joy to this project, as she has to my life.

Conversations	*Correspondence and Conversations of Alexis de Tocqueville with Nassau William Senior from 1834 to 1859.* Edited by M. C. M. Simpson. 2 vols. London: Henry S. King, 1872.
DA	*Democracy in America.* Translated, edited and with an introduction by Harvey C. Mansfield and Delba Winthrop. Chicago: University of Chicago Press, 2000.
DA (ed. Nolla)	*De la démocratie en Amérique.* Edited by Eduardo Nolla. 2 vols. Paris: Librairie Philosophique J. Vrin, 1990.
"État social et politique"	"État social et politique de la France avant et depuis 1789." Original French version of Tocqueville's 1836 essay published in *OC* (see below), vol. 2, pt. 1, 33–66.
Journeys	*Journeys to England and Ireland.* Edited by J.-P. Mayer. Translated by George Lawrence and K. P. Mayer. New Brunswick, N.J.: Transaction Books, 1988.
OC	*Alexis de Tocqueville: Oeuvres complètes.* Edited by J.-P. Mayer. 17 vols. in 28 pts. to date. Paris: Gallimard, 1951–.
OC (Beaumont)	*Oeuvres complètes d'Alexis de Tocqueville.* Edited by Gustave Beaumont. 9 vols. Paris: Michel Lévy Frères, 1864–66.
Oeuvres (Pléiade)	*Oeuvres.* Edited under the direction of André Jardin. 2 vols. to date. Paris: Bibliothèque de la Pléiade, 1991–.
OR, 1 and *OR,* 2	*The Old Regime and the Revolution.* Vol. 1: *The Complete Text.* Vol. 2: *Notes on the French Revolution and Napoleon.* Edited and with an introduction and critical apparatus by François Furet and Françoise Mélonio. Translated by Alan S. Kahan. Chicago: University of Chicago Press, 1998 and 2001.
Recollections	*Recollections: The French Revolution of 1848.* Edited by J.-P. Mayer and A. P. Kerr. Translated by George Lawrence. New Brunswick, N.J.: Transaction Books, 1987.

Review	"Political and Social Condition of France. First Article." Translated by John Stuart Mill. *London and Westminster Review*, 3 and 25 (April 1836): 137–69.
Selected Letters	*Selected Letters on Politics and Society.* Edited by Roger Boesche. Translated by James Toupin and Roger Boesche. Berkeley: University of California Press, 1985.
TA	Tocqueville Archives for *The Old Regime and the Revolution.* Tocqueville's manuscript notes for his book and unpublished sequel are contained in the following seven boxes, to which I have added each box's microfilm number(s) at the Bibliothèque nationale:

Box 39: "Handwritten MS" (9696)

Box 40: "Copy" (9697)

Box 41: "Proofs" (9698)

Box 42: "Sketches and drafts" (9699)

Box 43: "Reading notes" (9700–9703)

Box 44: "Sequel: the unfinished book—preparatory notes" (9704)

Box 45: "Sequel: the unfinished book—filed notes and initial drafted chapters" (9705–6)

Within box 43, "Reading notes," Tocqueville designated his work folders as follows:

A: "Feudal rights. Notes on administrative law"

B: "Turgot"

C: "Analysis of *cahiers*"

D: "Economists"

E: "M. Dareste"

F: "Old French laws"

H: "Archives of Tours"

I: "Old generality of Paris"

J: "France before the Revolution (miscellaneous)"

K: "Diverse ideas"

L: "Studies on England"

M: "Judgments of foreigners on the Revolution"

N: "Arthur Young"

O: "Statistical studies and others done at Tocqueville"

P: "Legislative and administrative power of the courts"

Q: "Studies on Germany"

R: "Diverse notes"

Within box 45, "Sequel," Tocqueville designated his work folders as follows:

AA: "Vague agitation of the human spirit"

BB: "1787: Various works on this year"

CC: "1788: Various works on this year"

DD: "1787, 88, 89 in Dauphiny"

EE: "1789: from the first of January to the reunion of the Estates-General"

YY: "Various notes to examine before giving a title to the folder"

TA (Beinecke)   Tocqueville Archives for *Democracy in America* at Yale University's Beinecke Library.

For my translations of Tocqueville's correspondence and *Democracy in America*, I have used *Selected Letters* and *DA* for applicable passages, with occasional changes where I saw fit. All other translations are my own. Within my text and notes, I refer readers to *OR,* 1 for passages from *The Old Regime and the Revolution*, volume 1, and to *OR,* 1 and *OR,* 2 for relevant archival documents for the book and its unfinished sequel.

TOCQUEVILLE'S HISTORICAL METHOD

Continuing Themes Shaped by

Discontinuous Means

> I think that I would do best to follow the method that I already
> used to write the book that just appeared [*The Old Regime*], and
> even the *Democracy*: . . . I take extraordinary pains to find on my
> own the facts in the documents of the time. . . . Having made
> this harvest so laboriously, I shut myself within myself, as if in
> a tightly enclosed spot, I examine with extreme attention, in a
> general review, all of these notions that I have acquired by my-
> self, I compare them, I link them, and finally I make the point
> of revealing the ideas that spontaneously have come to me in
> this lengthy process.[1]

In December 1838, revising drafts for volume 2 of his *Democracy
in America,* Alexis de Tocqueville thought to drop the persona
he had so effectively cultivated in volume 1, which melded political nonpartisanship with benign neglect of his academic peers.[2]
Within his pivotal practical chapters on local political institutions (*DA,* 485–88) and broad-based civil associations (*DA,* 489–
92), he considered launching a biting satirical sortie against the
Frenchman who reigned supreme in both the political and academic worlds of the time—François Guizot.

"A great publicist of our days," Tocqueville wrote in his draft
manuscript with reference to Guizot, had grasped the secret that
explained the Germanic barbarians' remarkable success in their
fourth-century invasions of Europe. No, the invaders did not
"exterminate" the remnant of Roman civilization in Gaul by
a strategy of direct confrontation. Rather, they simply "inter-
pos[ed] themselves" between Europe's civilized residents, thus
"isolating" them and "mak[ing] them strangers one to another."

"It is by a similar path," Tocqueville planned to warn his fellow Frenchmen, "that the men of our days could well return to barbarism, if they do not guard against it." In Tocqueville's perspective spanning fourteen centuries, France's present-day July Monarchy threatened to replicate the strategy— and the dire results—of the barbarian invaders who had destroyed early European civilization by pursuing policies that fostered political and social isolation among its populace. His satirical coup de grâce would show that it was the political Guizot—supporter of the controversial ban of 1834 on even the smallest French civil associations and of the repressive September laws of 1835—who bore a measure of responsibility for reproducing in Louis-Philippe's administration the very preconditions for barbarism that the professorial Guizot had so brilliantly limned in his earlier scholarly work. "End in this way [the chapter on] associations," Tocqueville wrote in the margin of his draft. "Turn G[uizot] against himself."[3]

To appreciate more fully Tocqueville's intended analogy of 1838, we must step back ten years to the Sorbonne, where, from December 1828 to July 1829, then-Professor Guizot delivered the second cycle of his celebrated course of lectures on the "History of Civilization in France" to a rapt audience of students that may even have included the young Tocqueville.[4] In his eighth lecture of this sequence, Guizot explained that the fourth-century barbarian invasions belied their contemporary Western victims' views of them as "*flood, earthquake, conflagration*"; rather, their true nature consisted of an insidious process of "dissolution and paralysis" that gnawed at the innards of society under an exterior of apparent normality. To be sure, the barbarians had destroyed some of the physical bonds linking Western civilization—a road here, a field there, all elements of the interdependence people had become accustomed to. But more important, Guizot emphasized, they had mutilated the psychic bonds that typically allowed each man to sustain a measure of self-awareness in space and in time. By their doing so, he concluded, "the social organization was attacked; the limbs were no longer attached to one another; the muscles no longer worked, the blood no longer circulated freely nor surely in the veins . . . as the most solid body is disorganized by the continual infiltration of a foreign substance."[5] It was his analysis of this disruption of society's "organic harmony" that marked Guizot's unique brand of philosophical history, providing his most precocious student with important lessons for his own future studies. It was the professor's inability in ensuing years to recognize its practical ramifications that precipitated that same student's strident censure.

When he finally published volume 2 of *Democracy in America* in 1840, Tocqueville reverted to his original impartial persona of volume 1, dropping from his text any reference to the contradiction he deplored in Guizot's teachings and actions on barbarism and association. He left only a single trace in II:2:5 of his extended twisting and turning of this theme, issuing an innocuous warning, stripped of all historical and political context, that a people who failed to acquire the skill of collaboration on great projects "would soon return to barbarism" (*DA*, 490). Although dismissed from Tocqueville's text, Guizot hardly disappeared from Tocqueville's rhetorical repertoire as a major, if often unacknowledged, disputant. I will return in chapter 2 to examine further the complicated nature of Tocqueville's historical debt to Guizot.

I have chosen to commence my study of Tocqueville's method and sources for *The Old Regime and the Revolution,* published in 1856, with this Guizotian anecdote from 1838, since I find it so characteristic of the craftsmanship that marks Tocqueville's entire career as a historian. In directing his rhetorical rapier at Guizot, Tocqueville demonstrated his propensity for "riposte," a strategy through which he sharpened and focused his own theses to combat a host of acknowledged and unacknowledged interlocutors. By ruminating for almost a decade on Guizot's portrait of a dysfunctional society invaded by foreign agents, he disclosed the protracted gestation that eventually gave birth to those singular historical analogies that we today find so striking and instructive. We see here as well his insistence on citizen participation as the precondition for a free and civilized society. We observe his anger at those who fail to recognize this precept. And we encounter an early example of his belief that the bonds uniting civilized men are tenuous and subject to rupture, with a "soft" version of debilitating psychic despotism peculiarly apt to cause civilization to revert to barbarism.

Beyond my own list of such constants, scholars have drawn attention to a host of other factors that testify to this striking continuity in Tocqueville's historical method and philosophical reflections throughout his career. François Furet asserts, for example, that Tocqueville conceived "an ensemble of problems . . . early on [that would] monopolize all of his intellectual activities from *Democracy* to the *Ancien Régime.*"[6] James T. Schleifer suggests that we should assume "no profound disjuncture of philosophy or methodology among Tocqueville's books."[7] Based on such parallels, Eduardo Nolla has even advanced the sweeping claim that he tends to find in Tocqueville's works "one *Democracy* that extends itself from 1835 to 1859."[8]

Nolla's claim goes too far, I believe, or at the very least it poses a risk in any review of Tocqueville's larger oeuvre. For it glosses over the discontinuous, unsettled, and we might even say quixotic qualities of Tocqueville's historical investigations, evident in both *Democracy in America* and *The Old*

Regime. Tocqueville's method—of both investigation and composition—is one of starts and stops, marked by conceptual blocks and writing blocks, with false leads to blind alleys followed by abrupt reversals based on new leads, often revealed through chance encounters with contemporary personal interviewees or prerevolutionary archival ones. Such shifts in his investigations led him in 1838 to "throw almost one hundred pages [of his drafts from 1836] in the fire,"[9] as we will see in our discussion of *Democracy in America* in this chapter. As we will see in chapter 7, such shifts in his strategy of composition led him sixteen years later to develop a ninety-page index encapsulating more than two years of archival probes *after* he had drafted the relevant chapters in *The Old Regime*.

Tocqueville listened to and learned from his "interviewees," but within conceptual frameworks shaped by his prior reflections. Thus, while in America he formulated the questions for his oral interviews by researching the "constitutive elements at home" of French society so that he might better "decompose [American] society a priori."[10] In turn, both of these research components fit within a preconceived system of ideas that was guided by his recognition dating from 1825 of society's inevitable march "toward an almost complete equality of conditions."[11] Back home in France, Tocqueville's probes of prerevolutionary voices for his 1836 essay operated within a similar conceptual system organized around the poles of "democracy" and "aristocracy," mentioned more than ninety times in the essay. As Tocqueville progressed in his historical work in the 1850s for *The Old Regime*, he became, I will argue, a more consciously "archival" thinker. To write the book that he believed needed to be presented to a public caught at that time in the despotic vise of Louis-Napoleon, he investigated different types of sources, relied on different epistemological methods for acquiring his principal ideas, and both envisioned and deliberately introduced into his text a different balance of ideas and supporting facts, although here too we will see that his investigations operated within preconceived limits. When it came to portraying himself in his two books separated by two decades, however, he used a common "inductive" persona, that of the inquisitive traveler developing his insights on American shores, portrayed in the opening paragraphs of *Democracy in America*, volume 1 (*DA*, 3), and that of the innovative archival explorer, marshaling his evidence in *The Old Regime*, volume 1, through painstaking herculean probes of heretofore unknown sources.

Tocqueville followed no fixed blueprints for any of the four volumes of his two great works. The books emerged in each case from a three-to-five-year gestation during which he worked mightily to achieve an appropriate blend of historical understanding, novel research, artistic balance of facts and ideas, and political persuasion. For *Democracy in America,* volume 1, he chanced upon the early features of such a constellation in Boston in September 1831.[12] For *Democracy in America,* volume 2, he integrated its appropriate components, as we will see in this chapter, during a period of reading and meditation in early 1838. For *The Old Regime,* volume 1, he settled on his topic and focus in the archives of Tours during the summer of 1853. And while Tocqueville never obtained a similar moment of definitive clarity in his vision for *The Old Regime,* volume 2, I will argue in chapter 8 that he was on the cusp of doing so when he died. In order to begin to recognize the distinctive elements of Tocqueville's historical method in *The Old Regime* to which I wish to draw attention, we need to scrutinize early manifestations in *Democracy in America,* volume 2, of his propensity to reconsider and reshape his work during its very formulation.

Seymour Drescher has been the most forceful proponent of the thesis that a dramatic break took place between the two volumes of *Democracy in America.* In his 1964 article "Tocqueville's Two *Démocraties,*" Drescher argued that "an intrusion of new social facts," gleaned principally from travels in England in 1835, allowed the successful author of volume 1 to forge the crucial link between democratic social equality and centralized government that would serve as volume 2's conceptual axis. Drescher described the change between the two *Democracies* as "less a sudden conversion than a slow percolation of new ideas into the old framework until they changed the framework itself," noting that "it is perceptible not only between the two books, but within the earlier and later chapters of the second."[13] Jean-Claude Lamberti popularized the notion of "two *Democracies*" with his book of that title in 1989, but he chose to emphasize a different point of rupture (between parts 3 and 4 of volume 2) and assign to it a different precipitating cause (a change in Tocqueville's understanding of the "revolutionary spirit" and of its proclivity to subvert liberty), thus deepening but also complicating the debate.[14] The "two *Democracies*" debate precipitated by these claims is not the only methodological prism through which we could begin our investigations of Tocqueville's historical method. But in examining Tocqueville's evolution in his work over time, we have a useful starting point for our own historical and genetic studies of *The Old Regime.*[15]

While I am sympathetic to the central thrust of both Drescher's and Lamberti's arguments, since they emphasize the subtle contributions of Tocqueville's particular historical investigations and since they highlight his capacity to make adjustments in dramatic and unexpected ways in the very midst of his composition, I am not inclined to posit a break in *Democracy in America* at either of the points they indicate. Contra Drescher, I believe that

Tocqueville was riveted upon the issue of administrative centralization and its connection to tutelary democratic despotism *before* his arrival in America. Contra Lamberti, I believe that Tocqueville's view of the "revolutionary spirit" was both more continuous with his earlier thought and more intricately interwoven within each of the earlier parts of volume 2. I also see a different rationale for the changes that Tocqueville did make and a different process of inquiry through which he sought to refine his various analyses.

But I too detect a major shift that took place during Tocqueville's writing of volume 2 of *Democracy in America,* one that can be pinpointed to a period commencing in the early days of January 1838. In September 1837 Tocqueville had suspended all work on the second volume of his book to stand for a snap election to the Chamber of Deputies. When his whirlwind candidacy ended in defeat on November 4, 1837, he struggled to resume his writing, with his difficulties compounded by his being sequestered in Paris in December for two discouraging weeks as a juror. When he finally returned to his book in January, he launched a new era in its formulation by reconceptualizing democracy's principal disease (the isolation of its citizens) and the type of government that would emerge to capitalize on that disease (a new form of subtle, sophisticated, worldly-wise despotism that would gull its citizens at precisely the point of their greatest weakness).

We will see in chapter 2 that the idea of a soft despotism instituted by a "tutelary power" standing at the end of democratic history was not a new one for Tocqueville at this time: he had articulated a clear and precise vision of it eight years earlier in a letter of April 21, 1830, to Charles Stoffels.[16] As he had ruminated for ten years starting in 1829 about Guizot's portrayal of past societal dissolution, so, apparently, he had ruminated during this same period about the velvet glove of future despotic tyranny. What was new was his determination to use the idea as his grand climactic vision for his book on American democracy. In one sense, the new focus was a natural product of his investigations and writing for volume 2 from 1835 to 1837: as he reflected for three years about democratic equality's influence on modern man's ideas (part 1), sentiments (part 2), and mores (part 3), he probed precisely those spheres into which this nightmarish new version of democratic despotism would insinuate its tentacles. In another sense, as Lamberti, Drescher, and Furet each rightly emphasize, Tocqueville despised the political spirit of the new regime that appeared to have gained a stable foothold in France during the years 1835–40; his new concluding vision thus represented a powerful cri de coeur against what he saw as the contemporary evisceration of public virtue that could pave the way for the new despotism.[17] And on still another level, his introduction of a new portrait of an old vision could well have been guided by his thirst for recognition and glory. Licking his electoral wounds during his dark December days in Paris, he had announced to his wife, "I struggle every day between the smallness of my means and the immensity of my desires," with the object of his desires consumed in his "immoderate, immense craving [*goût*] that leads [my soul] toward grandeur."[18] A new vision in a book that (as he would tell Henry Reeve after its completion two years later) had as its "principal object" to elevate "the idea of the individual" in the face of his democratic diminution[19] might well contribute to securing such glory.

These are, of course, speculations about the causes for Tocqueville's decision. We can state with more certainty the steps the author took to enhance his democratic vision and the ways he introduced it within his evolving text. Beginning in January 1838, Tocqueville initiated a self-taught "great books seminar" leading him to devour, most often for the first time and almost all in four months, a "confused and bizarre" collection of works that included Rabelais, Plutarch, the Koran, Cervantes, Machiavelli, Fontenelle, and Saint-Evremond. He also reflected on Plato and read Thomas à Kempis.[20] "For years," he told Beaumont at the conclusion of his course, "I have not read and thought as much about what I was reading as during these four months dedicated to the *Democracy*."[21] His readings led him to reflect on the enfeebled status of democratic man and the inculcation of "the great principles of the beautiful and the good" that could elevate him rather than complete his degradation—themes that had ever marked "the works of the human spirit which have most seized the imagination of the human race."[22] Believing that the tension between his key philosophical theme and his key rhetorical goal could best be resolved in dialogue, Tocqueville probed these same themes in steady correspondence throughout 1838 with his cousin, Louis Kergorlay, during which they exchanged reflections on Voltaire and d'Alembert, Saint Paul, Muhammad, Turgot, and Plato, as well as in conversations during Kergorlay's occasional visits and extended autumn residency at Tocqueville's château.[23]

Tocqueville thus solidified his elevated perspective during 1838 through this process of reading and meditation, aptly described to Duvergier in 1856 in his depiction of his method that I have used as the epigraph to this chapter. His "new" perspective guided him as he shaped and reshaped his book in three principal ways during 1838–39.[24] Beginning with chapter 3:17— "How the Aspect of Society in the United States Is at Once Agitated and Monotonous" (initially dated January 4 in his archives)[25]—Tocqueville gradually injected his new vision within the concluding ten chapters of part 3, all initially drafted from January to April 1838 during this period of his most intense democratic ruminations. [26] I do not wish to suggest that Tocqueville's new vision of democratic despotism now constituted the chief focus of his book: it did not and would not until he wrote his concluding political section, part 4. But we should look at each theme that he treated in these latter chapters of part 3 as now filtered through the author's new despotic prism, adding brilliance to his analysis but also producing unexpected and even conflicting rays. In these chapters, we thus see the beginnings of his portrayal of the dawning democratic age's future monotony, its lack of variety (DA, 588), its increasing diminution of a concept of honor, its deflation of ambition among the largest part of the population, and its "venal and servile humor" resulting from the pursuit of government patronage (DA, 605). Throughout the month of March when he was drafting II:3:21, recently celebrated by commentators on account of his prediction of the end of democratic revolutions, Tocqueville was simultaneously obsessed with his grand, long-term democratic vision of a "new, regular, placid society," formed by tyranny that was "bureaucratic, [supported by] scribblers, very repressive of élan," lulling its citizens to sleep in the arms of clerks and soldiers—"a sort of fatherhood without a view of bringing its children to manhood." [27] Thus, at the end of the chapter, he felt compelled to "correct" his conservative depiction of revolutions' obsolescence with his stirring closing oration, in which he issued a clarion call to renew precisely "those great and powerful public emotions that trouble peoples but develop and renew them" (DA, 616). [28] Assessing war in his final unit of five chapters (II:3:22–26), drafted in April, Tocqueville showed similar ambivalence: while war offered a dangerous pretext for governments to expand their central power, it also rejuvenated precisely the passions of national pride and individual self-esteem that were needed to combat "certain inveterate diseases to which democratic societies are subject" (DA, 621). On his famous democratic "balance sheet" in volume 1, Tocqueville had celebrated democracy's "peaceful habits" and prose (DA, 234–35); he now saw these same attributes as at best a mixed blessing, precisely because they lacked the "heroic virtues" and poetry that would be needed in the democratic future.

Tocqueville unveiled his new despotic phenomenon in his book's climactic political section (II:4:1–7), written at his Norman château during a three-month period from June to August. In his draft notes, he made it clear that to do this section justice, he must make it dovetail (s'emmanche bien) with his immediately preceding chapters, specifically those addressing ambition, revolutions, and the army. [29] In II:4:3, he introduced the new idea of democratic "individualism," which he adopted and adapted to describe democracy's most perilous new disease. [30] In II:4:5, Tocqueville sought to make the new idea more vivid for his readers by offering practical examples of the noxious effects of administrative centralization, examples he had accumulated for more than a year in a separate file that he titled "Unity, centralization, administrative despotism; mixing together [*Mélange*] of administrative and judicial power"[31] and that he would seek to supplement with Beaumont's help that July. And in II:4:7, he expanded his list of remedies to his enhanced democratic threat as part of his final statement of "what must be done to turn away this peril."[32] He incorporated his communal political remedies of II:2:4 within "secondary bodies formed temporarily of plain citizens" and a "provincial assembly" (DA, 667), recommended "elective officials," and extended his civil remedies of II:2:5 to include an even wider range of potent associations: "very opulent, very influential, very strong beings—in a word, aristocratic persons" (DA, 668). Tocqueville's final word on liberty highlighted the need for citizens to be vigilant and even feisty and combative as they sought to check the new despots' efforts to reduce men and women to servitude (*DA,* 673).

Tocqueville launched his third principal change in his book in September 1838 when he set out to revise the work's earlier chapters. During the ensuing year and several months, he reassessed all his former chapter drafts in light of his new vision, reentering "with a lighted candle" the spots through which he had previously "groped [in darkness]."[33] In autumn 1838, as I have mentioned, he consigned his work's first two chapters (II:1:1–2) to a literal fire. He rewrote them from scratch to clarify the homogenization of public opinion induced by democratic social conditions that would ultimately pave the way for the soft despotism with which he now knew his work would culminate.[34] In similar fashion, he rewrote II:2:1–2 in light of his explicit condemnation of "individualism" in II:4:3. Indeed, throughout his earlier text, he now injected the term "individualism" to describe the isolation and public disengagement that would serve as the new democratic era's most invidious social disease, making it a useful tool in our efforts to distinguish Tocqueville's earlier and later drafts in his archive. Tocqueville's revisions served on occasion to create two parallel essays written in two stages . . . essays that he then placed side by side within his final chapter. For example, he opened II:2:4, titled "How the Americans Combat Individualism by Free Institutions," with an 1838 "essay," which we quickly recognize as dating from this period, since Tocqueville used it to accentuate the ruses of his cunning new despot, now personalized, who shrewdly altered the natural meaning of words by extolling as "good citizens" those who isolated themselves from their fellows and gave silent obedience, if not love, to their master (*DA,* 485). This 1838 text continues in the chapter all the way to the start of his paragraph that introduces for the first time an American discussion (*DA*, 486), where he merges it with his earlier chapter draft, written in 1836.[35] Throughout his new chapters and revised text, Tocqueville incorporated various vignettes from his "great books" readings to help elevate and validate his new vision.[36]

Incorporated in these ways throughout volume 2 of *Democracy in America*, Tocqueville's new vision of despotism provided the dramatic pièce de résistance for the full work. He himself attested to its new central role by making his own case for two *Democracies*. Referring to his fullest portrayal of his new despotic vision in the note dated March 7, 1838, he contrasted it with his earlier version of the tyranny of the Roman Caesars in volume 1 (*DA*, 301), applauding the novelty, rhetorical power, and truth of the new version: "This one is the true and original tableau. That of the first volume was bombastic, ordinary, hackneyed, and false." [37] Four months later, he clarified for Beaumont that he had indeed achieved a new vantage point, describing it as "very much higher" than his previous one, from which he had viewed administrative centralization as emerging from the appropriation of secondary powers by the central power. Now he supplemented this view ("Je veux voir non seulement cela") with a far more frightening portrait of the death of the citizen, produced by "the state's successively seizing everything, injecting itself on all sides in the place of the individual, or putting the individual in tutelage, governing, regimenting, *rendering uniform* all things and all persons." [38] There was a "grandeur" to his new subject, he told Beaumont, one that evidently fulfilled the hidden craving he had expressed to his wife. Demonstrating the shift in his political objectives at this time, he sought to use his frightening new tableau to "strike" the senses of the somnolent citizens of the July Monarchy, as he documented the full extent of their progressive "bastardization." [39]

The challenge faced by students of Tocqueville's historical method is to weave together in a coherent fashion such diverse, often seemingly incongruous, and at times even contradictory features from his extensive oeuvre. Turning to *The Old Regime and the Revolution*, I will argue that Tocqueville settled both the form and the substance of his book in response to encounters with that profuse collection of archival sources that he had so ingeniously and assiduously compiled during his four and one-half years of preparatory studies. The record of these sources is woven within Tocqueville's some 3,700 pages of archival notes faithfully preserved in the family archives by his descendants for what is now almost 150 years.[40] For *The Old*

Regime, volume 1, we find in the archive his reading notes for the works of more than sixty authors, peppered with more than seventy dates when he conducted different facets of his research. For *The Old Regime,* volume 2, we find additional references to quite different kinds of sources, especially pamphlets and contemporary revolutionary works, replete with their own notations of more than twenty-five dates. In addition to indicating the identity of his sources and the timing of his work, Tocqueville's archive provides copious instances of his analyses of his readings, most often attached to particular passages of interest that he transcribed from the texts, and most often designated by the Latin notation "hic." Tocqueville's "hic" observations range from single words to full pages of extemporaneous analysis; by turn probing in their studiousness, irreverent in their pithy rejoinders, or biting in their sarcasm, they demonstrate his varying levels of engagement with his texts and his gradual testing of the principal themes that he would eventually incorporate within his book. My claims about Tocqueville's historical method in *The Old Regime* draw heavily on these "hic" comments in his reading archive, not because the works to which they are directed are his only sources (How could they be, when we have witnessed the extent to which he mulled over ideas drawn from readings conducted years, or even decades, previously?) but because they constitute specific sources, identified by author and edition, with references to precise passages that we can ourselves review with the benefit of his comments in front of us. What Beaumont rightly described as Tocqueville's "immense arsenal of ideas"[41] thus provides our most intimate—and accurate—picture of Tocqueville, the historian, at work.

In the archives for *The Old Regime,* we will find not one but several "books" that Tocqueville wrote, with clear signs of divergence between them and possible triggering mechanisms that may help explain his artistic and historical choices: his two initial chapters written in 1852 on the Directory; his book 1 of *The Old Regime,* volume 1, originally outlined in rough form in June 1853 as a short preface to a different, never completed larger work on the entire Revolution; his books 2 and 3 of the same volume 1, first drafted in 1854 at Tours and still joined as a single book 2 when published in 1856; and his unfinished sequel, for which he would return to square one in his analytical efforts. Mirroring his engagement with Guizot in *Democracy in America,* Tocqueville entered into spirited exchanges with various interlocutors within his notes that often shaped the connections within and between his "books." Close readers of *The Old Regime* have accorded Edmund Burke prominence as a principal foil for Tocqueville's arguments;[42] I concur with such a view and will show that Tocqueville's reading of Burke's works on the French

Revolution took place at a crucial juncture in the making of *The Old Regime,* volume I, provoking his arguments and providing a preliminary structure for its book I. I will add to such a list two interlocutors who are not recognized as having played a part in the formation of his book—Benjamin Constant and C. Dareste de la Chavanne—and another, Louis-Antoine Macarel, whom Tocqueville had read a decade earlier in preparation for a report to the Académie des sciences morales et politiques. Finally, in the case of Louis-Marie Prudhomme, I will argue that Tocqueville dropped, to his detriment, his customary caution in assessing the reliability of his sources and ended up being betrayed by the propagandistic fervor of this noted revolutionary pamphleteer who sought to reap political capital by publishing his hurriedly compiled collection of *cahiers* excerpts in the heated days of 1789 when the Estates-General first convened.

In keeping with a lifelong policy of "systematic" discretion,[43] Tocqueville never broadcast his links with his sources. He was consistent throughout his correspondence in the 1850s in preserving his highly secretive mode of operations, as when he admonished his nephew Hubert, in the heart of his studies, "I confide the details of my work to *absolutely no one.*"[44] Within his text itself, he chose to ignore the impassioned counsel of his two earliest readers, Gustave and Clementine de Beaumont, who urged him to be forthcoming with detailed citations of his sources: "Your proofs are so conclusive," they argued, "that it would be most unfortunate to suppress your sources."[45] He opted instead to impose a veil of secrecy, refusing to provide a single precise textual reference within *The Old Regime,* volume I, that would enable his readers to locate with assurance a single citation within a single historical work. While Tocqueville's veil undoubtedly contributed to the aura of mystery with which he enveloped his book, it undoubtedly also subtracted from a full appreciation of the novelty and ingenuity of his historical probes . . . and of their occasional deficiencies.

My account of Tocqueville's labors on *The Old Regime* commences in chapter 2 with a discussion of his early encounters with the works of two historians of the Restoration, Guizot and Prosper de Barante, since I believe his exposure to their historical thought—whether in the classes I have noted at the Sorbonne or in private readings—helped to shape his subsequent choices as a historian. In this chapter I assess Tocqueville's first efforts to establish the focus of *The Old Regime* in three venues: his installation speech to the Académie française in Paris in 1842, his ruminations at Sorrento in 1850–51, and his trial drafting of two chapters in Normandy in 1852.

In chapters 3–6, after presenting his 1836 essay as a benchmark for comparative purposes, I consider by turn four broad themes that came to shape

Tocqueville's investigations: feudal rights, a foreign perspective on the Revolution found in the writings of Burke, administrative centralization, and public opinion. The focus of these chapters is both epistemological, charting Tocqueville's initial encounters with his historical sources and tracing the evolution of his research from July 1852 through November 1853, and rhetorical, depicting his subsequent literary expression of these findings in his book.

In chapter 7, after analyzing the nature of Tocqueville's lifelong love affair with liberty, I describe a range of artistic choices affected by this passion, culminating in my portrayal of the potent persona he progressively crafted to help meld his dual historical objectives of truth and instruction.

If Tocqueville's post-1856 sequel to his first volume of *The Old Regime* demonstrates the continuity of that book's central themes, it also reveals the author's interest in probing new sources in his search for new evidence of liberty's persistent presence in France's revolutionary past. In chapter 8 I tell the story of those investigations and assess the new directions in which his work was moving when it was prematurely terminated by his death.

I attach to my chapters an appendix that lists Tocqueville's seventy-six endnotes for *The Old Regime,* volume 1, numbered consecutively for easier reference within this book. Apart from a study of the full reading archives—available, with the Tocqueville family's permission, for scholarly review on microfilm at the Bibliothèque nationale—Tocqueville's endnotes constitute the very best way to evaluate the many features of his historical method, since he drew them directly from his reading notes. Despite some pruning and rewriting of his endnotes in the galley proofs, often in unexpected ways, he largely preserved in his book their initial flair and provocative style.

TOCQUEVILLE AND NAPOLEON
Imperial History Deferred

[Napoleon] deprived [France] not only of liberty, but of the wish for liberty; he enveloped her in a network of centralization, which stifles individual and corporate resistance, and prepares the way for the despotism of an Assembly or of an Emperor. . . . He seized with a sagacity which is really marvelous, out of the elements left to him by the Convention, those which enabled him to raise *himself,* and to level everything else; which enabled his will to penetrate into the recesses of provincial and even of private life, and rendered those below him incapable of acting and thinking, almost of wishing, for themselves. . . . The History of the Empire and the History of the Emperor are still to be written. I hope one day to write them.[1]

In April 1842, Napoleon Bonaparte's posthumous grip on the French imagination extended to the packed chambers of the Académie française, where members and their guests attended to the words of its newest inductee, Alexis de Tocqueville. Delivering the standard eulogy for his predecessor, Comte Jean-Gérard de Cessac, a minister of state and war for Napoleon, Tocqueville used his speech to challenge, not champion, Napoleon's legacy. He minced no words in condemning Napoleon's imposition upon France of "the most perfected despotism" in the history of the world. Capitalizing on the people's appetite for order, Napoleon had deprived them of "liberty," defined by Tocqueville as the participation in public affairs that alone could have enabled them "to think together and act in concert." Only through such "powerful common emotions," leading in turn to the elevation of "souls above themselves," could people have transcended the monotonous routine of trivial daily pursuits and "petty thoughts" induced by the new democratic era. Napoleon's genius as an architect of order thus paled in the light of his legacy of spiritual depletion, making him "as great as a man can be," Tocqueville allowed, "without virtue."[2]

Tocqueville's caustic critique received a cool reception, we are told, as his audience turned a deaf ear to his familiar paean to liberty, previously voiced in the political arena but now framed within this historical context.[3] In his patronizing response to Tocqueville's talk, M. Molé affirmed that the French people had not only accepted but invited the very despotism that Tocqueville disparaged. They had shrewdly used Napoleon to preserve liberty in the long run while restoring immediate pride in their nation and preeminence among the powers of the world. That they had saved civilization in the process was but further proof of their perspicacity.[4] Tocqueville's critique of Napoleon thus floundered on two counts: it failed as history, since it underestimated the dire threat of dissolution faced by France before Napoleon's ascent, and it failed as theory, since it encumbered liberty with an excessive threshold of participation. Moreover, Tocqueville's speech failed politically, since it reinforced his status as a lonely sentinel on the margins of the political establishment, although the new Academician himself accepted such reduced standing as both the price of principled political leadership and an investment in the nation's future moral development.[5]

Ten years later, Tocqueville would indicate that his reflections at this time precipitated *The Old Regime and the Revolution*.[6] Such a claim does not surprise us: we can readily observe such a lineage both in his initial choice of topic for his book—Napoleon and his empire—and in his insistence on liberty as the best antidote to its "perfected" despotism. In its larger revolutionary analysis, his speech presaged important themes of his book, such as the primacy of ideas in the making of the Revolution, their conflict with existing mores, the people's resulting taste for servitude, and the interplay of general and accidental causes, even while it differed on others, such as the origins of centralization and the potency of the Revolution itself as a primary precipitant of change. Indeed, in tracing the contours of Cessac's entire life from 1752 to 1841, Tocqueville provided a rare panoramic overview of what he saw as the larger, and continuing, phenomenon of the French Revolution.

Tocqueville concluded his speech with a call for action. In our role as political leaders, he urged, we can still determine whether the legacy of the Revolution of 1789 will be liberty or servitude. We can help demonstrate whether men will have "the courage and intelligence" needed to "regulate and defend" their new taste for independence. In such a situation, our work as historians remains "premature": we cannot judge the Revolution, since "all of [its] products" are not yet revealed.[7]

1. Tocqueville's Historical Apprenticeship

Tocqueville's commitment to liberty thus inspired his public pronouncements even while ensuring their equivocal reception. He appraised French historical studies through a similarly distinctive lens, immersing himself in the resurgent field with early studies of Guizot and Barante and continuing to monitor it with a watchful eye throughout his life. He knew the renowned practitioners of French liberal history as colleagues in the Academies or the Assembly, where his own dual memberships often overlapped with their own, and he was all too aware of the enormous influence these writers exercised on the turbulent events of the time. In 1829, eager to place his own imprimatur on political events, he had perceived the writing of history as a stepping-stone to a political career;[8] in 1851, forcibly exiled from the public domain, he returned to history as a means of continuing that same career. He shared with his contemporaries the defining badge of liberal historiography—commitment—even as he reserved the right to differ with their ideological objectives and historical methods.

The ingenious ways French historians of the Restoration reenvisioned and transformed their craft have been traced with care and discernment by Lionel Gossman in his *Between History and Literature*. In Gossman's account, the work of Restoration historians was inextricably linked with "the premises and ideals—and contradictions—of liberalism in early nineteenth-century France."[9] Possessing great freedom in taking stock of the French eighteenth-century strains of antiquarian, philosophic, and naive narrative history, they investigated new sources and new themes, experimented with new means of composition, and wove their findings into a transcendent philosophy of history that explained the arrival and triumph on the historical stage of France's long-gestated bourgeoisie. Confronted by the return of the ultraroyalists in 1820, they diverted their fervor into writing the histories that proliferated throughout the 1820s. Buoyed by the triumph of their political agenda in 1830, they sought and received positions of power and influence, in turn precipitating vast new archival inquiries. Devastated by the splintering of popular consensus in 1848, they retreated from center stage, chastened by the setback to their constitutional and personal dreams. Their historical work mirrored their political fortunes, Gossman argues, for better and worse.

Alexis de Tocqueville's lifelong attention to history was similarly spurred by the vagaries of the same political era. A child of the Revolution's shifting fortunes, with both parents saved from the guillotine's blade by Robespierre's sudden demise, his general education and particular historical inquiries reflected his family milieu. His early intellectual interests were broad and eclectic. As a child, he participated in staging theatrical vignettes as family entertainment. On one memorable occasion, he greeted his father in a company that included his dead uncle's brother, Chateaubriand, disguised as an old woman.[10] Family members read aloud "every new book of any merit": they committed to memory the works of English novelists such as Richardson and Fielding, surveyed aristocratic tales from Froissart to Madame de Sévigné, and relished the romantic novels of Sir Walter Scott.[11] Weaned on the classics, Tocqueville was formally schooled in French literature and the classical oratory of Cicero, Demosthenes, and Quintilian.[12] In later years he would acknowledge four "great writers of the eighteenth century": Montesquieu, Voltaire, Rousseau, and Buffon. All their works had been present, Jardin tells us, in his father's library at Metz during his teenage years.[13] During the 1840s, he kept abreast through salon conversation and academy reports with the era's philosophical imports, such as Kant, Fichte, Schelling, Hegel, and Vico.[14] He conducted his own pilgrimages to Scott's Kenilworth ruins and the American wilds, de rigueur for romantics of the time, and his fascination with tomb and archive would inform the investigations and imagery of his books as he engaged in his own version of every historian's "sacred mission," seeking to "resolv[e] the riddles of the past, giv[e] a voice to its oppressive silences, [and] decipher its secret, forgotten or suppressed languages."[15]

Tocqueville cut his historical teeth on Guizot's three cycles of Sorbonne lectures, delivered from April 9, 1828, to May 29, 1830. Professor Guizot— detached and objective in an era that valued the credibility of science, erudite, careful to divorce himself from controversy, versatile in his use of both analytical and narrative modes of historical writing—had first inaugurated and then stood astride the emerging field of history in the 1820s.[16] Restored to his seat at the Sorbonne in spring 1828, during his initial cycle of fourteen lectures Guizot planted the seeds for the dramatic appearance on Europe's historical stage of his champions in the rise of Western civilization—the Third Estate. In his second unit of thirty lessons, delivered from December 1828 until July 18, 1829, Guizot turned his attention specifically to France and chronicled five centuries of struggle between Roman, Christian, and German barbarian principles, culminating in the emergence of modern French society in the tenth century. In his final unit of nineteen lessons that began on December 5, 1829, and continued through May 29, 1830, he traced the rise and fall of French feudalism between the tenth and fifteenth centuries, as it peaked during the Crusades and subsequently lost power and prestige in the face of encroachments by royalty and the communes.[17]

Serving with Beaumont as a young magistrate in the law courts of Versailles at this time, Tocqueville attended many of these famous lectures with his new friend, leaving carefully recrafted, polished résumés of seventeen of them, laced with his personal interjections.[18] While his notes are based on lectures in Guizot's latter two cycles of December 1828 to 1830, I believe Tocqueville attended or at least quickly digested the earlier cycle of 1828 lectures as well, since he appears both to incorporate and rebut several of Guizot's arguments in his own earliest reflections on English history, contained in his letter to Beaumont of October 5, 1828.[19] Tocqueville supplemented the coursework by reading during the summer of 1829 "the greatest part" of Guizot's works.[20] This included volumes of Guizot's compilation of *Mémoires relatifs à l'histoire de France,* portions of which the professor had excerpted in his lectures as part of his extensive edifice of supporting documentation,[21] plus, most likely, Guizot's parallel narrative history and supporting memoirs on the history of the English Revolution, published in 1826–27 and 1823–25, respectively, plus those lectures that Tocqueville had missed during the courses. Summarizing for Beaumont his impressions after reading Guizot's historical oeuvre, he famously effused: "Together, we must reread [Guizot's work] this winter, my dear friend, it is prodigious in its decomposition of ideas and propriety of words, truly *prodigious.*"[22]

In Guizot's extended history of the emergence of civilization in Europe and in France, Tocqueville encountered a historical model based on analysis and interpretation to which he instantly gravitated, since it complemented his own intuitions and previous studies.[23] Guizot's system of analysis commenced with the eyewitness accounts of contemporaries, including the more than fifty "memoirs," "poems," "histories," "chronicles," "lives," and "annals" written during seven hundred years that were contained in his *Mémoires.* Applying his own modern perspective to these accounts of early events, Guizot developed a multifaceted explanation for the causes underlying their tangled surface; he sought to capture, he said, "the general results, the linkage of causes and effects, civilization's progress, hidden beneath the surface events of history."[24] He proceeded by a method of "decomposition," through which he broke a historical entity into its constituent parts. In the case of the French feudal system, he progressively "decomposed" the whole so as to arrive at "its fundamental element . . . that primitive feudal molecule which cannot be split without abolishing the feudal character."[25] In the case of modern French "moral" society in the tenth century, he distinguished civil from religious society and then examined each according to its expression of the Roman, Christian, and Germanic principles that had been struggling for supremacy for five centuries. Once he had demonstrated the significance of each of these parts in its own right, he could then reassemble the pieces to elucidate the whole.[26]

Guizot thus helped train Tocqueville to analyze concepts by penetrating a web of surface "political" facts to unveil the underlying matrix of their "moral" causes. We can trace Tocqueville's fascination with such an approach in his notes, where his personal interjections identified the topics he found of special interest. In the last class of his first semester, he thus highlighted Guizot's claim that history must encompass the "whole man," interjecting his understanding that the manifestations of such history must be sought in his deeds, mores, opinions, laws, and the "monuments of intelligence."[27] In the first class of his second semester, when Guizot contrasted the missing "political" unity of the tenth century with its emerging "moral" unity, seen in France's common language, passions, and customs, Tocqueville took the distinction and embellished it as follows:

> Political unity is entirely external, exhibiting a type of ostentation in its power; *its existence strikes the view of the most unperceptive viewer, the wise man alone can predict its duration.*
>
> *[Moral unity], by contrast, operates secretly within the interior of societies, it hides, it evades observation and yet its influence is greater, it attracts, it unites, and it secretly binds hearts and souls.*
>
> *The former creates a power, the latter a people. [The latter] can endure on its own for centuries, [the former] cannot survive for long without its aid.*[28]

In his elaboration, Tocqueville used Guizot's conceptual distinction as a means both to deepen his own understanding and to cultivate its imaginative expression. He refined his views on other topics raised by Guizot with similar care, as in his treatments of popular literature, the nobles' isolation, the establishment of the "idea of rights," and the Third Estate's hatred of the nobles.[29]

Tocqueville's studies with Guizot helped to solidify and refine his preferred historical method.[30] Henceforth history, for Tocqueville, must be interpretative, or analytical, or what Guizot himself called "philosophical history," well described by John Stuart Mill as "the workings of the great determining causes traced through the complication of their multifarious effects."[31] Throughout his career he would denounce, on both analytical and moral grounds, the failure of historical writers to probe the complexity of historical causes, criticizing narrativists such as Penhoën, fatalists such as Gobineau, or narrativists and fatalists such as Thiers.[32] Each of these historians presented a unicausal or noncausal account of history, thus failing to do justice to the complications necessarily introduced by the free actions of free men.

Conversely, Tocqueville made a point of praising historical accounts such as those of the sixteenth-century Italian memoirist Benvenuto Cellini and the late eighteenth-century German historian and poet Friedrich Schiller, precisely because they did succeed in capturing the general causes of an event and the "movement of the ideas and passions that produced or sprang from it."[33] "After all," Tocqueville stated with reference to Schiller, "only [these general causes are] absolutely *sure* in history; all that is particular is always more or less doubtful."[34] These men delved below the surface of "doubtful" historical events and captured the underlying spirit that could explain them. They sought what Tocqueville would call in 1850 "the spirit of the facts" rather than the "facts themselves."[35] They received Tocqueville's approbation because they appraised history in the philosophical and conceptual manner that constituted, in Tocqueville's view, Guizot's "*prodigious*" legacy.

If Tocqueville was enamored by Guizot's analytical method and would restlessly define and redefine his own hierarchies of "decomposition" in ideas, mores, and laws throughout his historical career, he could not subscribe to his political message. In particular, within Guizot's account of the progressive emergence of civilization in England, Tocqueville objected to his professor's benign portrayal of the despotic Tudor regime as having played a useful role in inaugurating free institutions in England. Throughout Europe in the fifteenth century, Guizot explained, a new "epoch of political centralization" took place in response to the failure of feudal and communal liberties to "give to society [either] security [or] progress."[36] Carefully qualifying his claims about the new despotic regimes, in his final lecture of this cycle Guizot emphasized their pluses (their ability "to gather into the bosom of the central power the means of force existing in society") and minuses (their tendency to subvert local institutions). He denounced for his students Louis XIV's "powerful and splendid, but rootless" regime, explaining that its inability to survive in the eighteenth century was the result of its failure to promulgate free institutions.[37] But he never

deviated from his verdict on the role of such regimes in furthering civilization's progress, expressed most clearly in his eleventh lecture with respect
to Europe in general and each nation in particular: "It must be understood,"
he emphasized with reference to the Third Estate's voluntary relinquish-
ment of local liberties to the monarchs, "that this revolution was not only
inevitable, but beneficial [*utile*] also." [38]

In his 1828 letter to Beaumont, Tocqueville directly challenged such
a teaching. "Many people," he explained, "both among those who have
studied English history and those who have not," believed that the English
constitution had developed in a sequence of necessary stages, with each
era making its own contribution so that the final constitutional product
was "a fruit which every age has ripened." [39] "That is not my view," he
continued; the Tudor era in England constituted a "step backwards that
could not be more marked," a regression in the constitution's progress
toward liberal guarantees. To be sure, civilization's progress succeeded in
making men more aware of feudal vices, but in doing so, it "led all the
peoples to throw themselves, bound hand and foot, into the power of
their rulers to correct [those] vices." [40] Scathing in his sarcasm, Tocqueville disputed Guizot's fundamental trade-off through which the English
people, exhausted and demoralized by the Wars of the Roses at the end
of the fifteenth century, acquiesced to Tudor security while relinquishing
their traditional liberties. Tocqueville then used this voluntary surrender
of precious constitutional freedoms as an object lesson for Beaumont of the
dangers of "legal despotism" . . . and as a trigger for the most virulent expression of his own anti-English, pro-French chauvinism found anywhere
in his writings. [41] "I don't know who can see in this time an advance towards
the Revolution of 1688," he sniped at an unidentified target whom I take to
be Guizot. [42] In stark contrast, Tocqueville believed that the English Revolution as a whole challenged despotism rather than springing from its
supportive cocoon. It was made possible by the survival of hearty forms of
constitutional government among the Commons, "a circumstance that
marvelously aids popular movements." [43] Mired in popular lethargy induced by the Tudor brand of despotism, the Commons resurrected its
proud tradition of active and bold resistance to early aristocratic and subsequent royal encroachment—the very resistance that had been surrendered
in Guizot's "beneficial" revolution.

Tracing the tone and content of Tocqueville's personal interjections
within his course notes on Guizot's final four lectures of May 8, 15, 22, and
29, 1830, we detect similar discomfort in his response to Guizot's most extended analysis of the history of the French commune. Guizot's treatment

in these concluding lectures shifted in important ways from his 1828 analysis of the commune, primarily owing to his study of 236 royal acts of the twelfth and thirteenth centuries that led him to differentiate his earlier commune into three distinct classes. [44] In 1830 Tocqueville made clear in polite but firm terms his dismay with various aspects of Guizot's updated teaching: he would have preferred a more nuanced appraisal of how bourgeois and royal collusion paved the way for *"equality under a master";* a more forceful affirmation of the roots of the communes' liberty in insurrection, not royal concession; and a clearer recognition that it was the bourgeois, not the nobility, who were *"the true destroyers of communal liberties in France."*[45] Moreover, the new communes—in which "political liberty was nonexistent"—bred what Guizot described as the "bourgeois spirit": "a spirit [that is] honest, [a] friend of order, enemy of tumult and even of sound, supporter of authority still more from love than from fear, a spirit to boot [that is] excessively timid by nature and that takes fright at the very idea of energetic resistances." [46] Such a spirit, which Guizot had also depicted in his 1828 lectures,[47] in Tocqueville's eyes represented the very antithesis of the qualities of public virtue needed to build and sustain wise, energetic, and accountable government. It epitomized a frightening version of the new "democratic" man, conceived by a royal government that accorded rights and benefits in exchange for subservience. Soon imposing its character on "all of the French bourgeoisie," [48] this neutered creature embodied the same qualities that Tocqueville had pilloried one month earlier in the letter to Charles Stoffels we noted in chapter 1: "soft, sociable, [with its] passions calmed" by "this second providence . . . this tutelary power" that arrived to supervise society once civilization had attained "a very high degree."[49]

The royal government not only benefited from this passive acquiescence of its compliant citizens, it also enlisted a corps of bourgeois legists to legitimate the intrusion of royal power throughout the justice system, thus securing their complicity in forging their own bonds as they subverted judicial independence. In his lecture of May 1, 1830, on the "Development of the French Kingship," Guizot had revealed the origins of the "regulatory mania" of the French kings and the noxious overlay of administrative and judicial power, tracing both to the era of Philip the Fair (1285–1314). He indicated how the legists had established "extraordinary commissions" to protect the state from judicial action, a practice for which Tocqueville instantly drew the modern parallel, noting that its *"tyrannical usage has been perpetuated almost up to our days."*[50] Five years later, in volume 1 of *Democracy,* Tocqueville would draw on this teaching and date the French "taste for centralization and the regulatory mania" to the era "when legists entered the government, which takes us back to the time of Philip the Fair" (*DA*, 692). And in his 1836 essay of the following year, he embellished Guizot's historical account with his own commentary on the collaboration of kings and legists, who forged "a despotism which scarcely allows a breathing place to human nature."[51]

Tocqueville thus objected to Guizot's endorsement of a phase of despotism in history's progressive march that capitalized on democratic man's enfeebled status and made its shrewdest members the pliant architects of their quiescent fate. He insisted instead that a feisty local liberty was needed to inspire and train these complacent citizens to protect their national liberty by resisting the royal hegemony. Of course he recognized the need for a modicum of central efficiency, for national security, for national unity, for a national system of justice, for a level of civilization that would guarantee "the safety, the individual happiness" of its citizens.[52] For these reasons he drew his famous distinction in *Democracy in America* between governmental and administrative centralization (*DA*, 82–83) and clarified for Eugène Stoffels in October 1836 that "what I want is a central government energetic in its own sphere of action."[53] He recognized as well the extent to which in certain circumstances decentralized localities could be "instinctive, blind, full of prejudices, deprived of rules."[54] But the challenge for partisans of liberty was to find a balance between these two extremes: "either alternative has its advantages and its drawbacks," he told Beaumont early in his 1828 letter.[55] "No one perceive[s] the precise limits of the one [centralized government] and the other [administrative decentralization]," he added in his most extensive note from America in which he began to formulate his own strategies to correct this imprecision.[56] Of one condition, however, Tocqueville was ever certain: an appropriate balance could never include the wholesale surrender by a timid populace of its hard-earned liberties to an overbearing monarchy intent on muzzling once and for all a great, if temporarily depleted, aristocracy.

Tocqueville's prickliness on this issue was pronounced and ever present, as Sainte-Beuve discovered to his detriment in 1835 when he was skewered by Tocqueville for his flippant pleasantries regarding France's "Principles of '89."[57] It accounted for Tocqueville's belief that Montesquieu gave to despotism "an honor that it did not merit" (*DA*, 89).[58] And in line with it, Tocqueville insisted that the writing of history must support the instantiation of his view of liberty's essential components. Therefore, to the extent that bourgeois history segued into an endorsement of statist history, be it in the work of Guizot, Thierry, Mignet, or Thiers, Tocqueville took exception to this aspect of it. To the extent that populist history arrived at a similar conclusion, in the works of Michelet or Lamartine or Blanc, he similarly rejected it. The way a writer judged liberty became the sine qua non of Tocqueville's historical judgment, a Tocquevillian "liberty test" that he employed with reference to historians and theorists ranging from John Lingard to Plato to Voltaire to Hegel to the French historian Henri Martin,[59] as well as to the host of specific authors with whom we will see that he subsequently "debated" liberty's meaning in his preparations for writing *The Old Regime*. In Lingard's case, as he began his historical career in 1828, he referred to the author once by name in his letter to Beaumont, criticizing him as "[a] *cold fish*" in his accounts of the terrible scenes of devastation wrought during the Wars of the Roses. Lingard was oblivious, Tocqueville believed, to the wars' terrible consequences for liberty: the decimation of the landed nobility, the abandonment of the institution of Parliament, the failure of members of the House of Commons to function independently as checks on royal power, and the elimination of potential centers of resistance to tyranny in England, each of which contributed to the eradication of "oligarchic liberty" in favor of the government "of one man."[60] In Martin's case, as Tocqueville approached the end of his career in 1857, he reiterated this lifelong belief: "[Martin] belongs to the class of theorists, unfortunately not a small one, whose political beau ideal is the absence of all control over the will of the people—who are opposed therefore to an hereditary monarchy—to a permanent president—to a permanent magistracy—to an established church—in short, to all privileged classes, bodies, or institutions. Equality, not liberty or security, is their object. They are centralisers and absolutists."[61]

Three weeks after his rapturous report on his extensive reading of Guizot's historical works, and four days after his follow-up query for certain volumes of Guizot's supporting *Mémoires,* Tocqueville indicated to Beaumont that he had immersed himself in a "serious" reading of Prosper de Barante's *Histoire des ducs de Bourgogne.*[62] Tocqueville proceeded to express doubts about the merits of Barante's historical method, artfully delineated in the author's famous preface to his twelve-volume work.[63] In his preface, Barante inveighed against the politicians, orators, philosophers, and antiquarians who had intruded on the fabled domain of simple, direct, engaging French narrative history. In Barante's view, as the intruders sought to manipulate or dissect historical events for political or scholarly reasons, they vitiated the essential vitality of these events and limited their audience to a group of similarly detached philosophical observers. His solutions to this diminution of the interest of history? Remove any trace of an intrusive narrator armed with his self-serving commentaries; reproduce verbatim the engaging, if necessarily limited, eyewitness accounts of historical characters and chroniclers in all their naive simplicity; write narrative history, not conceptual history, tying events to a genealogical succession of important personages; remove all detailed references to sources and scholarly analysis of their merits; strive to "carefully efface the scaffolding" of the historical work.[64] In short, restore to history the spontaneous verve, passion, and engaging interest that once distinguished this proud offshoot of belles lettres by following Quintilian's sage advice: "Write to tell a story, not to prove a point."[65]

While Barante sought in these ways to resuscitate history's charm, he did not necessarily eliminate a more subtle interpretive role for himself as author. For in the way he chose a particular fact or event as representative of his era, or what Gossman terms a "synecdoche" for it,[66] and in the way he arranged these facts into a pattern showing the larger meaning of the historical story, he still fulfilled the great tradition of French narration: "Judge and narrate at the same time."[67] Indeed, his work communicated a potent political message of its own. On the one hand, Barante attributed broad importance to "the thought and voice of the people" that already exercised "an immense power" in France of the fourteenth and fifteenth centuries.[68] On the other hand, he directed attention to the two opposing trends in the fluctuating position of the Third Estate that Guizot had also noted in his lectures: the growth of the power of "this new people" in the court of Charles V, and its decline in the communes. Rendering a judgment on this process that differed from Guizot's, however, he lamented the way French historians had hidden the pitiful spectacle of the surrender of local liberties "under a monotonous flattery of royal authority and the nation itself."[69]

Guizot and Barante: two historians who treated at least in part a common era (medieval France), announced the ascension of a common new power (the bourgeoisie), but otherwise diverged sharply in historical method, artistic purpose, the use and portrayal of their original sources, and historical judgment. Two historians who thus engaged in the Restoration's debate over the purpose, method, style, and message of historical writing. Two historians who enjoyed broad popular success. Two historians who were read with intense interest by the young Tocqueville in the summer and fall of 1829.

Tocqueville wasted no time in giving Beaumont his personal verdict on the respective merits of the two models: "I do not know if you will share my opinion, but it seems to me that a history [the *Histoire des ducs de Bourgogne*] written in this genre is not complete. There are matters, the march of events, the development of revolutions that one cannot grasp well if one looks at them only in this way."[70] We are not surprised: Barante's history was "not complete" because it failed to address the underlying causes of the events of which it presented such a stirring surface rendition. It lacked Tocqueville's commitment to philosophical history, undertaken with what he would admiringly characterize to Beaumont as "the analytical spirit of Guizot."[71] Moreover, Tocqueville continued, even Barante's feisty endorsement of local liberty did not pass muster, since it evinced in too general a fashion a "partiality for the people against the great [men]."[72] Tocqueville thus made clear the broad parameters of his preferred historical method, even while leaving open for consideration the many issues he had encountered in such a provocative fashion in Barante's work—genre, style, the role of a narrator, the role of sources, and the role of citations to these sources. When the time comes for Tocqueville to write his own French history, he will reveal the mature results of these 1829 reflections on the Guizot-Barante debate as he chooses his own historical method, his own writing style, and his own rhetorical strategy for liberty.

2. Tocqueville's Tabula Rasa at Sorrento

Introduced in these ways to French history in the late 1820s, Tocqueville pursued its study during his lifetime with fierce individualism. His career as a historian gained momentum and prominence in inverse proportion to the decline of his political career. During the "critical years" 1848–51, when he believed that the very existence of civilization was at stake in the challenge socialist ideas posed to property and order, he committed his "peace and quiet and if need be my life" to the struggle for liberty in the face of them.[73] Initially, he continued his distinguished career in public service, with it now marked by a succession of further electoral victories under the new system of universal suffrage, election by his peers in the Constituent Assembly to the committee to draft a new French constitution, and tenure as French foreign minister from June 2 to October 31, 1849. This was a period of profound chaos and unpredictability in France that he subsequently described in his *Souvenirs* with wit and a rhetorical stiletto. He relished its life-giving energy, especially after eighteen years of experience with the political cabals and heavy-handed "divinity" of the Thiers-Molé-Guizot ministerial dynasty, even as he agonized over its consequences for liberty.[74] But when he found himself on the political sidelines after his abrupt dismissal with the entire Barrot cabinet at the end of October 1849, his thoughts increasingly turned to the writing of history as an alternative means to support liberty in this latest era of revolving Napoleons. He gave a preview of his plans for a historical work of his own in a conversation about Thiers's *Histoire de Consulat et de l'Empire* that he had with Senior in Normandy the following summer.

In light of his own public denunciation of Napoleon in 1842, we are not surprised that the Norman commentator found little positive to say to his English houseguest about Thiers's *Histoire,* in which "the First Consul emerge[d] as the saviour of France alike on the battlefield and in the cabinet."[75] "Too long and too detailed," Thiers's work was plagued by an excess of facts: "What do we care," Tocqueville asked rhetorically, "whether the Duke of Dalmatia marched on a given point by one path or another?" What the book slighted, inexcusably, was an account of the causes that might have precipitated those facts, both "intrinsic" ones resulting from the accidents of Napoleon's character and "extrinsic" ones due to the circumstances of his era. Thiers was blinded by Napoleon's surface successes: victories in war, restoration of political order, achievement of financial solvency. He failed to probe beneath this surface and discover the political tyranny and psychological destruction that Napoleon had wrought. Thiers slighted as well Napoleon's "defective" personal character, which accounted for his utter incapacity to judge men, women, books, or art. Louis Antoine de Bourrienne, author of the *Mémoires* of Napoleon, had captured many of these qualities; Thiers had not. "The History of the Empire and the History of the Emperor are still to be written," Tocqueville concluded. "I hope one day to write them."[76]

Four months later in November 1850, ever beset with concern caused by the violent advent of the Second Republic and its increasingly despotic tenor, Tocqueville and his wife settled in Italy within the "enchanted perspective" afforded by Sorrento's sparkling orange groves and adjacent mountains for four and one-half months of convalescent retreat during which he reflected deeply about his historical work.[77] Given his lucid statements to Senior, we are perhaps most surprised by Tocqueville's many doubts at Sorrento: doubts about his topic, about his method, and about his genre, intertwined with reflections on a host of subsidiary issues, such as his target audience and their reading habits, the validity of historical "facts," and the respective merits of primary and secondary sources. He recorded his evolving thoughts in his *Souvenirs,* to which he applied himself during his mornings, and in several letters, two general plans, and a specific chapter outline directed specifically to his new work.[78] Years later, after reading Tocqueville's remarkable "piece of psychological anatomy"—his letter to Kergorlay of December 15, 1850—Sainte-Beuve would marvel at the laborious, unflinching nature of the author's searches, exhibiting "such a host of anxieties and doubts!" Not even Montaigne, Sainte-Beuve proclaimed, stripped himself "more naked" than Tocqueville in this case.[79] Indeed, on the three key levels of his self-scrutiny—subject, method, and genre—Tocqueville chose to institute a historical tabula rasa, dispensing even with those parameters of his work he had so clearly outlined to Senior. After twisting and turning the factors involved in each case, he finally returned to his point of departure, concluding that a work judging the general causes of Napoleon and his empire would provide the most suitable focus for his efforts.

In his letter to Kergorlay, Tocqueville began his reflections by stating his intention to take on "a great subject of political literature." His first preference, he continued, was not to write a traditional history but to offer "an ensemble of reflections and insights on the current time," so as to provide "a free judgment" of modern societies and "a forecast" of their probable future. But Tocqueville was unable to integrate his disparate reflections on these topics, since he lacked, he said, the "knot" that could bind them together. In turning to the writing of history, with a special focus on the era of Napoleon's empire, he hoped to find "the solid and continuous basis of facts" to serve as the missing "woof" to weave these fixed and static threads into a composite cloth. Napoleonic facts were thus important as a catalyst for the integration of his finished "picture," as a means of sustaining narrative interest in his account, and as the building blocks of a contemporary topic that would allow Tocqueville to say all that he had in mind regarding the evisceration of citizenship in France and the disposition to voluntary servitude that he so rued among the modern French populace.[80]

To write such a history, Tocqueville similarly entertained a surprising point of departure. His "first thought" had been to redo Thiers's book in the vein of "*traditional history* [*l'histoire même*]" or "history properly so called": a lengthy, multivolume rendition of the Empire's history that presumably would correct, tit for tat, the errors of Thiers's vast work. We see the evolution of his thinking in this matter—as well as the seriousness with which he first entertained it—in his letter to Beaumont eleven days later. "While hiking through the mountains of Sorrento," he told Beaumont, he had gradually come to see that he should drop any connection to a history in the style of Thiers, opting instead for a much shorter work of judgment that would elucidate "the cause, the character, the significance of the great events that formed the principal links in the chain of our time." Indeed, he had already obtained during his meditative walks "many diverse views" that had not initially occurred to him.[81] Seeking causes beneath history's surface, Tocqueville thus returned to the type of investigation and analysis that he had prized in his Guizot lecture notes and at which he had excelled to such acclaim in *Democracy in America*. His new vision of his old history thus allowed him to settle these doubts about his preferred focus for his work.

Turning specifically to genre, Tocqueville again considered a surprising range of options. The traditional historian, now epitomized by the much-maligned Thiers, practiced a sophisticated art that consisted of weaving together "the fabric of facts," a woven cloth that captured the pattern, texture, and color of the events he sought to describe. "I do not know if this art is within my reach," Tocqueville told Kergorlay, leading him to consider a second option in which he would mix "history properly so called with historical philosophy." Tocqueville then expressed doubts over how he might achieve the elusive balance needed for such a mix, now envisioned within a brief, perhaps one-volume work that would most closely resemble Montesquieu's *Considérations sur les causes de la grandeur des Romains et de leur décadence*.[82] Montesquieu had had an easier assignment in his Roman work, Tocqueville argued, since he could garner his few carefully chosen, revealing facts from a vast time period. Tocqueville's own facts, restricted to a period of just ten years, must serve in his own variation of this genre as the powerful magnet propelling his readers "naturally from one reflection to another by the interest of the narrative." The judgments about those facts would now address precisely the "intrinsic" and "extrinsic" causes he had signaled as desirable to Senior: among eight prospective topics, Tocqueville expected to assess the causes of the Empire's foundation in postrevolutionary society, its enabling mechanisms, and "the *true* nature" of its founder, Napoleon.[83] In his more detailed chapter plan, he expanded these topics into ten chapters, with five devoted to Napoleon's psychological make-up and five to the circumstances that facilitated his ascent, helped consolidate his power, and precipitated his fall.[84]

Tocqueville's choice of Napoleon also met the requirements of his "singular" view of historical perspective, best described in his marginal note to his 1850–51 "Original Idea."[85] Tocqueville saw himself, he said there, as a "contemporary" of the events of the Empire—one of the "neighbors" of the era who could "still experience the last tremors in their minds or hearts" of the mighty Revolution and thus could better grasp "the true relation between the principal persons of distinction and principal facts, of the great historical masses between themselves . . . the general history, the general causes, the grand movement of facts, the current of opinion of which men placed too far away no longer form an idea." Where Thiers's view of perspective led him to distance himself from such contemporary emotions, so as to remove their undue power,[86] Tocqueville sought to familiarize himself with just those passions, since they constituted the essence of the history he sought to write.

With Napoleon as topic, Tocqueville thus succeeded in aligning at Sorrento each major component of his historical constellation. He resolved his doubts regarding subject, method, genre, and preferred historical perspective—only to reexamine each, we will now see, after his first prolonged endeavor to write his new book.

3. Tocqueville's 1852 Attempt to Initiate His New Book

Louis-Napoleon's cynical, violent, and repressive coup of December 2, 1851, inaugurated the next stage of Tocqueville's historical career by finally foreclosing his political one. As a duly elected deputy, Tocqueville acquitted himself bravely and decisively when the coup finally came, protesting in the Chamber, passing two nights in prison, and managing covertly to provide a letter to the *London Times* that urged international censure of Louis-Napoleon's constitutional violations. [87] Despite his immense political and personal despondency at this final forfeiture of "regular and moderate liberty," expressed most poignantly in his letters to Beaumont during the next four months, [88] he nevertheless picked up the threads of his historical work with remarkable speed, writing to a Norman constituent within two weeks of the coup: "I have had for a long time in my head the subject of a new book that, in anticipation of the events we have just seen, I had commenced at Sorrento last winter and that I was ardently wishing to have the leisure to continue." [89] True to his loyalty to France and its liberty, he added that he wished his newly acquired spare time had arrived in a fashion less costly for his country.

Tocqueville set to work in January 1852 on his new history in general and in particular the book's first chapter, clearly defined in his Sorrento chapter outline of the previous year: "Picture of the society formed by the Revolution that facilitated [Napoleon's ascent to power]." [90] To locate the all-important sources, he cast wide his initial archival net:

> To carefully study this history, I must divide it into compartments: war, administration, literature.
>
> Men to consult: Molé, Pasquier, Brévanne, d'Aunay, Mignet, Thiers.
>
> Documents:
>
> Printed: the *Monitor*, the *Bulletin of Laws*, histories, memoirs.

Manuscript: diplomatic papers, handwritten letters, unpublished memoirs.[91]

He subsequently made lists of readings recommended by Molé, d'Aunay, and others;[92] he also canvassed widely for "printed documents" at the Bibliothèque nationale, compiling various lists from miscellaneous catalogs encompassing the entire span of the Empire. During a five-month period from January through May 1852, Tocqueville used these lists to unearth a host of histories and political writings, newspaper accounts, and memoirs, as well as engravings, cartoons, and a list of the era's publications obtained from the librarian, Charles Richomme.[93]

Tocqueville transcribed more than 350 pages of reading notes on these assorted materials between January and June 1852, with a special focus on memoirs, both published and unpublished. Of particular interest are his extensive notes on Lafayette, transcribed in "February 1852," and his briefer but suggestive comments on three works written during the Directory by Benjamin Constant.

Tocqueville's notes on Lafayette's *Mémoires* demonstrate his interest in the numerous parallels in their personal situations dealing with Napoleonic coups separated by just over fifty years. On a substantive level, Tocqueville found Lafayette a blunt observer of the personality of Napoleon, his army, and the pre–18 brumaire spirit of France—"so enslaved, fed up, paralyzed."[94] Analyzing the nation, Lafayette saw the contradictions at the heart of the French character in its rising prosperity and declining patriotism, its rapacity and frivolity, its resistance to servitude even while grudgingly submitting to it. Lafayette labeled the mood "an agitated servitude," a term Tocqueville deemed a "(fitting remark)."[95] While Lafayette showed himself a bit too receptive to Napoleon's personal overtures, Tocqueville was clearly impressed by his assessment of his times, several aspects of which he would incorporate directly when he wrote his chapters, although without citing their author.[96]

Tocqueville also read and notated at this time Constant's 1796 and 1797 writings, *De la force du gouvernement actuel, Des réactions politiques,* and the latter's supplement, *Des effets de la Terreur.* Tocqueville had signaled the books for reading on two different bibliographical lists, including his most extensive one of 198 titles "pertaining to the subject that occupies me" assembled at the Bibliothèque nationale.[97] His two provocative pages of notes intersperse four passages of interest from the works with several personal comments. He first transcribed Constant's devastating portrait of those embittered men who had lost in the Revolution all that was dearest to them, leading them to pursue vengeance by whatever means possible, including criminal ones: "to generalize," he noted, "when I shall wish to speak of this party." [98] He highlighted Constant's warning to the Directory in his concluding chapter of *De la force* to adhere vigorously and precisely to both the laws and the forms of the new constitution. "It's infinitely more dangerous to make a revolution for virtue than for crime," Constant argued there. When scoundrels violate the constitution, the people will understand it as a crime; when "honest men," however, such as members of the Directory, violate the laws with impunity, they shake the very moorings of society and threaten its "overthrow," since "the people no longer know where they stand." "How true and even profound and well expressed to boot!" observed Tocqueville, adding that it would be "useful to use when I shall paint the state of mind of the French at the end of the Directory and its causes." [99] Having proffered such praise, Tocqueville subjected Constant to his standard "liberty test," chastising him in a wry aside for his inconstancy sixteen months later when he defended precisely the extralegal activity in the coup d'état of 18 fructidor 1797 that he here deplored. Tocqueville next transcribed Constant's statement in *Des effets de la Terreur* of France's irreparable loss owing to the Terror's "swallowing up" of the entire generation of the Girondins, a devastation that had left Constant's own generation "between the elderly in their second childhood and children of poor breeding." [100] Finally, Tocqueville noted, also without comment, Constant's reference to "an almost material impulsion" that was drawing his generation "at one and the same time far from liberal ideas and revolutionary crimes." [101]

With his note taking completed, Tocqueville left Paris in early June with a multitude of books for his family's château in Normandy, where he braced himself on June 15 to commence his writing: "I can't help but experience a bit of anxiety at the approach of this great test; because its success or lack thereof could exercise a huge influence on the rest of my life." [102] Beginning his writing on June 23, he chose to jump into that part of his work, based upon his notes from Paris, for which he had the most taste. [103] Within a month—by the end of the third week of July—he had completed his two chapters; [104] he delivered his own verdict on them to Beaumont, saying that they were "spirited enough, it is true, because it was almost contemporary emotions that I had to render," and adding that their purpose had been to gather a head of steam for his larger project. [105]

In his two chapters ("How the Republic Was Ready to Receive a Master" and "How the Nation, in Ceasing to Be Republican, Remained Revolutionary") Tocqueville analyzed "this internal and invisible malady that . . . was the state of minds and mores" of millions of Frenchmen during the period preceding Napoleon.[106] He depicts a pre-Napoleonic spirit full of contrary features: at once sullen and gay, tolerant of its governors but spiteful toward them, obedient but passively resistant. Working from a short index that he compiled of pertinent passages from Jacques Mallet du Pan, Antoine Thibaudeau, Lafayette, and Joseph Fiévée,[107] he uses his array of memoirists as expert eyewitnesses to document these conflicting strands of the French spirit. True to his intention to use Constant's "profound" insights of the political causes of this psychological imbalance, he first advances an explanation that highlights the people's disorientation in the face of the Directory's imposition of an increasingly harsh brand of legal terrorism. Constant had argued in *De la force* that the "corruption" of public opinion in 1796 was caused by "certain revolutionary habits" that had overturned all principles, perverted all opinions, and that now "weigh upon the society in mass, and on each individual in particular, at every hour and under every form."[108] In his first chapter, Tocqueville provides a similar diagnosis of the period that succeeded the coup d'état of 18 fructidor 1797, when Constant's worst fears were realized: the Directory—"so fertile in its invention of revolutionary procedures"—resorted to harsher and harsher extralegal measures, resulting in "a character of perfected atrocity."[109] It expected people to rally to its new institutions of terror; the people opted instead to withdraw from all political engagement, thus demonstrating the prescience of Constant's warning . . . and the futility of his advice.

We note that Tocqueville's explanation emphasizes the extraordinary political potency of the great Revolution of 1789. It was the Revolution, he states in his third paragraph, that had concentrated new power in the government, granting the Directory "greater power than had ever belonged to the kings whom the Revolution had overthrown." It was the Revolution, he continues, that had eliminated the old checks previously imposed on the government by "the laws, the customs and the mores." Initially, a residue of surviving liberty had caused fierce debate and elicited heated opposition to the imposition of the Terror. As the Revolution progressed, this liberty vanished: the press became "mute"; political representatives were selected by the government, not the people; local administrators were made to bend to the government's will; political accountability was nil. Revolutionary laws of the most extreme kind were now routinely passed without resistance, and routinely disobeyed by a people who had played no role in making them.[110]

In his sixth paragraph, Tocqueville broadens his argument by embedding it within a sociology of "violent revolutions." In such a revolution, laws and mores travel on opposite trajectories: laws progress from mildness to cruelty as public debate on their merits is progressively stifled, while mores, initially enflamed by popular passions, gradually succumb to lethargy owing to the same absence of liberty.[111] Tocqueville's sociology of revolutions disputes that of Adrien de Lezay-Marnésia, a detailed account of which he had encountered in Constant's pamphlet *Des effets de la Terreur.* There, in "all" revolutions—as Constant insisted in his own point-by-point rebuttal of Lezay's argument[112]—Lezay famously argued that Terror must serve as a "reinforcement" at the midpoint of a republic's development so as to ensure its successful transition from a position supported by popular "fervor" to one supported by popular "apathy." At either end of this popular spectrum, Lezay insisted (in a variation of the Guizotian argument that Tocqueville believed also attributed an unwarranted utility to despotism), a republic might survive; but during periods of unstable transition, Terror should be introduced to preserve that "excellent institution" to which the people could then be expected to rally. In Tocqueville's countersociology, he makes it clear that Terror at the midpoint of Revolutions could never rally the people, since it further degrades already enervated "public mores" and thus precipitates precisely the downward spiral of passive obedience and resistance in which the Directory found itself trapped. If the Directory had been shrewd, Tocqueville now says in his seventh paragraph, it would have dispensed with Terror and recognized instead "that great maxim of famous despots—a maxim we will soon see applied—that to put a people in servitude and hold them there, repressive legislation poorly applied is less effective than the mild laws of a perfected administration regularly applied, as of its own accord, every day to everyone." Such a soft despotism, to which Tocqueville had alerted his readers in his climactic political section of volume 2 of *Democracy in America,* would have served most effectively to achieve the "apathy" that Lezay actively sought, Constant naively encouraged, and Tocqueville resolutely abhorred.[113]

The French people as a whole were well prepared to accept the yoke of such a despotism, Tocqueville now argues in the rest of his two chapters, since they were irredeemably tainted by the "moral usury" that pervaded the nation as a whole.[114] On the one hand, they lived daily with the questionable legitimacy of their new wealth, acquired through purchase of confiscated lands and the fictitious reimbursement of prerevolutionary debts. On another, their consciences were troubled by the memory of atrocities large or small committed during the Revolution. On the whole, they suffered from self-contempt, "turn[ing] finally against themselves" and ridiculing the very enthusiasm and idealistic devotion that had formerly inspired their monumental revolutionary deeds. [115] Hating themselves, disoriented by revolutionary refashioning of their work schedules, calendar, units of measurement, and language—introducing "tyranny . . . more profoundly into private life than at any other time in history"[116]—they withdrew from one another, eschewing public participation of any kind. Tocqueville's deep dismay is evident in his account, for such a revolutionary legacy was responsible, he believed, for two eras of despotism, a first under Napoleon Bonaparte—still to be chronicled in his book—and a second under Louis-Napoleon that he lived with every day. Artfully building the suspense of his drama, Tocqueville saves even a mention of Bonaparte to the chapters' final sentence: trapped in a state of suspended animation, "turn[ing] its eyes listlessly from side to side to see if no one would come to its aid," the French nation, along with his readers, awaited the general's arrival to launch its next act, one that would usher in the new form of servitude for France and its people. [117]

Tocqueville never succeeded in raising the curtain on the Napoleonic era's "new play" for which he had set the stage in these ways. Two explanations seem plausible for his discontent with his first writing efforts. On three separate occasions, before, during, and after writing the chapters, he suggested to Beaumont that the problem pertained to his choice of "a subject."[118] The problem could not be his larger subject of the Revolution as a whole, so it appears that he referred here to his specific choice to begin with Napoleon and to dissect first the phenomenon of the society of apathetic and isolated individuals who endorsed his ascent to power. The Frenchmen of the Directory did not lack passions—indeed, they possessed a deeply entrenched hatred of the Old Regime that was in the process of transforming itself into "a permanent racial trait."[119] What they lacked was public virtue—the commitment to engage in the politics necessary to ensure stable, moderate, balanced liberty. So they stood on the sidelines, deferring to an army that did possess its own warped strain of public virtue, skewed to its desire for simple, clear, strong government that could dispense with inconveniences such as popular assemblies and other forms of "democratic" participation. Tocqueville's subject—combining in these ways economic, social, and cultural factors, [120] all intertwined with considerations of the French national character—thus caused him to push his investigations back not just to the early days of the Revolution but even further to prerevolutionary times.

In Furet's apt words, "He was in part impelled by the logic of all historical work, which is to proceed backward in time in search of origins." [121]

But such an explanation tells only part of the story. For Tocqueville's dissatisfaction was not just with the substance of his effort; in a July 16 letter to Beaumont, written as he was completing his first drafting efforts, he indicated that he would need his friend's help in establishing "the genre of the work and the style that is most suitable to adopt for it." [122] With respect to "genre" and its related issue of "style," Tocqueville's problem seems to be the same one that had worried him in his letter to Kergorlay from Sorrento: how to achieve the proper balance of facts and judgments. In these 1852 chapters, Tocqueville chose to organize his account within a sociological frame tied to the movements of revolutions. [123] At the same time, he resorted to psychological analysis heavily weighted with his own general reflections and theories about the mood of the period, often couched in vague terms: Paris's sleep, he said, was "disturbed by bad dreams"; "France to [her enemies] seemed to be raving mad." [124] In both cases, he chose to express his general ideas in a manner that was analytic and expansive, conveyed with omniscient assurance. It adduced facts but did not spring from those facts, a flaw in his historical method that he may have been calling into question in his letter to Beaumont. [125]

I would raise the additional possibility that Tocqueville was uncomfortable with his reliance on memoirs as his chief sources for this period of the Directory. For memoirs, he had emphasized at Sorrento, "cannot teach" the current of opinion and the more general history of an era. [126] But to Tocqueville's evident surprise, he found that contemporaries' observations contained considerable insight into "the great movement of facts" of their times. We have noted his respect for Lafayette's observations and his response to Constant's portrayal of the causes of the psychological dislocation of the period; he expressed similar interest in his reading of Mallet du Pan's *Mémoires,* finding his analysis of the Terror "better explained and even better depicted than I have ever seen." [127] These contemporaries, however, so full of insights of their own about the era's "spirit," [128] posed an unexpected challenge to Tocqueville's work, since they became a type of competitor to the novelty of his own account. If Lafayette, Mallet du Pan, and Constant had an understanding of the French spirit in this period, what topics should Tocqueville's own history focus on? Such a problem may have contributed to his general dissatisfaction with "the plan followed in the two chapters in question," [129] as well as to his upcoming decision to shift his research focus from memoirs to manuscript sources.

In these ways Tocqueville found the limits of an approach that privileged a history of Napoleon and his empire. By pushing back in time, as he now prepared to do, he hoped he would discover the roots of French public lassitude, as well as the sources that would allow him to claim for his own the field that analyzed its causes.

TOCQUEVILLE AND FEUDAL RIGHTS
A Bridge to the Old Regime

> You would laugh if you saw a man who has written so much
> on democracy, surrounded by feudists and poring over old rent
> rolls or other dusty records. . . . The boredom that this study
> causes me, combined with all the reasons I already had for not
> loving the Old Regime, ends by making me a real revolutionary.[1]

F rançois Furet has surmised that Tocqueville experienced
"a kind of conceptual block" when he sought—unsuccessfully—in 1836 and 1856 to move from his published writings on
the Old Regime to his planned sequels on the Revolution proper.
For Furet, Tocqueville's "block" resulted from a contradiction at
the heart of his historical vision, as he struggled to reconcile his
views of the Revolution's continuity, seen in its administrative
structures, and its radical ideological transformation, evident in
pamphlets and the *cahiers*.[2]

At a number of crucial junctures in writing *The Old Regime*,
Tocqueville indeed encountered various kinds of "blocks" that
forced him to reappraise his work in different ways—in July 1852,
as we have just seen, but also in June 1853, fall 1856, and spring 1858.
Most often the blocks involved a combination of factors, I find,
as in 1852 when Tocqueville set aside his seven-month inquiry
that had brought him to the cusp of the Napoleonic era and
chose to step back instead to a new analysis of the prerevolutionary period. At Sorrento in 1850–51, Tocqueville thought he
had determined an appropriate configuration of the elements
necessary for his history; in Paris in spring 1852, he sought to fashion it; in Normandy in late July 1852, he embarked on a new effort
to recalibrate its parameters.

Pushing back in time from the era of Napoleon to that of the Revolution's origins, Tocqueville encountered the same prerevolutionary period to which he had previously addressed scholarly attention in his 1836 essay.[3] Some scholars have seen this overlap in subject matter as contributing "an enormous advantage" to Tocqueville's new work, since "it enabled him to use again the analytical framework he had constructed for his essay."[4] To be sure, Tocqueville's "analytical framework"—shaped in his courses with Guizot—served him well in both instances. But Tocqueville himself saw no advantage in thus retracing his steps, since his new project emerged from a new intellectual phase in his own life and a new political phase in the life of his nation. Indeed, we have seen in chapter 2 how his historical method led him repeatedly to seek to reenvision its correlated parts. He thus looked back to the essay as a singular product of a separate compartment of his earlier life, no longer relevant to his new endeavors: it might be, he would only concede in 1856, "rather curious to reread in my idle moments."[5]

But despite Tocqueville's own dismissive attitude, we benefit from examining the essay for what it can tell us about the evolution in his historical thought during the twenty-year heart of his historical career. Such an examination of his conceptual development over time has been a staple in Tocquevillian studies since at least the 1960s, when Drescher published his pioneering article.[6] The progressive exhuming of Tocqueville's archives for The Old Regime has led to similar such comparisons between volume 1 and the unfinished volume 2 of his later work.[7] The 1836 essay and The Old Regime, volume 1, constitute a third pair of such Tocquevillian "doubles" possessing its own rich pedigree, dating back to Minnie Senior and Gustave Beaumont's posthumous republications of the essay in the 1860s that served to expand its audience to France and America and identify it for the first time as Tocqueville's work.[8] Senior and Beaumont each presented the essay as a remarkable example of Tocqueville's intuitive genius, containing "the same thought . . . at bottom" as The Old Regime.[9] In line with the famous quip cited by their contemporary, Sainte-Beuve, that Tocqueville "began to think before having learned anything,"[10] their arguments tended to maximize Tocqueville's deductive brilliance and minimize the importance of his archival toils in the 1850s, since these latter investigations for The Old Regime served to validate but not "supersede" his earlier views expressed in his essay.[11]

A close examination of Tocqueville's two works yields a more complex view of his historical method, however. Tocqueville's devastating critique in the essay of the growth in the Old Regime of "administrative tyranny" (in which he followed Guizot's lectures by explaining how "the people and the *tiers-état* . . . even gave up, voluntarily, all their rights")[12] masks a far more complicated process of gestation in his understanding of this issue by the time he wrote *The Old Regime,* as we shall see in chapter 5. In chapters 6 and 8, we will likewise see how Tocqueville revised in *The Old Regime* his early view of liberty's powerful presence in eighteenth-century French opinion where it had flourished as "the modern, the democratic, and, I venture to say, the only just notion of liberty."[13] In the 1836 essay, such "democratic liberty" not only benefited from its remarkable suffusion throughout society but also incorporated within itself all of France's surviving particles of long-standing local liberty, including both its communal and its aristocratic variants. Given such deep roots, it presented a powerful antidote to absolute royal despotism, forcing kings to take note of it and "the royal power [to stop] as it were of itself" in the pursuit of its administrative hegemony.[14] In the 1850s Tocqueville reconsidered this portrait of democratic liberty triumphant, for two reasons. First, political events portrayed a far less salubrious view of liberty's deep instantiation within the modern French mind. Second, Tocqueville's archival research tended to highlight in the documents he perused a new strain of ubiquitous zeal for government solutions, resulting in individual and community dependence and leading to a type of opinion that was neither just nor free. Both shifts led to a less optimistic portrayal in *The Old Regime* of liberty's pervasive presence and future prospects.

In this chapter, we will see a third significant deviation in Tocqueville's 1856 revolutionary understanding owing to his studies of the mentality of the French peasant. In his 1836 essay, Tocqueville had recognized that French landholdings "were already remarkably divided" before the Revolution, a finding he would confirm in his 1852 investigations. But in the essay he attributed to France's small landed proprietors a "mental tranquillity . . . this calmness and simplicity in their desires, this habit and relish of independence" that he saw as crucial to the development of the era's new democratic institutions.[15] The individual liberty assured by property in the countryside aided the era's democratic revolution in France; in his chief rhetorical message of 1836 to his elite English audience, he urged them to accept division of their own excessive properties and thus avoid the French Revolution's violent denouement. Twenty years later, Tocqueville's studies for *The Old Regime* revealed a French peasant who no longer epitomized the peaceful independence that forestalled revolutionary excesses but now embodied the violent rage that precipitated them.

1. Tocqueville and Peasant Economic Gain

In late July 1852 Tocqueville began his explorations of how the Revolution "enormously increased the well-being of the people"[16] by listing seven categories of peasant financial gain mentioned in his second Napoleonic chapter, outlining a general approach to an investigation, and then seeking to develop specific sources or inquiries that could help answer the questions thus posed.[17] The seven categories were purchase at a low price of confiscated lands; reimbursement of debts with a fictitious money; payment of rents with this same money; raising of salaries; abolition of feudal rights; abolition of certain taxes and equalization of those maintained or created; and nonpayment of taxes. He turned to friends and acquaintances for help in locating sources that would shed light on each category. A mid-July letter to his cousin, Le Peletier d'Aunay, brought information on where to find the "nomenclature" of suppressed taxes.[18] In conversations with a former deputy, Jacques-François Hervieu, and with the intendant of Tocqueville, Birette, he explored the elimination of debt and jump in salaries of agricultural workers.[19] A rapid exchange of four letters in eleven days with Gallemand produced two books by the feudist Joseph Renauldon, advice to consult two experts—M. Cordhomme, a property specialist and Valognes Council member since the days of the Revolution, and François Dubosc, the departmental archivist—plus crucial information regarding the importance of the "records of properties [états de section]" required by the law of 1790.[20] Tocqueville's most important correspondence on his feudal project took place with Kergorlay, since it was his cousin who articulated the limits of such an investigation and proposed a useful model for realizing a crucial part of it.

Writing on July 22, 1852, just as he finished drafting his two Napoleonic chapters, Tocqueville broached two separate but related questions that had been stirred by his "painting of the epoch that preceded 18 brumaire and the state of minds that brought about this coup d'état": What was the financial profit of the peasantry during the Revolution, and what was their degree of property ownership before it?[21] The two questions were, of course, related: financial profit produced by the Revolution would include new ownership of property, unless such ownership predated the Revolution. Kergorlay answered in a sober letter framed by his reaction to the death of their friend Eugène Stoffels and an account of his severe personal financial problems.[22] Regarding a calculation of the material gain of the peasantry, Kergorlay opined prophetically: "What strikes me is that I believe it insoluble." "It would require an army of Benedictines to discover those unknown times," he added, doubting that Tocqueville as one researcher could even begin to make sense of this "abyss." He predicted that Tocqueville would be constrained to accept only general, secondhand notions of the peasants' gain.[23]

With respect to peasant property ownership, Kergorlay reported that by looking at prerevolutionary land plans of his own and neighboring towns in the Oise, he could readily recognize that the number of plots was about the same then as now, and that the names of peasant owners before and since the Revolution had remained constant, thus demonstrating little change in ownership. He then presented several options by which Tocqueville might "generalize" this snap investigation: he could seek out property experts who might know something about the larger arrondissement or department; he could wait and explore the archives of the ministry of finance in Paris where, after all, the key to all of these questions must exist; or he might consider sending a questionnaire on these matters to fifty of his former colleagues in the legislature.

Tocqueville made an intense and sustained effort, especially during the next two months, to prove Kergorlay wrong by demonstrating that his solo, original archival work could measure up to the hypothetical efforts of Kergorlay's Benedictine army. His dogged twisting and turning of this issue can be seen in the variety of sources he assembled, in his methodical consideration of variables affecting a number of his seven potential sources of economic gain, and in the application of his research to a functioning seigneury of the eighteenth century—that of his own family. "Imagine," he suggested, "a parish like T[ocqueville] under the Old Regime and myself as seigneur." [24] Using a family inventory of the revenue received from its properties in 1780, he estimated that as many as sixty small property holders would have subsequently been relieved by the Revolution of at least 3,485 livres of seigneurial rent "abolished without indemnity," plus another 925 livres representing payment of the feudal *champarts*, also abolished without compensation.[25] However, despite his best efforts, Tocqueville was increasingly forced to acknowledge the wisdom of Kergorlay's advice on these matters, even while engaged in the heart of this research: "I plunge deeper and deeper into these matters without touching bottom; and I begin to believe, as you do, that there is no bottom. It's the ocean one hundred leagues away from shore." [26]

In assessing peasant land proprietorship, Tocqueville would fare better as he replicated Kergorlay's simple model in studies of various communes in his own canton of Saint-Pierre-Église.[27] Tocqueville's elaboration of Kergorlay's study consisted of five steps:

1. Obtain a count of property holders during the Revolution, using the "records of properties" recommended by Gallemand and required by the law of November 23–December 1, 1790.
2. Seek to verify that this revolutionary figure could be applied to prerevolutionary times as well, by controlling for the sale of *biens nationaux* from either the church or émigrés.
3. Obtain a current count of property holders in 1852, using a written or oral interview with a local public official.
4. Seek to control for population growth between 1788 and 1852, which could provide an alternative explanation for a rise in property ownership, by asking the public official or consulting 1847 census figures.
5. Compare the two counts from steps 1 and 3, after taking into account the control data, to assess the relative numbers of pre- and postrevolutionary landed proprietors.

Tocqueville's research plan worked best in the small neighboring commune of Réville, where the town's mayor—legitimist leader and former legislative colleague Comte Henri Duparc—responded helpfully to a five-question survey submitted by Tocqueville.[28] He indicated that the town had 685 property holders in 1852, and he responded to the second of Tocqueville's "control" questions by saying that there had been no population growth since the Revolution. Tocqueville knew from the 1791 inventory that there were 405 property holders at that time; since their total was not inflated by revolutionary sales of confiscated property, except for very limited sales of *biens d'église* indicated by Duparc, he was able to conclude that prerevolutionary property owners numbered approximately 405/685 of the current figure.[29] Consistent with Kergorlay's advice, Tocqueville recognized the need to generalize these results; thus, after summarizing them for Freslon on September 7, he added: "But in order for such research to mean something, it must be applied to a great number of different points of the country and that is what I will succeed, I hope, in doing."[30]

In a related study, seeking further confirmation of how the sale of *biens d'émigrés* affected local property ownership, Tocqueville investigated such sales in the full canton of Saint-Pierre-Église. Using an 1824 document provided by the local office of registration, he examined the disposition of thirty-eight properties of émigrés in the canton. He found that many of the smaller properties were purchased, especially in the cases of emigrant priests, by local family members, some of whose names he recognized. The largest lots were taken by buyers from the larger towns of Saint-Pierre,

Cherbourg, and Valognes. The châteaus, factories, grain mills, and oil mills were purchased by industries from Cherbourg.[31]

As part of his parallel effort to determine "the extent of pecuniary charges" still weighing on the peasant in 1789, Tocqueville requested from Gallemand a suitable reference work for eighteenth-century feudal "practitioners" that would give the exact nomenclature, the relative importance, and the collection procedures for the vast array of extant feudal rights.[32] Gallemand provided Tocqueville with Renauldon's *Traité historique et pratique des droits seigneuriaux* (Paris, 1765), a work for which Tocqueville laboriously compiled copious, often verbatim textual summaries that he would subsequently incorporate into *The Old Regime* as his concluding "general feudal rights" endnote. Tocqueville seemed to have applied himself to this reading immediately on receiving the book at the end of August, for he told Freslon on September 7 that despite his "intellectual indigestion from documents of great weight and little substance," he had gained a "very clear and fairly exact" knowledge of the specific nature and weight of these charges.[33] But in keeping with Kergorlay's prediction, he also indicated to Freslon the declining prospects of arriving at any precise economic calculations of peasant profit from abolition of these rights, citing their geographic variability as the chief obstacle to such a broader assessment. Writing to Madame de Circourt on September 18, he spoke of the benefit now afforded his historical perspective by these prerevolutionary studies; he also hinted at the limitations of a reading approach so closely tethered to his archival facts: "But I do not yet know . . . how to direct myself in this ocean of the French Revolution. I study, I strive, I try to squeeze the facts more tightly than it seems to me has been attempted up until now, in order to extract the general truth they contain."[34]

It was in the midst of this investigation of the fifth point of his original outline—"abolition of feudal rights" as a potential source of peasant economic gain—that Tocqueville discovered a preferred means for assessing these feudal remains: the discussions, committee reports, and subsequent legislative acts of the Constituent Assembly, Legislative Assembly, and Convention that sought to implement the decrees of August 10, 1789. Using *L'ancien moniteur* and, most likely, *L'histoire parlementaire* of Buchez and Roux, he traced the evolution of this issue from the initial decrees until the final law of July 7–18, 1793, which suppressed all seigneurial dues and feudal rights fixed or casual, without indemnity.[35] Arriving at the crucial decree of May 15–28, 1790, which abolished personal feudal obligations but preserved the necessity of redeeming contracted property rights, he employed a *Dictionnaire de droit* of 1749 to define successively each term encountered there.[36]

Tocqueville believed that the advantages of this new line of inquiry were manifold, with the committee reports, in particular, helping him "to come to know best what remained of feudalism in 1789. Better than all the studies I made of heavy and outdated books." [37] In them, Tocqueville could view with confidence the precise feudal rights existing at the commencement of the Revolution, thus eliminating the twenty-four-year time gap presented by Renauldon's 1765 tome. Moreover, the very focus of the early debates—which attempted an economic analysis of rights to determine the various costs of reimbursement—directly aided Tocqueville's own calculations. Finally, and perhaps most important, Tocqueville found in these debates the beginning of a new approach to feudal rights, one best seen in his brief notes on Sieyès's speech of August 10, 1789, regarding abolition of the *dîme*.

In his notes on that speech, which he termed "a masterpiece of logic," he began by contrasting Sieyès's estimated figure of "70 millions" of collected *dîmes* with Mirabeau's "100 millions"; Sieyès's underestimation demonstrated again the difficulty of establishing reliable financial data owing to the ideological perspectives of the calculators, in this case the renegade priest and the count. [38] Tocqueville went on to note how tenant farmers had "the illusion" they would gain from the *dîme*'s abolition, whereas it would in fact be only the property owners who would gain; he added, however, that in a revolution, "the illusion . . . is worth the fact." [39] The peasants' perception of the injustice of the *dîme* then gave rise to another Tocquevillian observation that tied together the two separate research tracks on which he had first embarked in his letter to Kergorlay:

> But my research establishes more and more that the number of
> these small property owners was already immense at the time of
> the suppression of the *dîme*. Reason why this tax was more odious in
> France than anywhere else. . . . The small property-owner . . . who
> sees his harvest seized without compensation . . . and who depends
> on this harvest to survive, is so placed as to feel the weight of this tax
> more than anyone else. The substance and the form hurt him. [40]

Tocqueville here recognized how the high level of property ownership among French peasants exacerbated their remaining feudal burden; rather than welcoming their new status, the peasants were incensed by their new burdens. With this realization, Tocqueville achieved the conceptual breakthrough that would guide his chief feudal rights thesis in *The Old Regime:* the paradoxical notion that the peasants' feudal hatred increased with the lessening of their feudal obligations. The passage also prefigured his famous personification in *The Old Regime* of the embittered, isolated peasant property owner (*OR*, 1:117), economically more independent but psychologically more irate than his European counterpart.

The conclusions of Tocqueville's Normandy investigations were well expressed in a summary note he wrote during this period,[41] subsequently incorporated as endnote 14 in *The Old Regime*. In the note, based, as he stated, on his summer of investigations in Normandy, Tocqueville focused on the pervasive breadth of the feudal system that affected "men's pecuniary interest in almost all of their affairs." It was not the absolute amount of the financial burden that was most important; it was the universal experience of its continuing weight that piqued a new level of ire owing to the presence of so many independent property owners.

Bastions of independence and tranquillity in the 1836 essay, these small landed proprietors now seethed with pent-up frustration, awaiting a revolution to settle their hatreds and a master to secure their economic gains.

2. Tocqueville and Dareste

Tocqueville's investigation of feudal rights would continue unabated for four years. Although for reasons of health he could not sustain his hoped-for focus and consistency, he persisted with a multifaceted approach, ready to seize upon new books or articles that might expand or corroborate its reach. He was aided in this effort by the clear vision of his principal thesis achieved during his summer in Normandy, allowing him to direct his research toward explaining the paradox of peasant feudal hatred. In this vein, he turned to eyewitnesses of the prerevolutionary period who traveled in the French countryside (such as Arthur Young), political leaders who sought to formulate policies there (Turgot and Necker), insurgents who instigated events there (Pierre-François Boncerf), agricultural societies and peasants who described life there, and even eighteenth-century "experts" who reported facts from there (Guillaume-François Le Trosne and François Quesnay). These readings were often rich and anecdotal, providing grist for future endnotes. Tocqueville especially relished contact with unassuming, unknown writers who made up in enthusiasm what they lacked in style; one such example was Gaultier de Biauzat, an author "who possessed no authority and merited none" but who provided "several interesting pieces of information on the doings and ideas of his contemporaries."[42] Apart from the special case of Young, who as an agricultural expert viewed the countryside with an especially practiced eye, memoirs were noticeably lacking from Tocqueville's new printed sources.

When Tocqueville turned to study the European context of feudal rights, he dispensed with these assorted barometers intended to take the measure of eighteenth-century sentiments and relied directly on feudal experts. For Germany, these consisted primarily of the professors he encountered in his stay at Bonn, whom he queried extensively on German feudal rights in his conversations with them. [43] For England, Blackstone and Macaulay helped him to probe "this English point of departure, which explains so much and which, by incredible luck, has been barely noted." [44] Tocqueville sought in England a counterpoint to the French nobility's abject surrender of responsibility for local affairs in the French countryside, a key emerging plank in his explanation of peasant hatred there. While the French nobility succumbed to the allure of the king's court, the English stayed firmly planted in their country homes. While the French nobility insisted on preserving those pecuniary and honorific privileges most inclined to inflame local sentiment, the English nobility surrendered theirs. While the French "caste" remained closed, the English "aristocracy" opened its ranks to newcomers. It was in Blackstone, in particular, that Tocqueville sought and found confirmation for these theses. [45]

Many of these supplementary sources for feudal rights were noted in *The Old Regime;* Tocqueville's chief feudal rights instructor—the thirty-three-year-old C. Dareste de la Chavanne—was not.

It was as a member of the Académie des sciences morales et politiques that Tocqueville encountered an 1852 text of Dareste submitted to the Académie in response to its prize competition of that year. The Académie's 1852 question to which Dareste responded read as follows:

> Research what was the condition of the agricultural classes in France
> from the thirteenth century up to the Revolution of 1789. Indicate
> through what successive stages they passed—whether they were in
> full servitude or whether they had a certain degree of liberty—until
> their complete emancipation. Show the successive obligations to
> which they were subjected, marking the differences produced in this
> regard in different parts of France, and drawing upon writings of
> jurists, texts of old and reformed customs, general and local, printed
> and manuscript, royal legislation and writings of historians, as well as
> titles and old leases that could throw some light on the question. [46]

The question, in the same terms, had been formulated originally for the 1850 prize competition, when Dareste was its sole, albeit unsuccessful, respondent. [47] Dareste submitted his revised and expanded response by the deadline of October 31, 1852, titled "Mémoire sur l'état des classes agricoles depuis le XIII siècle jusqu'à 1789," and was judged victorious among four contestants in an announcement by Guizot on April 30, 1853. Guizot's comments to the winner were double-edged: although praising Dareste's work for its "rare knowledge of sources" and "skilful analysis of facts," Guizot made a point of expressing the judges' displeasure with its failure to capture "the moral laws that preside over the enchainment of facts, and that govern them in binding them among themselves. . . . It is necessary to demonstrate, at the heart of these facts, the secret bond and movement that unite and nurture them, and that are providential laws."[48] True to his beliefs articulated twenty-five years earlier in his course at the Sorbonne, Guizot thus affirmed his conviction that history must articulate the hidden "moral laws" that accounted for the linkage of surface facts; by focusing on just the facts, however diligently and capably, Dareste had failed to explain their underlying causes.

Reading Dareste's essay in the late spring of 1853, I believe,[49] Tocqueville benefited in multiple ways from the Lyons professor of history's carefully crafted, richly documented, heavily footnoted text. First, he used it as a bibliographic treasure trove. With the Académie having designated the sources to be studied, Dareste's task, as he subsequently noted, had been rather straightforward: "I had to gather together these documents, often incoherent and dispersed, study them and make sense of them."[50] Tocqueville's job was even easier—to plumb Dareste's work thus assembled, not only to take note of Dareste's extensive repertoire of feudal sources (including a number of authors whom Tocqueville would subsequently read with considerable interest at Tours, such as Le Trosne, Quesnay, Boncerf, Baron August von Haxthausen, and Marquis Victor Riqueti de Mirabeau),[51] but also to assess the way the author wove his sources together, as in his concluding chapter, "On the Central Administration in Its Relations with the Rural Population."[52] Indeed, it was in this chapter that Tocqueville first encountered a reference to the seventeenth-century expert on the commerce of wood products, Charles de Lamberville, whose hunger for a government job he would subsequently immortalize in The Old Regime.[53]

In addition to utilizing Dareste's work as an invaluable catalog of sources, Tocqueville benefited from the diligent author's feudal expertise. He paid special heed to Dareste's efforts to clarify the whole range of the baffling feudal vocabulary that Tocqueville himself had encountered in his field studies and in his readings of the eighteenth century feudists at Tocqueville. Although he did not always agree with Dareste's formulations—taking issue, for example, with his too theoretical definition of the distinction between a seigneur's land and governing rights[54] —he welcomed the opportunity to learn from a modern-day feudist.

The thrust of both the Académie's question and Dareste's extended answer emphasized the progressive lessening of the feudal burden in the French countryside over six centuries. This change was the result of "that long-hidden and imperceptible revolution" that had altered country life "by emancipating men and the soil and opening new perspectives to progress, be it material or even moral."[55] Instigated and aided by this progress and the combined efforts of royal initiatives and seigneurial accommodations to lessen the feudal burden, the countryside's hidden original revolution produced in Dareste's view a noteworthy solidarity among the classes of the Old Regime: "Among all members of a common nation, regardless of the class to which they belong, . . . there exists, as between all members of the same family, a solidarity that is much tighter than is generally supposed."[56] Yet Dareste's work was no panegyric to centralization. He limned both the positive and negative ramifications of these political policies.

Tocqueville noted Dareste's feudal sympathies without judging them.[57] But as we have seen, his other studies at this time were leading him to develop a different interpretation of rural conditions that featured isolation, not harmony. Where Dareste saw a prosperous peasant enjoying the benefits of civilization's progress under a seigneurial government "much less intolerable than is commonly supposed,"[58] Tocqueville saw a struggling one, isolated even in the face of such progress. Where Dareste saw increasing harmony and solidarity between the rural classes, Tocqueville saw increasing hatred and hostility. Where Dareste saw a beneficent central administration instituting reforms to assist agriculture and reduce feudal inequities, Tocqueville saw a despotic one weaning the countryside from its institutions of liberty. Although such a government claimed to serve the needs of the small farmer, Tocqueville challenged even that benefit, pointing to the ability of "true liberty" in England to provide rural improvements with "greater efficacy and power."[59]

Dareste's book provided an ideal sounding board for Tocqueville's probe of the issue of feudal hatred.[60] Using his evolving system of commentary prefaced by "hic," he took Dareste's rural "facts" and interpreted them in light of how they contributed to a particularly virulent strain of feudal hatred developed over the centuries. Dareste described the decline of the seigneurial taille; Tocqueville contrasted its functional utility for local public works with that of the unjustified royal taille, by now simply folded into a general fund for prefects, subprefects, and mayoral administration.[61] Dareste discussed the negative effects of seigneurial absenteeism; Tocqueville elaborated by noting how it increased rural polarization. [62] Dareste discussed the lessening of abuses of *péages;* Tocqueville commented on how the seigneurs still managed to exempt themselves from paying any taxes for the repair of roads. [63] Dareste analyzed the rash of property transfers and the role of new farming leases; Tocqueville saw how this would lead to middlemen intent on squeezing every ounce of profit from their newly acquired feudal rights, while at the same time removing once and for all the justification for such rights in seigneurial service.[64] Most important, Dareste attested throughout his treatise to the gradual moderation of feudal exactions; Tocqueville recognized the paradox that this very lessening made the burden "more hateful and more unbearable . . . which makes perfect sense but is almost inconceivable at first glance." [65] As the nobles withdrew from the countryside and the peasants increased their landholdings there, Tocqueville thus found "two grand causes of the particular violence of revolutionary thought in France . . . [and] of the Revolution." [66]

3. Feudal Rights in *The Old Regime*

Tocqueville's two chief feudal rights chapters in *The Old Regime* (book 2, chapters 1 and 12) spring directly from the feudal rights facts that he so patiently assembled. They are the most heavily documented chapters in the book, both in their internal citations and in their endnotes, thus demonstrating Tocqueville's debt to his archival investigations. Taken together, the two chapters explain prerevolutionary peasant hatred in the eighteenth-century French countryside.

As we have seen, Tocqueville's chief argument is counterintuitive: French peasant hatred increased at the very time that the absolute burden of feudal rights decreased. He makes his case through a systematic geographic comparison in II:1 and an analogous temporal one in II:12. The chapters serve as "bookends" for book 2, framing Tocqueville's intervening ten chapters on royal centralization and the dissolution of civil society; together they establish the context and show the effects of these key long-term causes of the Revolution. In both chapters, Tocqueville attributes the wellsprings of the peasants' fury to the nobles' desertion of the countryside in the eighteenth century. This theme of noble absenteeism thus becomes both the bridge between the two chapters and a unifying theme for the twelve chapters of book 2 as a whole.

In II:1, Tocqueville develops his argument within the geographic framework posed by the chapter's title: "Why Feudal Rights Had Become More Odious to the People in France Than Anywhere Else." Tocqueville answers his own question by claiming that there were two revolutions in France that preceded the Revolution of 1789: in the first, the French peasant had become a freeholder of property, and in the second, he had been released from the government of his feudal lords. The first revolution contributed directly to the peasant's hatred by exposing him to every residue, however small, of the once extensive feudal burden; the second revolution contributed indirectly by removing the established, on-site pillars of a strong, active, committed nobility that traditionally had given the system meaning and commanded the loyalty of its participants. The two revolutions reinforce each other, since the destruction of the system's political legitimacy magnifies the perception of the breadth and scope of its unjust exactions. Together they render the system, however scaled back it may be, "one hundred times more odious" (*OR*, 1:118).

On four occasions in the chapter, Tocqueville adduces evidence from his European sources to solidify his arguments explaining why the French peasant's hatred was so acute. He marshals German evidence to show the remaining vestiges of serfdom there (*OR*, 1:111–12); English and German evidence to show their relative paucity of property holders (*OR*, 1:113); English and German documentation of how the countries' respective landholders maintained an active role in the governance of their rural districts (*OR*, 1:115); and English and German examples to demonstrate the comparative vigor of feudal rights still exacted from those populations (*OR*, 1:116). In each case, Tocqueville's succinct evidence has but one purpose: to buttress his comparative claims that the French peasant had least to resent yet was most apt to hate.

The conceptual core and stylistic crown of the chapter is Tocqueville's mustering of "all sorts of testimonies" to "prove" the pervasive fact of peasant proprietorship (*OR*, 1:112). Tocqueville develops his case in a brilliantly efficient and compact résumé of twelve sources and three endnotes, organized chronologically and presented symmetrically. After an opening reference to agricultural societies in 1769, Tocqueville's case study is framed by the expert testimony of Turgot (in a quotation and endnote) and Necker (in a single observation, given twice). In the first half of his study, comprising six "testimonies," Tocqueville cites five witnesses; as his fourth reference he injects his own finding of a "secret" seigneurial report, and as his fifth, he describes his personal "infinite labors" (*OR*, 1:112) to investigate the prerevolutionary landholdings discussed in section 1 above so as to confirm peasant proprietorship at the time. In the second half, comprising six additional references to his sources, he adds his comparative evidence from outside France through an English traveler's testimony and one English and two

German findings, the latter backed by endnotes. In endnote 8, he emphasizes that he obtained the German evidence "in person" and that he has held a part of it "in his hands"; in his fifth internal reference, he repeats his role in the study as original researcher, emphasizing his great "patience" (OR, 1:113) to obtain the information we noted above on the disposition of *biens nationaux*. The two halves of the study are thus balanced by the expert testimony of Necker and Turgot, his personal uncovering of documents, and his own painstaking studies of prerevolutionary ownership patterns; they are bridged in the middle by quotations from the agricultural expert Arthur Young.[67]

Tocqueville concludes his chapter with his famous interactive portrait of the embattled French peasant, in which he seeks to engage his readers through four direct overtures to them: "Imagine to yourself. . . . Observe for yourself. . . . Figure for yourself . . . calculate, if you can" (OR, 1:117). Tocqueville had announced in his chapter title that he would explain the hatred evoked among "the people of France" by feudal rights; in his portrait, he telescopes his topic from this larger class to a single individual, in order to personalize and magnify the psychological toll of the existing feudal burden. His individual portrait derives its power from its connection to the sources noted in this discussion; indeed, Tocqueville renders this link explicit, exhorting his readers: "Observe for yourself [the French peasant] as the documents I have cited depicted him." As a result of the thoroughness of his prior expositions, Tocqueville can dispense with technical feudal language and present the peasant's burden in clear, simple, personal language, articulating both his dreams and his frustrations. Nine times he personalizes the oppressors who were the cause of the peasant's problems: his ubiquitous "neighbors." Having recounted their depredations, Tocqueville moves to those of their clerical counterparts, the men "dressed in black" who collected the *dîme*, portrayed by Tocqueville in his notes to Sieyès's 1789 speech. Having masterfully reduced his four years of prodigious feudal research to two simple, moving paragraphs, Tocqueville concludes with endnote 13 that deftly allows his peasant to verbalize his own fury in the colorful "philosophical and literary tirade" written to an intendant.

Tocqueville's treatment in this first chapter thus progresses from the general to the particular, from "the people" to the individual peasant. In II:12, he reverses this flow: he begins with the individual peasant in his title and first paragraph but quickly places him and the other rural actors back in the context of their class, since "history regards classes only" (OR, 1:181). As in the first feudal rights chapter, the title of II:12 suggests the principal comparative framework within which the book's central argument will unfold:

"How, despite the progress of civilization, the condition of the French peasant was sometimes worse in the eighteenth century than it had been in the thirteenth." Tocqueville's chapter title encompasses the precise period designated for study by the Académie and addressed in Dareste's "Mémoire" that dated back to the reign of Saint Louis (1226–70): it differs only in its antithetical conclusion.[68] For Dareste, the progress of civilization, marching hand in hand with the spread of royal centralization, had brought a balance of steady improvement to the French countryside, allowing the peasant to join with other segments of society in realizing "the benefits of a progressive civilization."[69] Tocqueville's chapter constitutes a harsh rejection of this rosy rural scenario—and of his own more favorable view in his 1836 essay— as he directs the full bite of his sarcasm against all "progressive" arguments and their advocates. In his analysis, the class of the peasantry is not a winner in civilization's march but the biggest loser: "Nothing can better demonstrate the sad condition of the people of the countryside: society's progress, which enriches all other classes, discourages them; civilization turns against them alone" (*OR*, 1:187).

As with chapter II:1, chapter II:12 is rooted in Tocqueville's research. As "proof" of the nobles' desertion, for example, he offers four succinct sentences (*OR*, 1:180). In his first sentence, he uses an anecdote from Péréfix, drawn from Dareste,[70] in which Henri IV voices the complaint of noble abandonment of the countryside. In his second, he claims the support of "all of the documents of the time" for the desertion, citing the works of the political economists, intendants, and agricultural societies. His choice of witnesses—king, economists, intendants, and agricultural societies—is ironic, of course, since all bear a measure of unintended responsibility for the trend they are lamenting. In his third and fourth sentences he caps his argument with "the authentic proof" from an unbiased source gleaned from his own research: the place of collection for the capitation, a head tax.

As he had summoned his readers to view the embattled peasant at the end of II:1, Tocqueville now calls us in II:12 to regard his larger class: "Come and observe now what an abandoned class becomes" (*OR*, 1:183). It is in the ensuing class portrait that Tocqueville puts on display the full panoply of his research on feudal hatred. He uses much of the framework and several of the particular issues developed in his reading of Dareste, but he has now tailored them for his own use through his subsequent collection of original source material. Thus, where Dareste had cited an example from Rousseau of a peasant's being forced to disguise his wealth in order to avoid the scrutiny of his neighbor, the tax collector,[71] Tocqueville supplies his own original document from the Agricultural Society of Maine to confirm the destructive effect of the taille (*OR*, 1:184). Where Dareste had described the lingering onerous burden of corvées, using as his chief source Turgot's efforts to combat them during his intendancy in Limoges,[72] Tocqueville applies six of his twelve chapter endnotes to this topic, exhibiting the full range of his own findings regarding corvées. In each case, Tocqueville had received a solid history and useful sources from Dareste's work; in his subsequent investigations, he developed his own fresh documents, designed to support many of the same facts as Dareste, but with a different series of connections between them. Chapter II:12 is his résumé of these searches and these connections.

&

In two of his most detailed analyses of *The Old Regime*, Furet poses the question why Tocqueville framed book 2—his discussion of the Revolution's long-term causes—with his treatments in chapters 1 and 12 of the peasantry and feudal rights.[73] Based on my account of Tocqueville's investigations of these topics, I can advance several answers to Furet's question.

Observing the evolution of his "subject" from his 1842 overview at the Académie française to his 1850–51 plans at Sorrento to his 1852 initial writing and subsequent further investigations in Normandy, we have witnessed his preoccupation with a common puzzle: Why did the French population as a whole acquiesce to despotism at the expense of their traditional liberties? Not only did such a puzzle connect with ruminations throughout his life on this same issue—in Tudor history, Roman history, futuristic American "history," Napoleonic history—but it also tied directly to the contemporary period. For what class had been more decisive in shaping events in France since 1848 than the peasantry? On the one hand, to be sure, Tocqueville was proud of the peasants' role as independent rural proprietors who united to resist urban "demagogic agitation" and revolutionary socialism.[74] But on the other hand, taking advantage of universal suffrage, their votes had installed a conservative majority in the Constituent Assembly of 1848, thus removing Tocqueville's modest hopes for a moderate Second Republic; subsequently, their overwhelming mandates had elevated Louis-Napoleon to president in 1848 and then ratified his coup and his empire in the national plebiscites of 1851 and 1852. By spotlighting in his "bookend" chapters the cascade of injustices endured by the peasantry in the Old Regime, and by pointing to a common precipitating cause for the simmering cauldron of accumulated grievances—the nobles' absenteeism—Tocqueville both explained the peasantry's loyalty to the new order and accentuated local liberty as the needed antidote to their despotic tendencies.

Tracing the development of his historical method, we have seen the way Tocqueville's earliest, novel, tangible research with primary sources allowed him to discover "all of the subsoil of the field that we have been plowing for sixty years" revealed in startling ways, as he reported to Freslon in September 1852.[75] Incorporating his results regarding peasant proprietorship and peasant anger in book 2, chapters 1 and 12, Tocqueville prominently displayed for the first time his own historical credentials in these matters, tied closely to his unveiling of new sources. The chapters thus served as an announcement to his readers of the appearance of a new contender in the heated arena of revolutionary studies. Through his blunt rejection of the orthodox view of six hundred years of French rural history—epitomized in the work of the young Dareste with his portrayal of rural liberty's steady expansion during this period—Tocqueville countered this "progressive" thrust of liberal historiography . . . and threw down the gauntlet to the pantheon of France's elite historians led by Guizot who had both posed the question and awarded the prize for such a mistaken view.

4

TOCQUEVILLE'S BURKE

From Foreign Observer to Primary Protagonist

You see this destruction of all individual influence and you seek
the causes of the Revolution in accidents![1]

Tocqueville's high hopes "to draw something from [him]-
self"[2] during the six months following his summer research
efforts at his family château fell victim to "a true tempest"[3] encountered as he and his wife were returning from Normandy
in early October 1852. His carriage delivered him to Paris on the
tenth of October in "the sad shape" that would mark his health
for the next year.[4] Tocqueville's illness—an acute pleurisy in-
flaming his lungs—consigned him to bed for much of October
and November. Despite a change of residence and a brief resump-
tion of work in December,[5] Tocqueville was stricken again in
January and February of the new year with recurring stomach
ailments. His wife's alternating bouts of grippe sealed their decision, first announced to Beaumont on April 8, 1853, to seek to
relocate for a year "in some very tranquil, small corner of a province."[6] With substantial help from their prospective neighbor,
Beaumont, they found a suitable site near Tours in the Loire Valley, to which they would shift their household of six, including
two domestic servants and two dogs, on June 1, 1853.

Tocqueville's initial illness in October and November 1852
"rupture[d] suddenly the heart of all [his] thoughts"[7] on his book,
terminating the efforts he had envisioned to generalize his Norman studies of peasant proprietorship and to further probe other
vestiges of the feudal system's lingering influence within civil, as
well as political, society. Frequently exhausted and consigned to
"an arduous and very tedious existence," Tocqueville remained

determined to persevere in "the work [that] is my sole refuge." [8] But he deemed it negligible during these eight Parisian months of illness and partial recuperation, resisting any efforts to exaggerate its progress:

> This so-called book is not, as a matter of fact, begun; and I do
> not even know if it is doable. I am still only at the stage of *aspiring*
> *author*. I have, it is true, a powerful desire to put myself to work. But
> preoccupations, sickness, and especially the difficulty of the subject
> that I have in view have prevented me, up until now, from writing
> anything. I have limited myself thus far to reading what others have
> written. [9]

Tocqueville chastised even the loyal Beaumont in early April for an inno-cent compliment on his writing of several new chapters, assuring him that "I have not *written one line* since we parted." [10]

Tocqueville struggled in various ways to maintain the thread of his research efforts during this difficult period as he undertook a broad and eclectic reading program. While consigned to bed, he consumed escapist travel literature and prerevolutionary correspondence and memoirs. [11] In late November he found comfort and "a bit of air and light" in reading Montalembert's *Des intérêts catholiques au dix-neuvième siècle*. [12] In December he sought the government's reports on its scientific explorations in Algeria during 1840–42, and he read M. Nicolas's *Du protestantisme et de toutes les hérésies dans leur rapport avec le socialisme*. [13] Hearing that Beaumont wanted to pur-sue a major historical work of his own on Austria's Hapsburg empire, he presented his friend with Macaulay's *History of England* as a New Year's gift, praising it for its "rapidity of pace, sobriety of language, rigorous choice of facts." [14] And during his abbreviated attempt to return to work at year's end, he tackled the first chapter of the seventeenth-century legal scholar Jean Domat's *Traité des lois,* praising to Corcelle the "great intellectual enjoy-ment" afforded by such a monumental effort to achieve a synthesis of civil and divine law. [15]

In the 1853 segment of his fitful Parisian convalescence, Tocqueville did manage to inaugurate two new lines of research, both of which would even-tually contribute rich dividends to *The Old Regime*, although in unexpected ways. In keeping with the breadth of his original Napoleonic plan of study with which his new investigations would eventually dovetail, Tocqueville expanded his probe of the prerevolutionary French mentality beyond the economic factors studied in Normandy to social, political, and cultural elements as well. Tocqueville thus invested the most productive weeks of his convalescence "lost in an ocean of research"[16] in the regional archives of Paris's Hôtel de Ville, where he studied "the France of the Old Regime at the moment the Revolution surprised it, the state of the people, the habits of public administration."[17] He quickly noted the intrusion of the royal administration into the local communal affairs of the Île de France, with its intendants supplanting the traditional power and influence of the seigneurs.[18] He marked for further investigation the evident parallels of these elements of the Old Regime's administrative system with Napoleon's subsequent fabled one: "The administrative regime of the Consulate and Empire is not a creation; it's a restoration—probe deeply this very true idea."[19] The insinuation of monarchic control into local affairs was blurred, however, by Louis XVI's administrative reforms of 1787 and 1788, which gave the seigneurs reasons to return to their parishes to be candidates for the new local assemblies.[20]

Moreover, the Parisian files tended to be concentrated only in that period of 1787–88, leading Tocqueville to comment on the folder's title page: "Unfortunately, these cartons contain very few documents before 1787, and beginning in this epoch, the old administrative constitution was profoundly modified, and one enters the transitory and not too interesting period that separates the administration of the Old Regime from the system of administration created by the Consulate that governs us still."[21] Tocqueville's search for documents preceding this period would contribute to his choice of a location near a major administrative center of the Old Regime for his upcoming retreat from Paris.[22]

In a second initiative, Tocqueville wrote on January 2, 1853, to Charles von Bunsen, the Prussian ambassador to London and a future historian of primitive Christian liturgy, who was recommended as a contact by his English friend Harriet Grote. He requested Bunsen's help in finding German sources that would allow him to view the French Revolution from the perspective of foreigners: "I seek to situate myself at the period of the [Revolution's] birth and to gain a clear idea of the first impressions, the first thoughts suggested to foreigners by the still hazy view of this great movement. I would like to pick up the trail of the different judgments that influential men of the time, the writers, the statesmen, the princes entertained about it from abroad during the years 1787, 88, 89, 90, 91, and 92."[23] Tocqueville suggested to Bunsen that memoirs, collections of letters, or collections of diplomatic documents might provide such a perspective. Bunsen did not respond until April 21, 1853, when Tocqueville was otherwise occupied in his studies and already in the process of confirming his plans for Tours.[24] But Tocqueville did announce to Bunsen in late May his intention to visit Germany in 1854 to gain a firsthand view of these issues, making his visit contingent on his learning the German language during his upcoming sojourn at Tours.[25]

It was within the context of this desire for a foreign perspective on the emergence of the Revolution that Tocqueville first encountered the English political polemicist Edmund Burke. Within weeks of his letter to Bunsen, he chanced upon two articles by Charles Rémusat in the January 15 and February 1 issues of the *Revue des Deux Mondes,* titled "Burke: Sa vie et ses écrits."[26] In the second article of February 1, Rémusat presented in considerable detail a chronological rendition and analysis of Burke's foreign perspective on the French Revolution. He demonstrated the significance of Burke's first public speech on the event and its pivotal role in realigning both British and international opinion. He traced the political contexts of each of Burke's subsequent speeches and letters, their substance, and their immense consequences both for the aging statesman, Burke, and his targeted audience, the English elite. He carefully delineated his own lines of disagreement with Burke's thought, and he concluded by analyzing the larger issues of Burke's consistency and prophetic intuitions. Most important, he brilliantly brought Burke to life—as a private man, as a key reformer of the British Parliament, and as a frank and acerbic critic of the Revolution whose statements stood as its seminal dissenting view, unsurpassed in clarity and resonance for sixty years.[27] He summoned his readers to engage the public Burke, saying of his *Reflections:* "You must read it to admire it, and analyze it to combat it."[28]

Tocqueville responded enthusiastically to Rémusat's clarion call for attention to Burke's withering critique of the Revolution. He used Rémusat's article of February 1 to establish a bibliographic list of nine of Burke's writings on the French Revolution dating from the years 1790–96.[29] Based on Rémusat's comments, he assigned priority to Burke's *Reflections on the Revolution in France,* designating it as "the one I must read first, along with his first speech and especially his correspondence." He took special note as well of Burke's *An Appeal from the New to the Old Whigs,* highly recommended by Rémusat, and of his "Letters on a Regicide Peace" of 1796, noting that "they demonstrate the movement of public opinion that pushes for peace." He even listed works by other authors cited within the article, including one by Sir James Mackintosh, who vigorously defended the French Revolution against Burke's blasts.[30] Using Rémusat as his guide in this way, Tocqueville thus prepared for his own bearding of Burke.

1. Tocqueville's Reading of Burke

During the spring or early summer of 1853,[31] Tocqueville read in their original English the complete corpus of Burke's speeches, public letters, and private correspondence on the French Revolution.[32] Taking his cue from his notes on Rémusat's article, he began with Burke's early "Speech on the Army Estimates" of February 9, 1790, continued with the *Reflections,* interjected the correspondence, and then proceeded chronologically through the second "Letter on a Regicide Peace," published in October 1796. He transcribed some seventy-five passages of special interest,[33] freely interchanging Burke's English with his own French translations of it. At this stage of Tocqueville's reading, he had not yet fully developed his system of "hics" as a consistent means to designate his personal observations. We can follow his reading emphases, however, in his choice of passages to transcribe, the titles he gave them, and the various notes he appended either at the end of specific passages or in their margins; in three cases, moreover, he concluded his readings of particular works with summaries of his reactions to them.[34]

To delve deeply into a foreign viewpoint on the Revolution, Tocqueville undertook a sober, balanced assessment of how Burke, graced with the superior vantage point and "practical wisdom"[35] afforded by a lifetime's immersion in his country's liberal institutions, was able to discern so much yet mistake so much in his view of French revolutionary events. Tocqueville assigned Burke high marks in many areas, peppering his reading notes with comments of "well seen" and "well perceived." Burke was particularly astute, Tocqueville found, at judging the frailties of France's new political institutions, shaped by its inexperienced political innovators. He recognized the leveling tendencies of the new institutions as they sought to obliterate intermediate orders, and he saw clearly that "a despotism without precedent" could result from such an extreme "crush[ing] together,"[36] especially if a monarchy should ever again reign supreme in France. At the same time, Burke understood immediately—"since 1790"—the Revolution's special radical character evinced in its desire to "refashion" laws, mores, ideas, language, and man's very nature.[37] Burke correctly perceived that the Revolution's affirmation of "the rights of man" made it *"a revolution of doctrine and theoretic dogma."*[38] Although Burke was at first oblivious to the universal appeal of such a doctrine, he soon recognized its seductive power, transforming itself into a "proselytism" that fed on the "poison" existing in the heart of all European nations.[39] Burke understood the essence of that "poison," seeing that the hatred driving the Revolution targeted "not the despotism of a Prince but the condition of a gentleman."[40] And he saw that the French

Revolution bore its closest resemblance to prior religious, not political, revolutions that similarly had swept irresistibly across national borders.

Although Burke thus got much right, he finally missed, Tocqueville believed, what was most important in the Revolution and presented but a limited, mistaken verdict on it. His account was "filled with true touches, but very false on the whole." [41] To begin with, Burke overestimated the redemptive potential of "the almost obliterated constitution of your ancestors," [42] seeing in it a model France could have retrieved and recycled for current use; he failed to see, Tocqueville emphasized, that the current Revolution "must entirely abolish this ancient law." "He is in touch with the event," Tocqueville added, "and doesn't see it." [43] Second, without detecting the true nature of the assault on "Europe's age-old aristocratic law," Burke viewed the Revolution as but "a French accident," [44] triggered by "art and impulse" and manipulated by its leaders into their own sinister channels. [45] In such a view, a French cabal perpetrated a willful and skillful deception leading to a despotic tyranny over the vast majority of the well-meaning but naive French people, still loyal to the leadership of the three bastions of its old French constitution—the king, the nobility, and the clergy.

In his running commentary on Burke's texts, Tocqueville challenged every aspect of such a portrait. France may once have had such an old constitution commanding the respect of its populace, Tocqueville said, but "it was a chariot that still rolled along, although it no longer possessed impulsion or a motor." [46] All the parts of this old machine were encrusted with age, deformed from their original function, stripped of influence, and out of synchrony with each other. By stressing the Revolution's origins as an accident—"a work of art alone" [47] —Burke was oblivious to "the general character, the universality, the final significance" of the Revolution, [48] and he missed as well its chief, long-term, fundamental causes: "The real weakness of the nobility, envy, vanity in the middle classes, misery, the torments of the feudal system among the lower classes, ignorance—all these were the powerful and ancient causes." [49] Confident in his own understanding of the nation's spirit, instincts, and passions at the time of the Revolution thanks to his research to date, Tocqueville repeatedly rejected Burke's avowed causes, labeling them as "accidental." When Burke targeted, for example, "fanatical atheism" as "the principal feature in the French Revolution," Tocqueville acknowledged the horror such fanaticism induced in the spirits of observers, equating it to their reaction to "a stray visitor from hell if one had arrived in our world." He urged himself never to forget this "philosophical character" of the French Revolution, but he concluded that however great its importance, it was still only a "transitory" cause. [50] When Burke cited the Revolution's attack on private property, Tocqueville termed it an "accidental force." [51] Burke, trapped in his benevolent view of the old aristocratic world, could see only the short-term fireworks caused by the Revolution; he was unable to comprehend the longer-term fuses leading to their explosion.

Tocqueville's notes on Burke thus reflected his growing recognition of the value of his "historical distance," as he saw that his own retrospective understanding of the Revolution exceeded that of a contemporary observer, even one with such evident political sagacity and skills. His study of Burke was a study of contrasting perspectives: Tocqueville coolly observed Britain's aging political leader as Burke passionately reacted, and at times overreacted, to the events of the unfolding Revolution. He took note of shifts in Burke's perspective, observing dryly his evolution from 1790, when he expected France to be devastated by its Revolution and reduced to a long period of powerlessness, to 1793, when the terrible energy of the Jacobin Revolution threatened all of Europe: "This barely resembles any more the hatred mixed with contempt that led [Burke] three years previously to consider France reduced to nothing." [52] In the same vein, in 1796, when Burke registered the surprise of "common speculators" that France had become the scourge of Europe, Tocqueville commented wryly that Burke himself had been just such an uninformed speculator "at the beginning of 1790." [53] Throughout his reading, Tocqueville made frequent note of various expressions of Burke's belief in the "new, extraordinary, unprecedented character of the Revolution." [54]

Within his perspectivist study, Tocqueville showed, for the most part, a marked sympathy with the limits imposed by Burke's viewpoint. Thus, when Burke described as incomprehensible the seizure of ancient clergy property to pay revolutionary government debts, Tocqueville clearly, carefully, and artfully delineated how Burke's blind spots prevented him from placing in context the longer-term meaning of the event: "[Burke] does not see the whole spirit of the Revolution there. The property that they seized violently was booty from the ancient world, the destruction of one part of the old feudal edifice. These [modern] debts for which they showed a perhaps exaggerated respect did not represent a more exceptional right, but one that was common to all citizens. They robbed an aristocratic property to pay religiously a democratic debt." [55] He then demonstrated how Burke's view of the Revolution's exceptionalism was necessarily a function of his contemporary perspective, accounting for his mistaken notion of the events' actual significance: "This seemed *extraordinary and unnatural* to Burke. He can comprehend nothing in this matter and for good reason—because he is not at the true point of view of an observer."⁵⁶ Burke was wrong because he lacked the needed detachment of an "observer" that would have allowed him to grasp the deeper, historically rooted French passions and furies that drove their revolutionary appetites.

However, Tocqueville's sympathy in his notes gave way on two occasions to intense flashes of anger at Burke's myopia. In these cases, Tocqueville dropped his even-handed, objective references to Burke in the third person and addressed him directly—as a second-person interlocutor. In the first case, in his 1791 "Thoughts on French Affairs," Burke noted the lack of potential centers for organized resistance to the Revolution in France; he attributed their absence to a policy of the kings that "had so much abstracted the nobility from the cultivation of provincial interest." ⁵⁷ In thus depriving France of its local leaders, the government had ensured that "no man in France exists, whose power, credit or consequence" would enable him to gain support in even two contiguous districts. ⁵⁸ Tocqueville exploded at Burke's failure to draw the logical consequences of his own argument, attacking him personally: "You see this destruction of all individual influence and you seek the causes of the Revolution in accidents! You who see a great aristocracy live before your eyes, do not perceive that the aristocracy here is not just sick but dead before one touches it!!" ⁵⁹ Burke should have been able to dispense with his contemporary blinders and correctly discern the Revolution's true causes, Tocqueville charged, since he was personally familiar with the great English aristocracy and since he wisely recognized royal complicity in the destruction of local liberty in France. A page later in his notes, Tocqueville responded with similar second-person vehemence to a similar Burkean condemnation of the failure of rural leaders to resist revolutionary tyranny, this time in Jacobin times. Again, he took the occasion in his notes to state clearly the reasons for such timid capitulation: "[The nobles] had lost all contact with the population for a long time; no bond existed any longer between it and them; left to itself, an aristocracy is never but a handful of men." ⁶⁰ The extinguishing of local liberty had left France's aristocrats and the countryside they once served isolated and helpless in the face of revolutionary tyranny.

Having vented his anger, Tocqueville regained his own detachment as an "observer." Near the end of his notes, reading Burke's first "Letter on a Regicide Peace," he calmly contextualized Burke's fury: "The hatred and horror of Burke for the Revolution increases with his years . . . ; I must read this in order to understand the horror that the event inspired in certain religious and honest people who were unable to conceive where it was heading." ⁶¹ Tocqueville's overall verdict on Burke was thus a sympathetic and respectful one, recognizing his sincere, if misdirected, terror in the face of revolutionary despotism.

2. Tocqueville's "Initial Outline" of His Book at Tours

Tocqueville arrived at Tours on the first of June 1853, determined to plunge into "the work in retirement [that] alone can restore my body and soul to the condition of equilibrium that I desire." [62] His initial notion of an appropriate balance was a highly demanding one: he told Freslon on June 9 that his daily regimen was reminiscent of his days in the foreign ministry. "Know that I am short of time," he said to his friend, stressing the accuracy of such a claim, however surprising for a man on convalescent retreat. [63] Tocqueville at Tours was driven to launch his book, still in dry dock because of conceptual blocks and his lingering health problems.

Propelled by his self-imposed timetable, Tocqueville distributed his efforts in June in multiple directions. Reporting within days to the local provincial archives, he introduced himself to the archivist, Charles de Grandmaison, and quickly immersed himself in a perusal of eighteenth-century administrative correspondence between intendants and various royal ministers. [64] Seeking to augment his understanding of feudal rights and seigneurial responsibilities throughout Europe, he reread Blackstone to study these issues in mid-eighteenth-century England. [65] Consuming "many readings that connect from afar to my subject," he also prepared to study German. [66]

Tocqueville's anxiety in these initial days at Tours, reflected in this rapid sounding of so many sources, resulted from his lack of a clear picture of his book as a whole. Without such a picture, he worried about how to assign priority to the relevant research on each of its parts without losing sight of his larger canvas: "The composition of a book is similar to that of a painting. What's important is not the perfection that one could give to a part, but the exact relation of all the parts from which the general effect is born." [67] With this in mind, how could he justify spending his days at Tours producing "a mountain of notes, from which will finally emerge only a small chapter of thirty pages?" [68] by which he still meant a short introductory chapter to his larger work on Napoleon and his empire.

Vexed by these concerns, plagued by doubts about his progress, unable to give himself freely to his archival studies, Tocqueville resolved to confront the central question of his book's focus and direction: he set out to formulate its introductory chapter in a precise, detailed manner. Anxiously preparing for these first sustained writing efforts in almost a year, on June 19 he expressed to Ampère his doubts whether such a new initiative was the best use of his time: "If the chapter that I am about to write fails to have some value, I will have lost time and intellectual energy in preparing its elements."[69]

Tocqueville's first drafting efforts at Tours consisted of two preliminary sketches for his book's intended first chapter.[70] One was a general sketch, dated "26 June 53," showing the larger themes of the chapter as well as where and how it would fit within a five-chapter book. The other, undated but contemporaneous,[71] was a specific "order of ideas" for the chapter, specifying three steps to follow in writing it, corroborative sources, and an evolving conceptual plan to guide its architecture. The general sketch revealed Tocqueville's interest in a study of revolutionary perspective for judging both the strengths and the vulnerabilities of institutions of the time. The specific sketch showed how he intended to weave together his readings of Young, Mirabeau, and three "great enemies of the Revolution"—de Maistre, Mallet du Pan, and Burke—in a separate, preliminary case study of contemporary perception at the Revolution's outbreak. The importance Tocqueville attached to these sketches is revealed in a note he subsequently appended to them: "Initial outline of the chapters that were destined to contain the book and its founding ideas. (Saint-Cyr 1853) To reread with care before the final *review* because all of *the spirit, the movement,* and *the linking together* of the work shows itself there, better than anywhere else."[72] In both documents, thus accorded such prominence in the author's retrospective views, we can readily detect the powerful influence of Tocqueville's reading of Burke.

Tocqueville began his general sketch of June 26, 1853, by stating his larger objective: "It's the entire movement of the Revolution that I must paint."[73] To portray this larger movement, he proposed five chapters—the first he was poised to write, and the fourth he had completed the previous summer:

> Chapter 1—general physiognomy of the Revolution
> Chapter 2—the Republic at home
> Chapter 3—the Republic abroad
> Chapter 4—how toward the end of the Republic France was ready to receive a master
> Chapter 5—the 18 brumaire[74]

His first chapter, positioned in this way as the gateway to the larger book, received the general title, "What Particularly Characterizes the French Revolution among All Revolutions." It should indicate what was "new and *unprecedented*" in the French Revolution. Using comments and conclusions

developed in his notes on Burke, Tocqueville planned a rhetorical conceit to frame the various views of this question. To its contemporaries, the
revolution veered between two extremes: it appeared first as an accidental
event of little note, then shifted to an equal if opposite exaggeration of
"something superhuman, diabolical." In neither case did contemporaries,
in France or abroad, perceive the Revolution clearly: its "true physiognomy" disappeared "under the contortions of the moment." Tocqueville
contrasted such lack of understanding at both extremes with the "point of
view where we are," from which "we only begin to be well placed to judge"
both the Revolution's "general" characters and its "particular" ones. Its
true physiognomy, revealed in a proper understanding of these general and
particular elements and of the relation between them, was thus only now
accessible, "such as time has revealed it." Tocqueville noted his satisfaction
with such a matrix of differentiated viewpoints, accenting his own objective
one: "good start," he appended to his sketch. [75]

Having established the importance of such a perspectivist prism ema-
nating from his reading notes on Burke, Tocqueville planned to add in this
first chapter two additional discoveries from other lines of his research. Both
disclosed the paradox that popular fury increased in inverse proportion to
the lessening of repression in political or civil society. In the first case, probed
in his March explorations in the archives of the Hôtel de Ville, Tocqueville
planned to argue that Louis XVI's 1788 administrative reforms increased people's hatred of his regime rather than diminished it. "If you ask me why the
French showed such a furious hatred toward their government" at the very
time it was becoming more liberal and less harsh, he proposed rhetorically,
the answer is that such a "phenomenon" is common to "all the history of
the world": one challenges governments only "when they begin to become
less oppressive." [76] In the second case, based on Tocqueville's feudal rights
studies and reflections on his reading of Dareste, he would show that hatred
of feudal rights was exacerbated even as those rights grew less burdensome
to the people:

> Often in this, as in many other matters, it was the destruction of
> a part of the evil that had rendered the existence of the rest more
> visible, less easy to justify, and more unbearable. The charges and
> the [unreadable word] burdens of feudalism, as applied to property,
> were experienced more acutely in proportion to the destruction
> of its authority over the people. The hardship was smaller, but
> since it appeared without justification, they accepted it with greater
> impatience. . . . In 1789, feudalism weighed heavily *nowhere,* but it made

itself felt a little bit *everywhere*. It oppressed no one, but it bothered
everyone, which is the most dangerous situation for an institution
and the best preparation for a Revolution. It was powerless and
odious.[77]

Taken together, the two examples illuminated a central Tocquevillian insight: what counts in revolutions are people's expectations, and these may
be inflamed rather than appeased by measures to relieve oppression.

In a final sheet of notes in this June 26, 1853, sketch, echoing his personal
exchange with Burke, Tocqueville suggested that his chapter would culminate in a resounding affirmation of political liberty, which alone could
have forced the French aristocracy to intertwine its interests with both the
people at society's bottom and the intermediate classes above them. For
Tocqueville, such liberty could have served as the needed antidote to the
nobles' natural inclination to pursue their own passion and interest. Dis-
missing as "a joke" any claim that government on its own would act in the
interest of the governed, he argued: "We forget that men, kings, or nobles
continually fail to do what is in their duty, but rather do what is in their
passion and interest. Taken in mass and with a long view, they are good
only in exact proportion to the necessity of being so. An aristocracy draws
itself near to the people and treats them with consideration only when it
has need of them; and it feels this need only when free institutions exist."[78]
Liberty alone could ensure accountability, Tocqueville argued; without it,
those in power would abuse their position. Tocqueville planned to prove
this argument by a concluding contrast with the English aristocracy, confirmed in his recent readings of Blackstone. Never, he said, would such an
aristocracy—"by nature the proudest, the most exclusive, and often the
harshest of all nobles"—have opened its ranks and guaranteed the people's
rights unless forced to do so by its participation in the British Parliament. By
contrast, with its participatory destiny foreclosed by monarchic absolutism
and the 140-year absence of political institutions, the French aristocracy had
no reason to engage itself with the people and thus became "egoistic and
indifferent."[79]

Moving to his specific sketch and the more detailed elaboration of an
"order of ideas" for his first chapter, Tocqueville adduced "citations, facts,
traits"[80] to support three components of his opening perspectivist matrix.
He signaled that he would use Burke for his proofs in his second step, in
which the view of the Revolution shifted to regard it as an event "so extraordinary, so inexplicable as to be superhuman . . . a direct agency of hell."[81]
Having established this conceit, designed as we have seen to bring into focus

his own objective perspective of the Revolution, Tocqueville adopted another organizing principle elaborated in his reading notes on Burke to further illuminate this perspective: "What is fundamental and what is accidental. What is born naturally and necessarily from the character of this Revolution, from its nature, from its purpose, and what emerges from a particular accident of the time, a people's character, anterior facts, established opinions, the particular acts of particular men, the unexpected twist of certain events."[82] Using this new axis as a conceptual divider, Tocqueville went on to distinguish the Revolution's "fundamental" quality: "Destruction of the old aristocratic fabric. Foundation of equality."[83] He then considered case by case the commonly attributed causes of the Revolution, denying by turn their fundamental status. Its antireligious fervor? "Accidental."[84] The attack on the right of property? "Accident."[85] The weakening of the power of the state? "Much more accidental than all the rest,"[86] since it should have been increasing. The expression of political liberty? "Accidental."[87] Working through his analysis step by step in this way, Tocqueville applauded its usefulness, suggesting that such an approach could serve as an organizing principle for his chapter: "Perhaps begin by successively casting off all that is accidental and then arrive, after thus setting aside all of the accidents, at the fundamental: What is indeed the fundamental character of the Revolution?"[88] By a process that successively eliminated accidental features, he suggested, the fundamental kernel of the Revolution, in France and throughout Europe, could be isolated: its inexorable march to equality. With that revealed, he noted that he would immediately shift his question to a second inquiry: "Then immediately research what accounts for the fact that this fundamental Revolution began in France, rather than elsewhere?"[89]

Tocqueville's conceptual architecture for his first chapter, developed step by step in June 1853 along such promising lines, came apart when he sought to categorize the issue of revolutionary violence: "How to explain this degree of almost unprecedented violence of the Revolution?"[90] He speculated that the violence may have resulted from its "democratic" character, perhaps referring to the new regime's ability to institute sweeping reforms with no chance of their being checked by legitimate popular institutions.[91] But such a formulation missed the uniquely French manifestation of this violence—its "bloodthirsty character from the very first day" and its intemperate scorn for "rules, precedents, morality, the idea of right."[92] Such excesses were linked, Tocqueville believed, to the "role of the French character": "Why, at one and the same time, [the Revolution] attacked the government, social state, beliefs, administrative habits, language—elements that were political in scope and those that were the furthest from it? There is in all this much of the French fury, independent of general causes."[93] "The French fury" defied ready categorization in Tocqueville's schema. It was "independent of general causes," but its ferocity and the all-encompassing scope of its attack precluded viewing it as just an accident. Tocqueville's analysis of the French character was further complicated by the juxtaposition of the "low civilization of the people . . . at the heart of the most civilized nation in appearance"[94] with the upper classes beset by "corruption on high" and "philosophical irreligion," allowing them to visualize the revolution but not implement it in a way that could provide a stable transition to liberty. Violence, clearly tied in Tocqueville's view to the French character and to this split in perception between France's two societies, necessitated further study to grasp its meaning: "Within this phenomenon, there are highly complicated causes that I must research, find again, and analyze."[95]

Tocqueville's first writing effort at Tours—"blocked" in this case by the historical complexity of his subject—thus ended in frustration and defeat, sending its architect back to his drafting board for further exploration of additional sources. On the first of July, he initiated one step in his renewed research, writing to Beaumont in Paris and asking him to collect on his behalf additional books on feudal rights and on the role of seigneurs noted from Dareste's text.[96] On July 2, he wrote to Senior for help in understanding the divergence in histories of the French and English aristocracies and urged him to discuss this question with Macaulay if the opportunity presented itself.[97] On July 3, Tocqueville expressed to Corcelle his huge disappointment at this time, although, with his customary reticence in matters of his book, he made no mention of his failed drafting efforts: "I am without news and, I would add, almost without ideas; because the research work that I do at this time gives me none at all."[98]

3. Tocqueville's Treatment of Burke in *The Old Regime*

Tocqueville assigns Burke pride of place as his primary interlocutor in *The Old Regime*, acknowledging his central role from the very beginning of the book until its very end. He refers to Burke by name eleven times in eight passages within the body of his text, second only to Turgot as a cited source, and includes six quotations from five of his works. On each occasion, he introduces Burke to argue against him, either explicitly or implicitly. He constructs I:1 around the juxtaposition of two quotations from Burke. He introduces and concludes I:5 with two more, the only such references in the chapter, thus creating a Burkean frame for book I as a whole. Returning in III:8, his book's final chapter, to contest Burke one last time, again as his sole cited source, he expands his Burkean frame to the book as a whole, completing the symmetry of his references to Burke and confirming the English polemicist's intended status as his book's chief disputant.

In I:1, following the plans of his "Initial Outline" but expanding Burke's place in it, Tocqueville introduces two of Burke's heated comments on the Revolution, carefully selected to complement each other through a common image of death and resurrection that bridges their six-year lapse in time. In the first quotation, taken from Burke's earliest "Speech on the Army Estimates" of 1790, Burke sounded the death knell for revolutionary France, indicating that politically speaking it should be "considered as expunged out of the system of Europe" (OR, 1:94). [99] In the second, drawn from his first "Letter on a Regicide Peace" of 1796, Burke restated that early prediction of France's demise; he then retracted it, depicting instead the "vast, tremendous, unformed spectre . . . that hideous phantom" that had sprung from the tomb of France's "murdered monarchy" and proceeded to overpower and terrorize the world (OR, 1:95). [100] In his own explanation of how Burke's quotations exemplified the shift in the era's "point of view," Tocqueville mirrors Burke's vivid apotheosis of the Revolution in satanic form, using language developed in his "Initial Outline" to describe "the terrible physiognomy of the monster's head," its "murderous maxims," and its intent "to assail even God himself" (OR, 1:94). [101] Having derided both Burke's initial dismissal of the Revolution and his subsequent exaggeration of it, Tocqueville ends the chapter by making explicit the advantages of his own modern perspective: "We are placed today at that precise point from which one can best perceive and judge this great object. Far enough from the Revolution so that we experience only feebly the passions that blinded the view of those who made it, we are close enough to be able to enter into and understand the spirit that led it" (OR, 1:95). Freed from the passion yet able to grasp the spirit of the revolutionary era, Tocqueville has achieved his "true" historical perspective. He can now pose the central question of his first book: "What was the real meaning, what the true character, what the permanent effects of this strange and terrible revolution?" (OR, 1:95).

His objective perspective duly emphasized with the help of his Burkean conceit, Tocqueville proceeds to implement his conceptual schema first advanced in June 1853. In chapters 2, 3, and 4 of book I, he takes four components judged by Burke as essential to the Revolution—its antireligious character, its anarchic quality, its propagandism, and its rejection of the old European constitution—and distinguishes, as he had planned, the "fundamental" and the "accidental" characteristics of each. The goal of his rhetorical strategy is to draw attention to the difference between apparent and genuine revolutionary causes, as well as between revolutionary and modern perspectives; it is not to dismiss the importance of the role of the contingent factors that retain, as he will show throughout his book, their own significance in history.

In chapter 2, after acknowledging that the Revolution left a general philosophical residue as "the most fundamental, the most durable, the truest portion of its work" (OR, 1:96), Tocqueville argues that its concurrent attack on the church was due instead to a contingent political factor: the excessive and incestuous liaison of the church with the state. The Revolution's attack was on this overt, political encrustation, not on the church's inner, spiritual mission. It was thus but "a temporary product of ideas, passions, particular facts that preceded it and prepared the way for it" (OR, 1:96), a conclusion validated by the ease with which French religious life was rejuvenated and indeed strengthened once the Revolution had severed it from its unseemly political attachment. In the rest of chapter 2, using the younger Mirabeau's "profound" quotation, long held ready for just this moment,[102] Tocqueville demonstrates that the Revolution's appearance of anarchy was equally misleading, even though we should not be surprised that it was perceived as such by contemporary observers (OR, 1:97–98). Reflecting a long-held insight, he argues that its outer "anarchic" accident masked a more fundamental, underlying consolidation of central power.[103] In chapter 3, Tocqueville acknowledges that the Revolution's proselytism contained a universal character in its embrace of abstract rights, making it comparable to religious revolutions.[104] But he argues that its powerful role in the French Revolution was nonetheless a contingent one, requiring "pre-enacted changes in the condition, customs and mores of men [that] had prepared the human spirit to allow itself to be penetrated in this way" (OR, 1:101). Finally, in chapter 4, Tocqueville recognizes the former prevalence of that "old constitution of Europe" but asserts that "in the eighteenth century, it was half-ruined everywhere" (OR, 1:103). Such a constitution had once rendered the laws of all of Europe uniform, but at the time of the Revolution it no longer held sway, since "all which lives, acts, produces is newly-minted, not only new but opposed [to the old]" (OR, 1:104). Tocqueville makes a special point of refuting the presence even in England of such an old constitution: "In England, where it would appear at first glance that the old constitution of Europe is still in force, it is indeed similarly in ruin" (*OR*, 1:105).

Thus, in each of the four cases, Tocqueville acknowledges a certain plausibility in allegations of their status as fundamental causes, but he insists that such a contemporary view is mistaken. Given the "unprecedented" character of the events, it is not surprising that contemporaries mistook appearances for reality, a confusion that Tocqueville's book will now correct.

Tocqueville begins his culminating chapter 5 of book 1 with a summary list of these apparent causes, perceived as fundamental by the revolution's contemporaries; he now refers to them as "all of the accidents that momentarily changed the physiognomy [of the Revolution] in different epochs and diverse countries." He uses one direct quotation in his list—that of "one of its principal adversaries" who claimed that the Revolution had tended to *"methodize"* anarchy (*OR*, 1:105). Given our tracing of Tocqueville's rebuttal of Burke as his chief organizing principle of book 1, we are not surprised that the quotation is his. [105] Tocqueville then provides his own view, informed by his own insights of the Revolution's fundamental cause: ten generations of a process that he defines simply as the replacement of aristocratic, feudal institutions with "a more uniform and simple social and political order which had equality of conditions for its base" (*OR*, 1:106). [106]

To conclude book 1, Tocqueville now reintroduces Burke by name as a foil against whom to summarize his chief arguments. He first reemphasizes the key point with which he began the book—the superiority of modern observers to those revolutionary contemporaries mesmerized by surface events: "It is surprising that what seems so easy to discern today remained so entangled and veiled to the most clairvoyant eyes" (*OR*, 1:106). He chooses the vivid quotation he had recorded in his reading notes to dramatize the unqualified support of one such contemporary—Burke—for the very feudal edifice whose collapse would necessarily have taken place even without the Revolution, owing to its progressive erosion by the forces of social and civil leveling. [107] Lest we mistake the conclusion of such an argument, Tocqueville makes it for us: "Burke does not see what is right before his eyes—that it is the Revolution that must abolish precisely that ancient common law of Europe; he does not perceive that that, and nothing else, is the crux of its meaning" (*OR*, 1:107). The Revolution's fundamental objective was the pursuit of equality; it could allow nothing to impede its course, least of all the old hierarchy of orders, so beloved by Burke.

In book 1, Tocqueville thus uses Burke overtly as a foil to establish the superiority of his modern perspective, covertly as a spokesman for the primacy of the Revolution's "accidental" causes, each of which Tocqueville scrupulously dissects and sets aside, and overtly as an advocate for the sustained viability of Europe's old constitution . . . the demolition of which Tocqueville argues constituted the very essence of the revolutionary project. What one reviewer has called "the Tocquevillian debate with Burke" is rapidly becoming a one-sided mismatch![108]

Having defined the Revolution's fundamental characteristic as its pursuit of equality, Tocqueville advances, as he had planned in his "Initial Outline," to his "second question": "But why did this Revolution, everywhere prepared, everywhere threatening, break out in France rather than elsewhere?" (OR, 1:107). In Tocqueville's two ensuing books, originally combined as a single unit of twenty consecutive chapters in the first edition of 1856, he addresses this second, coequal question of the specifically French character of the Revolution. Chapters II:1–12 discuss long-term causes, in which his description of the Old Regime's administrative centralization is framed, as we have seen, by his feudal rights chapters; III:1–7 describe short-term causes, including the role of literary men of the time, irreligion, and the unintended effects of the government's economic and administrative reform policies of 1787 and 1788; III:8 is a summary chapter. In these chapters, Tocqueville mentions Burke on five occasions, with his treatment now adapted to the new, specifically French focus of his investigation.

Tocqueville's five references to Burke in books 2 and 3 are bound by a common theme—the death of local powers in the French countryside, with special attention to the fate of the aristocracy. The first and last quotations (OR, 1:147 and 1:243) express Burke's "surprise and horror" at the ease with which the revolutionary government imposed its will on the countryside, first by severing France into eighty-three new administrative districts and second by arresting its political opponents and transporting them to Paris for execution. Burke presumes these to be revolutionary atrocities; Tocqueville argues in each case, as he had in his notes, that such atrocities were made possible by an earlier royal policy usurping local offices and excluding local participation, resulting in a quiescent countryside with no possible sources of resistance to the Revolution. Burke's contemporary revolutionary atrocities thus become, in Tocqueville's view, ancient monarchic ones. Tocqueville's middle three citations are not quotations but comments representing various Burkean views of the French nobility. Burke argues that entails still maintained the nobility's prosperity (OR, 1:150), that the nobility was open to the entry of commoners through the purchase of offices (OR, 1:157), and that it still held sufficient status in the country to be viewed by Louis XVI as his chief threat (OR, 1:198). Tocqueville pointedly demonstrates in each case how Burke mistakenly perceived these surface features as signs of health, when in fact they concealed the nobility's deep, lingering, terminal malady caused by political atrophy.[109]

To highlight his differences with Burke, Tocqueville resorts again to corporeal imagery. A human society can appear to be functioning normally, but without a transcendent force to give life to the parts, it may in reality be dying: "One could say that in human institutions as in man himself, there is a central and invisible force which is the very principle of life, independently of organs that perform the various functions of existence. When this life-giving flame is extinguished, though the organs seem to act as before, the whole languishes at once and dies" (OR, 1:150). Burke and his contemporaries, Tocqueville says, saw only the French eighteenth-century corporate exterior, and they presumed it to be healthy. Tocqueville, thanks to his modern investigation of the body's "vital principle," can see that its surface contortions were its death throes. According to Burke, it was the French revolutionaries who destroyed French vigor and normality: "I believe the present French power is the very first body of citizens who . . . have chosen to disseever [their country] in this barbarous manner" (OR, 1:147).[110] Tocqueville again chooses his own corporeal imagery to distinguish his view from Burke's: "It did look as if they had torn living bodies, but in reality they had only dismembered corpses." The revolutionary violence was perpetrated upon a citizenry that was already dead, its vital principle extinguished by the French monarchs. Tocqueville sees not one but two stages of murder, separated in time and place; he uses Burke's horror at the second murder to highlight his own horror at the first.

It is in his summary treatment of Burke in his book's final chapter that Tocqueville weaves together the themes and images he has inaugurated thus far in book 2. Chapter III:8 is a summary of the preceding nineteen chapters of books 2 and 3; it is not, nor does it purport to be, a summary chapter for The Old Regime as a whole. No such larger summary exists, presumably awaiting the completion of Tocqueville's larger book. Chapter III:8, in seeking to provide a résumé of the specifically French character of the Revolution, thus has a function similar to that of I:5, which provided a synopsis of the fundamental qualities of the European Revolution. Burke's status as the exclusive cited source in each summary chapter enhances his importance in the book as a whole, allowing Tocqueville a final chance to emphasize the distinctions between their respective views of the Revolution.

Given Tocqueville's preoccupation in his "Initial Outline" with "the French fury," and the difficulties he encountered in explaining it, we are not surprised to find his final comments on Burke enmeshed in a consideration of the causes of the French Revolution's ferocity and violence. Nor are we surprised to find that Tocqueville saves for his culminating rebuttal of Burke the second of the two passages that had so intensely provoked his ire in his reading notes:

> I never yet heard, that a *single man* could be named of sufficient force or influence to answer for another man, much less for the smallest district in the country. . . . We see every man that the Jacobins chuse to apprehend, taken up in his village, or in his house, and conveyed to prison without the least shadow of resistance; *and this indifferently,* whether he is suspected of Royalism or Federalism, Moderantism, Democracy Royal, or any other of the names of faction which they start by the hour. (*OR,* 1:243) [111]

He then summarizes his chief dispute of books 2 and 3 with Burke, emphasizing how ancient royal policy undermined the chances for collective rural action and resistance, leading residents to rely on their own violent means to avenge their own perceived wrongs: "Burke had poorly understood the conditions in which the monarchy he regretted had left us to our new masters. The administration of the Old Regime had removed in advance from the French the possibility and the desire to help each other" (*OR,* 1:243). [112] In his reading notes, transcribed in 1853, Tocqueville had thundered at Burke's blindness. Now, two years later, he adds a new dimension to this characterization. Burke not only misunderstood the fundamental causes of the Revolution, he also missed the degree to which they contributed to the very violence he decried. The Revolution was violent because the people had been stripped of local means "to check or even delay for an instant" the central power after it had "exchanged mildness for ferocity" (*OR,* 1:243). By eliminating local institutions, the monarchy had thus sealed its fate on two levels, facilitating both the advent of the Revolution and its subsequent veering to violence and regicide. Only local liberty, in making resistance to the Revolution possible, could have served as a brake upon its final ferocity.

Tocqueville's treatment of Burke is a highly efficient one, stripped to the essentials of Burke's thought on the Revolution and adapted to the rhetorical purposes of Tocqueville's argument. Chancing upon an unanticipated and peerless foreign observer of the Revolution, Tocqueville uses Burke to spark his "Initial Outline" and embolden his successor text, book 1 of *The Old Regime.* He does so by highlighting Burke's shortcomings as a contemporary observer, even as he takes pains to ensure that his own treatment is straight-forward, sober, and even-handed, in no way imitating Burke's rhetorical flights of anger or fancy. Tocqueville thus makes sure to acknowledge Burke as a target, if cryptically on occasion; he quotes him accurately, if at times liberally in his French translations; he relishes his dreadful images of the Revolution's satanic features as well as its corpses and tombs, freely adopting them for his own use; he takes care to blunt the bite of his criti-cisms with expressions of respect for Burke's "clairvoyance" (*OR*, 1:106) and "eloquence" (*OR*, 1:243); and he even, as we have noted, corrects his draft language to reflect more accurately the nuances of Burke's thought.

But Tocqueville's treatment of Burke is ultimately biased. "Always crit-iciz[ing] [Burke's] illusions," [113] he fails even to mention the broad areas of congruence in their respective revolutionary analyses, glossing over their common disdain for the Revolution's abstract theorists, their common recognition of the parallels of the French Revolution with earlier religious revolutions, their common support for independent provincial institu-tions, such as in Languedoc, their common insistence that liberty requires restraint, and their common belief that France must retain elements of its old constitution—aristocratic elements—in order to secure liberty. In-deed, we will see that Tocqueville's fixation on many of these issues will only intensify as his studies progress for *The Old Regime,* volume 2. But in none of these later discussions—either in his writings or in his voluminous notes—does Tocqueville credit, or for that matter even mention, Burke, except with the intention to discredit him. [114]

I would advance two explanations for Tocqueville's puzzling reticence. First, Burke clearly violated Tocqueville's "liberty test," failing to recognize the multiple reasons for the French nobles' inability to protect liberty in the French countryside and thus incurring Tocqueville's smoldering reproach. Second, for all the merits of Burke's observations, he advanced them within the context of an unapologetic defense of an old world order that was irre-trievably compromised, as Tocqueville had spent the better part of two vol-umes of *Democracy in America* demonstrating. In Tocqueville's view, Burke's persuasive strategy was inapplicable to the political and moral exigencies of the modern world, however much he might agree with elements of its spir-ited program. Central to Tocqueville's challenge, especially for the second volume of *The Old Regime,* would be developing his own rhetorical strategy that would allow him to argue convincingly for the resurrection of "aris-tocratic" institutions in a nation that by 1856 had sought to eradicate them root and branch.

TOCQUEVILLE AND ADMINISTRATIVE CENTRALIZATION

Detecting Its Deep Roots in the Archives of Tours

> Without you and your archives, I would not have been able
> to write the book I have just published. All that my previous
> studies had taught me was unconnected. Next to you, I found
> the linking together of rules [*l'enchaînement des règles*] that I was
> seeking.[1]

D espite an all-too-spirited welcome from bedbugs ensconced
in the domestics' quarters, Tocqueville's choice for his and
his wife's convalescent retreat of "Les Trésorières" in the small
village of Saint-Cyr-sur-Loire on the outskirts of Tours proved to
be a felicitous one. Situated within hearing distance of the city's
clock bells, by which Tocqueville set his watch, the spacious villa
afforded easy access by foot to the prefectural archives of Tours
four kilometers away, opportunities for "extensive walks" in the
adjoining valley of the Choisille River, and a point of embarka-
tion for neighboring châteaus.[2] Most important, its location under the lip of the north ridge of the Loire Valley provided both
maximum exposure to the sun and protection from the north-
easterly winds that had damaged the couple's health the previous year. With these many advantages, the Tocquevilles chose
to remain in residence for a full year, from the beginning of June
1853 until the end of May 1854.

Tocqueville was aided in his recuperative program at Saint-
Cyr by the fortuitous presence next door of his doctor, the lung
specialist Pierre Bretonneau. Despite recurrences of stomach and
respiratory problems, including an attack that immobilized him
for a month in the late spring, he made steady progress in re-
building his frail constitution. Reinforced sufficiently to under-

take a trip to Germany after leaving Saint-Cyr at the end of May, Tocqueville reported to his American friend Theodore Sedgwick in July 1854: "I left Saint-Cyr at the end of last May, having achieved almost completely the goal I had envisioned in settling there . . . : I completely reestablished the health of my wife, and I restored my own to its condition of two years before."[3]

Tocqueville sought and found mental relief at Tours as well, with his new "hermitage" making possible a solitude he craved. To be sure, he and his wife enjoyed visits from their closest family and friends, and on occasion they entertained Grandmaison, the local archivist, and Cardinal Morlot, the bishop. They, in turn, departed for a week in both fall and spring to visit the neighboring Beaumonts; Tocqueville himself spent a day in Saumur in December to resolve a delicate dispute provoked by his nephew's amorous pursuits[4] and another in Paris in May for an election of the Académie française. But by restricting all local contact to news provided by his barber, and by refusing even to subscribe to a French newspaper, Tocqueville and his wife obtained "a perfect tranquillity" in their secluded outpost, variously referred to by Tocqueville as "a deserted island," "a walled-up burial vault," and a "fortified château."[5] Explaining his "misanthropy" of this era, Tocqueville told Madame de Circourt: "The solitude is sometimes a bit profound: but in the times in which we find ourselves, it is still better for me than the crowd."[6] Through his self-imposed seclusion, Tocqueville thus gained both relief from the craven obeisance of his fellow citizens to Louis-Napoleon's despotic regime and the freedom he needed to establish the strict and stable regimen essential to his health and his work.

Tocqueville's daily routine underwent various modifications during his stay at Tours. We have already noted the intense focus and activity with which he had arrived at Saint-Cyr on June 1, proclaiming to Freslon after his first week that "I am short of time." After the disappointment of his initial writing efforts at the end of June, Tocqueville adopted a summer routine in July and August, best described by Grandmaison, in which he walked each day to the Tours archives.[7] At "Les Trésorières" this was a time of conviviality, conversation, and good humor, with friends Ampère, Corcelle, Beaumont, and Rivet all in residence on various occasions, the first for a stay of six weeks.[8] Fall brought another flurry of visitors, including Tocqueville's father and brother, but it also marked Tocqueville's inauguration of his "voluntary *treadmill*,"[9] consisting of studies at home plus two or three trips each week to the archives. By late October, with visits from friends reduced to a minimum and with a target date selected for a new attempt to launch his book, Tocqueville adopted the full "exact and symmetrical manner" that would govern his ensuing life at Tours.[10] He described his daily schedule for Mrs. Grote in one of their February conversations:

> Our lives revolve in the most inflexible routine possible. I rise at half-past five, and work seriously till half-past nine; then dress for *déjeuner* at ten. I commonly walk half an hour afterward, then set to on some other study—usually of late in the German language—till two p.m., when I go out again and walk for two hours, if weather allows. In the evenings I read to amuse myself, often reading aloud to Madame de Tocqueville, and go to bed at ten p.m. regularly every night.[11]

Despite the division of his day into such concise segments, each contributed in a different way toward the making of his book, with even the evening readings intersecting with his archival interests.[12]

It was during the second phase of Tocqueville's Tours tenure—July and August 1853—that he delved most deeply into the district's immense intendants' archives. To be sure, in the early days of June he had sampled the archives' offerings sufficiently to be able to announce to Freslon the discovery of "not exactly a rare treasure, but a precious deposit."[13] But we have noted how he saw his investigation of the archives at that time as just a stepping-stone to his larger project, meant to lead only to "a small chapter of thirty pages." While he needed to know the Old Regime "through and through," he had told Freslon,[14] he did not intend to write at length about "centralization," as we have seen in his "Initial Outline" of June 26. We have also seen that, frustrated by the tangled issue of revolutionary violence and unable to achieve a satisfactory formulation of either his "small chapter" or its place in his larger book, on July 1 and 2 he launched a further phase of his work by requesting from Beaumont and Senior new resource materials and information, especially in the field of feudal rights. It was not until early July, as we can tell from the dates he affixed to his archival reading notes, that Tocqueville commenced in earnest his studies of the intendants' correspondence . . . studies that by the end of the summer would contribute to a complete reformulation of the concept and scope of his book on the French Revolution.

1. Tocqueville's Investigation of the Intendancy of Tours

When he first presented himself in early June for admission to the Tours archives, Tocqueville was not a neophyte in the study of intendants' papers. After all, he had spent April immersed in the Paris archives studying just such documents, and he had also read and noted with particular care six volumes of Turgot's collected works, including those focusing on his 1761–74 intendancy at Limousin.[15] But each of these portrayals of intendant activity failed to provide a base on which he could build a larger project. As we have noted, Tocqueville found to his dismay that the papers in the Parisian archives chiefly covered a period just before the Revolution, when Louis XVI's most recent reforms sought to reverse his administration's historical monopoly of French communal affairs. And Tocqueville knew that Turgot's works had already been digested and used as source materials by others, as he had seen in his own readings of Dareste.[16] The archives of Tours, by contrast, presented a wealth of precisely the older documents he needed to view the administration in its unreconstructed and most hyperactive form; moreover, they were untapped, having been largely neglected since 1790 when the king first ordered their assembly.

Tocqueville's scrutiny of documents at Tours was facilitated in its selection, scope, and analysis by the young director of the collection, Charles de Grandmaison. Grandmaison was already familiar with Tocqueville when he appeared on his archival doorstep, having observed him at Institute meetings and in conversation with one of his superiors during his own apprenticeship at the Bibliothèque nationale in early 1852; he had read his books as well.[17] Since his arrival at Tours, Grandmaison had worked to reorganize the vast collection that he had found in such chaos; indeed, in a subsequent 1867 report he would describe the full extent of this chaos, showing how feudal documents had been requisitioned and burned on public bonfires in 1793 and how "the most beautiful and best preserved of our charters" had been appropriated during the Directory to serve as cartridge bags for the artillery.[18] Thrilled to have a visitor of Tocqueville's stature appear at Tours, Grandmaison gradually succeeded in winning the confidence of his illustrious guest, first by his own evident familiarity with the collection, second by providing his personal office, with a view of the prefectural vegetable garden, for Tocqueville's work, and third by expressing in their early conversations his support for "liberty such as [Tocqueville] understood and loved it."[19] Nurtured in these ways, an unusual collaboration blossomed between the older and younger men, driven by shared service to Tocqueville's so far stillborn book.

In his retrospective account of their relationship, Grandmaison emphasized the familiarity and openness with which Tocqueville shared his observations about his book: "The most common subject in our conversations was quite naturally the book that monopolized his attention at that time."[20] Tocqueville's unusual willingness to be forthcoming on this subject reflected, of course, his need for Grandmaison's help: the more Grandmaison understood Tocqueville's goals, the better he could tailor his selection of documents. The fervor of Grandmaison's response is equally understandable, as he spared no effort to please the intensely private guest whom he came to admire and even revere: "I spared nothing in seeking [documents] for him in the chaos that was still poorly sorted out at the heart of our intendancy."[21] Bound by these complementary objectives, the relationship developed its own rhythm and place within the larger pattern of Tocqueville's life at Tours. Arriving at the archives, Tocqueville allocated precisely one-half hour for general conversation with his young assistant. Grandmaison then brought him the folders he would review and notate during the day, with Tocqueville often reporting on the results of his reading and requesting technical advice. In contrast with his deployment in 1834 of his two young American assistants for *Democracy in America,* volume 1, Tocqueville never sought Grandmaison's direct help in his note taking. "My role limited itself," said his aide, "to seeking and providing the pieces I thought likely to interest him and lead him to his goal."[22]

Thus abetted by Grandmaison's able assistance, Tocqueville reviewed and notated a broad swath of the intendants' correspondence in the larger Tours archives. In their early conversations, Grandmaison argued that Tocqueville must forgo his initial intention to study documents dating back to the fifteenth century; Tocqueville heeded this advice, Grandmaison tells us, in deciding "to limit himself to the depiction of the epoch immediately preceding the Revolution that was specially named 'Old Regime.' "[23] Even with these limits, Tocqueville transcribed some 330 pages of reading notes during July through November 1853. His notes on the intendants' files are separable into twenty-two subsections, each representing from four days to four weeks of work with a distinct dossier of correspondence unearthed by Grandmaison.[24]

Tocqueville's reading style lent itself well to the random and diffuse collection he found at Tours, which included, despite Grandmaison's best efforts, "an enormous amount of useless dust to swallow."[25] Fluid and adaptable, he sifted and sorted with an eye toward seizing the unexpected fact, the curious twist, the revealing directive, or the surprising tone of the private correspondence passing before his eyes. These findings in turn triggered his more general observations integrated freely throughout his notes regarding the larger lessons to be derived from the materials. Since Tocqueville provided precise dates on eighteen of his twenty-two subfiles, we can follow the evolution of both the facts and the themes that captured his attention in the archives at Tours.[26]

Tocqueville's first great interest was the parallel he quickly detected between the conduct and objectives of the Old Regime's system of management and those of its successor system in his own day, an observation he had already flagged in his Parisian notes for further "digging." On the first page of his first file of Tours reading notes, he emphasized that entreaties to the state for highly prized tobacco licenses were a constant in both eras; on his next page, he asserted that the royal intendants acted "absolutely as prefects of our day."[27] In his second file, he equated the royal bureaucrat's desire to be judged by a special court with "what the same official would claim in our day," and he observed how the local intendant prefigured his modern counterpart by serving as the exclusive local agent for the delivery of all national services.[28] In his first "general remark" at the end of this second file, Tocqueville summarized these connections: "What is striking in reading this correspondence for the years 1772, 1773, 1774 is the extent to which, from this moment forward, the government and its unique representative, the intendant, were absolutely the center of all, as in our day; how particular persons were trained to see only him and address themselves only to him; some for a road, others for public aid."[29] Tocqueville's eager desire to document these parallels between the two eras would persist throughout his note taking at Tours.

At each point of his reading, Tocqueville sought to discern the way the royal administration intersected each day with the lives of the French populace. On one level, he was interested in how the administration treated its citizens, both to their faces (as in its style of addressing them) and behind their backs (in its surveillance of their activities, its critique of their character, and its paranoia about their organizations).[30] On another level, he sought to determine the practical effects of the regime's activities, so difficult to discern given the shifting character of its regulations, the extraordinary discretion it vested in its intendants, the differential treatment it accorded various sectors of the French population, and the erratic way it enforced its own highly detailed and often stringent laws. On a third level, he tried to assess the expectations and customs that such administrative behavior engendered in the French people.[31] Only through a case-by-case scrutiny of repeated instances of daily contact revealed in the intendants' files could Tocqueville build his subtle case for the curious anomalies of the system's conduct and its effects on the population as a whole; only in this way could he document the inherent contradictions and calamitous, if unintended, effects of a regime that was "arbitrary, violent, mild, and feeble at one and the same time."[32]

Such contradictions invited explosive reactions. To study these, Tocqueville took special interest in early August in a dossier titled "Subsistences," which chronicled the government's efforts to address the food shortages and mob riots of 1772. Here he observed the way "the welfare state" readily established itself as the sole actor and claimant in such a situation of dire emergency, thus inadvertently creating two conditions that would result in the eventual flowering of violence in the Revolution. First, in its construction of "an immense empty space between [the government] and the people," it established the vacuum within which mob activity could flourish, since such activity alone could provide "a common passion" denied to the people by the suppression of local liberty. The people thus gravitated from "a sort of imbecilic obedience to an insurrection that was no less so."[33] Second, it provided a model for future revolutionary leaders who found that they too could impose despotic controls without fear of local resistance exercised through legitimate channels: "The revolutionary measures of the *maximum* and others are born of memories and habits of the Old Regime," he asserted.[34] Tocqueville found this early precursor of the revolutionary spirit so compelling that he would return to this file for a second reading in the fall.[35]

By viewing documents spanning the full period from 1750 to 1788, Tocqueville could measure the degree to which the royal administrative machine "perfected" itself, achieving greater and greater supremacy during the forty years preceding the Revolution, always at the expense of local participation. "It is curious," he observed in a letter to Freslon on September 23, "to see at what point the government of 1780 is already different from the one of 1750. . . . Those who are governed and those who govern are already changed beyond recognition."[36] To analyze these changes, in October Tocqueville studied a file containing correspondence dating from 1750 in which he observed local resistance to the new taxes and central management imposed by the government in the construction and maintenance of roads.[37] It was precisely this local opposition and independence that he would find missing in later files, suppressed by the government through its policies of tutelage. One such instance of well-intentioned government intrusion was the founding of agricultural societies, seen in documents from Tours of 1761. The government conceived, authorized, selected, and operated the agricultural societies; its monopoly on all such functions ended by creating a situation where "the true farmers are very nearly absent from them."[38] The government's myopia in these matters was also epitomized for Tocqueville in its failed efforts to launch a gazette reporting on local news throughout the kingdom. Despite its huge competitive advantages, the newspaper collapsed from an unusual and unexpected cause—it was unable to gather enough instances of local activity to fill its pages.[39] The government's energetic efforts to preempt vigorous popular participation eliminated the mediating institutions needed to sustain it, leading Tocqueville to suggest in October that he would prefer outright tyranny, since it might incite resistance, to this insidious sapping of the people's participatory spirit by government tutelage. In an argument that mirrored the same soft despotism and the same prescription of feisty liberty that he had projected as part of the democratic future in *Democracy in America,* volume 2, he wrote: "It's not tyranny but tutelage that makes us what we are. Liberty can take root and grow in the first. It knows neither how to be born nor how to develop itself in the second. The former can give rise to free nations, the latter can produce only revolutionary and servile peoples."[40] In a reading that culminated on the last day of November, yielding his final animated notes from the intendants' archives two days before he began writing his book, Tocqueville would find further evidence of the erosion of popular participation when he examined the corresponding decline of political and civil life in the nation's cities.[41]

In his reading of the intendants' files at Tours, as shown in these examples, Tocqueville took full advantage of the unique opportunity afforded by his unrestricted access to these heretofore hidden materials. Finding himself presented with the equivalent of a retroactive Freedom of Information Act, issued in his name alone without restrictions for a period of more than one hundred years, he probed every nook and cranny of the Old Regime's bureaucratic edifice. His studies benefited from his own contemporary political experience, which prepared him for the subtleties of government "meddling [*friponnerie*]," that universal tendency of bureaucratic administrators.[42] Tocqueville had no need to acquire a specialized vocabulary here, as he did in his study of feudal rights, since his legislative and administrative experiences had already schooled him in its finer points! On top of these many advantages, Tocqueville received a personal Freedom of Information officer— the sympathetic Grandmaison—to recommend and locate the materials he sought. Tocqueville's "precious deposit" at Tours, rendered accessible in these ways, showed every sign of yielding rich discoveries.

Thus possessing a private key to unlock the innermost secrets of the Old Regime's administrative apparatus, Tocqueville decided in the late summer of 1853 to shift his focus to a full-length book on the period preceding the Revolution. Grandmaison described the gradual process through which Tocqueville arrived at this momentous decision: "But this thought [of painting the Old Regime] entered his mind only little by little, as the pieces and documents passed before his eyes and as the interest and especially the novelty of his subject unfolded before him." [43] Tocqueville confirmed his decision, Grandmaison reported with evident self-satisfaction, at the end of August when he announced it at dinner at "Les Trésorières" with Grandmaison, Madame de Tocqueville, and Ampère all in attendance:

> Toward the end of the summer, M. de Tocqueville honored me by inviting me to dine at his *hermitage*. . . . A number of other subjects were touched on; we spoke notably of the work in which Tocqueville was engaged, and he wished to say clearly to Ampère that it was not only in scouring the archives but also in conversing with the archivist that he had settled his ideas—up until this point a bit fluid—and set out the plan of the book that he had decided to detach from his great work and give separately to the public. [44]

Tocqueville's proposed full, separate book on the Old Regime would in no way replace his "great work" on the larger Revolution, Napoleon's place in it, and their affiliations with his own era; it would constitute a complementary volume that would set the stage and provide the novel impetus for this subsequent work. [45] This new strategy, developed during the summer at Tours, would provide him, he wrote to Mrs. Grote on November 22, with an indispensable advantage over other writers on the larger Revolution: "I believe I see clearly that what those who wished to speak of the French Revolution and even of our current time have most lacked are true and just ideas of the preceding period. I will possess, I believe, over them this advantage, and I hope to take full advantage of it." [46] Tocqueville's advantage, as he thus envisioned it, was made possible by his access to the individual voices of the Old Regime—both "governors" and "governed"—found in the Tours archives as well as in his other readings of the period. [47] These voices stated for his unique benefit the aspirations they entertained, the passions they felt, and the deeds they enacted at the presumed peak of the Old Regime's strength and influence. They thus articulated at the same time its supposed strengths and its secret weaknesses, the twin factors that would contribute to its demise.

2. Tocqueville's Study of Administrative Law

In addition to his experienced administrative eye, Tocqueville trained a legal lens on the archives of Tours, well-focused through his formal education of 1824–26 and almost four subsequent years of practice as a *juge auditeur* and *juge suppléant* at the bar in Versailles. He sought in particular to untangle the respective responsibilities of the French state and the parlements in matters of administrative law, complicated by their often overlapping, shifting, and competing jurisdictional claims.

Tocqueville's desire to scrutinize these matters at Tours is not surprising, given a long history of special interest in this topic. For example, in *Democracy in America,* volume 1, published in January 1835, Tocqueville had written several paragraphs and the footnote X probing this terrain and explaining the confusion introduced by unnamed despots who sought to turn to their advantage its blurred topography (*DA,* 92, 692–93). By characterizing centralization as "one of the great conquests of the Revolution," which had put an end to royal favoritism and the absurdities of monarchic administration, these "friends of absolute power" sought to mask their own despotic aspirations in the popular antiroyal rhetoric of the day. Tocqueville had used his footnote X—bearing Guizot's historical imprint, as we noted in chapter 2—to expose the errors of this rhetoric by demonstrating that the roots of centralization in fact stretched far back into the monarchy. "It is not right to say that centralization was born of the French Revolution," he began; "the French Revolution perfected it but did not create it" (*DA,* 692). After indicating its earliest manifestations in the reign of Philip IV, Tocqueville then cited a 1775 remonstrance of Malesherbes exposing and criticizing the intendants' domination of communal administration by their control of expenditures, authorization of lawsuits, and ability to bring complaints before special tribunals. By concluding that administrative centralization's insinuation into local life under both Louis XIV and Napoleon was "still the same principle, extended to more or less distant consequences," Tocqueville aimed to expose the rhetorical duplicity of those, past and present, who applauded the Revolution's "*conquests*" to justify their own centralizing ambitions (*DA,* 693).

Tocqueville's subsequent probes of administrative centralization led him on a circuitous route, with his studies at Tours finally returning him to his 1835 point of departure.[48] His greatest detour occurred in 1845 when he presented a report to the Académie des sciences morales et politiques on a work titled *Cours de droit administratif,* by the legal scholar Louis-Antoine Macarel, in which he expressed a position directly at odds with his earlier and later analyses.[49] For in Macarel's work Tocqueville encountered a scholarly view that traced the origins of France's modern administrative system not to the Old Regime but to the monumental work of the National Assembly of 1789: "In 1789, after having set down the first bases of the country's

new constitution, [the National Assembly] wished to create and organize a
new political body out of the incoherent debris of the old monarchy, and
to raise on a common foundation the double edifice of national representation and internal administration."[50] In the first paragraph of his own report
presented to the Académie in 1845, Tocqueville adopted the chief thrust of
Macarel's analysis:

> The French Revolution, which introduced so many innovations into
> the world, created nothing more novel than that part of our political
> law that relates to actual administration. There, nothing resembles
> what preceded it; almost everything is of recent date: functions as
> well as functionaries, duties as well as immunities. But what is more
> novel than all the rest is the methodical order that presides over this
> vast organization and the rigorous and logical binding together that
> makes a single body of all these parts.[51]

In his second paragraph, Tocqueville restated this view that "the French
administration of our day does not resemble the one that existed in the Old
Regime." He went on to endorse for his audience Macarel's findings that the
modern French administrative system originated with the Constituent Assembly: "Almost the whole of our administrative organization is the work
of the Constituent Assembly: it is the Assembly that set forth all of the principles on which it still rests; it is [the Assembly's] hand that formed, defined,
and activated almost all of the powers constituting our modern administration, and that placed them in the relative position they occupy.[52]" In light of
the Assembly's great work, Tocqueville placed Napoleon's own subsequent
administrative contributions in their proper, diminished perspective: "One
readily discovers, in glancing through this succinct history, that Napoleon
innovated far less than one supposes and recounts in administrative matters."[53] In his concluding comments, Tocqueville reiterated that what his
Macarel findings thus subtracted from Napoleon should redound to the
accomplishments of the Revolution:

> What must be of surprise, gentlemen, is that it is the Revolution that
> rendered all these things not only doable but easy and necessary to
> do; this unprecedented Revolution that was able to overturn all the
> small or great powers that had existed up until that point, to abolish
> all the special privileges, all the local franchises, all the individual
> prerogatives, and to make disappear almost all the differences that
> had separated the citizens, in such a way that they were forced to

recreate in one fell swoop according to one plan, the entire system of public administration.[54]

Having accepted this core of Macarel's historical analysis, Tocqueville proceeded in the body of his speech to dispute Macarel's political assessment of it. According to Tocqueville, the pioneering system of the Constituent Assembly was "conceived and fashioned by liberty," since it contained three vital measures guaranteeing freedom: executive councils that made decisions, councillors who were elected, and officials at all levels of the administration who were subject to ordinary justice. But Napoleon distorted the spirit and substance of "this vast machine" by appropriating it "to the needs of absolute power." He replaced the councils by a single agent, elections by executive appointments, and judicial review before the "ordinary courts" by a principle of inviolability for officials, with their cases reserved for special courts,[55] all the while shrewdly cloaking his despotic apparatus with a facade of unelected councils. Tocqueville vigorously criticized Macarel for failing to see through Napoleon's sham, especially in the matter of "reserved justice [la justice réservée]" applying to cases to which the government was a party. Macarel saw this feature as a standard feature of "ordinary" justice; Tocqueville saw Macarel's benign acceptance as perpetuating a dangerous precedent that had established a beachhead for tyranny within the French legal system.[56]

With his report, Tocqueville thus sought to counter Macarel's position by warning his fellow academicians of the danger of an administrative system unchecked by elected officials and independent judicial review. Macarel's unsuspecting apology for despotism was particularly dangerous, Tocqueville believed, because such a legist's comments on the general principles of the laws were apt to be "eternal and fecund," as opposed to the more limited range and consequence of the laws themselves. Moreover, in the short term his comments would be received and digested by generations of students taking his course and using his textbook. Tocqueville concluded his report with a final plea to reject Macarel's view of the French administrative system as "a perfect whole" and to recognize the way political influence had infiltrated and corrupted it. Calling for a book on the topic that could span both of these "neighboring but distinct" worlds, he concluded with a final, none too veiled swipe at the failure of Macarel's book to reconcile "the principles of our administrative law with those of our political law": "There is a subject that still awaits a book. Such a book, gentlemen, would, in my opinion, be one of the greatest works to which our generation could apply itself."[57]

Tocqueville's plea for such a book would be fulfilled only with the publication, ten years later, of his own book—*The Old Regime*, volume I—in which he would provide a key chapter and frequent related comments that addressed just this issue, as well as a specific refutation of Macarel and his colleagues (*OR*, 1:133–34). His critique resulted from his ensuing archival studies that forced him to abandon Macarel's historical framework, which he had embraced in his 1845 report, and led him to reestablish the roots of administrative centralization squarely in the Old Regime.

During Tocqueville's very first archival probes, undertaken at the Archives nationales in 1852 when he was investigating the Directory, he conducted a brief "Examination of various *arrêts du conseil* rendered in 1785" in which he observed that there is "nothing new with us in matters of centralization."[58] A year later in April 1853, in his first extensive encounter with Old Regime administrative documents in the Parisian archives, he studied the repercussions of France's "administrative revolution" of 1787–88. His studies of these documents provoked, as we have noted, his observation that "the administrative regime of the Consulate and Empire is not a creation: it is a restoration."[59] In the same file, viewing an intendant's use of an *arrêt du conseil* to quash a parlement's judgment against a commune's higher officials, he added: "Nothing is new in our current regime. It's the Old Regime restored in perfecting itself."[60] And in his subsequent reading of Turgot, while studying an instance of "administrative jurisdiction," he again registered surprise that this example of judicial preemption by an intendant should have been common in the Old Regime: "The principle that I thought modern—that the administration must judge those legal proceedings that are triggered as a consequence of its own actions—is simply the principle of the Old Regime."[61]

It was at Tours that Tocqueville most pointedly and repeatedly studied the Old Regime's intrusions into judicial affairs. In his very first file, he noted an intendant's description of his unwarranted detention of beggars in a poorhouse as a form of "*administrative correction*";[62] he subsequently recorded repeated examples of such "administrative justice." Tocqueville soon connected the intendants' extraordinary powers to their official judicial position in the monarchy: "What facilitated things was the judicial origin of the intendant and of the council—both judicial and administrative—of which he had always been part. It was always clear in the official words—*a departed commissioner*."[63] In a file of August 6 titled "Ministerial correspondence," Tocqueville studied the whole issue of Old Regime evocations, in which the intendants justified their exceptional powers to try separately administrative cases involving their own officials. After a concluding summation of the "judicial character of the intendant," Tocqueville noted to himself: "Pursue carefully all of these filiations in order to show clearly all the roots of centralization [unreadable word] in the Old Regime."[64]

After his first six weeks of intense investigative work in the archives of Tours, Tocqueville told Freslon on August 10 that his studies of the competing assertions of power between the state and the parlements in the matter of administration had revealed "the continual intervention of the administrative power within the judicial sphere."[65] He then stated his surprise at such a finding: "I had had up until now the simplicity of believing that what we call administrative justice was a creation of Napoleon. It's *pure Old Regime preserved.*" Tocqueville concluded his letter by summarizing the escalating differences of his findings from those of the legists, known to him from his 1845 report:

> In reading the correspondence of Louis XV's ministers and their subordinates, we seem to see a crowd of small embryos destined to become the professors of imperial administrative law—the Cormenins, the Macarels, the Boulatigniers—splashing about in a spermaceutical state. Thus it is true that if we knew the Old Regime better, we would find that the Revolution was very far from accomplishing all of the good and the bad that one claims, and that it agitated society still more than it changed it.[66]

Tocqueville's antipathy toward Macarel and his associates was no longer just political, as it had been in 1845; his ire now encompassed their deficiencies as historians. For by failing to detect the ancestry of their own field of administrative law in the Old Regime, or by refusing to attribute it to that time, they had contributed to an exaggeration of the achievements of the Revolution, specifically in the area of administrative centralization—an exaggeration that Tocqueville himself fell prey to after his first reading of one of their works. Through his studies of prerevolutionary administrative law and practice in the archives of Paris and Tours, Tocqueville determined the correct roots of modern administrative law, thus uncovering "this truth [that] emerges from the ground on all sides, as soon as we dig into the ancient soil."[67]

While Tocqueville continued to focus on this intrusion of the central administration into the justice system,[68] he scrutinized at the same time the justice system's own attempts to usurp administrative policy through the actions of the parlements. His early probings in the Parisian and Tours archives and in Turgot's papers from Limousin revealed his initial view of the parlements' protestations as forming "an *irregular* and *unhealthy* liberty, but one that was great in France."[69] "Observe how justice strikes fear!" he subsequently noted approvingly on August 6 at Tours in viewing the administration's anxious response to an *arrêt* of August 22, 1777, of the Parlement of Paris.[70] But as he summarized for Freslon on August 10, his study revealed a justice in retreat in the eighteenth century, "imperceptibly driven back into [its natural sphere]" by an administration intent on exercising its full judicial prerogatives.[71] On January 13, 1854, he would write to Dufaure seeking books relative to the "*arrêts de règlement* issued by the Parlement of Paris," with particular interest in those extending into "the domain of administration properly so called."[72] Three months later, reading Isambert's *Recueil général des anciennes lois françaises,* he would conclude that the political and administrative interventions of the parlements could best be seen as occasional, specialized, intermittent cases, since they lacked "a habitual, detailed and continuous influence on the administration or the government."[73]

Tocqueville's probing of the respective jurisdictions of the parlements and state in matters of administrative law sustained his attention throughout his sojourn at Tours. In addition to his status reports to Freslon and admonitions to his favorite nephew, Hubert, who was contemplating a career in government,[74] he alluded to his studies in letters to other friends as well. With his archival work peaking in the fall of 1853, he told Rivet on October 23 that his studies had prepared him "to open a course on the study of administrative law under the Old Regime."[75] Eight days later, on October 31, he quipped to Lavergne that he was qualified to assume his very own "chair" in the subject.[76] Tocqueville's confidence in his credentials flowed from his prolonged and productive archival studies. His belief in the necessity for such a course of study stemmed from his disdain for the current holders of these chairs: Macarel and the other imperial apologists who had done so much to legitimate the cause of despotism. Tocqueville's own proposed course would seek to undo the harm caused by the mistaken views of Macarel and his associates by properly directing the study of administrative law back to its despotic roots in "the ancient soil."

3. Administrative Centralization in *The Old Regime*

In his portrayal of "administrative centralization" in *The Old Regime,* Tocqueville derives both his authority and, on frequent occasions, his facts from his intendancy studies at Tours. Throughout books 2 and 3, in which he focuses on why the Revolution originated in France, he injects his facts from Tours to support his arguments, either as illuminating vignettes, as surprising anecdotes, or, in twenty-eight cases, as corroborative endnotes. Tocqueville relishes the versatility of his Tours discoveries, since they can support not just his comments on centralization but also his theses ranging from feudal rights to the taille to the dearth of popular participation in the countryside and cities to the "revolutionary education" of the people.

However, Tocqueville's investigations at Tours provide more than the illustrative facts needed for his case studies. They also serve as the underpinning for his principal substantive arguments regarding administrative centralization, contained in a compact, thoroughly integrated six-chapter unit in II:2–7. In this unit, the first three chapters introduce three key elements of the administrative system, the fourth summarizes the way they took root among the feudal ruins, the fifth describes the system's methods of operations, and the sixth situates its locus in Paris. Indeed, in his drafts of these chapters, Tocqueville envisioned II:2–5 as a single unit, with II:6 and II:7 as correlated revelations of centralization's broad effects.[77] Tocqueville progressively unveils in his unit the defining administrative mechanism of the Old Regime—a streamlined pyramid, concealed within the old feudal system, that allows the instant transmission of decisions from its apex in the Council of State at the side of the king to its base, represented by a syndic and a collector in every French commune. It was his Tours findings that revealed the system's thorough instantiation in every community and documented its strategic significance there.

Tocqueville believes that his unearthing of the modern system's roots in the Old Regime is a major new discovery, one that repudiates the common notion that the system is a product of the Revolution. He thus seeks in his unit to awaken in his readers the same surprise he experienced in discovering the ancient roots of the modern system in his own archival searches. His title to II:2 summarizes his central theme for the unit as a whole: "That Administrative Centralization Is an Institution of the Old Regime, and Not the Work of the Revolution or the Empire, as Is Commonly Said." Tocqueville frames each of his two succeeding chapters with a title and concluding sentence emphasizing this modern parallel (*OR*, 1:124 and 131; 1:132 and 135). "This will certainly surprise those who think that all we see in France is new," he adds (*OR*, 1:128). In his recapitulation in II:5 of his first three chapters, he asks pointedly: "What is this but the centralization with which we are acquainted?" (*OR*, 1:135). In II:6, he emphasizes three times the parallels between government administrators and their customs and those "of our day," adding that "who reads a prefect reads an intendant" (*OR*, 1:139). History, he affirms, is "a picture-gallery in which there are few originals and many copies" (*OR*, 1:141). He concludes II:7, and his entire unit, by stressing that Paris's influence on modern revolutions mirrors its former influence on the original Revolution (OR, 1:148). Tocqueville's drumbeat regarding the neglected affinity between the two eras never abates, as it seeks to elicit a responsive chord in his modern audience.

Within his unit, we have no trouble locating Tocqueville's polemical nemeses, those expert legists who in their wisdom traced the origins to the Revolution of what they portrayed as a modern, efficient, clearly demarcated administrative system: "The modern legists assure us that we have made great progress in administrative law since the Revolution: 'before, the judicial and administrative powers were intermingled,' they say; 'but since then, we have unraveled them and restored each to its proper place' " (OR, 1:133–34). In II:4, Tocqueville repudiates these legists by showing, first, that the intrusions of the judicial and administrative powers in the Old Regime were reciprocal and, second, that subsequent governments, up to and including that of his own day, have never desisted from their administrative intrusions into the judicial sphere. Such administrative interference causes particular harm, he says, since it "depraves men and tends to render them revolutionary and servile at one and the same time" (OR, 1:134).

Tocqueville's internal consistency within his unit, apparent in his principal sources, modern message, and modern protagonists, benefits from his decision to relegate three potentially discordant discussions to later sections of his book. First, he defers until the end of III:3 his acknowledgment of a vibrant rebirth of local liberty beginning in 1770. Second, he avoids any reference throughout his unit to the sweeping administrative changes of 1787 and 1788, noted particularly in the Parisian archives, reserving for his penultimate chapter the revelation that a king's edict "had overturned the order of justice in all its parts" (OR, 1:234) and created provincial assemblies authorized to supersede the intendant "in most circumstances" (OR, 1:236).[78] Tocqueville presents "this first revolution" (OR, 1:239–40) in the context of the short-term causes of the Revolution in book 3, emphasizing its tendency "to stir up each citizen in the very heart of his private life" (OR, 1:234), disturb the equilibrium of the nation, and thus pave the way for the larger explosion of 1789.[79] By segregating it in a separate, later compartment of the book, he benefits in two ways: he gains a potent concluding explanation for the shocking ease with which the Revolution of 1789 dislodged the nation from its fractured base, and he preserves in an uncontaminated form his idealized model of the Old Regime's centralized system presented in his earlier unit of II:2–7.

Third, Tocqueville relegates the issue of administration in the *pays d'état* even farther to the back of his book—this time to a concluding appendix where he dramatically shifts his treatment from his first forecast of it. At the very beginning of his centralization unit, he announces his reasons for setting apart his description of the *pays d'états:* "I ask that you permit me first to put aside what were called the *pays d'états,* that is to say the provinces that administered themselves, or more precisely gave the impression of at least still partly administering themselves" (*OR,* 1:118). With most of the *pays d'états* possessing only the semblance of legitimate local government, Tocqueville will demonstrate, he says, "how far the central power had subjected even them to common rules" (*OR,* 1:118).[80]

When Tocqueville does provide his appendix at the end of his book, however, he presents an argument that diverges sharply from this anticipatory announcement of it. After four paragraphs that address the purported topic in a brief and disjointed fashion, he devotes the bulk of his appendix to a portrayal of the province of Languedoc, describing it as a model of local liberty in the Old Regime, a self-governing entity that managed to function politically, harmonize socially, and prosper economically despite the government's continuing controls. Midway through the appendix, he offers a glowing assessment of Languedoc under royal rule:

> The more I study the general regulations with respect to that portion of extant public administration established by the states of Languedoc with the permission of the King, but ordinarily without his initiative, the more I admire the wisdom, equity, and mildness revealed there; the more the procedures of local government seem superior to me than all that I have just seen in the *pays* administered by the King alone. (*OR,* 1:253)

Tocqueville thus shifts his appendix into an account of local liberty triumphant, a testament to the political, social, and economic benefits of legitimate local assemblies. Deferred to the end of the book and elevated to a full separate appendix rather than an excerpt within an endnote, Tocqueville's portrayal of local government in Languedoc seeks to leave his readers with a vision that can serve as a corrective to the relentless expansion of pervasive royal centralization exposed in his earlier centralization unit.

In each component of Tocqueville's centralization discussion in *The Old Regime,* including its unified body and three divorced appendages, his project is an educational one. True to his earlier teachings in *Democracy in America,* volume 2, part 4, he seeks to prepare his readers to recognize the pervasive grasp and debilitating effects of the Old Regime's unique form of benevolent government tutelage, so difficult to discern because it simulates the features of liberty: "Almost all princes who have destroyed liberty, from Augustus to our day, have tried first to maintain its outer forms; they thus flatter themselves that they can combine the moral force that public approval always gives and the conveniences that absolute power alone can provide" (*OR,* 1:127). His chapters, in seeking to expose the deceit of such a system, thus must distinguish the appearance from the reality of credible local liberty. At first glance, France of the Old Regime is a polyglot of seemingly independent, self-assertive bodies with "a diversity of rules and authority, a jumble of powers" (*OR,* 1:118). A deeper view, Tocqueville tells us, is needed to bring to light the central government's strategy in preserving this surface heterogeneity as a mask for its pursuit of an underlying uniformity. This is true in the case of the justice system, where the king and his legal apologists have instituted "a type of more dependent tribunal, that presents to [the king's] subjects some appearance of justice, without causing him to fear its reality" (*OR,* 1:132). This is true in the case of the nobles, where they are permitted to monopolize the king's court and direct the country's army and navy even while being stripped in the provinces of their local power and influence by faceless intendants (*OR,* 1:121). It is especially true in the case of local political assemblies, both in municipalities and villages, where the government preserves the forms of political representation while denying their substance. Citizens are still called to vote, in the cities as part of "general assemblies" (*OR,* 1:126), in the villages at special town meetings convened by the hallowed ringing of the local church bell. Municipal bourgeois have learned to abstain from participating in such assemblies (*OR,* 1:127), Tocqueville says, but village residents still cling to these "most hollow forms" (*OR,* 1:131) of a once vibrant local life. Beguiled in this way, the lifeless peasants are but shadows of their ancient forebears . . . and of their vigorous, hearty counterparts in the New England township whose system of local government Tocqueville had discovered so fortuitously in America (*OR,* 1:129).[81]

Tocqueville's revelations of the sham that marks the Old Regime's system reinforce the timeliness of his centralization unit's primary message. Put aside your blinders, he fairly shouts. Stop exaggerating the Revolution's so-called achievements. Recognize its tainted royal roots, which have given birth to our modern despotic system. Centralized government was omnipresent in the Old Regime, depriving its citizens of their liberties, insinuating its own agents into positions of power, and unknowingly creating a fertile field for revolutionary agitation and violence, unimpeded by intermediate institutions. This same centralization, resurrected by two Napoleons, is the keystone of our modern regime, enervating citizens, protecting its agents, and paving the way for our own brand of violence and our own cycles of revolution. Louis-Napoleon and his despotic govern-ment are singularly incapable of curing these problems, since they are the problem. Avoid the blandishments of such concentrated power. Choose to counteract it by insisting on legitimate local government, such as that once provided in the assemblies of Languedoc.

꙳

In his 1856 letter of thanks to Grandmaison, cited in the epigraph to this chapter, Tocqueville affirmed the essential contribution of the archivist and his archives to the making of his book. Without them, his previous studies lacked focus and cohesion. With them, he was able to achieve the "link-ing together of rules that I was seeking." Tocqueville's words of praise are validated by what we have noted of his early experiences at Tours. In late June his studies were indeed disconnected and unfocused, leading him to abandon in frustration his initial drafting efforts, noticeably devoid of a sin-gle reference to administrative centralization. Proceeding in July and Au-gust to his most intense reading of the intendants' archives, he certified the existence of this phenomenon and began to appreciate the ways it could serve as a foundation for his book, given its accessibility and novelty and the modern parallels conducive to his intended message. Most important, as Tocqueville said to Grandmaison, it provided the missing set of causal connections for his work, linking back to his feudal studies and forward to his studies of opinion. Given these multiple developments, all achieved in the context of a busy social summer, we are not surprised by Tocqueville's biggest decision on his road to *The Old Regime*—determining at the end of August 1853 to devote a separate volume to a full analysis of the Old Regime.

TOCQUEVILLE'S STUDY OF OPINION

Assessing Prerevolutionary "Spirit" in France

> I must first take the French spirit as the Old Regime had formed
> it, that is to say its opinions, tastes, natural tendencies in mat-
> ters of government (quite well represented by the economists),
> and then follow the jostling and transformation (never the de-
> struction) of these first elements in all that followed.[1]

In his 1842 speech at the Académie française, Tocqueville had
argued that a philosophical revolution had already been
launched and accomplished in France by 1770, the date of Cessac's
achievement of "manhood [*l'âge viril*]."[2] This first revolution, to
which he had also intended to alert his readers in an opening section of six paragraphs that he subsequently dropped from his 1836
essay,[3] infused the whole populace with new ideas that denied
the validity of traditional or revealed truth and insisted on each
individual's right to determine his or her own version of it. Freed
in this way from tradition, nursed by abstract ideals, possessed of
boundless confidence in their ability to realize vast aspirations,
the French had been transformed by the victory of the "new
philosophy," leading them to pursue the subsequent political
and social revolutions of 1789. "Deeds are but the outer structure
[*corps*] of thought," Tocqueville had asserted in his preparatory
notes. Youthful "ideas" thus trumped outmoded "mores," eventually triggering and shaping the Revolution.[4]

Ten years later, consigned to his sickbed in Paris by his respiratory illness of October 1852, Tocqueville again attested to the
power of these ideas, although this time with a different emphasis, pointing to their corrupting effect. In a vitriolic summation
of his impressions of Madame du Deffand's letters to Horace

Walpole, he denounced to Corcelle the way "the philosophy of the eighteenth century" had "ravaged" Deffand's soul during sixty years: "What a hideous ruin! The radical destruction of all moral forces; a profound egoism, a universal indifference, a consuming ennui leading to a disgust for life itself, mixed with the fear of dying, a vague and incessant restlessness that does not allow her a moment of repose, although all action is indifferent or uncomfortable for her."[5] Madame du Deffand's will for action had been broken, he declared, by her singular infatuation with the century's new philosophy. What had been a source of power and enlightenment in 1836 and 1842 had now become, at least in her case, the cause of disease and destruction.

In three readings in the spring or early summer of 1853, Tocqueville made little effort, however, to delve more deeply into an investigation of these different manifestations of the new ideas of the eighteenth century. Reading Turgot, he concentrated on his practical initiatives as both an intendant and a royal minister, choosing to skip entirely those volumes of his *Oeuvres complètes* in which the renowned physiocrat revealed his intellectual affiliations.[6] Assessing Burke, he noted his flamboyant polemics against the men of letters and his contention that they conceived, managed, and presided over the Revolution. While flagging the crucial importance of the antireligious fanaticism of the Revolution, he emphasized, as we have seen, its "transitory" quality: "Never forget the philosophical character of the French Revolution, its *principal,* though *transitory,* character."[7] In like manner, studying Dareste's "Mémoire," Tocqueville encountered a series of generally positive references to economists and physiocrats, especially Le Trosne, Quesnay, and Mirabeau, whose work shed light on rural questions and helped to free the countryside from absurd and outmoded market constraints. Tocqueville noted this "influence of economists, physiocrats, and learned men on social renovation,"[8] made pertinent bibliographical citations, but otherwise avoided an in-depth investigation of these actors in Dareste's account.

Tocqueville's seeming neglect of the influence of ideas on the Revolution was mirrored in his "Initial Outline" of June 26, 1853. In these draft notes for what he anticipated would be his larger work's introductory chapter, he focused on the economic and social factors leading to the Revolution, especially those detected in his feudal rights studies and reinforced by his recognition of Burke's mistaken views. The Revolution's "powerful and ancient causes" were those he had emphasized in his notes on Burke, as we have seen: the nobility's surrender of power, the bourgeoisie's envy and vanity, and the lower classes' misery and ignorance, exacerbated by their rising expectations[9]—none of which required an extended investigation of the era's philosophic crusaders. Having stated to Freslon, as we have noted, that he needed to know the Old Regime's administrative apparatus "through and through," and while possessing, we will now see, a similar desire to probe its prevailing ideas using books he took with him to Tours, he nonetheless omitted plans in his "Initial Outline" for a serious treatment of either centralization or the philosophical tenor of the era.

1. Tocqueville and Opinion in the Economists

Taking advantage of the references he had found in Dareste, Tocqueville took with him to Tours two of the three principal books that he would use to study one group of ideological crusaders, the "economists" or "physiocrats." [10] In "(June 53)," he took the measure of the first of these books— *De l'administration provinciale et de la réforme de l'impôt*, by Guillaume François Le Trosne; [11] in July, he began studying the second book—a collection of economists' writings titled *Physiocrates*, compiled by Eugène Daire. In an opening "Notice," drawn from Daire's own "Notice" in *Physiocrates*, Tocqueville remarked that Le Trosne was responding with his book to a question posed by the Académie de Toulouse, making him a practitioner of "the *literary politics* that characterized France in the eighteenth century." [12] Tocqueville culled an assortment of facts and figures from Le Trosne's work, especially in matters of tax policy, the proliferation of offices, and the financial burden of extant feudal rights. But in marked contrast to his reading notes of Le Trosne's contemporary Turgot, where Tocqueville had been frequently respectful of the energetic intendant's reform initiatives, he here expressed increasing impatience with Le Trosne's ill-conceived speculative schemes. "The situation in France is infinitely superior to that in England," Le Trosne claimed in one instance, referring both to agricultural production and to the king's ability to institute reforms "that will transform in an instant the condition of the country." Tocqueville exploded in response: "What ignorance! . . . What inexperience in practical politics! . . . What naive and incredible confidence in himself! What a revolutionary taste for enormous reforms made in one fell swoop!" [13] When Le Trosne went on to advocate the creation of a system of provincial assemblies, Tocqueville disputed the plan on two grounds. First, despite its ostensible intention to revivify rural political life, Tocqueville impugned the sincerity of "all the economists" in this matter, suggesting that they were simply seeking a

venue for implementing their massive reform plans and would have preferred not to be bothered by popular input at all: "In Le Trosne's case, as with
all the economists, we see that he desires social and administrative reforms
far more than political liberty. All these men visibly dread the assemblies
for fear of being bothered by them in their own reform schemes. . . . They
hardly possess a greater idea *of rights* than the government itself and thus
already have the true revolutionary temperament." [14] Second, Tocqueville
saw Le Trosne's willingness to eradicate existing territorial units, names
and all, as naive and dangerous in the extreme, exhibiting the "same taste
[of Turgot] for the system of the tabula rasa." [15] And when Le Trosne subsequently argued that voting rights should be extended to men performing
charitable deeds, such as raising orphans or donating cows to poor farmers,
Tocqueville disdainfully dismissed such "philanthropic nonsense": these
"speculative and literary" dreams of the period revealed no comprehension of the "more general, less sentimental" benefits of a system of suffrage. [16]

Taking stock of Le Trosne's arguments, Tocqueville revealed how
greatly he was struck by the credulity of such a "revolutionary": "Le Trosne
is a peaceful magistrate, a friend of order, justice, and religion, rather respectful even of acquired rights, and yet, in the tranquillity and heart of
his private office, he sketches plans of reform in which he fails to detect
the great Revolution that they bear." [17] Le Trosne's ambitious schemes for
France, conceived without political experience, showed how "revolutionary ideas were in the heads of the philosophes before entering those of the
demagogues." [18] Juxtaposed by Tocqueville with the philosophes, Le Trosne
thus became a first and prime example of what Tocqueville would immortalize in *The Old Regime* as his "literary men of politics."

In July, Tocqueville adopted a chief theme of his reading of Le Trosne—
the economists' disdain for popular participation and political liberty—as
the organizing principle for his ensuing studies, labeling it the "antiliberal
tendency of the eighteenth-century economists." He applied the principle
as a heading on his very first page of reading notes on François Quesnay's
Maximes générales du gouvernement économique d'un royaume agricole. [19] Quesnay, the
private physician of Louis XV and a confirmed statist who believed that the
royal government must institute vast reforms in French agriculture, [20] argued in his first maxim for a single sovereign authority to unite the nation
in pursuit of its reforms. "The system of checks and balances in a government is a terrible idea," he added, since it causes dissension among the great
leaders and overwhelms the lesser participants who are unprepared for such
responsibility. After taking note of the economists' energy, efficiency, and

honesty as revolutionaries, Tocqueville revealed the emerging focus of his studies of them:

> It is instructive and frightening to see from the beginning in their minds the germ of the true and final spirit of the Revolution. The view of the inconveniences of classes, orders, and inequality drove them on the basis of theory to seek an absolute government (revolutionary, in truth). How passions born of equality led the masses instinctively and practically to acquire the taste for such a government.[21]

The economists, Tocqueville found, were partisans of absolute government and as such served as the literary counterparts of the intendants, whose work to institute such government was evident on every sheet of correspondence in the Tours archives that Tocqueville was perusing during the same period.[22] While both promoted absolute government, they did so as agents of the principal "passions" of their time, those born of the nascent drive for equality manifest throughout their eighteenth-century culture. Given this passion and their zeal, Tocqueville was not surprised by the result: a contempt for popular participation resulting in the death of local liberty.

Tocqueville's narrow focus on the "illiberal tendencies of the economists" became even more exclusive as he read works of Mercier de La Rivière and Abbé Baudeau, again found in Daire's *Physiocrates:* he now commenced five consecutive pages of notes with this very heading.[23] On one level, his readings of these writers were thus highly selective and biased, since they served as a catch basin for examples to support his preconceived thesis about their aversion to liberty. Nor did the two economists disappoint him: they served up belabored expressions of support for "legal despotism," flowery praise for China's "true theocracy," stylistic foreshadowings of modern administrative directives, and a general amassing of "literary nonsense, in place of true understanding of men!"[24]

But on another level, Tocqueville's reading of the economists was unexpectedly nuanced—even, at times, sympathetic. He attributed to Baudeau a fundamental respect for individual rights, property, and liberty, engraved in a natural law superseding all particular laws of a sovereign authority.[25] He took pains to suggest reasons for the economists' inexperience in political matters: positive models of local liberties were lacking, since the "fertility" and "grandeur" of England's free institutions were hidden at the time to the untrained foreign eye, and negative models were abundant, with France's "detestable constitution" accounting for a host of such corrupted entities.[26] Given these factors, Tocqueville suggested, it was not surprising that the economists might have viewed the sovereignty of the people as incompatible with the division of power.

In a similar measured vein, Tocqueville concluded his notes by summarizing the economists' significance for the Revolution. They were not, he said, the great architects of the Revolution; indeed, based on his readings of Dupont de Nemours's letter to Say included in Daire's collection, it was clear that they were a marginal force in 1789 owing to their unpopularity.[27] Moreover their ideas, while certainly contributing to the destruction of the ancient edifice, could best be viewed as a product of the social conditions and opinions of the time, "springing naturally and peaceably from the state of mind, institutions, and mores of the nation, from its education, its history, and from what was most potent among its impressions and memories of the Old Regime."[28] Their illiberal tendencies, on which Tocqueville had focused his readings, were of special interest because they exhibited "what one could call the natural tendency of the nation of their time."[29] The economists thus reflected the nation; they did not lead it. Their thought must be examined, Tocqueville suggested, as a representative sample of the prevailing opinion in prerevolutionary France—"the permanent base of our instincts in politics," ready to mix and be mixed into the new institutions of society soon to appear.[30] Given the inherent illiberalism of this opinion, it would pull the nation toward despotism despite the best efforts of "the real revolutionaries, those of 1789 and the succeeding years" and thus would cast doubt on the possibility of a sustained realization of liberty.[31]

Using Dareste one more time as a bibliographic source, Tocqueville had requested two books of "Mirabeau the father" from Beaumont in Paris on July 1.[32] Beaumont quickly responded that he had located one of the books, L'ami des hommes (Avignon, 1756–58), in two volumes, and that he would deliver it to Tocqueville at Tours on July 5.[33] Tocqueville's subsequent reading of Mirabeau, which culminated his study of the economists, consolidated his previous findings of the ways the "public spirit" had infused and influenced their writings.

As with the other economists, Tocqueville read Mirabeau as a reflector, not a progenitor, of new "democratic" ideas prevalent in prerevolutionary society. He clearly stated this in his brief introductory comments:

> What is most curious in reading the works of the Marquis de
> Mirabeau is to observe the ideas that spring from equality and are led
> by the social revolution, penetrating within the mind of a man in the

midst of a swarm of aristocratic prejudices, pride, and noble insolence
that fill his head, and taking there the bizarre and unexpected forms
bestowed upon them by a place so little prepared to hold them.

There is nothing more singular than this invasion of democratic
ideas within a feudal mind.[34]

He summarized his findings of the peculiar mutations within Mirabeau's
spirit in a detailed list, drawn from throughout Mirabeau's two volumes,
of "what the Marquis de Mirabeau takes from his century and the economists."[35] While Mirabeau supported a small liberal core of natural rights, his
overall philosophy owed little to individual liberty and much to a belief that
royal authority should shape society and its subjects, since it alone possessed
"the supreme power . . . to transform men to its liking."[36] In 1758, the date
of publication for *L'ami des hommes*,[37] Tocqueville thus found early evidence of
the same soft despotic tutelage that he had anticipated for the democratic
future in *Democracy in America,* volume 2. It remained simply to shift the state
into the position of Mirabeau's king to obtain a "just" and "true" picture
of the way the eighteenth century featured "the greatest, most extensive,
most detailed influence of the government on affairs and even on ideas."[38]

On two occasions at the turn of the new year, still at Tours but now
immersed in writing his book, Tocqueville would spell out for his friends
the significance of his economist studies. Responding to comments from
Corcelle, he wrote on the last day of 1853:

> I read, pen in hand, the works of Turgot of which you speak. As
> you remark and as I had noted with the greatest care, he and all his
> school—which you perhaps do not know as well as I do—are the
> true precursors of the Cormenins, the Macarels, the Boulatigniers,
> the Viviens (before December 2). In reading them, I thought I was
> living with these moderns. It is they who in the eighteenth century
> best represent the true spirit of the Revolution and provide the
> clearest view of how equality of conditions can lead to centralization
> of power.[39]

Tocqueville took this occasion to formulate retrospectively two links for
Turgot, neither of which he had explicitly considered in his reading notes.
First, he now identified Turgot clearly with the group of his contempo-
raries consisting of Mirabeau, Quesnay, Le Trosne, La Rivière, and Abbé
Baudeau, defining them as "all his school." Second, he described this group
as preceding and laying the groundwork for Macarel and the other legists

of Tocqueville's own time, thus establishing a one hundred year circuit through which coursed "the true spirit of the Revolution." From Mirabeau to Macarel, Tocqueville suggested, the writers assisted in the formulation of despotism. Products of the new "equality of conditions," they helped move the nation toward the logical extension of these conditions—the "centralization of power"—by articulating a philosophy on which it could be based.[40]

Six weeks after this letter to Corcelle, Tocqueville was visited for ten days at Tours by Mrs. Harriet Grote, a political observer, author, and friend from his 1835 English travels. She recorded Tocqueville's comments to her about his economist studies in the following terms: "Alexis thinks that the writers of the period antecedent to the revolution of 1789 were quite as much *thrown up by* the condition of public sentiment as they were the exciters of it."[41] Consistent with the findings of each of the studies of economists that we have examined in this section, Tocqueville here confirmed the presence in the Old Regime of a preexisting "democratic" public opinion that both shaped and was shaped by the writers of the time.

2. Tocqueville and Opinion in the *Cahiers de Doléances*

During his early studies at Tours, Tocqueville showed interest in the separate phenomenon of an emerging public opinion, representing a new, potent, independent force in the Old Regime. In June he attached a description of "new power" to Le Trosne's assertion, "It is public opinion that governs,"[42] and in August he introduced as "nascent power" Finance Minister Comte Mollien's description of public opinion in his memoirs: "The ministers were all surprised to find a new power, the judgments of which they could neither direct nor defy."[43] In reading during the same period Jacques Necker's *De l'administration des finances de la France* of 1784, he noted "the supreme power of public opinion at the approach of the Revolution," this time with reference to Necker's description of "an invisible power, that . . . gives its laws to the city, the court, and even the kings' palaces."[44] The antidote to both the potency and volatility of such opinion, Tocqueville stated in his notes, was to strengthen people's personal convictions through their participation in intermediate institutions.

While continuing to pursue his interest in the intendants' correspondence during June, July, and August 1853, Tocqueville thus simultaneously broadened his studies to investigate the substance of public opinion in the Old Regime, whose political tendencies were "quite well represented by the economists,"[45] and the manner of its circulation in society, as noted by contemporary observers and actors. All three investigations revealed the same characteristic present in the Old Regime—a comprehensive, uniform, faction-free, rationally constituted political philosophy that promoted the expansion of a comprehensive, uniform, faction-free, rationally constituted political state. All three investigations showed the government's myopia in understanding the volatility of such opinion, since its monopoly of all functions in society caused it to be oblivious to differing opinions and to make itself subject to the absolutist whims it had itself created. In August in particular, he assessed the revolutionary repercussions of this blindness. [46] At the end of the summer, as we have seen, Tocqueville announced his decision to write a separate book on the Old Regime, the pieces of which had thus appeared and coalesced during the summer months. In September he set a deadline of "about October 15" to begin writing it. [47] Although he kept rescinding the deadline, moving it back in time to allow for library recall notices and a flurry of new studies that provoked his attention, Tocqueville apparently meant it to accommodate one further reading that would allow him to test and refine his summer's findings: that of the *cahiers de doléances.*

That Tocqueville took up the *cahiers* for a study of opinion at this pivotal moment just before he started writing *The Old Regime* should not surprise us. He was already familiar with a three-volume *Résumé général, ou Extrait des cahiers* published by Louis-Marie Prudhomme in 1789, [48] having usefully employed it to probe various levels of prerevolutionary opinion in preparation for his 1836 essay for Mill's *London and Westminster Review.* In January 1836 he had transcribed nine pages of notes based on his study of the *Résumé général,* including both reading notes and drafts of sketches describing divisions between the nobility and the Third Estate on the eve of the Revolution, several of which he would incorporate into his essay. [49] Returning now, almost eighteen years later, to the same *Résumé* for a further reading of the *cahiers,* Tocqueville again demonstrated his continuing confidence in its value to his studies, a confidence made clear in Mrs. Grote's account of his February 1854 description of it: " 'Cahiers,' published in 1789, contain the whole body of instructions supplied to their respective delegates. . . . Of this entire and voluminous collection (which is deposited in the archives of France) three volumes of extracts are to be bought which were a kind of *rédigé* of the larger body of documents. In these three volumes De Tocqueville mentioned, one may trace the course of public sentiment with perfect clearness." [50]

Tocqueville's reading in October 1853 of thousands of the *cahiers* excerpts that he found so conveniently cataloged in the *Résumé général* was a particularly spirited one, punctuated by a succession of outbursts that ranged from unqualified admiration to undisguised disgust at what he observed in the grievances of the three orders. Indeed, in no other reading file do we find him interacting so frequently with his materials.[51] On one level, with its enthusiasm, fluidity, and interactive quality, Tocqueville's reading of the *cahiers* in the *Résumé général* resembled his readings of the intendants' correspondence. Both sources allowed Tocqueville to "eavesdrop" on citizens making passionate pleas to official authorities in the Old Regime, in formats free from interpretation or commentary by third parties. Both sources were largely untapped by revolutionary observers, thus satisfying his quest for archival novelty.[52] Both provided barometers of opinion in the Old Regime, seen from below, which was Tocqueville's preferred perspective. And both were conducted at a time of his intensifying interest in the Old Regime, as it evolved to become the new focus of an initial separate volume of his proposed book.

However, Tocqueville's reading of these two sources was distinguished by two major variables. If the format of the intendants' correspondence had been necessarily shifting and unpredictable, dependent on the daily tenders of Grandmaison, the format of the *Résumé général* was fixed and predictable, equipped by its authors with detailed tables of contents, chapter and section heads, and a combined index and number table. If the intendants' archives had "an enormous amount of useless dust to swallow," the presentation of the *cahiers* in the *Résumé général* was highly sifted and sanitized.[53] If Tocqueville's system of study in the intendants' archives had been necessarily unplanned and spontaneous, here it could frequently be guided by major thematic categories for which he was seeking "new proof."[54] If his goal there had been to explore new data on the regime's inner functionings, here it was often to confirm theories he had already developed on the nuances of opinion on the eve of the Revolution.

The second key variable distinguishing the two readings was that in treating the *cahiers,* Tocqueville engaged not in a new reading but in a reexamination of a work with which he was already well acquainted. His familiarity with the *Résumé général* from his studies for his 1836 essay is evident at every stage of his note taking. Thus, on his title page for the entire file he affixed a prospective work objective for the readings as a whole, then added his anticipated result: "Establish the concordance of the *cahiers* of the three orders; I will come to find a great resemblance of demands and a more or less explicit *identity* of sentiments and general ideas."[55] On the second page of his first reading file of notes on the clergy, he commented on their gravitation "toward all of the liberal and innovating ideas," adding that "we are going to see" more proofs of this as his reading continues.[56] On his first page of notes on the nobility, he observed a call by the nobles of Metz and of Montargis for the elimination of the clergy as a separate order; "we will see many more" such signs of hostility against the order of the clergy, he added with the foresight conferred by his familiarity with the entire volume.[57]

Tocqueville's third reading file on the *cahiers* of the Third Estate was particularly remarkable for his anticipation of the themes he expected to encounter there. "Here," he said on the file's very first page, "before entering into detail, [are] the general remarks that the reading of the *cahiers* of the Third suggest to me." He then listed twelve fully developed themes drawn from his reading of the Third's *cahiers,* all written before he recorded thirty-two and one-half pages of corroborating details.[58] On the first page setting forth these details, anticipating the issues he knew lay ahead, he indicated that "we will see the Third Estate just as preoccupied with closing the door of the nobility as the middle classes in England are desirous of opening that of the aristocracy."[59] On his second page, he again alluded to the importance of his previous reading: "This idea is expressed in the *cahier* of Rennes. This *cahier* will be repeated constantly and remains in my mind as the one that is most filled with absolute ideas in the matter of the Revolution, the most aggressive in innovation, the most hateful against the privileged, and, in sum, the one where we can already best sense the epoch that is to follow."[60] Tocqueville's recall of this *cahier* of Rennes is not surprising; he had paraphrased in his 1836 essay the quotation this note is based on when he alluded to the Third's self-sufficiency as "a people complete unto itself alone"; he now also drew explicit attention in his notes to its status as a "commentary on the words of Sieyès."[61]

Given such a "deductive" framework within which Tocqueville's 1853 *cahiers* readings took place,[62] we may usefully ask if he learned anything new in his 1853 rereading of *cahiers* excerpts in the *Résumé général.* Tocqueville's 1836 reading had been marked by an emphasis on incipient civil war in France between mismatched opponents—an ascending Third united in contempt of the nobility, into whose order it possessed "no desire to introduce itself" and of whom it spoke with a "singular harshness of style,"[63] and a declining nobility engaged in internal recrimination and retaliation. The orders showed themselves capable of transcending self-interest and self-preservation, however, and when they did they displayed a "very robust" spirit of liberty, revealed in their common support for "*very liberal* principles" and "inalienable and imprescriptible" rights.[64] Using number counts provided in the appendixes of each volume of the *Résumé général,* Tocqueville even sought to construct a simple "concordance" that documented specific examples of common support for liberal principles among the three orders.[65]

Where Tocqueville had used the *cahiers* in 1836 to gain a surface snapshot of the distinct agendas of the three orders in 1789—containing both disparate and common elements—he studied them in 1856 to analyze French opinion at a deeper, less subjective, and less conscious level. In particular, he probed the relation between decentralizing "ideas" and centralizing "mores" that allowed him to splice together the three chief strands of opinion that he had identified and scrutinized at Tours during his summer of investigations.

The first strand was that of decentralizing "ideas," the most durable legacy of the eighteenth-century Enlightenment. Within his *cahiers* reading notes, Tocqueville showed a special interest in these "liberal innovations" of the time, defining them as "(the philosophical ideas, guarantees for properties and persons, the rights of the nation, the destruction of abuses and of the old institutions)." [66] Throughout his readings of each of the orders, he noted such Enlightenment concepts, either in the "inalienable rights of man" (including freedom from slavery, from *lettres de cachet,* and from arbitrary judicial detention) or in the new "social compact" of the nation (requiring regular meetings of the Estates-General, voting of all taxes, and strict accountability of royal ministers). [67] On eighteen occasions within the margins or text of his nobles' *cahiers* notes, Tocqueville emphasized that the nobles were "of their time," by which he meant that they were thoroughly imbued with these concepts and that they used Enlightenment language to express them. [68] Within his clergy reading file, he likewise accumulated eleven pages of notes especially designed to show "*Liberalism of the clergy. Innovating spirit. Fear of arbitrariness. Belief in the rights of the nation. Democratic theories. Hatred of special courts and, in general, of administrative justice.*" [69] The Third, "for the strongest reason," endorsed these same liberal precepts as well, [70] with Tocqueville commenting on these "rights" throughout his readings of its grievances in folder C.

Tocqueville's second variation of opinion embraced liberty too, but it advocated sweeping government reforms to accomplish it; it reflected the nation's centralizing mores as he had observed them in his summer studies of the economists. Advocating a uniform, rational system to erase the diversity and traditions of anachronistic Old Regime institutions, it quickly merged with despotism, as Tocqueville noted in his clergy reading file: "I must observe here: . . . all of the ideas of centralization and tyranny that reign in the spirit of this nation and that are going to overthrow everything in the name of liberty. . . . the revolutionary spirit, in a word, even in the least revolutionary class." [71] Tocqueville subsequently found examples of "the spirit of tyranny for the greatest good of society" in efforts by the nobles to restrict the number of farmers' plows and to force them to use stud farms, by the clergy to enforce common religious rites, and by assorted representatives of each order to mandate bureaus of charity for the poor, jobs for all able-bodied workers, a uniform standard for weights and measures, or reform of the monastic orders.[72] In Tocqueville's view these were "measures and habits that announce and lay the groundwork for centralization."[73] In each case, the state was called on to regulate existing institutions and practices in the name of the public good.

Throughout his *cahiers* readings, Tocqueville sought to clarify the relation between these two strands of opinion, linked in theory but leading to such different political outcomes. He took the opportunity to do so when the clergy of Colmar and Schlestadt called for villages and communities to elect their own municipal officers: "It is curious to see these two intellectual customs of the French spirit of 1789. One is superficial, arising from liberal instincts and theories that contain . . . the ideas of decentralization. The other is profound, sprouting from the habits, the mores, the past, the social state, where all the ideas of centralization have been deposited and stand in the way of all the movements of intelligence."[74] The depth and durability of centralizing "habits" and "mores," Tocqueville suggested, would ultimately thwart the "superficial" intellectual construct born from liberal instruction and decentralizing theories. Tocqueville clarified his formula as "extreme decentralization in the spirits, centralization in the mores."[75]

In addition to these first two "intellectual customs," Tocqueville noted the pervasive presence within the three orders of a third form of opinion, which he also labeled "democratic," now using his civil or social definition.[76] Such "traits" or "tendencies" or "passions" reflected the deeper, pervasive slide of the society as a whole toward equality, a move so central and irrefutable in Tocqueville's analysis that he saw no special need to comment extensively on it. "Democracy" for him in this case could encompass arguments for small farms and private canals; calls for the suppression of seigneurial justice, *banalités,* and royal *garde-chasses,* and for increased military professionalism; and a plea for the abolition of a law of substitutions containing testamentary obligations.[77] It was the link of these "democratic" traits with the centralizing mores that constituted the chief genetic imprint of the nation and posed the central threat to liberty. Responding to a demand of the Third of Saint-Quentin for uniformity of religious practices, Tocqueville summarized his view in the following terms: "Observe how the taste for uniformity works on men's minds in all matters. Signs of the times. Enough social equality so that the idea of equality lays siege to all intellects. Not enough political equality to prevent this idea from becoming a passion."[78]

A Tocquevillian summary of these findings on the three strands of opinion in the *cahiers* can be found embedded within his "General remarks on
the *cahiers* of the Third Estate," containing the twelve projected themes of
his subsequent reading.[79] There Tocqueville suggested that the Revolution
was doubly fated before it began. Its purported legacy of universal equal
rights was already achieved, with virtual homogenization—"nearly ABSO-
LUTE IDENTITY"—of the enlightened opinion of the upper classes of the nation. But this intellectual attachment to liberal principles was simultaneously being subverted by a still deeper attachment at the level of mores to
democratic social equality, induced and supported by the seductive charms
of a central state that "has a hand in everything, works toward [doing] everything, encourages, creates, impedes."[80]

3. Tocqueville's Use of the *Résumé Général*'s Number Tables

Gilbert Shapiro and John Markoff, moderating Taylor's more acerbic characterization, gently chastise Tocqueville's method in his *cahiers* reading for
The Old Regime, explaining that even such a talented reader could go only so
far with an "informal process" that failed to include "self-conscious record-
ing in explicitly defined categories . . . [of] detailed comparative frequencies," or what they subsequently denote "the technical paraphernalia of
content analysis."[81]

But unknown to readers—of his generation or our own—Tocqueville
did possess such precise recordings of grievance frequencies: the number tables appended by the editors of the *Résumé général* to each order's assembled
"grievances."[82] Each "TABLE OF CONTENTS CONTAINED IN THIS VOLUME, with
the unanimity or the number of bailliages supporting their demands," constituted a vast compendium of itemized grievances. Under the single letter
A in the table of the Third, for example, we find thirty-five such grievances,
ranging from "Absolution" to "Avocats du roi [lawyers of the king],"[83] with
frequent subdivisions under individual grievances refining still more precisely the shades of opinion measured. Virtually every grievance, and every
subsection of every grievance, was accompanied, as promised, by a separate
number count; eight hundred such counts exist for the nobles' grievances
alone, each purporting to represent the number of *cahiers* that articulated
the particular grievance. At the head of each table, the editors carefully explained the basis for their counts: "(una) designates *unanimity;* the figures between two parentheses, the *number of bailliages* when there is no unanimity."
In addition to presenting counts of grievance frequency, the tables served

as the books' indexes, with a page number referring back to a representative
sample within the body of the text for each stated grievance.[84]

On the first page of the first file of his *cahiers* reading notes, Tocqueville
took the measure of the tables:

> For what relates to the unanimity of bailliages, I followed what is
> indicated in the book's table. But I have my doubts about the perfect
> exactitude of the statements of this table, because in certain instances
> where the table indicated the unanimity of bailliages, I found *cahiers*
> whose tenor evidently deviated from this presumed uniformity, and
> without being precisely contrary, differed from what was said to be
> the unanimous wishes. I fear that the editors took for unanimous not
> those demands found in all the *cahiers*, but those expressed in some
> that were not contested by any other.[85]

Tocqueville's reservations in this case were methodological ones, unre-
lated to the editors' trustworthiness or credibility. When the tables indicate
"una," or "unanimous," he asked, were they referring to support of the entire collection of the respective order's *cahiers* for a particular grievance? Or
were they simply indicating concurrence within a smaller subset, provided
that no dissenting grievances had been found in the rest of the collection?
In both cases, Tocqueville assumed that the editors had plumbed the entire
corpus of *cahiers*—he counted 168 for the clergy and 166 for the nobles in lists
at the front of their respective volumes—to collect their information and
determine their "una" counts. He concluded his comment by stating that
even if unanimity existed only within an unchallenged subset, this would
provide information that was "still very important to know, it is true."[86]

Having registered his query, Tocqueville proceeded to his reading of the
cahiers, a reading that relied heavily on the tables. In 175 instances, representing more than 40 percent of the total number of grievances he chose
to record, he cited the editors' number count for a particular grievance.
On more than 100 occasions, the counts Tocqueville chose to use were the
"una" ones: "The table says that this demand is unanimous," he would say
in one case; "all demand . . ." in many others; "unanimity" in still more. To
be sure, on several occasions he indicated a gnawing distrust in the reliability of the tables, based on either internal or external evidence he adduced
for a particular grievance.[87] But he invariably returned to his use of them,
even complaining on occasion that the editors had chosen not to include a
count for a demand of particular interest to him.[88] The tables' findings, he

thus believed, added a further vital dimension to his study of the *cahiers*, since they allowed a particular grievance of a particular order in a particular part of the country to be instantly generalized to provide a snapshot of opinion in the country as a whole.

The *Résumé général* that Tocqueville perused with such interest in October 1853 was conceived and executed with skill and audacity in the fiery days surrounding the convening of the Estates-General on May 4, 1789. At that time, Louis-Marie Prudhomme—a transplanted Lyonnais, secondhand Parisian bookseller, Cordeliers and Jacobin club member, and prolific radical pamphleteer[89]—took on the bold project of summarizing for the deputies, and the nation as a whole, the results of France's recently completed preparation of its *cahiers de doléances.* Prudhomme was one of the few Parisians who could even have entertained, let alone implemented, such a project. Overseer of a five-person "Society of Men of Letters," flush with funds from his lucrative illicit pamphlets, and soon to be a rare owner of his own printing presses, Prudhomme possessed incomparable resources for the undertaking.[90] Moreover, he recognized the unique importance of the *cahiers* as a way to give voice to "that which must be the great regulator, public opinion."[91]

Prudhomme's most eloquent formulation of his heady objectives for his new work occurred in the "Prospectus" he issued on May 20, 1789, seeking subscribers.[92] Using images of light, he described the anthology of *cahiers* excerpts as "the product of the wisdom and enlightenment of the age," which could now infuse each citizen and each deputy with the knowledge and inspiration to address "all of the questions that are about to be debated in the Assembly of the Estates-General." As the first, unique statement that would contain the "germ" of "all the elements of a perfect legislation," the *cahiers* would constitute the indispensable guide that could lead the French nation toward "its regeneration."

Within his prospectus, Prudhomme acknowledged the largest problem faced in this process of transmitting the nation's enlightened will to its deputies: the *cahiers* collection was "so voluminous" that the cost of reproducing it would be prohibitive. Moreover, readers of such a collection would soon experience "a sort of disgust," given the essential homogeneity of the *cahiers,* in which "the same ideas, the same objects return so often." Prudhomme then justified the need for an "extract" that would collect and organize by theme both general and particular ideas and views that were "scattered in more than five hundred *cahiers.*" The work would be conducted with scrupulous "exactitude" and "fidelity," making sure not to tamper with the integrity of the texts being presented. Prudhomme completed his prospectus by assuring subscribers that they would be acknowledged by name in his work; surprisingly, in this promotion of his book on May 20, he made no mention of the work's proposed number tables.

We must turn to another document of the same period—a letter from secret police files of a prerevolutionary police informant, the "director of the publishing house, Maissemi"—to gain a fuller understanding of the climate of surveillance and royal censorship within which Prudhomme drafted his prospectus. Identifying for the police those booksellers whom he believed were in violation of the law, Maissemi said:

> One is the man named Prudhomme, who runs his shop under the name of Monsieur Dupuis, who himself is absent from Paris. This Prudhomme, a secondhand bookseller, lives on Jacob Street, opposite Saint-Benoît. . . . It seems evident that it is this Prudhomme who is in charge of the distribution of the bulletin titled *Estates-General* and that he is accustomed to peddling all that is most reprehensible. I would happily send there the Syndical Chamber; but as this Prudhomme may have stores separate from his shop, it would be essential that the visit be made by a commissary and one of your inspectors, with the greatest care and secrecy. . . . He circulates as well a prospectus with the title *Résumé général, ou Extrait des cahiers des bailliages,* for which one subscribes at the house of M. Laurent de Mézières, 28 Saint-Benoît Street, faubourg Saint-Germain. It is probable that Prudhomme has something to do with this work. This would also be an object to look for and seize.[93]

Unmoved by the noble public spirit Prudhomme voiced in his prospectus, the informant thus articulated his distrust of any work that bore the imprint of the revolutionary pamphleteer. His suspicions portend questions that have accompanied Prudhomme's labors on the *Résumé général* to the present day.

"Object of an incessant surveillance,"[94] Prudhomme published a book that did its best to dispel fears of its radical content. The first paragraph of its "foreword" set forth the impartiality of its objectives even while openly acknowledging the power possessed by the authors of such an anthology: "The collection we present to the nation is its own work. It is the exact and faithful *résumé* of all of the instructions that it gave to its deputies. The only choice belonging to the editors is the order in which we thought we must present them to the public."[95]

The work then presented a vast compendium of *cahier* passages, transcribed verbatim, without commentary or analysis by the authors. Thanks to its tables of contents, readers could readily locate thematic categories of grievances; its meticulous indexes facilitated reference to several thousand particular grievances. Its compilation of passages was not one-sided, since it made a clear effort to include various points of view; passages of contradictory intent thus often appeared consecutively.[96] Despite spelling and transcription errors, the book's professionalism and breadth were remarkable, especially given the haste with which it had necessarily been compiled to meet the needs of deputies sitting at Versailles, debating the future of the nation and awaiting just such a summation of the words their constituents had spoken.[97]

We have noted that in his prospectus Prudhomme promised that excerpts for the *Résumé général* would be drawn from "more than five hundred *cahiers.*" Within the text itself, however, a careful count demonstrates that Prudhomme in fact drew on only 186 *cahiers* for the entire selection of quotations that made up his three volumes. Moreover, the vast majority of such excerpts are drawn from an even smaller sampling of available *cahiers.* As shown in table A (pp. 128–29 below), 86 percent of the *Résumé général*'s excerpts for the clergy were taken from just twenty *cahiers;* for the Third, 77 percent; and while an effort was made to incorporate a broader sample for the nobles, more than half of the volume was still a digest of just twenty *cahiers.*[98]

We need only turn to modern content studies of the *cahiers* to cast still more doubt on the extent and veracity of Prudhomme's claimed computations. When Prudhomme cited "una," or 100 percent, for the nobility's demand that venal purchase of positions be abolished, Guy Chaussinand-Nogaret finds the same grievance in only 44.77 percent of the nobles' *cahiers,* and Sasha Weitman in 45 percent.[99] When Prudhomme again cited "una" for the nobles' demands for the abolition of serfdom, Chaussinand-Nogaret records 5.22 percent and Weitman 4 percent.[100] Raising Tocqueville's own cautionary note, it is possible that when Prudhomme cited a count as "unanimous" he may have been referring only to those *cahiers* that articulated the particular grievance. But not only is such a rendering at odds with his own definition of "una" at the heading of each table, Prudhomme's non-"una" counts are also at odds with modern number counts. Thus, as shown in table B (pp. 129–30 below), when the *Résumé général* shows eighty-nine *cahiers* of the nobles advocating the redemption of *banalité* rights, Chaussinand-Nogaret finds only seven such *cahiers.*[101] On all fronts, then, Prudhomme's own counts seem fraudulent.[102]

Thirty-five years after the turbulent events of 1789, Prudhomme provided a succinct synopsis of the fate of the book in which he had invested such hopes:

I published, in three volumes in octavo, a general résumé of the *cahiers* and powers given by the bailliages to their deputies to the Estates-General. The minister had the edition seized. On my protestations that it was the voice of the nation, he responded that this was true; but that the king did not wish for it to be made public. More than eight hundred deputies protested this arbitrary act. The work was returned to me. [103]

Despite his extraordinary efforts to give voice to a unified French public opinion while investing his results with an aura of impartiality, in 1789 Prudhomme failed his ultimate test of convincing a skeptical king to allow the distribution of the book in an arena where his number tables could have helped to promote his legislative agenda. In the ensuing years, however, unknown to him, his book did achieve a widespread, if unacknowledged, distribution. In 1825 François Grille took Prudhomme's *cahiers* excerpts, reorganized them, and produced a vast "tableau comparatif"; he made no mention of his debt to Prudhomme. [104] In 1834 P.-J.-B. Buchez and P.-C. Roux, again without attribution to the now deceased Prudhomme, presented their own "Résumé des cahiers," drawn from the excerpts and number tables of the *Résumé général*. [105] And in 1856 another historian of the Revolution—Alexis de Tocqueville—published *The Old Regime*, in which he used Prudhomme's *Résumé général* to authenticate his own numerous claims about opinion in the Old Regime. Enamored by the "perfect clearness" with which it presented such opinion, he was ultimately betrayed by the partiality and manipulations of the Revolution's master polemicist.

4. Opinion in *The Old Regime*

Within books 2 and 3, presenting the long- and short-term causes of the Revolution in France, Tocqueville unveils the results of his investigations of opinion in the Old Regime. He does so in two distinct units of three chapters each, the first documenting the presence of centralized mores in all classes of the Old Regime (II:8–10), the second showing the potency of new philosophical ideas that mesmerized and guided the entire French populace (III:1–3). Consistent with his findings in his *cahiers* studies, he presents the existence of the mores as a long-term cause, discussed in book 2, and the infatuation with ideas as a shorter-term one, initiating book 3. In both units Tocqueville traces the origins of the opinion described to a common factor—the absence of political liberty. And in both units he concludes his discussions with spirited defenses of a resilient, competing strain of liberty in the Old Regime: in book 2 he assigns this affirmation to a separate succeeding chapter (II:11), while in book 3 he places stirring perorations on liberty's abiding presence at the end of his unit's latter two chapters (III:2 and 3).

In II:8–10, Tocqueville's analysis reveals two simultaneous, seemingly contradictory tendencies produced by the administrative centralization defined in his preceding unit (II:2–7): in the first, centralization molded the politically relevant parts of the French population into a "uniform crowd" (OR, 1:149), and in the second it created artificial barriers within and between this enlightened elite and the population as a whole, causing jealousy, resentment, division, and conflict. Tocqueville's three chapters, buttressed by comparisons with Germany and England, are unified by their central claim: that political actions of the French state irresistibly and "inevitabl[y]" (OR, 1:152) dictated these strains of prerevolutionary French opinion.

Highlighting the resemblance of the privileged classes, II:8 contains the results of Tocqueville's findings of the "unanimity" of French opinion on the eve of the Revolution. He based his argument on his *cahiers* readings: "Nothing highlights this more than reading the cahiers presented by the different orders in 1789. Those who write them differ profoundly in their interests, but show themselves alike in all else" (OR, 1:149). Such a conclusion accurately represents, as we have seen, the results of his close scrutiny of the *Résumé général* and its number tables. Tocqueville found such similitude in the underlying mores of the French upper classes, encompassing their "ideas," "habits," and "tastes" (OR, 1:152); it existed at a deeper level than simply that of ideas, and it clearly was not caused by such ideas, since it resulted, Tocqueville emphasizes in his conclusion, from a lack of political liberty due to the restraints imposed by "the government of one person" (OR, 1:152). It was the absolute monarchy of France, possessing both legislative and executive power, that monopolized the exercise of power and precluded society from diversifying its convictions through independent action. It was the monarchy that thus produced a generic breed of men who were "similar among themselves and mutually indifferent to the fate of others" (OR, 1:152). Such homogeneity stands in stark contrast to the differences between the Third and the nobility evident in previous Estates-General, where the two orders seemed "still to belong to two distinct races" (OR, 1:150).

In II:9 and 10, Tocqueville analyzes a different symptom traceable to the same cause. Class divisions proliferated at every level of prerevolutionary French society; they resulted from the "detestable institutions" (OR, 1:169) of the Old Regime, now personified by Tocqueville in particular kings who made particular decisions to meet their particular financial needs. The kings' tax policies, exemptions, and collection procedures, transacted in private and without accountability to voters, split the society apart, as demonstrated by the Third "in its grievances" (*OR*, 1:158) and by Turgot, Necker, Le Trosne, Young, and the intendants in the archives at Tours. The root cause of this "crime of the old monarchy" (*OR*, 1:170) was the absence of political liberty, which could have rid society of these institutions "if it had been permitted to debate them" (*OR*, 1:169). The absence of political liberty, Tocqueville thus argues in this three-chapter unit, led to the French Revolution in two ways. In II:8, it ensured not just the ease of the rupture but the totality of the ensuing collapse of French unity, proving that the bond of national assimilation had been merely superficial. In II:9–10, it created an intensely selfish preoccupation on the part of all men with the interests of their own splintered groups, an effect that Tocqueville labeled "collective individualism" (*OR*, 1:163). This led to the animosities inherent in the society as a whole, most clearly manifest in a shared hatred of the nobility, and to an inability to unite for a public purpose. When these classes with this history came together in 1789, "they first touched only through their raw sores" (*OR*, 1:171).

Tocqueville maximizes the power of this unit on centralized mores by reserving his discussion of liberty in the Old Regime for a separate, succeeding chapter (II:11). Tocqueville's resurrection of liberty in II:11 thus bears a double burden: it must counter the flow of nine consecutive chapters stripped of dissenting perspectives so as to spotlight centralization's appropriation of the vital organs of the Old Regime, and it must overturn the very premise these chapters were based on: the absence of an active, participatory tradition of local liberty.

Faced with this daunting challenge of his own making, Tocqueville engages in a point-by-point reappraisal of his earlier discussions, now finding, by turn, protections for liberty in the limitations and timidity of the government, in the character of the nation's elite, and in the motley collection of archaic institutions that were still "strongly resounding with voices, even though political liberty was nowhere to be seen" (*OR*, 1:176). Tocqueville recaptures the presentist orientation of his early chapters on centralization, quickly informing his readers that this assessment of liberty in the Old Regime will show "a kind of singular liberty, not easily understood today" (*OR*, 1:171). The chapter, which contains Tocqueville's first extended exposition of his "men of '89," is thus inspirational in intent: "Would to God," he says, "that we could recover, even with their prejudices and their faults, a little of the greatness [of the men of the eighteenth century]!" (*OR*, 1:179).

Tocqueville uses the *cahiers de doléances* as his chief source for his findings of liberty in two of the three orders: the nobility and the clergy. With

reference to the *cahiers* of the nobility, he says: "In the midst of their prejudices and errors, we feel the spirit and several of the great qualities of aristocracy" (*OC*, 1:173). He then refers his readers to endnote 44 for his full "analysis" of these *cahiers,* an endnote in which he presents his most extensive
portrayal of both his *cahiers* sources and the nobles' spirit he had found in
reading them.

Tocqueville was not the author of this portrayal of the nobility in endnote 44: Alexis Stoffels—his godson and namesake—researched and wrote
it.[106] Stoffels's summary was a straightforward synopsis of the nobles' grievances. He incorporated more than one hundred specific grievances, every
one of them derived from the *Résumé général.* He used nine direct unidentified
cahier quotations in the endnote, all traceable to the *Résumé.* Restricting all
interpretative commentary, he pieced together excerpts from throughout
the *Résumé* to produce his finished product.

Stoffels's endnote does bear Tocqueville's editorial imprint, however, in
a variety of ways. It was Tocqueville who wrote the three paragraphs that
introduced the texts he had used for his *cahiers* studies (*OC*, 1:287). It was he
who removed all references to particular sections of the *Résumé général,* as
well as to individual *cahiers.* It was he who injected the more than thirty numerical quantifications, citing "some," "many," "a great number," "almost
all," or "all," drawn in each case from the *Résumé*'s number tables. Indeed,
on two occasions he drafted specific sections that contained the largest part
of these quantifications, including the single case in which he used a precise
numerical count traceable to the *Résumé*'s number table.[107] And it was he
who provided the paragraphs of interpretation within the endnote, including the final one in which he summarized the eighteen examples we have
noted in his own *cahiers* reading notes of how the nobles' spirit and language
were representative "of their time": "What is most striking in reading the
cahiers of the nobility, but what no extract would know how to reproduce,
is to what extent these nobles are indeed of their time: they possess its spirit;
they employ very fluently its language" (*OR*, 1:294).

"I began the study of the old society full of prejudices against [the
clergy]," Tocqueville says in *The Old Regime,* adding that he completed his
study "full of respect" for them (*OR*, 1:175). We can trace this transition in
his *cahiers* reading notes, which he began with comments on the clergy's
Faustian bargain with the monarchy[108] and concluded with the inventory
we have noted of their liberal attributes. Tocqueville listed twenty-two such
attributes (*OR*, 1:174–75) that he presented as enjoying the consensus of the
clergy; his compilation did not follow his own notes but drew on those
of Stoffels, who used the *Résumé général* to prepare a report of the clergy's

grievances analogous to his synopsis of those of the nobles.[109] As with the nobility, Tocqueville's claim of the clergy's consensus on particular grievances appears to be tied to the *Résumé*'s number tables, since sixteen of the twenty-two attributes he mentions are counted as "una" in the tables, with thirteen recorded as such in his notes.

Tocqueville attributes the superior citizenship of the clergy to their status as property holders, an idea developed as an "*important* general remark" in his own *cahiers* reading notes.[110] As property holders, they had a powerful commitment to liberty and to France; when their property was seized during the Revolution, this spirit was replaced by political indifference and a loyalty to Rome. Tocqueville argues that this finding, also revealed in his readings of the reports of the provincial assemblies, demonstrates the essential ephemerality of opinion and its dependence on social forces, thus exhibiting "the revolutions that can be wrought in men's minds by changes arising in their condition" (*OR*, 1:174).

Where the clergy's spirit of liberty was made possible by their "condition" as property holders, the Third's was contingent in similar fashion on the possession of its own version of property: offices held from the king. Since these offices were at that time immune from government tampering, they protected the dignity of their holders by providing them with a means to avoid being placed "at the mercy of the ruling power" (*OR*, 1:176). Even the small cliques of II:9–10, with their narrow and fierce provinciality, are now reappraised by Tocqueville and assigned a useful role as centers of resistance to the central government, since they gave men a forum within which to hatch plans, defend them, and be held accountable by strident public response (*OR*, 1:176 and endnote 48).

In II:11, Tocqueville thus seeks to moderate his extreme portrayal of centralized opinion by introducing competing arguments, often drawn from the same sources, to demonstrate the continued existence in the Old Regime of "an irregular and intermittent kind of liberty . . . stunted and deformed [but] still fertile" (*OR*, 1:179). Such liberty was tenuous at best, given the weaning of the nobility from the countryside, the venal compromises between the clergy and the monarchy, and the attaining of middle-class respectability by the Third. Such liberty will be even more difficult for modern Frenchmen to fathom, Tocqueville acknowledges, since political, economic, and social changes within society have further eroded its bases by destroying the nobility, confiscating church property, and politicizing the tenure of administrative offices. But its eradication in modern times, he argues, should not cause readers to lose sight of the fact that it had formed an essential, if endangered, element of French national character in the Old Regime, resisting the ever-increasing attempts of centralization "to equalize, soften, and deaden the characters of all" (*OR*, 1:179).

In III:1–3, Tocqueville argues that French literary men both inspired and led the Revolution, first by infecting the population with "their ideas . . . their temperament and their humor" (*OR*, 1:201) and then by offering themselves as leaders to implement the bold projects thus inseminated. Tocqueville presents this situation as a function of circumstances peculiar to France: "Voltaire's spirit had long existed in the world, but Voltaire himself could hardly have indeed reigned except in the eighteenth century and in France" (*OR*, 1:204). It was caused by an absence of political liberty, not just among the purveyors of ideas (*OR*, 1:197) but also among those who received them and took them to heart: the masses (*OR*, 1:197), the aristocracy (*OR*, 1:198), and government officials (*OR*, 1:199), all of whom would have responded differently to events if their own ideas had been forged by free institutions. One element of "Voltaire's spirit" thus unleashed was its ferocious distaste for religion, again caused by the confluence in France of exceptional circumstances (*OR*, 1:204). Another element was its abhorrence of the very idea of "public liberty properly so called" (*OR*, 1:209), best exemplified in the writings of a smaller, less conspicuous, less influential subset of writers of the day—the economists or physiocrats.

Despite the simple overarching premise of his argument, Tocqueville's unit shows evident signs of the difficulties he encountered in writing it, subsequently summarized for Beaumont when he said that its first two chapters were "the ones that cost me the most in reflection, work, and worry."[111] We see an awkwardness in the repetitive nature of a number of the arguments he advanced, as when he repeated a similar triad of questions posing a similar introductory premise for both III:1 and 2 (*OR*, 1:196, 203–4). We note confusion in his inability to distinguish clearly the "men of letters" in III:1 and 2 from the economists and physiocrats of III:3 as he chastised the work of both, although for different reasons.[112] We detect ambivalence in his judgments on the merits of the "men of letters," with the severity of his critique drawing measured rebukes from his friends Clémentine de Beaumont, Harriet Grote, and John Stuart Mill.[113] When forced to defend his portrayal against Madame de Beaumont's censure, he would tell Beaumont in 1856 that he had not wished to "bring action against" eighteenth-century ideas, or at least "the just, reasonable, applicable portion of those ideas, which, after all, are my own."[114] And we see an inability to clarify the chief factors responsible for the opinion he so ardently sought to define: Did "men of letters" shape this opinion through their unique brand of political education that contributed "more perhaps than anything else" (*OR*,

1:201) to the nation's "ideas, temperament, and humor"? Or were previous social and political transformations of the nation chiefly responsible for the French people's receptivity to these new ideas, so antithetical, Tocqueville emphasized, to their national character (OR, 1:202)?

One way of grasping Tocqueville's many difficulties in the unit is to trace his evolving conception of it. In his first draft of its initial chapter (III:1) prepared at Tours,[115] Tocqueville gave it two possible titles:

> How the absence of all public life favored the birth and hastened the development of the philosophical doctrines that produced and characterized the French Revolution.

> The general philosophical doctrines that produced and characterized the French Revolution and why they developed in France more rapidly than anywhere else and seduced more completely all minds here than in other countries.

In each case, the chapter was intended to focus on political or social factors explaining the reception of the philosophical ideas; it stressed longer-term, institutional causes for the peculiar receptivity of the French to philosophical ideas, dovetailing with his earlier portrayal of a centralization that had stripped the nation of those local institutions that might have led people to consider the new ideas with a more realistic and savvy spirit. Tocqueville minimized the role in these early formulations of those men who were the purveyors of these literary ideas.

When Tocqueville subsequently altered the chapter's focus and broadened its scope to include a full treatment of the "literary men of politics," a move that he characterized in his notes as "more perceptible and pleasing to the average readers,"[116] he was hampered by a general lack of analysis in his reading notes of their personal motives, reforming zeal, religious hostility, or political capacities, since these issues had formed little part of his original studies. He possessed no thorough notes on the philosophes in general and only a single assessment of the character of one literary writer, the economist Le Trosne. He had made no specific investigation of the fierce religious hostility of some of the writers. Moreover, the readings he had conducted were often limited in focus and skewed to consider a single aspect of the writers evident in their work—their eschewing of political liberty. When Tocqueville transcribed a brief set of notes on Voltaire, for example, he did so with the intent to capture only the illiberal aspects of a selection of his letters.[117]

With their gaps and one-dimensional focus, Tocqueville's reading notes thus lacked the breadth to accommodate his chapters' shifting concerns. One way to detect this inadequacy is to view the endnotes he chose to include for the unit: for his three chapters surveying the philosophes, irreligion, and economists in *The Old Regime*, he selected only three reading note excerpts to append as supporting endnotes (endnotes 63, 64, and 65), with endnote 64 subsequently adapted to focus more on feudal abuse than on church-state collusion.[118] He did not select a single endnote from his central reading file for the unit—folder D on the economists. He appended little because his notes for this section of his book provided little; they were selective, frequently condensed treatments that often lacked the more provocative, nuanced assessments of the rest of his reading files.

Tocqueville's diligent reworkings of these chapters, conducted over two years, masked many of these disjunctions in *The Old Regime*. What they could not hide was the biggest flaw of the unit—and arguably of his book as well—that resulted from his excessive reliance on an imperfect source: the *Résumé général*. Prudhomme, consistent with his self-proclaimed role as a modern-day Aeneas assisting the birth of a new French nation through his preservation and presentation of the people's grievances,[119] extensively edited the *cahiers*, selecting those texts that highlighted their luminous role as beacons for the nation's new political constitution. To provide evidence of widespread support for such claims, he attached his number tables to each of his three volumes. His text as a whole had the effect of exaggerating the *cahiers*' liberalism, in ways that we can witness by looking again at table B (pp. 129–30 below). In every instance in the table, Prudhomme's specific number count overstates the presence of the respective liberal grievance in the *cahiers*. Tocqueville, pursuing objectives of his own that included highlighting liberal attributes of the nobles and clergy and demonstrating the abstract philosophical tenor of the era, gladly availed himself of Prudhomme's texts and tables. In so doing, he further liberalized what was already a highly liberalized *cahiers* anthology, creating a multiplier effect leading to an inflated portrayal of the *cahiers*' enlightened demands.

Such inflation helps explain Tocqueville's view of the *cahiers*—to use Furet's felicitous characterization—"as a corpus of revolutionary texts."[120] In 1836 it contributed to his view of liberty's pervasive presence in French opinion. In 1856 it solidified his case for noble and clergy enlightenment and for the broad consensus for change among the nobles and the Third. In each case it led him to overstate the continuity between prerevolutionary and revolutionary France; by extension, it thus led him to understate the rupture introduced by the Revolution itself.

Tocqueville's argument regarding the political naïveté of the revolutionaries is similarly flawed. In *The Old Regime,* he presents it in famous terms:

> I read attentively the cahiers drafted by the three orders before meeting in 1789; I say the three orders, those of the nobility and clergy, as well as that of the Third. I observe that here one demands the change of a law, there of a custom, and I take note of it. I continue in this way to the very end of this immense task, and, when I come to add together all of the particular demands, I discover with a sort of terror that what they demand is the simultaneous and systematic abolition of all the laws and all the customs prevailing in the country; I see at once that one of the vastest and most dangerous revolutions that the world has ever seen is about to unfold. Those who will be its victims tomorrow suspect nothing; they believe that the total and sudden transformation of such a complex and old society can take place without a shock, with the help of reason and by its sole efficacy. (*OR,* 1:199)

Tocqueville bases his comments in *The Old Regime* about the imminence and totality of the impending revolution on his own careful, detailed reading of Prudhomme's *Résumé général* of *cahiers* excerpts. [121] We have seen that the *Résumé* was a condensation that necessitated a rewriting of France's hundreds of general *cahiers.* It accumulated more than 3,700 grievances from a slender sampling of the total *cahiers* and then accentuated them, staccato-like, in dozens and dozens of thematic categories chosen by the authors. By definition it distorted the *cahiers,* since it took each grievance out of its original context and placed it in a new one created by the editors. The effect of reading the *Résumé général* is thus very different from that of reading a collection of individual *cahiers:* one is bombarded by a succession of grievances in a format that fails to capture the idiosyncratic nature of each particular *cahier* . . . a nature that can by turn, even in the same *cahier,* be defiant or supplicating, local or national, venal or public-spirited. [122] This textual distortion was compounded, as we have seen, by the *Résumé's* fallacious, inflated number tables, which multiplied wildly the purported numbers of grievances, a distortion Tocqueville necessarily incorporated when he "add[ed] together all of the particular demands." It was the *Résumé général's* repetitive drumbeat of demands, unmitigated by local idiom and falsely amplified by the number tables, that explained his "terror" in reading them and contributed to his conclusions regarding the naïveté of France's literary leaders and the credulity of their philosophically inclined followers. [123]

We must be careful, however, not to overstate the ramifications of such flaws. Chaussinand-Nogaret arrived at a similar view of the nobles' "new and explosive proposals" and potent liberal agenda in his extensive study.[124] He and others have emphasized the homogeneity of elite French liberal opinion on the eve of the revolution.[125] We must remember, too, that Tocqueville engaged in multiple types of probes of the Old Regime and the Revolution, using multiple sources beyond the *cahiers*—indeed, it is precisely the validity of these probes that many modern *cahiers* studies have tended to confirm.[126] Moreover, we have seen that Tocqueville used the *cahiers* for a variety of investigations—such as his observations, contra Burke, about the Third's increased hostility to the nobles based on their perception of a French system of caste, even though the barrier between classes was in fact permeable. Such investigations, themselves confirmed by modern studies,[127] relied on Tocqueville's reading of particular grievances and on his intuition, and thus were not affected by Prudhomme's distortion.

꙰

In a letter to Corcelle of September 17, 1853, Tocqueville recounted the emphasis of his political studies in famous terms: "Don't you know my ideas well enough to realize that I accord institutions only a secondary influence on man's destiny? . . . I am quite convinced that political societies are not what their laws make them, but what sentiments, beliefs, ideas, habits of the heart, and the spirit of their members prepare them in advance to be, as well as what nature and education have made them."[128] As a summary statement of his interpretation of the French Revolution, Tocqueville's declaration encapsulates his fundamental view of its practitioners' central failing: to the extent that they sought to create a new political society from the ground up, their Revolution was destined to fail, given the constraints imposed by intractable kernels of preexisting opinion. As a résumé of his historical method, it demonstrates as well his lifelong commitment to a history of underlying causes, to which he had been exposed so persuasively in Guizot's lectures twenty-five years previously and for which he possessed such natural affinity.

Advanced at this pivotal juncture of his conceptualization and research of *The Old Regime,* Tocqueville's statement is curious, however, in its apparent rejection of a political interpretation of the Revolution. By September 17, 1853, Tocqueville had read Burke, arguing strenuously in his notes for a recognition of the dire consequences of the monarchy's suppression of political liberty. He had read Dareste, arguing similarly that peasant hatred had been fueled by the political vacuum caused by noble absenteeism encouraged by monarchic policy. He had read the economists, studying them as reflectors of a new French opinion that embraced the prevailing belief in the vast regenerative powers of the state. He was in the midst of reading the intendants' correspondence, from which he was daily gaining graphic evidence of the state's suppression of popular participation, both deliberately to counter imagined competitors and innocently to lull the populace with well-intentioned welfare programs. All of these readings contributed to a political interpretation . . . one that he seemed to blithely dismiss in his comments to Corcelle.

Two explanations may be helpful, I believe, in considering this quandary. First, Tocqueville responded in his letter to his friend's construal of a conversation they had had during Corcelle's recent visit to Tours. Without Corcelle's letter, we do not know precisely how he chose to render Tocqueville's claims in that conversation about his work. But Tocqueville's natural reticence in such matters, accentuated perhaps by lingering doubts of Corcelle's reliability following the 1849 Roman debacle,[129] may have led him here to overstate his corrections of what he perceived to be Corcelle's initial misinterpretations.

In a more important sense, Tocqueville wrote this letter at a time of crucial transition in the making of his book. Having just determined that he should write a separate work on the Old Regime, he was engaged in formulating this work's new focus and new parameters. Having encountered at Tours the wealth of primary evidence of the debilitating effects of an undivided political state, accountable only to itself, he was weighing in particular the repercussions of such a monolithic system on the behavior and spirit of the French people. Reading Necker this same summer, he expressed the difficulty that accompanied any such investigations in terms that I find more reflective of his beliefs at this time: "[But is it the institutions that made the mores, or the mores that made the institutions? Eternal question!]."[130]

Arguably, in September 1853 Tocqueville's book was in transition from the more economic and social analysis of his "Initial Outline" to the more political and ideological analysis that we are familiar with in *The Old Regime* and that he was poised to seek to substantiate in his reading of Prudhomme's *cahiers* excerpts. Seeking the roots of Napoleonic despotism—both as a historian and as a critic of its contemporary resurrection—Tocqueville provided Corcelle with a simplistic rhetorical summary of a view that was soon to be superseded by his ever evolving investigations.

5. Tables on the *Résumé Général*

Table A   Predominance of Excerpts from the Twenty Most Cited *Cahiers* in Each Volume of Prudhomme's *Résumé Général* of 1789[131]

Name of Bailliage or Sénéchaussée	RG, volume 1 (Clergy)	RG, volume 2 (Nobility)	RG, volume 3 (Third)
Agen		32	
Angers			31
Auxerre	80	57	
Aval		25	
Bas-Viverais		30	
Calais			34
Château-Thierry		35	
Châlons-sur-Marne			29
Clermond Ferrand		20	33
Colmar	40		
Cotentin			40
Dijon	34		
Dourdan	34	36	41
Dunkerque			29
Evreux	33	22	
Laon	27		
La Rochelle			78
Limoges	22	30	
Lyon	56	37	45
Mantes	91		
Meaux	30		
Melun	34		
Metz	27		
Montargis	33	31	
Montford l'Amaury		20	
Nantes			81
Nivernois			76
Orléans		29	
Paris-hors-murs	51		120
Paris-entre-murs	70	38	68
Ponthieu			42
Reims		30	37
Rennes			181
Rodez	22	21	
Rouen	41		47

continued

Table A   *Continued*

Name of Bailliage or Sénéchaussée	RG, volume 1 (Clergy)	RG, volume 2 (Nobility)	RG, volume 3 (Third)
Saint-Quentin			32
Saumur	31		
Tours		24	
Troyes	35	18	151
Vannes			60
Vermandois		33	
Vitry-le-François	59	38	
Number of excerpts from twenty most cited *cahiers*	850	606	1,255
Total number of excerpts	992	1,123	1,633
Percentage of total number of excerpts from twenty most cited *cahiers*	86%	54%	77%

Table B   Prudhomme's Inflated Number Counts in the *Résumé Général* of 1789: A Comparative Study for Twenty Liberal Grievances of the Nobility[132]

Grievance	Number Count: Prudhomme (1789)	Number Count: Chaussinand-Nogaret (1985)
Defending counsel to be created	"una"	23.88% (32)
Labor service, or dues in kind, or common obligations (*banalités*) to be bought out	89	5.22% (7)
Annual publication of expenses	"una"	48.50% (65)
Criminal prosecution to be in public	"una"	9.70% (13)
Relief (*franc-fief*) to be abolished	63	17.16% (23)
Absolute freedom of trade and traffic in grain and goods	68	19.40% (26)
Consent to taxation	"una"	90.29% (121)
Justice to be free	"una"	5.22% (7)
No interference with private mails	"una"	50.00% (67)
Apanages of royal princes to be abolished, suppressed, or modified	78	14.7% (19)
Military life to be given fixed laws	72	31.34% (42)
Ministers to be answerable	"una"	85.07% (114)
Restriction of death penalty	"una"	9.70% (13)

continued

Table B *Continued*

Grievance	Number Count: Prudhomme (1789)	Number Count: Chaussinand-Nogaret (1985)
Venal nobility to be abolished; nobility to be the reward for service	81	44.77% (60)
Soldier's position to be improved or pay raised	"una"	8.20% (11)
Bastille and other state prisons to be destroyed	"una"	11.19% (15)
Prisons to be improved	"una"	5.97% (8)
Uniformity of weights and measures	"una"	20.14% (27)
Salt monoply to be abolished	"una"	43.28% (58)
Suppression of corvées	"una"	13.00%[a]

[a]For this final grievance, I am using Shapiro and Markoff's count of the percentage of the nobles' *cahiers* that demand the abolition of corvées (*Revolutionary Demands*, p. 256). Citing Tocqueville's claim that "all" *cahiers* demand such abolition, they conclude: "By our findings, these claims are very wide of the mark." See too ibid., p. 593, note 9, where they say that Tocqueville "wildly exaggerates" on this and other counts.

TOCQUEVILLE'S ELUSIVE BALANCE
Art in the Service of Liberty

> I believe that the books that have made men reflect the most
> and have had the most influence on their opinions and their
> actions are not those in which the author has sought to tell
> them dogmatically what is suitable to think, but those in which
> he has set their minds on the road leading to truths and has
> made them find these truths for themselves. If God leaves me
> the time and strength necessary to finish my task, no one will
> have any doubt, be certain of that, about the goal I had in view.[1]

Tocqueville's liberalism has been called by turns "strange," in
that it borrowed from both conservative and radical democratic traditions,[2] and "eccentric," in that it sought to resurrect
ancient political participation as a guarantee for modern individual freedoms.[3] Each of these depictions recognizes in its own
way Tocqueville's fierce independence, evident throughout this
book, in his pursuit of liberty—"the prime good" that guided
both his public and his private lives.[4] In view of it, we should resist the temptation to situate Tocqueville too neatly as a protégé
or disciple within any larger tradition of liberal or Doctrinaire
thought, even if such a strain of liberalism might be "unortho-
dox and unconventional" in its own right.[5] Tocqueville's view of
liberty was sui generis, in ways we must now seek to define.

Bred of Norman aristocratic stock, Tocqueville hated above
all "the hand of power weighing on my brow" (*DA*, 410). During his lifetime of writing—stretching from his Beaumont letter
of 1828 to his concluding sketches on the French Revolution of
the late 1850s—he meditated on the nature of that heavy-handed
power and on the best means of protecting himself from it. While

his means shifted in ways calculated to reflect the fluctuating events of his political era, the essence of such liberty could not and did not change. It was a taste (*un goût*)—a determination to think, write, and act without interference—a capacity, states Isaiah Berlin, "for positive choice, without which there is no moral life." [6] All men possess the ability to experience this taste; regrettably, the lesson of Tocqueville's lifetime was that few men chose to exercise it fully.

The key to the preservation of such liberty lay in a correct calibration of forces that could solidify primary national liberty with the aid of secondary local liberties. National liberty (encompassing, at a minimum, divided government, independent judicial review, and freedom of the press) would always engage just a handful of principal citizens (*DA,* 487). Local liberties (including elected provincial and communal assemblies) were thus the chief forums within which to train citizens to equate their interests with those of their neighbors so as to establish, as needed, stable centers of cohesion, interest, and resistance to central encroachments in society as a whole. Tocqueville would work throughout his life to provide deep roots for both levels of liberty within the French nation. Thus his search for models of bracing local vitality through his studies and his travels—in America and England and Germany and Switzerland and Italy. Thus his tenure as an elected member of the conseil général of Manche from 1842 to 1852, serving as its president from 1848 to 1852. [7] Thus his service as French foreign minister in 1849. And thus his shifting strategies tied to France's unstable political fortunes. Faced with the threat of socialism posed by the February Revolution and the workers' revolts of June 1848 and 1849, he looked to national institutions to provide order and stability. Faced with Louis-Napoleon's cavalier abuse of such institutions, he supported a nationwide fight in 1851 to pass resolutions in each conseil général to endorse his own defeated constitutional amendments. [8] Faced with Louis-Napoleon's mockery of the provincial councils after the 1851 coup—rendering them "bodies without soul," as he told Corcelle in 1856[9]—he resigned his council presidency in protest on April 29, 1852, and shifted his attention to his research for *The Old Regime.*

Writing to Auguste de La Rive in fall 1856, Tocqueville summarized the high hopes he had attached to "the peaceful and effective way I saw [the conseils généraux] develop themselves from 1830 to 1852." [10] The government of Louis-Napoleon perpetrated its greatest crime, he added, when it "put its foot on this fertile germ [of local liberty] and crushed [it] right down to its root."

This shifting balance in France in the 1850s shaped Tocqueville's message for liberty in *The Old Regime.* His target audience for his book was precisely those "enlightened classes" who had played the crucial role of moderating French revolutions in years past and who were uniquely qualified by their intellectual abilities and training to perform the work of liberty, both locally and nationally. But this group, he told Freslon in 1858, had been rendered personally mute (*insensibles*) by long, disillusioning experience with revolution. They had been rendered politically moot (*détrônées*) by the displacement of power to popular French actors and classes, specifically those "who read nothing at all" or, as Tocqueville corrected himself, who read only newspapers. [11] The astute Napoleonic regime, recognizing this shift of power to a new class, carefully censored the periodical press. Recognizing the marginalized status of the onetime leaders—Tocqueville and his peers—it left them free to write what and to whom they chose.

Tocqueville thus possessed an uncensored opening, an elite if demoralized audience, and a pressing period of need. In light of Napoleon's position of supremacy, he told Corcelle on September 17, 1853, specific proposals to heal France were of little value. If "man's true grandeur lies only in the harmony of the liberal sentiment and religious sentiment, both working simultaneously to animate and restrain souls," Tocqueville necessarily must seek to animate souls on the "liberal" side of this equation, since this was the great need of the day. To do so, however, he would write his book in decidedly nondogmatic fashion, since his audience was one that must regain that simple taste of thinking, writing, and acting that constituted liberty's essence. [12] He could "set their minds on the road leading to truth"; they would have to do the rest. But of course, if he did his job properly, his readers would arrive in their voyage of self-discovery at the same destination that he had had in mind for them all along, well expressed to Odilon Barrot a month later: "that pride in themselves, that habit of speaking and writing freely, that need at least to dispute their servitude, which is in the spirit of the age and the most ancient instinct of their race." [13]

This is not to say that Tocqueville believed the French would gain their freedom during his lifetime. He did not, as he told Beaumont in 1858: "I am convinced that, in our day, we will not see a free society in France, at least what we understand by that word." [14] But by reawakening the dignity and pride of his French audience, he could provide the essential catalyst for liberty's future revival.

1. The Evolution of Tocqueville's Writing Style

As part of his retrospective assessment of his book in the summer and early fall of 1856, Tocqueville engaged in an exchange of eight letters with

Kergorlay regarding the quality of the writing. Kergorlay offered general praise for Tocqueville's style in the book, saying in his first letter that it had "gained in facility and suppleness."[15] But as the correspondence and his own repeated readings of the book progressed, Kergorlay sought to convey diplomatically to his cousin a significant "defect in your style": his tendency "to wish to explain in a too thorough and detailed manner" the many nuances of his complex thoughts. In his second reading, Kergorlay employed his own test to detect instances of such "entanglement," dropping words or phrases and finding that he could still capture the essence of Tocqueville's meaning. Tocqueville overestimated the sophistication of his reading public, Kergorlay believed; desiring to demonstrate his own extensive knowledge, he tended to overwhelm the "young lads who are barely in a condition to learn their four rules." Tocqueville would be well advised to please his audience with "literary charm," not fatigue them with ideas of too fine a calibration.[16] After his third reading, he asserted that Tocqueville's style lacked the nimbleness, dexterity, and resulting grace of the great French writers. If he was to elevate his writing to their level, he "must live on Voltaire."[17]

Tocqueville responded with enormous interest to Kergorlay's suggestions, acknowledging that in writing *The Old Regime,* he had expended "huge efforts" to make his style more natural.[18] Despite his endeavors, however, Tocqueville recognized that he had not achieved the fluidity he sought. The problem—"this tendency to include all sorts of nuances of ideas within the same phrase"—was not easily resolvable, however, since it was precisely the deep, lengthy twisting and turning of each idea in his mind that had permitted its development and that accounted for its "true value." Tocqueville's challenge, he believed, was to meld "a spontaneous drafting with a long-ripened thought." It was this obstacle of reconciling these opposing tendencies that he knew he would have to surmount "to rise from the crowd into the ranks [of great writers]."[19]

Tocqueville's dedication to achieving a succinct, fluid style to convey the weighty, intricate subject matter of his book manifested itself throughout his drafting efforts for *The Old Regime.* To aid these efforts, he transported to Tours a small, highly specialized library comprising twenty-five short volumes of the original great masters of the French language. At Tours he sampled "sometimes one, sometimes another at random. It's almost as if I was conversing with their authors."[20] Writing to Corcelle on December 31, 1853—four weeks after commencing his own definitive drafting efforts for his book—he praised one member in particular of this "great and fine company," the seventeenth-century Jesuit preacher Louis Bourdaloue. Tocque-

ville applauded Bourdaloue's use of his own preferred educational form—
the sermon—to engage and move his audience, as well as his gift for choosing the uniquely appropriate word to capture and communicate the full
meaning of each thought:

> What admirable language! What consummate art in this sainted
> man! . . . The skill with which he varies the forms of language to
> sustain and refresh the attention of his listener is truly marvelous. . . .
> And in the qualities still more substantial than those I mention,
> the gift of choosing the necessary word (there is never but one)
> and of emptying so to speak the thought of all that it contains
> so as to expose these other elements in sharp relief, he is no less a
> master.[21]

Bourdaloue's gift served as Tocqueville's goal as the aspiring historian of the
Old Regime defined and refined his own self-conscious art at Tours. We can
best observe his efforts by viewing his initial drafts for *The Old Regime* prepared
at Tours between December 2, 1853, and the end of May 1854.

Tocqueville's drafts from Tours demonstrate his preoccupation with selecting his own unique "necessary word," a determination Beaumont attested to years later in telling Senior that he had watched his friend "rewrite
a phrase twenty times";[22] they also reveal his interest in refining his strategy to "charm" his audience. His first draft of his first chapter (I:1) flowed
smoothly in a version virtually synonymous with that of his final text: we
are not surprised, since we have witnessed his careful planning of it in his
"Initial Outline," developed when he first arrived at Tours six months previously. Turning to I:2, in which he would introduce the first of the Revolution's "accidental" qualities, again in keeping with the organizing axis of
his "Initial Outline," Tocqueville paused to clarify his writing goals: "Force
myself, in all these chapters, to avoid . . . the *abstract* style—so as to make
myself well understood and, especially, read with pleasure. Make a constant
effort to enclose the abstract and general idea in words that offer a precise
and particular image."[23]

This effort to concretize his ideas in words that would generate precise
referents for his readers might detract from his intended meaning, he concluded in a marginal note, but such trade-offs were unavoidable, since he
must keep in mind the larger context of his work: "But one writes to please
and not to attain an ideal perfection of language." Tocqueville's striving for
specificity was thus a component of his strategy for capturing and sustaining
his audience's attention and interest.

Tocqueville intended these early drafts to serve only as "unformed sketches, a first effort of the thought seeking to free itself."[24] Constituting an unembellished initial distillation of his ideas, they could be converted, at a later date, into a polished final tableau. Tocqueville summarized his strategy in an additional note he affixed to I:3: "In general, tighten, quicken the pace. My actual chapter is full of *meanders*. . . . One can see clearly, especially on this page, how my thought veers and scatters itself. . . . Take this chapter again later and redo it in a rapid burst as if I had not already written it." With a first draft that successfully crystallized his ideas, Tocqueville could subsequently strive to mask his immense initial labor in a fresh second draft that gave the appearance of spontaneity.

At Tours, Tocqueville adopted a further strategy that would dramatically affect his evolving text: he chose to exclude from this preliminary distillation of his general ideas the particular "facts" he had so meticulously assembled in his reading notes. Having worked for two years to garner these facts, and having pondered "with extreme care, in a general review, all of these notions that I acquired by myself,"[25] Tocqueville now deliberately set them aside as he commenced his writing at Tours. To be sure, he began his writing of book 1 with a page containing "several passages of Burke that I can draw on." Arriving at I:2, he similarly listed quotations directly from a text of Mirabeau's *Correspondance*.[26] But his writing of the rest of his first draft from Tours was marked by his rigorous exclusion of source citations, as he left holes in his text for their subsequent incorporation: "Draw on part of Burke here" (I:1); "Find here two phrases to cite . . . then recommence" (I:5); "Introduce here the text of my most striking notes" (II:1). The decisive moment for determining such a strategy seems to have been at the end of December, after he had completed his draft of what he now recognized as "the first chapter of the book"—book 1. At the turn of the new year, as he plunged into "the second chapter" that would contain "the product of the immense labor of notes that I have done for a year"[27] —what would become books 2 and 3—Tocqueville was forced to resolve his dilemma, first articulated at Sorrento, regarding his preferred method for integrating his facts into his text. He posed the crux of the problem to Ampère, saying that he would welcome his friend's assistance: "This mountain of notes crushes me, it suffocates me. . . . It's at this time that I would constantly . . . entreat you to tell me the precise point where the facts cease to interest and begin to fatigue the spirit of the reader; what I must include to make my general ideas understandable, what I must mix with them so that they inspire reflection." Adding that "all the art is there," Tocqueville suggested that his work was stymied.[28] But in a letter to Beaumont of December 28, 1853, he hinted that he had glimpsed a way out of this dilemma posed by the enormous weight of his notes: "Little by little, I seemed to have perceived how I could make a path for myself."[29] Tocqueville's new "path" appears to have consisted of the startling decision to deny himself any recourse to his reading notes for his entire first draft of the chapters of books 2 and 3 that he would now set out to write at Tours during the ensuing four and one-half months.[30]

Seeking specificity for his ideas by deliberately refraining from reliance on his voluminous notes, Tocqueville patiently delineated the key arguments of his second book. At times, his system affected the pace and quality of his writing, as he indicated in this note to II:2–5: "All of this very *slow* [*mollasse*] and poorly expressed. It can be done well only in a comprehensive view and after a new study of my notes." At other times it affected the presentation of his argument, as he commented on two occasions in II:6:

> I must consider all that follows as only *barely sketched out*. The retrieval of facts from my notes can alone permit me to paint a picture. . . .
>
> Unfortunately this chapter can have originality only through the cited facts—and I will have these facts present in my mind only after reviewing my notes.

Tocqueville's system bestowed upon his drafts from Tours a curiously disembodied character, readily apparent to readers familiar with *The Old Regime*. Thus, in II:6 we quickly recognize his assertions regarding bureaucratic mores—the ministers' penchant for detail, surveillance of individuals, taste for statistics, style of writing, and excessive regulatory desires—but we look in vain for his accompanying grid of corroborating facts. But even with these drawbacks, Tocqueville tenaciously adhered to the system, insisting on completing this first stage of his writing before using the profusion of novel facts contained in his notes. In a marginal note to II:3, he summarized this determination: "All of this unfortunately is still confused in my mind. But I must review my notes and study anew this material only after the first draft."

Aided by these decisions, Tocqueville was able to tell Beaumont by the end of January that the full outline of the book "appears to take shape quite clearly in my mind."[31] In early March he recounted its progress to his nephew Hubert: "Its form and its limits become, in my mind, more and more precise, and all of the first part, that is to say about a half volume, will, I hope, be completed when I leave this retreat in the month of May."[32]

"All of the stones of my facade are in place," he told Grandmaison in March with reference to one of his chapters, adding that "nothing remains to consider except the decorative and ornamental parts."[33] And by May 20, as he prepared to leave Tours, he was able to announce to Ampère: "All the chapters are *constructed;* but at least two months of work will still be necessary so that the book is presentable and can be read."[34]

Experiencing "the absolute need of a quite intense distraction, before taking up again my scribblings and painting the genuine picture,"[35] Tocqueville left Tours at the end of May and embarked, in June, on his long-planned journey to Germany. Tocqueville's German expedition enabled him to confirm "by the detail of facts" the validity of general ideas previously arrived at "only by abstract reasoning."[36] His firsthand exposure allowed him to confidently integrate Germany into his European framework, as he discovered evidence of active German seigneurs, local resistance to a unified central government, moderate feudal rights, high peasant property ownership, and a general "spirit of innovation and change." "All of this is *capital* for me," he exclaimed with reference to the issue of the local influence of seigneurs;[37] he might well have been commenting on how far his German findings in general reinforced his anticipatory ideas, many of which had already been included in his Tours drafts.

Rejuvenated by his five-month sabbatical, although frustrated by the abrupt termination of its German leg because of his wife's acute rheumatism in her wrist, Tocqueville collected "all my papers and books" from Paris at the end of October and prepared to resume his work in a small, sun-drenched house that he rented at Compiègne in the Oise near his father's home at neighboring Clairoix.[38] "Like a snail in my shell,"[39] Tocqueville would remain in residence at Compiègne for five months, during which time he expected to complete his book: "I expect to spend my time at Compiègne in a great surge of work which will permit me to conclude all that was only a draft when I left Saint-Cyr."[40]

Since he had deliberately set aside his reading notes once he began writing at Tours, we are not surprised that he resumed his work at Compiègne by directing his long-suppressed attention to just these notes. His comprehensive review allowed him to reassess his subject both "in detail" and in its entirety, affording immense pleasure and benefit: "I can only carefully reread my notes, which is not a small affair since they form more than one thousand pages. I experience great pleasure in seeing them again pass in detail, and I believe that in retracing the route across all of the ideas that came to me on this subject that has consumed me for two years, I am drawing notions that are more assured in specifics and more comprehensive in their entirety."[41]

In conjunction with this review, Tocqueville now constructed an elaborate matrix of interlocking indexes, with his ordering and collation of his notes requiring three separate steps. First, he created a central numbering system, which he accomplished with his seventeen folders, alphabetized and numbered from beginning to end. Next, he compiled his voluminous "great index"—a more than ninety-page catalog of facts referenced to specific sheets within his folders, encompassing notations to all but two of his reading files.[42] Organized broadly into thematic categories linked to his principal chapter themes,[43] the index typically included from twenty to thirty entries per page with as many as fifteen specific file notations for each entry. In his third and final step, using the almost 3,900 notations contained in this master index, Tocqueville recorded lengthy sheets of "excerpts" from his notes. In December 1854, for example, he compiled twenty-six pages of excerpts from seven folders on the theme "administration of towns and parishes." In January 1855 he supplemented these with thirteen pages of further pertinent passages for "parish administration," as well as with twelve pages of citations "on administrative justice and the immunities of public officials."[44] These lists of topical excerpts, accentuated by self-reminders such as "letter to cite" or "excellent to cite," provided the reservoir of facts that he would need both to validate his general arguments and to corroborate them with specific examples in the rewrites he was now poised to undertake.

Index and excerpts in hand, Tocqueville refashioned all of his existing chapters during his five-month residence at Compiègne. His renewed access to his notes clearly did not affect book 1 in the same way that it did book 2, since he rewrote book 1 making only a single reference to his reading notes.[45] This shift in his use of facts in book 2 no doubt contributed to his subsequent reassessment of book 1 in his letter to Beaumont of March 17, 1856: "When I wrote these five small chapters [of book 1], I was very pleased with them. They now seem to me the most mediocre and least novel part of my work."[46] Throughout his new drafts of books 2 and 3, he peppered his sheets with file references (e.g., "Q.5" or "J.32") to identify new quotations or to legitimate existing ideas. In II:1 he commented: "I have not made for this section as I did for the other the methodical excerpting from my notes. Undertake this work before proceeding to the definitive review of this section." In II:12 he observed: "I will find very readily the elements in rereading attentively the index." In III:1 he similarly emphasized, "Reread what is in the index." At Compiègne, Tocqueville thus transformed his Tours drafts into "factual" ones, with the index serving as the vital bridge to carry his wealth of facts to his skeletal text.[47] In some cases his access to his notes contributed

in striking ways to the presentation of his arguments, as in his assertion in
II:1 of the high incidence of peasant property ownership in prerevolutionary France.[48] In other cases it inflated the length of proposed chapters, contributing to Tocqueville's eventual decision to split several of them into separate units worthy of independent status.[49] In the case of his discussion of the
economists, it provided the fresh insight that allowed him to bring closure
to his argument.[50] And in still other cases it assisted in the development of
new chapters that he now decided to introduce into his work.[51] Throughout
the nineteen emerging chapters of book 2 (II:1–12 and III:1–7), Tocqueville's
facts—constituting the reclaimed bounty of his archival investigations—
surged into his text. As he wove them together within the frame provided
by his previously distilled general judgments on them, Tocqueville culminated his drive to achieve the blended genre of history to which he had as-
pired at Sorrento.

On January 11, 1855, Tocqueville had expressed to Beaumont his hopes
that he would complete within two or three months "all that must form
the first part of the book,"[52] by which he meant his entire projected volume of *The Old Regime*. Despite his "*blazing* ardor" in his efforts, his timetable
proved overly optimistic, primarily because of a "diabolical difficulty" encountered most likely in his drafting of III:1–2.[53] His problems led him to
break away again from his writing for a period that would stretch into four
months. Relocating to Paris, he conducted further research and handled
affairs of the Académie française in April and May; in June he visited the
Beaumonts and the Corcelles; and at the end of the month he returned to
Tocqueville for the first time in three years. There he immersed himself in
long neglected duties as the château's absentee landlord, seeking, among
other projects, to winterize his home for year-round habitation. Although
he was encouraged by a favorable reception of his reading of several chapters of the book at the Beaumonts' house in June, Tocqueville was plagued
by self-doubts as he returned to it after his break: "I am absolutely like a
man who, after having regarded his object through the small end of his field
glasses, arrives next at considering it through the large end. It's always the
same object, but seen in one way, it seems greater, and in the other, smaller,
than it really is. I would like very much to put my eye back on the end that
enlarges my view."[54]

Faced with a topic that had thus contracted in size, confronted with at-
tacks of discouragement and severe stomach ailments,[55] Tocqueville only
gradually managed to regain his preferred perspective, allowing him to proceed "obstinately, passionately, and sadly" to complete his book.[56] This final
six-month period of seclusion, lasting until the end of January 1856, brought

resolution to his difficulties in III:1–2, the completion of the remaining chapters of book 3, including a troublesome concluding III:8,[57] and the incorporation of the whole into a final manuscript.[58] Throughout this phase, Tocqueville's reading notes continued to be the indispensable catalyst for his writing efforts; his manuscript, for example, contained more than 240 specific references by file and page number to passages within his notes, a far cry from his initial draft at Tours that contained, by his deliberate choice, nary a one.

2. Tocqueville's Construction of His Persona as Archivist

At Tours in the early months of 1854, Tocqueville had first sketched the preliminary draft of his famous passage in *OR*, 1:199 in which he had argued that philosophical doctrines found fertile soil in prerevolutionary France, in part owing to the political inexperience of the nation:

> It is impossible in reading with one breath the cahiers of the Estates-General of 1789 not to be struck by two things.
>
> 1. When one reads separately the different cahiers of the Estates-General of 1789, it seems that they only call for a few reforms. But when one reads them all in one breath one sees that they demand nothing less than the simultaneous change of all existing institutions. That the legislative power run the nation, that (1) . . . what they demand in a word is that all existing institutions be simultaneously and suddenly changed. The second striking feature is that the same men who write the cahiers haven't the least idea of questioning for an instant that what they demand can produce the most immense and terrible Revolution ever seen among men.

We look in vain in the draft for any characterizations of the author himself—either as diligent archivist, terrified observer, or prescient analyst. Tocqueville's objectives at Tours, clearly indicated in the accompanying marginal note (1), were precision and persuasion, not the prominence of his own persona.[59] Such neglect was consistent with the focus of his entire Tours draft: it contained limited facts, limited references to his sources, and a limited role for Tocqueville himself as a dramatic figure in his book.[60]

As he subsequently wove his facts into his evolving text, first at Compiègne in 1854–55 and then in his final phase of composition at his Norman château in the fall of 1855, Tocqueville increasingly directed attention to his own role as the enterprising discoverer of those facts: "I find in a circular," he commented on one occasion; "I have read a great number of petitions," on another; "I remember the first time I examined the archives of an intendant's office," on a third; "I have seen property registers of the fourteenth century, which are masterpieces of method, lucidity, neatness, and intelligence," on a fourth. Reporting on the intendants' tendency to subvert elections, he introduced a multiplier clause that would become a common refrain in the book: "Of this course I have noticed a thousand examples" (OR, 1:131). And against those who might question his conclusions, Tocqueville reminded his readers that he possessed an ultimate and ubiquitous trump card: "I hold the facts in my hand" (OR, 1:233). In each case, Tocqueville injected himself into his text in conjunction with the introduction of facts from his sources. Drawing attention to the facts, he highlighted his own pioneering role as their indefatigable excavator.

But it was not until May and June 1856 that Tocqueville the author most fully incorporated Tocqueville the master archivist into his text. Having departed from his Cotentin château for Paris in early February 1856, braced for "many disagreeable sensations and all sorts of agitations of spirit," Tocqueville had already "crossed the Rubicon," signing a contract with Michel Lévy publishers and receiving a first installment of 2,000 francs based on a minimum sale of 2,000 copies. He had recopied his entire manuscript, judged "illegible" by his printer, and redistributed it to eight typesetters. He had agonized over the choice of a title and consulted half a dozen friends for their advice, only to find the decision made for him by the editor, who had injected the book's galley title into a prospectus mailed to several thousand potential subscribers.[61] Aware of the need to verify facts, he had spent time in the Archives nationales and sought books from the Bibliothèque nationale. From mid-March to mid-May, with printer's proofs becoming available in stages, he had established a relay system with Beaumont and his wife whereby they received proofs, commented on their form and substance, and returned them to Tocqueville in Paris, all with a turnaround time of six days to comply with his publishing contract.[62] With the date of publication drawing near, Tocqueville had even begun to strategize with his friends regarding preferred reviewers. Only at this late date, with the book thus poised for publication, did Tocqueville finally direct his attention to the book's endnotes and preface, each of which he now used, in ambitious and surprising fashion, to augment his expanding persona as archivist supreme.

Tocqueville commenced his work on his endnotes in mid-May after he had finished correcting the proofs for his twenty-five principal chapters and appendix. In a letter of May 18, 1856, to Henry Reeve, his English translator,

Tocqueville stated his goal of selecting "about 100" pages of endnotes to supplement his "333 to 340" pages of text;[63] he thus compiled his notes with a fixed quantity in mind, presumably connected to a proportion he deemed appropriate between his notes and his text.[64] His problem, he said to Reeve, had been to limit these endnotes: "I could add indefinitely to [them], because in notes taken on *manuscripts* I have the equivalent of at least two volumes."[65] Two weeks later, in a letter to Beaumont, Tocqueville explained that "the choice and arrangement" of the endnotes had caused the delay in the book's anticipated publication, since this "enormous enterprise . . . demanded an immense effort so as not to be done in a most mediocre fashion."[66] Tocqueville's efforts were devoted to choosing and arranging the supplementary endnotes within the one hundred prescribed pages; they were not, as we have said, intended to provide documentation for sources he had cited within his text.

In more than one-quarter of the endnotes thus compiled, Tocqueville chose to incorporate an explicit reference to his own role as archivist. His intention of spotlighting his assiduity as researcher can best be detected in his drafts of endnote 44, his famous treatment of the *cahiers.* In his initial "Copy" prepared for the printers, Tocqueville penned a draft introduction to the *cahiers* synopsis of young Stoffels in which he suggested, misleadingly, that his own research had taken place with the "very vast series of volumes in folio" that constituted the full *cahiers* collection at the Archives nationales, adding: "I made on these very documents the analysis of the cahiers. I give here that of the nobility. I believe this analysis exact, and I think that it makes known with exactitude the sentiments held by the great majority of those who wrote the cahiers at that time."[67]

Correcting these first printer's proofs, Tocqueville subsequently revised this exaggerated claim, adding a "section (a)" that comprised the three introductory paragraphs we are familiar with in endnote 44 in *The Old Regime* (*OR*, 1:287). Although he now mentioned an unnamed "extract in three volumes"—which we know to be Prudhomme's *Résumé général*—he again exaggerated his role by asserting that he had conducted a comparison between it and the full *cahiers* collection, finding "the greatest resemblance between the grand tableau and the abridged copy."[68] It was in this same second printer's proof that Tocqueville injected into the Stoffels text his two new paragraphs that contained the bulk of his explicit references to counts of various *cahiers* proportions. Tocqueville was evidently determined that we picture him immersed in the Archives nationales with his notepads, making his way through hundreds of general *cahiers* in order to quantify their specific demands.

Tocqueville's preface, written in May 1856 and revised in early June, likewise revealed a progressive buildup of his own persona. In his first preface draft, he highlighted his own role as a discoverer of new sources, but he commented on only one source he had made use of: the intendants' archives.[69] In his second draft, written after June 6, Tocqueville sought to respond to a critique by Louis de Loménie, who had said of the preface that "taken in its entirety [it was] too dry [trop sec]."[70] He enlivened his account, in part, by now enumerating the full array of sources that he used in making his book, including little-known books, public documents, and the cahiers (OR, 1:84).[71] Mirroring his vacillating portrayal in endnote 44, he once again artfully sought to imply that his cahiers studies had been with "the originals [that] form a long series of handwritten volumes" (OR, 1:84). In addition, Tocqueville now inserted his equally artful claim that his studies of numerous intendant archives had allowed him to extrapolate his observations throughout "the greatest part of the realm" (OR, 1:257). With these final flourishes, he sought to generalize his research throughout the cahiers and throughout the intendants' archives in all of France, thus expanding the efforts of his industrious persona so as to accentuate the universality of his historical message.

Step-by-step, Tocqueville thus heightened his own presence in his book as his work progressed. Amiable interviewer of fellow farmers in his first draft, he transformed himself in his subsequent draft into the confident, innovative archivist who had discovered and distilled a dozen new sources documenting the widespread property ownership of such farmers. Generalist observer of trends throughout medieval Europe in his early draft, he became the particular surveyor of the clarity of particular property registers from the fourteenth century (OR, 1:103).[72] Investigator of intendants' archives in his first preface draft, he chose to add spice to his account by expanding his portrayal of his sources and generalizing his studies of their applicability throughout France. Anonymous reviewer of cahiers described in his earliest Tours draft, he transformed himself in both endnote 44 and his preface into the dedicated personal inspector of the full collection of cahiers ranged at the Archives nationales—every one of them, in its original form, drawn from every bailliage and sénéchaussée in France. Such a transformation, accomplished with equal shares of bravado and artistic license, culminated in Tocqueville's apotheosis as the masterful archivist in his own book. In these ways he solidified the "rhetorical" power of his own persona as well as that of his sources themselves, making them indispensable features of his art in his book.[73]

3. Tocqueville's Instruction on Liberty in *The Old Regime*

Tocqueville's preface recounts the story of his career as an unswerving apostle of liberty. Flashing back to *Democracy in America,* where he had revealed both threats and safeguards for liberty in the dawning democratic age, and projecting forward to *The Old Regime*'s sequel, where he will chronicle liberty's spirited resistance but eventual demise in France owing to the too eager thirst of revolutionaries for equality under a despot, he draws attention to the common passion that has spanned and unified his career. Some may accuse him of showing "an almost unlimited taste for liberty" (*OR,* 1:86), but even such opponents, he replies, would choose laws of their own making before capitulation to a capricious despot, provided they could be certain that their nation possessed "the virtues necessary to make a good use of liberty" (*OR,* 1:88). It is Tocqueville's aim in his book to inculcate just these virtues to support just this proper practice of liberty.

To achieve this aim, Tocqueville envisions twin complementary strategies: "My goal has been to paint a picture that was strictly exact and which, at the same time, could be instructive" (*OR,* 1:86). Truth, he claims, will support his intended instruction in the service of liberty. Tocqueville's dogged pursuit of truth is evident in his chief historical theses that we have watched him develop through his immense archival labors and reflections. His instruction, he announces, will draw attention to two conflicting attributes of his nation's character, the interplay of which will determine its prospects for liberty: its independence and greatness, described as "manly virtues," and the laws, ideas, and mores that have consistently undermined such virtues (*OR,* 1:86). Tocqueville equates his role as instructor to that of an anatomist, seeking to dissect France's corpse so as to study "the laws of life" (*OR,* 1:86) of the Old Regime in limbs that had been calcified in extremis for sixty-five years. By throwing light on the causes of the Old Regime's death, Tocqueville might aid liberty's rejuvenation in a contemporary France afflicted with its own version of rigor mortis.

In his preface's first seven paragraphs, Tocqueville introduces the corpse of old France that he must venture "to interrogate in its tomb" (*OR,* 1:83), the reasons for its demise, the preventive steps that might have saved it . . . and the prerevolutionary voices resurrected through his sources that allow him so confidently to pronounce the shocking results of his autopsy. Untouched by artifice, often shielded from the glare of publicity, these voices reveal the "secret" lives—public and private, in Paris and the provinces—of the men and women of the Old Regime.

Tocqueville privileges one source above all others as he performs his autopsy: "I especially made great use of the cahiers prepared by the three orders in 1789" (*OR*, 1:84). The *cahiers*—the final words and testament bequeathed by a generation of Frenchmen, now deceased—constitute the missing document in the case of mystery and intrigue that Tocqueville constructs in these opening paragraphs of his "study" (*OR*, 1:83). They are the statement, lost for years behind the bedroom dresser, of the French victim's frame of mind, of its desires, and of its final intentions. Read now, they can enable the right examiner to interpret them so as to determine the true cause of its death. Tocqueville intends to be that interpreter; the *cahiers* provide the indispensable tool that will allow his autopsy to be successful.

Commandeering our attention in this way, the naturally retiring Tocqueville makes himself a central figure in his own text. By inserting his own dramatic persona, wedded so closely to his sources, he hopes to gain our confidence as the industrious and impartial discloser of the precise tableau of the Old Regime. At the same time, by investing his persona with a caustic and biting edge, he seeks to challenge his readers to take note of his arguments and refashion their attitudes toward liberty. Introduced in the book's first sentence, he will dominate it in these ways until its last, when he finally relinquishes his stage, even while alerting his readers again to anticipate his central casting in his book's sequel (*OR*, 1:247).[74]

Tocqueville devotes the bulk of books 2 and 3 to exposing liberty's impediments in the Old Regime, as he delineates the Revolution's causes: the isolation and simmering hatred of the peasant in the countryside (II: 1 and 12), the steady intrusion of sweeping administrative centralization (II: 2–7), the simultaneous homogenization and division within and between classes (II: 8–10), and the receptivity of the people to broad, often irreligious philosophical ideas advanced by political neophytes (III: 1–3). For each broad cause, we have seen how he weaves its roots into a common narrative on liberty, since each results from the absence of a viable, sustained tradition of participatory local government, occasioned by the failure of a national Estates-General to meet for 175 years and the curtailment or co-optation of local assemblies. Tocqueville's relentless account fulfills one objective of his instructional strategy, since it demonstrates "the trace of several of the vices that, after devouring the old society, still torment us" (*OR*, 1:86). "All of my book has the goal," he will tell Beaumont on April 24, 1856, "of bringing out the abuses that condemned the Old Regime to perish."[75] By chronicling the Old Regime's mistakes, especially with respect to its systematic dismantling of local liberty, Tocqueville reveals the reasons for its slide to despotism . . .

and the liberty that was needed in prerevolutionary times, as it is needed in the Second Empire, to correct it.

Writing each section of his historical argument at maximum pitch, Tocqueville gives his book a decidedly "anti–Old Regime" temper. [76] On two occasions he interjects chapters clearly designed "to attenuate the effect produced by the accusatory chapters." [77] In II:11, using the *cahiers* as his principal source, he presents a corrective to support his case for a resilient if stunted surviving strain of liberty at the time of the Revolution. After nine further chapters that conclude his book, he presents his appendix on Languedoc, altered in focus from its original conception, to furnish his readers with a concluding French model of the benefits of local liberty in action. Placed at these critical junctures of his text, he intends these two insertions to sustain a positive view of liberty in the face of his withering catalogue of causes accounting for its demise.

If one part of Tocqueville's instructional strategy serves as tough tonic for his fellow Frenchmen, administered unsparingly by "a brutal surgeon," [78] its second part emphasizes the disinterested public virtue of his "men of '89." He splits this portrait between three chapters: II:11, III:2, and III:3. Variously referred to as "the men of the eighteenth century" (*OC*, 1:178), "the French who made the Revolution" (*OC*, 1:208), and "our fathers of 1789" (*OC*, 1:216), Tocqueville's heroes in his book are men of high energy, purpose, and commitment, displaying none of the sensual slackening common to their democratic descendants. "These vigorous souls, these proud and audacious geniuses" (*OC*, 1:179), however, were riven with contradictions. Bold visionaries, they lacked practical skills. Espousers of the new philosophical ideas, they failed to comprehend their consequences. Partisans of a local liberty that they imagined but had never known, they embraced a centralized government that would destroy it. Inventors of "a sort of new religion . . . a more sincere, disinterested, truly grand patriotism" (*OR*, 1:208), they extirpated the old religion that provided cohesion for the old society. Embodying a "grandeur without precedent," they produced a Revolution that inspired "at one and same time admiration and terror" (*OR*, 1:179).

While drawing attention to these proud if deformed bearers of liberty's surviving strain, Tocqueville chooses to forgo a more reasoned analysis of the essential character of their chief virtue. At the end of his pivotal III:3, which he had planned to use as his concluding chapter in his earliest plan for his book, he rejects an instrumental definition of liberty for different nations, saying that it cannot be viewed chiefly as a means to ends such as toppling corrupt governments or acquiring vast riches. He insists, rather, that liberty is a natural good, felt by "the great champions of liberty throughout history" who cherished for its own sake "the pleasure of being able to speak, act, breathe without restraint, under the sole government of God and the laws" (*OR*, 1:217). But when it comes to analyzing "this sublime taste," he declines to do so, arguing that true liberty can be experienced only by "peoples made for being free" (*OR*, 1:216). Tocqueville thus bases his book's central argument for its central commodity on the dual powers of dignity and shame, appealing to his readers' elevated instincts and pride, not their reasoned self-interest. Kergorlay aptly characterizes the thrust of Tocqueville's instruction on liberty when he says: "One could say, in a certain sense, that the whole book is [contained] in that phrase where you state that the taste for liberty is something that cannot be proven and that this taste consists of loving it for its own sake."[79]

In his concluding chapter, returning to the topic that had thwarted him in his "Initial Outline," Tocqueville attempts to explain the fury of the Revolution as it sprang from the succession of causes he has now outlined. One part of his explanation reassembles these causes, pointing to their common origin owing to the suppression of local liberties (*OR*, 1:241–44). A concluding segment places in brilliant relief the role of the French national character in contributing to these causes and sparking their explosion (*OR*, 1:246–47), even though Tocqueville privately retained doubts about such a depiction.[80] A substantial midsection, consisting of seven famous paragraphs (*OR*, 1:244–46), eloquently synthesizes Tocqueville's treatment of liberty and its place in the Revolution's gestation.

Tocqueville's peroration on liberty in his concluding chapter is added in the eleventh hour in response to Loménie's stinging criticism that Tocqueville had slighted its spirit in his book. "You have made too feeble a defense of the spirit of liberty," Loménie had said to a clearly chagrined Tocqueville.[81] The seven new paragraphs in the conclusion (*OR*, 1:244–46) are added in tandem with two new paragraphs in the preface (*OR*, 1:85–86).[82] Bound in their portrayal of liberty and in their common culminating use of Tocqueville's corporeal imagery, the "Loménie additions" serve as a crucial frame to Tocqueville's existing book and a valuable expression of his intentions in his next. Their ideas about liberty are not new to the book but build on his earlier abbreviated version in III:3 (*OC*, 1:216). In all three conceptions, liberty and equality exist in a fragile and ultimately untenable balance, since political liberty, despite its glorious legacy, is consistently undermined by the habits of dependence and community division instilled by the government of the Old Regime. Tocqueville's final words in *The Old Regime* are thus true to the overall spirit of the book, in which liberty faces what may indeed be bleak prospects for the immediate future in France. The twin passages in the preface and conclusion do emphasize, however, in analogous terms, the generosity and sincerity of the early phases of the Revolution itself, elevating it as an inspirational model for all Frenchmen and establishing it as the focal point for the next phase of his research and writing.

ᕀ

Richard Herr, in *Tocqueville and the Old Regime,* argues that although Tocqueville clearly believed his book supported liberty, he failed to comprehend its true message that "of course, it did nothing of the kind." Owing to his "considerable quality for self-deception," he thus "unconsciously . . . connived with his hope and his craving to obscure the lesson taught by his reason."[83]

Sheldon Wolin, in *Tocqueville between Two Worlds,* makes a parallel claim of Tocqueville's despair, impotency, and self-delusion in writing *The Old Regime.* "Close to being a broken man," Tocqueville introduced a nostalgic teaching in his final book that "focus[ed] upon the re-creation of an archaic world located somewhere between the late Middle Ages and the first half of the eighteenth century."[84] "Grub[bing] in the past in search of sources of political renewal," he emerged "with a work that seemed to refuse engagement with the political present." In so doing, he violated his own stated mission and disappointed his countrymen's high expectations by failing to "offer some clues about the course to be followed by those who cherish liberty and find themselves deprived of freedom."[85]

I vigorously disagree with both conclusions, since they belittle the central purpose of Tocqueville's entire project, which was to confront the French people with the true reasons for their current servitude. Tocqueville clearly expressed his lucid awareness of the stark instructional message of his book in his letter to Corcelle of November 15, 1856:

> I was unable to claim to paint a pleasant picture, only a likeness, persuaded as I am that the only opportunity nations, like individuals, have to heal is to first study the reality of their illness. Then it sometimes happens, it is true, that after having seen and known it, one succumbs to it nonetheless. But without knowing it, one is certain not to heal. Few men would persist in their failings if they could have a clear view of them, see their source, and measure the results of them.[86]

For all its severity, Tocqueville issued his instructive medicine with the objective of curing his French patient, not serving it with Herr's "strong dose of opium"[87] or Wolin's "*mytheoreticus et politicus*" that constituted "an entry in the story of modern powerlessness."[88] He sought with his book to prod his countrymen to action, to inspire them to rise to the challenge he had posed with his portrayal of liberty's precarious status. That French readers responded enthusiastically to what he termed "the *free* spirit of the book," snapping up the entire first edition of two thousand copies in just seven weeks, vindicated his strategy, he believed, and suggested that "liberty [in France] must not be as dead as many believe and some hope."[89]

Tocqueville delivered his austere message in a concrete, compact writing style that he hoped would garner both attention from his readers and eventual glory for himself. Beginning at Sorrento, where he envisioned "a rather short book,"[90] and continuing through his research at Tours, where he told Kergorlay that "it's a matter of knowing an enormous number of things and saying very few of them,"[91] he adhered to this objective. Terseness would translate into readability and action, he believed, as he adapted his book to what he took to be the reading capacities of his ever preoccupied, often listless, and often timid elite audience in France's Second Empire.

Tocqueville crafted a persona within his book that featured himself as its chief spokesperson for liberty, metamorphosed into the larger-than-life archivist whose herculean labors resurrected the often anonymous, often "secret" voices of the Old Regime. His earnest persona invited his readers to share in his relentless probes of hidden sources. As Tocqueville sought to lift the veil masking the mysteries of the Revolution, we seek to lift that veil. As Tocqueville surveyed its sources, we survey them. And as Tocqueville liberated long-suppressed voices recounting liberty's loss in the Old Regime, we listen . . . and can learn from them.

To maintain his persuasive grip on his readers' limited attention, Tocqueville dispensed with source citations. Responding on August 13, 1856, to Lewis's criticism of his strategy, he explained that he had done so to advance his book's rhetorical objectives in a time of "intellectual and moral exhaustion." "I was obliged, in this goal," he claimed, "to reduce all of the weight of the details and not fatigue [my readers'] attention and turn it from the text by multiplying my notes."[92] Running the risks warned against by the Beaumonts, incurring the censure of at least one perceptive reviewer, Pierre-Sébastien Laurentie, for thus "offend[ing] the liberty of the reader,"[93] Tocqueville imposed in this way a further level of mystery on a text that he had already cloaked in mystery, while forging a useful shield to conceal his artistic exaggerations.

TOCQUEVILLE AND HISTORY

Telling Liberty's Revolutionary Tale

> Reason, then, [about] these politics by fixed rules, by consider-
> ations drawn from the ordinary logic of facts, when the object
> of your study is a passionate being who escapes repeatedly from
> these fixed laws![1]

In August 1860, sixteen months after Tocqueville's death, Beaumont joined Senior and his wife for breakfast in Paris. With
their discussion naturally gravitating to their late great friend,
Beaumont solicited Senior's advice on his own imminent publication of an initial selection of Tocqueville's works. Should
he organize Tocqueville's correspondence chronologically, he
queried, or group the letters thematically, separating, for example, the political from the personal ones? Moreover, for the
personal letters, might it not be appropriate to distinguish those
addressed to Tocqueville's most intimate friends, Kergorlay and
Stoffels? Senior—friend of twenty-six years, correspondent,
intended memoirist, and houseguest of Tocqueville's at Paris,
Tocqueville, Sorrento, and Tours—had never heard of Tocqueville's earliest and dearest friends: "Who were Kergorlay and Stoffels?" he could only sheepishly respond.[2]

Tocqueville's tendency to compartmentalize his life went
well beyond his splitting of new friends from old. Fastidious, discreet, punctual to a fault, he separated work from leisure time,
country life from city life, and political activity from his writing
of books. A superb conversationalist with peasants and princes,
he displayed "a certain antipathy" for philosophical topics and
refused altogether to broach matters of religion.[3] Studying his
nation's great authors, he applauded their method or style . . .

and disparaged their message for liberty. In keeping with his credo that life was "of value only insofar as one uses it to do one's duty," [4] he lucidly defined his objectives and then pursued them with single-minded devotion, in a manner reminiscent of his walking style in Sorrento's open country: "In order to follow the straight line that seemed his natural direction, he jumped as needed over a hedge, a ditch, sometimes a wall." [5]

Tocqueville conceived, researched, and executed his mature masterpiece, *The Old Regime and the Revolution,* with equivalent rigor within a series of self-imposed compartments. At Sorrento in 1850, he instituted what I have termed a tabula rasa, returning to square one in assessing all aspects of his proposed historical work. He chose to direct his attention to the phenomenon of Napoleon Bonaparte and his apotheosis as the strongman craved by the French peasantry, with their bond formally consecrated in 1799 by a measure of universal suffrage. Tocqueville's commitment to his subject would intensify as political events conspired in his own era to elevate a new Napoleon to power. But propelled back in time by the logic of his historical probes, he detoured first to the years preceding Napoleon—the Directory—and then to the period preceding the Revolution—the Old Regime. Finally settling the focus of his book at the end of August 1853, he envisioned it in exclusive sections that cleaved to a simple thematic axis: the Revolution's origins in the broad context of an egalitarian social revolution (book 1) and in the narrower theater of France (books 2 and 3). He researched it in compartments as well, shunning "the contact of others' ideas [that] agitates me and distresses me to the point of making such reading painful," [6] while relentlessly pursuing his own novel encounters with original sources through a broad array of fields, subsequently organized in his seventeen discrete folders. When he finally commenced his writing, he tenaciously adhered to a strategy by which he would first complete a full draft of the book's precise conceptual framework before embellishing it with supporting proofs. Similarly, he wrote his preface and endnotes only after the rest of his book was in galley proof. But he used these outlying texts for an additional purpose as well: to solidify his book's greatest rhetorical device . . . his own presence as meticulous archivist, innovative historical theorist, and fervent apostle of liberty. Tocqueville was thus an efficient and economical artisan in the making of his book: he deliberately sought to achieve borders and depths, leading to "profundity," while avoiding open spaces and shallows, leading to "superficiality." [7]

The long-awaited publication of *The Old Regime and the Revolution* on June 19, 1856, proved to be a bittersweet event for Tocqueville, as he mourned the sudden death of his father a week earlier. In our investigation of his historical method, the book's publication signals a watershed of a different sort, since it effectively freed its author to open a new compartment in his vast historical project: his study of the French Revolution proper. He had held such a study in abeyance in his first volume, he told Montalembert on July 10, 1856, since he had not yet had as his goal "to seize [the Revolution] in its proceedings and judge it in its finished works." Indeed, his first study had been the easier one, since in treating the Old Regime "one operates on a dead man." Now, as he prepared to engage the Revolution itself, he was obligated to "touch the living person," forcing him to undertake a host of "more varied and more extensive studies" that alone could enable him to "approach the ideal that I have in my mind."[8] For almost three years, until his death on April 16, 1859, Tocqueville would make a sustained effort to grasp that palpable essence of the living Revolution.

In his investigations for *The Old Regime,* volume 1, Tocqueville had encountered a world of specialized, often archaic, most often unexamined facts, all requiring his close attention to a variety of novel sources for their discovery and comprehension. "In general, let nothing appear on these specialized matters without having consulted beforehand the specialized books," he had noted to himself with reference to his Old Regime studies.[9] In *The Old Regime,* volume 2, Tocqueville entered a new world in which, as he confided to Duvergier, the facts were already largely plumbed: "It is crystal clear that one cannot hope these days to discover what one could call *new facts* on the French Revolution."[10] The focus of Tocqueville's research thus shifted from discovering novel facts in a relatively neglected era to fashioning "a new manner" in which to treat heavily sifted facts in a much scrutinized era.[11] Central to this new project would be his reading of the political brochures and pamphlets of the revolutionary period. His notes on these constituted more than half of his reading archive, supplemented by comments on revolutionary newspapers, on official documents such as ministers' letters and remonstrances of the parlements, on reports of local associations, and on four general *cahiers.*

Tocqueville's reading of brochures in 1857–58 was judicious and balanced. While he refrained from explosive expressions of surprise or dismay such as marked his 1853 readings of Le Trosne and Burke, he commented with wit and animation on the pamphleteers' arguments and conscious and unconscious political choices. He even adopted the second person in the epigraph

I have chosen for this chapter, wryly criticizing one anonymous writer's reliance on "fixed rules" to govern unfixable human behavior. Especially in his notations on writings of 1789, Tocqueville tended to correlate the brochures' political arguments with the era's unfolding political events: "All of these different phases [of the fight]," he noted with reference to a brochure of Péthion's, "are visible in the pamphlet when one reads it with attention and perfect understanding of the facts of the time." [12] His readings in 1857 of the era's principal pamphleteers (Brissot, Condorcet, Rabaud Saint-Etienne, Péthion, Mounier, Roederer, Barnave, Sieyès) most often coolly assessed their spirit of grand philosophical presumption, with even his reading of Sieyès marked as much by admiration for his subject's political genius as by disdain for his "pretended profundity." [13] In 1858 Tocqueville digested a further collection of "political brochures," addressing these same themes, and then turned to a host of often anonymous, often unheralded pamphlets that he usefully plumbed for facts on social and economic conditions, military conduct, and the early stirrings of the revolution's new principal actors—the people—and their rabid, if naive, bourgeois patrons.

Taken as a unit, Tocqueville's 1857 and 1858 reading of brochures constitutes a subtle study of how revolutionary language reflected social leveling and political absolutism in the Old Regime, while presaging future revolutionary violence and ferocity in its own dramatic transformation. Lynn Hunt has argued that Tocqueville studied revolutionary language as "a vehicle of political self-deception." His investigations were "vertical" in nature, she says, as he stripped away layers of rhetorical fluff to unmask the unrecognized motives of revolutionary actors. By contrast, her own "horizontal" studies sought to situate political discourse within a broader context of political culture. [14] I see both vertical and horizontal elements in Tocqueville's study of language. To be sure, he frequently commented on the underlying forces that negated actors' intentions, as when Rabaud expressed his "exalted love of the king . . . when logic and political passions are moving continually in the opposite direction" or when Péthion articulated decentralizing sentiments even while he was "drawn toward administrative centralization by the substance of [his and his contemporaries'] ideas and of their system." [15] His 1853 study of the Marquis de Mirabeau's 1758 *L'ami des hommes* had documented the same bridle of "democratic" constraints that curbed actors' intentions. Revolutionary language for Tocqueville—whether in 1758 or 1789—thus revealed "powerlessness when [the chief actors] are not swept along by the tide." [16]

But that is not Tocqueville's final word on such language. In his brochure readings he was every bit as focused on the way the interplay of revolutionary language contributed to and shaped the era's political events. In reading the 1787 and 1788 brochures, Tocqueville often commented on the moderate and respectful language of the writers, even while they expressed the "true revolutionary spirit" of philosophical presumption, an approach he labeled "Violence of the Moderates" or "Radicalism of the Moderates" or "Revolutionary Spirit of the Moderates." [17] These leaders in 1788 were not, for the most part, revolutionary provocateurs, or at least not initially; they became radical, however, as they listened to the flagrantly "rude" official language of the Parlements in their remonstrances and to the king in his strident replies; the fierce polemical battles over the composition of the Estates-General; and the brilliant efforts by the provocative few, exemplified by Sieyès, to use language to "give a coloring and form to the passions that existed in germ . . . in all hearts." [18] By 1789, as a result of these factors, Tocqueville noted the transformation in language evident in its "violence and ferocity . . . that followed the victory" at the Bastille, with even the efforts of moderates such as Abbé Fauchet to control the workers' insurgency in Faubourg Saint-Antoine now fueling the fire of the Revolution's rhetoric. [19]

As in 1853, Tocqueville again saved his reading of the *cahiers de doléances* for a pivotal moment in his research—June 1857, at the conclusion of his studies of the fights against despotism by the Notables and parlements—and he again utilized a familiar *cahiers* source—the same initial tomes of the 174-volume collection of the full general *cahiers* at the National Archives that he had scanned in 1856. [20] In this latest and final reading, Tocqueville established—for the fourth time in twenty-one and one-half years!—the existence of a host of "identical ideas among the three orders," this time with a particular focus on their common support for provincial institutions. What the *cahiers* shared was a commitment to "free institutions, the government of the nation by itself," with the wishes of the three orders "not only analogous but *identical*" in this matter. [21] What the *cahiers* "absolutely and universally rejected" was the "idea of *administrative* centralization." To be sure, they supported a central national government with certain clearly defined tasks, such as establishing a national educational system. But harking back to his distinction developed first in America, and illustrating the abiding importance of the American model of local liberty to his political thought, Tocqueville did not find such a desire for national political unity "incompatible with decentralization (see America)," even if it rendered it more difficult. In the *cahiers* of the three orders of Amiens, in particular, Tocqueville lauded their universal commitment to provincial liberty and liberal principles, their common support for "*social* economies" that placed liberty and equality "side by side," and their calls for freedoms for the church. He also

applauded the "conciliatory spirit" between the orders that led them to exchange visits, compliments, and courtesies, even while downplaying areas
of potential disagreement. "Should I make," he wondered, "a tableau of this
momentary disposition of the orders to understand one another and take
Amiens as a model?"[22]

In January 1858 Tocqueville was able to announce to Freslon, "I have thus
written without verve; but assiduously enough to have finished the first
book of my new work."[23] Tocqueville's seven chapters of his sequel's book 1
depict the brief but incandescent reign of "an active passion" (OR, 2:35) that
erupted in France in 1787. The passion was unique to France, even though
all European nations shared a general commitment to the "new cosmopolitanism," a transnational spirit of humane compassion that he defined in his
first chapter. It appeared in France in the form of a powerful thirst for "political liberty" (OR, 2:35) that preceded the drive for "equality of rights" in
the Revolution proper. Its principal advocates were the nobles, priests, and
upper bourgeoisie, with the "timid and indecisive" majority of the bourgeoisie largely absent from the fight, as they sought rather to "caress the
[central] power" (OR, 2:47). Galvanized by events in Dauphiny, which themselves were the product of traditional local liberties, these leaders defiantly
resisted in the Assemblies of Notables and the parlements the king's efforts
to impose his despotic rule. Although this aristocratic-inspired first revolution was quickly defused and supplanted by the "true spirit of the Revolution" (OR, 2:55), it attested to liberty's continuing ability to arouse and unite
the French nation. Indeed, Tocqueville concluded book 1 with a testament
to that liberal zeal: the drafting of the *cahiers*, marked by the three orders'
temperate postures and their proud and liberal grievances.[24]

With this climactic description of "the hearts that drew near to one another" on the eve of the reunion of the Estates-General, Tocqueville returned to the same moment with which he had concluded *The Old Regime*,
volume 1. But where in his first work's preface and conclusion he had relied
on his rhetorical skills and the concept of national character to make his
strongest case for liberty, he had now built a powerful historical argument
for liberty's potent role in an earlier, previously unacknowledged Revolution. As the year turned, he charted three directions for his ensuing work.
First, in a December 1857 "chapter plan," he designated three precise research
topics that would guide his 1858 investigations.[25] Second, he developed three
sheets listing eighteen specific "headings of ideas" for book 1, chapters 3–
7, on which "I must make a new examination and a new classification of
notes."[26] The specific topics contained in these "headings" each flow from

Tocqueville's text; they in turn help dictate the length and specificity of the corresponding indexes for the chapters in question. Thus it appears that he crafted the "headings" and indexes for at least these five chapters in 1858 *after* his initial drafting of book 1, thus hewing to the strategy that had served him so effectively in *The Old Regime,* volume 1.[27] Such a view of Tocqueville's timing—one that looks *ahead* to the definitive drafting of these chapters after a major reexamination of his notes—is consistent with his statement to Kergorlay on February 27, 1858, that the seven chapter drafts were "at the stage of drafts too imperfect for me even to share them with you."[28] Third, he began to cast his eye in preliminary fashion forward to his larger book, making clear that he still envisioned it as stretching all the way to the Consulate.[29]

Tocqueville's enthusiasm for all three facets of his planned endeavors enabled him to tell Ampère on February 18, 1858 that he had "emerged from the regions of shadows where I groped for a very long time," allowing him to "proceed more quickly" upon a clearly perceived "way" toward a clearly perceived "objective."[30] Writing to his wife in May, he announced that he had indeed regained his literary momentum: "It's the first time since the printing of my first book that I feel truly at my work and thinking of it from morning to night."[31]

Tocqueville's new "way" in 1858 led him back to the familiar intersection of two historical paths. On the one hand, he planned to continue his story of liberty's potent presence, now in the Revolution proper. For during the summer of 1789, liberty played a central role in the Constituent Assembly's activities—in the "near unanimity of the resistance" in July, in the "most extraordinary" display in history of public virtue evidenced in the Night of August 4, and later that month in the Declaration of the Rights of Man and the Citizen that, flawed and pretentious as its deliberations might have been, still revealed "to what extent [it] establishes *liberty* even more than equality."[32]

Tocqueville planned to culminate this tale of liberty's abiding presence with an explicit statement that would specify the meaning of "the Principles of '89," thus responding to the charges of friends and critics alike who had found his earlier portrayal deficient in *The Old Regime,* volume 1.[33] He stated his intention to define those principles in the third and final subsection of his December 1857 "chapter plan."[34] He then pinpointed four additional specific passages in his notes for this climactic discussion, using a common flagging device—"To the principles of 1789 [*Aux principes de 1789*]"—to direct the comments to this pivotal chapter-section. In each case the passage referred in a different way to his vision of the bold, inclusive, temperate, self-regulating ideals of 1789.

In the first reference, he state clearly that the ideals were necessarily based on "democracy . . . in the true sense of the word [in which] the people take a more or less extensive part in government." Their sense was thus "intimately bound to the idea of political liberty."[35] Second, in contrast to their perversion in the decadent Roman Empire, they allowed the people genuinely "to act, speak, write, and . . . think" for themselves in a society that was "free" and "civil."[36] Third, they reflected the breadth of the prerevolutionary belief in decentralization, embraced even by the future revolutionaries, since "all the brochures published . . . in 1788 and 1789 [were] entirely enemies of centralization and favorable to local life."[37] Tocqueville here designated for special consideration Condorcet's anonymously published brochure of 1788, *Essai sur la constitution et les fonctions des assemblées provinciales,* in which the author called for popular restraint and the slow, peaceful evolution of the newly established provincial assemblies as preferred strategies that might lead to the constitutional regeneration of the monarchy. The single quotation from the brochure that Tocqueville copied in his notes attests to Condorcet's surprising moderation; it also provides a striking example of Tocqueville's indexing of his liberal arguments to particular historical circumstances, as he here looked approvingly on Condorcet's cautious recommendation to suppress headstrong pursuit of bold objectives: "Let us even fear to surrender to those noble and proud sentiments that have produced the rebirth among so many peoples of brilliant rather than tranquil days [and produced so many great actions and so little happiness]."[38] Finally, Tocqueville designated for possible inclusion in his discussion of the principles of 1789 a quote of the younger Mirabeau that he had first encountered in his research for volume 1 when reading *De la monarchie prussienne sous Fréderic le Grand:* "There are only INDEPENDENT SENTRIES that can stop despotism." Mirabeau's evident recognition of the "necessity of a nobility or at least of a body of property owners taking part in government" would have assisted Tocqueville's difficult rhetorical argument for preservation of an aristocratic element in society . . . and served as a further example of his lifelong strategy of long-gestated riposte.[39] The principles of 1789, explained in these ways, grew from the desire of every man to manage his own destiny, and they found a natural home within the French national character. Linked with the revolutionaries' early commitment to decentralization, they swept France and astounded the European world. Properly corrected by Tocqueville's modifications, they might have served as the basis for a regular, stable, moderate liberty for France in the future.

But Tocqueville's studies also revealed liberty's immense difficulties in the spheres of politics, ideology, culture, and national character. Politically, liberty possessed many theoretical proponents but no active practitioners, on either a national or a local level. Moreover, he noted in June 1858 that France suffered from the "length and intensity of the fight" that "enflames, embitters, exacerbates, perpetuates" the hatred between the classes.[40] Liberty's cause was also damaged by the Constituent Assembly's inability to suppress anarchy, a task for which it possessed no electoral mandate.[41] In the world of opinion, liberty quickly encountered the similarly widespread but more powerful axiom of democratic theory, bestowed by Rousseau: "the idea of a crowd made up of equal elements and representatives of *number*."[42] Politics became a numbers game in 1789 as the society debated whether to double the Third or vote by head; such fascination with numbers crystallized in the "ultrademocratic" notion of universal suffrage that suddenly "fell into everyone's head"—ready to rupture a society of traditional orders defined by limits of class.[43] On the cultural level, moderate liberty was subverted by the nation's mores, as Tocqueville had already chronicled in volume 1, making them the back door through which "centralization was reestablished."[44] Finally, the French national character bred a "new race of revolutionaries," a "virus" unlike any seen in history. An explanation for their character—"immoderate, violent, radical, desperate, audacious, almost mad, and nonetheless powerful and effective"—remained "veiled" to Tocqueville's probes, preventing him from touching or even seeing it, despite his final intense efforts in May 1858.[45] Buffeted by such forces, liberal France succumbed, ushering in the new "demagogic and egalitarian" revolution that eclipsed its "aristocratic and liberal" predecessor.[46]

The Revolution's "double character: liberalism, democracy," evident in these contrasting descriptions, metastasized during the summer of 1789 in ways that would shape, for better and worse, the political events of Tocqueville's lifetime. Tocqueville planned that such a portrayal in his book would "lead me bitterly back to the present," allowing him to conclude his chapter on the "Principles of '89" by demonstrating to his contemporaries what they must renounce and what they must preserve of its potent legacy.[47]

In this chapter's epigraph, Tocqueville criticized a revolutionary pamphleteer for failing to recognize that "the object of your study" was "a passionate being who escapes repeatedly from fixed laws!" The pamphleteer's philosophical presumption, reinforced by his political inexperience, led him to seek to impose—to liberty's detriment—tidy and reasonable solutions on unpredictable political problems complicated by human passions.

A number of Tocqueville's readers have thought that he, in his role as historian, did likewise. Investing his own studies with "considerations drawn from the ordinary logic of facts," he ended by denying his passionate human subjects—the revolutionaries of 1789 and, by extension, his contemporaries—their own ability to shape the politics of their respective eras. He admirably demonstrated that "the French Revolution had invented nothing," in Gobineau's words; [48] he was preoccupied "with origins and outcomes," in Hunt's words; [49] he was caught in the undertow of his book's "ocean current," in Herr's words; [50] he was engaged in a mission wherein "the logic of facts is thus mobilized to discredit the heroic image of 1789," in Wolin's words. [51] In each case, his critics argued, he ended by depreciating the possibilities of human enterprise, thus ironically harming his supreme good and highest calling—the cause of liberty.

As I have sought to demonstrate in my own study, Tocqueville believed that liberty must be produced by an imperfect process of a complex, untidy, passionate politics. He defined such liberty with care during his lifetime, seeking to calibrate the critical point where national and local institutions and interests could meet and reinforce one another. One's contributions to the politics needed to produce such a liberal balance could take many forms for him, be it distinguished service as a local provincial councillor, national deputy, or French foreign minister—or the writing of a great book that disseminated, in its own way, political ideas within a nation's "intellectual atmosphere" so as to furnish both governors and governed with "the principles of their conduct." [52] Of course there were constraints on the ability of politics to ensure the realization of liberty: economic ones (such as those we have studied in the French countryside in chapter 3); cultural ones (such as those contained in a nation's centralized "mores" viewed in chapter 5); ideological ones (such as those introduced by philosophical pundits or revolutionary pamphleteers that we viewed in chapters 6 and 8); and rhetorical ones resulting from overt efforts, such as that of Burke that we studied in chapter 4 and Sieyès in this chapter, to shape an era's political discourse. But Tocqueville never saw such powerful forces as limiting man's capability to act; arguably, his need to act increased in direct proportion to the potency of their grip. In his final investigation of the political events of 1789 at the end of his life, Tocqueville increasingly focused on revolutionary politics—on the legislative battles of the Constituent Assembly, the jockeying of the classes for positions and power, the surge of peasant activity in the countryside, and the drive to influence and control the discourse of the day. Liberty—defined as direct participation in local and national politics—and only liberty could address the threats he had already outlined.

In my own study, I too have encountered "a passionate being who escapes repeatedly from these fixed laws!" In 1838, writing *Democracy in America,* volume 2, Tocqueville evinced a new "democratic vision" that transformed every aspect of his three years of previous work on the book. Writing *The Old Regime,* he chanced upon Edmund Burke and the Tours archives, leading him to decide to undertake a distinct volume 1 in late summer 1853 . . . in which he would articulate the very vision of tutelary despotism that he had predicted for democracy's future in *Democracy* but would now find in the monarchic past. Assessing Tocqueville's work on his sequel in 1858, we must recognize his capacity for change, since a new constellation of form and vision might similarly have led him to transform his final book in dramatic fashion. Arguably, he was again rethinking a number of his central premises in late May when he reported to Beaumont that he was searching for "a new way to arrive at [his] subject."[53] Arguably, he was reassessing his stylistic choices for his final draft as he read Gibbon's autobiography in English seven weeks before his death in 1859.[54] The only claim we can make with confidence—following Beaumont in his posthumous "Notice sur Alexis de Tocqueville"—is that his sequel would have affirmed the author's "faith in [liberty]," since he would have "broken his pen rather than give a discouraging conclusion."[55]

For all his archival anxieties—indeed, perhaps precisely because his labors reflected in their quixotic quality liberty's quixotic quest—Tocqueville's design and execution of *The Old Regime* constitutes an extraordinary success story, testifying to the artful achievement by a great historian and ardent champion of liberty of his intended consequences. The rebirth of liberty in France, he had argued in *The Old Regime,* would have to be led by determined, devoted partisans; he could offer no easy formulas for such local instantiation, just a clear appeal to the instincts and pride of his readers . . . and the powerful example of his own commitment to liberty's service. As recounted by Françoise Mélonio in *Tocqueville and the French,* Tocqueville's defense of liberty in *The Old Regime* indeed contributed to liberty's rebirth in France in the decade following his death, when he became "the Liberals' Posthumous Leader."[56] A century later, at the time of their Revolution's bicentennial, his work enabled the French, led by their historians, to advance liberty in new ways by discrediting the Marxists' revolutionary interpretation.[57] Most recently, during the 1990s in America, his prescient view of the tendency of citizens in democratic societies to withdraw from political and civil life has served as a touchstone for American thinkers and activists in a national debate on civic disengagement. Tocqueville's readers have thus continued to respond to his appeal to use their passion for liberty to transform democracy into a boon for their own generation . . . and for those yet to come.

Note Number/ Page Number[1]	Book/ Chapter in *OR*	Short Description of *OR* Endnote	TA File/ Page Number
1, 265–66	I, 4	Power of Roman law in Germany	Q, 89(b)–90, 108–9
2, 266	I, 4	Kings' "golden age"	K, 20[2]
3, 267	I, 4	Decline of free German cities	Q, 54–55
4, 267–68	II, 1	Dates of abolition of serfdom	Q, 92
5, 268	II, 1	Severity of serfdom in Slavic Germany	Q, 27(b)–28
6, 268–71	II, 1	Code of Frederick the Great	Q, 82–88
7, 271–72	II, 1	Free peasant property owners in Germany	Q, 35–35(b)
8, 272	II, 1	Nobility and peasant property owners along Rhine	Q, 35
9, 272–73	II, 1	Effect of usury laws on division of property	B, 12
10, 273	II, 1	Bitterness caused by *dîmes*	H, 105(b)
11, 273	II, 1	Clergy's divorce from people	H, 104(b)–105
12, 273	II, 1	Priests' feudal rights	A, 25
13, 273–75	II, 1	Peasants' feudal fury	H, 49–51
14, 275	II, 1	Feudal system's effect on every private interest	A, 40–40(b)
15, 275–76	II, 2	State's favoritism—public charities	H, 61–61(b)
16, 276	II, 2	Administration of charities	J, 70
17, 276–77	II, 2	Intendant's power to regulate manufactures	I, 15–16
18, 277	II, 3	Louis XI's city constitutions	"Drafts"[3]

(continued)

Note Number/ Page Number[1]	Book/ Chapter in *OR*	Short Description of *OR* Endnote	TA File/ Page Number
19, 277–83	II, 3	A city government (Angers)	H, 38 ([4]–[10])
20, 283	II, 3	Variability of city rules	K, 60(b)
21, 284–86	II, 3	A village government (Ivry)	I, 10(b)–13
22, 286	II, 3	Municipal maladministration	B, 36
23, 286	II, 3	State oversight of convents	H, 123(b)
24, 286–87	II, 5	Administrative centralization in colonies (Canada)	J, 92–93
25, 287–88	II, 5	Government's intrusion in courts	H, 104(b)
26, 288	II, 6	Language of provincial assembly (Guyenne)	J, 71–71(b)
27, 288	II, 6	Fervor for tobacco licenses	H, 159
28, 288	II, 6	Extinction of local life	"Drafts"
29, 288–89	II, 8	Feudal rent variations	B, 17
30, 289	II, 9	Importance of agricultural societies' discussion	H, 54(b)–55
31, 289	II, 9	Dependence of local liberty on general liberty	K, 31
32, 289–90	II, 9	Tax exemptions of nobility	B, 41
33, 290	II, 9	Tax collection inequality	B, 41(b)
34, 290	II, 9	Tax collection inequality	H, 91
35, 290	II, 9	Tax collection inequality	B, 8
36, 291	II, 9	Tax collection inequality	H, 135(b)
37, 291	II, 10	Young's defense of English tax plan	N, 7(b)–8
38, 291–92	II, 10	Pleas for tax exemption by Marquis of X	H, 131–131(b)
39, 292	II, 10	"Respect" for rights in Old Regime	K, 7
40, 292	II, 10	Pleas for rent redemptions by agricultural societies	H, 53–53(b)
41, 293	II, 10	Tax exemptions for public officials	H, 148, 167
42, 293	II, 10	Limited venality in Germany	Q, 95
43, 293	II, 11	Public/private judicial overlap	"Drafts"
44, 293–301	II, 11	Analysis of *cahiers* of nobility	[Stoffels]
45, 301	II, 11	Levels of government in an ecclesiastical province	H, 56–56(b)

(continued)

Note Number/ Page Number[1]	Book/ Chapter in *OR*	Short Description of *OR* Endnote	TA File/ Page Number
46, 301	II, 11	Spirit of clergy in assemblies (Haute Guyenne)	J, 65(b)
47, 301	II, 11	Clergy's liberality	J, 75
48, 301–2	II, 11	Resiliency of civil society's bonds	B, 29
49, 302	II, 11	Defiant tone of courts	I, 2
50, 302	II, 11	Duties of a free citizen	K, 51
51, 302–3	II, 11	Lack of loans in Old Regime	K, 29
52, 303	II, 12	Harshness of farmers-general (Mayence)	H, 135(b)
53, 303	II, 12	Protest of Prince of Rohan	H, 136
54, 303	II, 12	Clergy's insistence on pecuniary rights (Noisai)	H, 132
55, 303–4	II, 12	Complaints regarding collection of taille	H, 75
56, 304	II, 12	Government's admission of superiority of *pays d'états*	H, 143(b)–144
57, 304	II, 12	"Progress of civilization" in *corvées* for roads	H, 158
58, 304	II, 12	Imprisonment for *corvées*	H, 64
59, 304	II, 12	Two means for construction of roads	B, 40
60, 305	II, 12	*Corvées* for transportation of convicts	H, 160
61, 305	II, 12	Turgot's sketches of *corvées*	B, 10
62, 305–6	II, 12	Multiple uses of *corvées*	H, 160(b)– 161(b)
63, 306	III, 1	Disdain of philosophers for people	K, 68–68(b)
64, 306–7	III, 2	Ill treatment of peasantry	H, 130(b) and H, 162–162(b)
65, 307	III, 2	Frederick the Great's lack of understanding of utility of religion	L, 37–37(b)
66, 307–8	III, 4	Parallel spirit of progress in Germany and France	Q, 47–47(b)
67, 308–10	III, 4	Checks provided by English court system (Blackstone)	L, 19(b)–22

(*continued*)

Note Number/ Page Number[1]	Book/ Chapter in *OR*	Short Description of *OR* Endnote	TA File/ Page Number
68, 310	III, 4	Extra charity for Paris	I, 3
69, 310–11	III, 4	More active political life just before the Revolution	K, 35
70, 311	III, 5	Secret tax increase (Tours)	H, 142
71, 311	III, 5	Turgot's words for peasants	B, 24
72, 311	III, 6	Price controls in 1779 on straw	H, 105(b)
73, 312	III, 6	Government's refusal to indemnify (Tours)	H, 122(b)
74, 312	III, 7	New "democratic" spirit before the Revolution	B, 4
75, 312	III, 7	Administrative conflicts (1787)	I, 9
76, 312	III, 7	Burdens of a syndic	I, 3(b)
77, 312–21		General feudal rights endnote	A, 2–15(b)

1. To facilitate reference to Tocqueville's endnotes, I have assigned each a consecutive number in the order in which it appears in *OC*, II, pt. 1, pp. 265–321. The page number(s) cited are those within the *OC* text.

2. Page numbers are difficult to ascertain in folder K; I have used the numbers appearing on each sheet, even though they fail to fit into a larger numbering plan.

3. "Drafts" refers to TA, box 42, "Sketches and drafts," which contains a rough draft by Tocqueville of this endnote. I have been unable to locate this note, as well as notes 28 and 43, within a particular reading file.

ONE

1. Tocqueville to Prosper Duvergier de Hauranne, September 1, 1856, *OC* (Beaumont), VI, pp. 332–33.

2. For this dating, see Tocqueville to Gustave Beaumont, December 5, 1838, *OC,* VIII, pt. 1, p. 328. Tocqueville indicated to Beaumont while working on his revisions that he hoped "soon to be in the middle of the first volume," by which I take him to refer to parts 1 and 2 of his 1840 *Democracy,* initially published as a separate volume in that work's two-volume set.

3. TA (Beinecke), C.V.g., vol. 3, "Manuscript Notes and Drafts," folder for II:2:5 (*DA* [ed. Nolla], 2:103n). Tocqueville also considered placing this analogy in II:2:4 on local political institutions where it would have been, he noted, "less satirical, but more *just* and more *striking*" than in his chapter on associations (ibid., folder for II:2:4).

4. We have no confirmation that Tocqueville attended this particular lecture, although we do know he attended six of the later lectures in this same cycle (see his "Notes on Guizot's course on the history of civilization in France," *OC,* XVI, pp. 441–77). Even if he did not attend this lecture in person, he certainly read Guizot's lectures afterward, as we will see in chapter 2.

5. François Guizot, *Histoire de la civilisation en France depuis la chute de l'empire romain,* 12th ed., 4 vols. (Paris: Didier, 1872), 1:236, 239–40.

6. François Furet, "The Intellectual Origins of Tocqueville's Thought," *Tocqueville Review* 7 (1985–86): 118.

7. James T. Schleifer, "Tocqueville as Historian: Philosophy and Methodology in the *Democracy,*" in *Reconsidering Tocqueville's "Democracy in America,"* ed. Abraham S. Eisenstadt (New Brunswick, NJ: Rutgers University Press, 1988), p. 146.

8. Eduardo Nolla, "Introduction of the Editor," *DA* (ed. Nolla), 1:liii (note).

9. Tocqueville to Beaumont, December 5, 1838, *OC,* VIII, pt. 1, p. 328.

10. Tocqueville to Hervé de Tocqueville, June 3, 1831, *OC*, XIV, pp. 99–100. Two weeks earlier, Tocqueville had asked his friend Ernest Chabrol to send him his volumes of Guizot's lectures to assist in this research project (Tocqueville to Chabrol, May 18, 1831, cited in Edward T. Gargan, "The Formation of Tocqueville's Historical Thought," *Review of Politics* 24 [January 1962]: 54).

11. Tocqueville to Louis de Kergorlay, undated but assumed by editor to be "end of January 1835," *OC*, XIII, pt. 1, p. 373 (*Selected Letters*, p. 93).

12. George W. Pierson, *Tocqueville and Beaumont in America* (New York: Oxford University Press, 1938; Johns Hopkins Paperbacks edition, 1966), part 5 ("New England: The Heart of the Experience"), 347–454; Robert T. Gannett Jr., "Bowling Ninepins in Tocqueville's Township," *American Political Science Review* 97, no. 1 (February 2003): 1–16.

13. Seymour Drescher, "Tocqueville's Two *Démocraties*," *Journal of the History of Ideas* 25, no. 2 (1964): 202, 216. Drescher subsequently updated his argument in "More Than America: Comparison and Synthesis in *Democracy in America*" in *Reconsidering*, ed. Eisenstadt, pp. 77–93.

14. Jean-Claude Lamberti, *Tocqueville and the Two Democracies*, trans. Arthur Goldhammer (Cambridge: Harvard University Press, 1989), pp. 209–10, 227–30.

15. For an excellent summary of the terms and stakes of the "two *Democracies*" debate, including his own rebuttal of its central thesis, see James T. Schleifer, "How Many *Democracies?*" in *Liberty, Equality, Democracy*, ed. Eduardo Nolla (New York: New York University Press, 1992), pp. 193–205. Other approaches to Tocqueville's methodology in the *Democracy* include George W. Pierson's description of Tocqueville's "pre-determined—and to him scientific—series" of observation-induction-deduction in *Tocqueville and Beaumont in America*, pp. 758–61; Robert Nisbet's examination of his "ideal types" in "Tocqueville's Ideal Types," in *Reconsidering*, ed. Eisenstadt, pp. 171–91; Edward T. Gargan's and Roger Boesche's investigations of his prognosticatory powers in (Gargan) "Tocqueville and the Problem of Historical Prognosis," *American Historical Review* 68 (1963): 332–45, and (Boesche) "Why Could Tocqueville Predict So Well?" *Political Theory* 2, no. 1 (February 1983): 79–103; Marvin Zetterbaum's depiction of Tocqueville's "facade of neutrality" in *Tocqueville and the Problem of Democracy* (Stanford, CA: Stanford University Press, 1967); Françoise Mélonio's portrayal of his analogical reasoning in her twin introductions in *Tocqueville* [three works] (Paris: Robert Laffont, 1986), pp. 9–37 and 397–425; and Harvey C. Mansfield and Delba Winthrop's remarks on his "political science" in "Editors' Introduction" to *DA*, xliii–xlix.

16. Tocqueville to Stoffels, April 21, 1830, *DA* (ed. Nolla), 2:323. In "Tocqueville and the Political Thought of the French Doctrinaires (Guizot, Royer-Collard, Rémusat)," *History of Political Thought* 20, no. 3 (Autumn 1999): 476–77, Aurelian Craiutu portrays this letter as Tocqueville's "first sketch" of his vision of the soft despotism to which he will address such attention in *Democracy in America*, volume 2. Schleifer cites other early instances of Tocqueville's treatment of this theme in "How Many *Democracies?*" in *Liberty*, ed. Nolla, pp. 197–99.

17. For Tocqueville's view of the July Monarchy during this period, see François

Furet, *Revolutionary France, 1770–1880,* trans. Antonia Nevill (Oxford: Blackwell, 1988), pp. 354–55.

18. Tocqueville to Mary Mottley, December 26, 1837, *OC,* XIV, p. 410.

19. Tocqueville to Henry Reeve, February 3, 1840, *OC,* VI, pt. 1, pp. 52–53.

20. Tocqueville to Beaumont, April 22, 1838, *OC,* VIII, pt. 1, p. 293 (*Selected Letters,* p. 131). For his reading of Kempis on February 11, 1838, see *DA* (ed. Nolla), 2:202n. For a further commentary on the "grandeur" he found in these readings, see Tocqueville to Francisque de Corcelle, March 19, 1838, *OC,* XV, pt. 1, p. 97.

21. Ibid., p. 291 (ibid., p. 127).

22. Ibid., p. 292 (ibid., p. 130).

23. Tocqueville to Kergorlay, letters of March 21 and August 8, 1838, *OC,* XIII, pt. 2, pp. 28–29, 40–41; Kergorlay to Tocqueville, letters of January 22, March 18, April 17, June 25, August 3, 1838, ibid., pp. 9–10, 25–26, 30–31, 33–34, 39.

24. The best way to follow Tocqueville's 1838 transformation of his text is by reading the various notes he composed in the process of writing it (DA [ed. Nolla], 2:190–282). On twenty-seven separate occasions, Tocqueville dated his miscellaneous ruminations and drafts to the specific period of January through the first week of September 1838, encompassing the time during which he drafted the final ten chapters of volume 2, part 3, and the first seven chapters of part 4. For this important purpose, Eduardo Nolla's critical edition is superior to James Schleifer's annotated text (see "Notes and Variants" in *Oeuvres [Pléiade],* 2:1084–1181), since Nolla includes passages from Tocqueville's "rubbish" while Schleifer incorporates only relevant variations from Tocqueville's manuscript. Nolla's edition is marred, however, by the haphazard way he chooses the point in Tocqueville's final text to which he references the author's earlier ruminations, apparently basing his decision on his own judgment of a correlation rather than on any indication of a connection signaled by Tocqueville himself.

25. *DA* (ed. Nolla), 2:190n.

26. For this dating, see *DA* (ed. Nolla), 2:190–235, plus Tocqueville's comment to Beaumont on April 22, 1838: "I am putting at this moment the finishing stroke to the *penultimate* chapter," by which he meant the totality of his chapters in part 3 (*OC,* VIII, pt. 1, p. 291 [*Selected Letters,* p. 127]).

27. Tocqueville note, dated March 7, 1838, *DA* (ed. Nolla), 2:264n.

28. In *Two Democracies,* Lamberti was the first to refocus attention on this chapter, one that clearly held special significance for Tocqueville since he selected it for advance publication in the *Revue des deux mondes* of April 14, 1840. According to Lamberti, Tocqueville wrote his chapter as "a pamphlet directed against Guizot" (*Two Democracies,* p. 202), using it to rebut Guizot's political trump card of the specter of imminent revolution raised to justify the government's repression of associations and the press. I disagree with Lamberti's assertion on any number of grounds, the main one being that when he wrote it Tocqueville was engaged in formulating his work's great concluding vision that far eclipsed Guizot's short-term fear-mongering. Making clear in near-violent terms his political disgust with Guizot at this time, Tocqueville

clarified for Corcelle that his distaste was for Guizot's lack of "*morality*" and willingness to abjure his principles, not for his particular political acts that indeed were drawing him closer to Tocqueville as he reversed field to resist the Molé ministry in spring 1838 (Tocqueville to Corcelle, March 19, 1838, *OC,* XV, pt. 1, p. 98). For Drescher's own rejection of Lamberti's claim of an anti-Guizot polemic, see " 'Why Great Revolutions Will Become Rare': Tocqueville's Most Neglected Prognosis," *Journal of Modern History* 64 (1992): 435–37.

29. *DA* (ed. Nolla), 2:237n.

30. Schleifer dates Tocqueville's first use of "individualism" to April 24, 1837 in *The Making of Tocqueville's Democracy in America* (Chapel Hill: University of North Carolina Press, 1980), p. 252; he notes as well its initial positive usage. Tocqueville shifted the meaning he assigned to "individualism" as he mulled over his need for an apt description of despotism's isolating tendencies. Indeed, he also sought—unsuccessfully—to invent a comparable new name for his "administrative despotism" (*DA* [ed. Nolla], 2: 265n).

31. Tocqueville to Beaumont, July 8, 1838, *OC,* VIII, pt. 1, pp. 311–12. Excerpts from this file, found in TA (Beinecke), C.V.g., vol. 4, are presented by Nolla in *DA* (ed. Nolla), 2: 244, 247–49, 254–56, 258–61, 270, and 285.

32. I am using here Tocqueville's initial draft title for II:4:7 (*DA* [ed. Nolla], 2:270n), one that he dispensed with in his book since he found it promised more than he could deliver.

33. Tocqueville to Pierre-Paul Royer-Collard, November 20, 1838, *OC,* XI, p. 73.

34. Tocqueville to Beaumont, December 5, 1838, *OC,* VIII, pt. 1, p. 328. Lamberti argues based on his manuscript review that Tocqueville rewrote his first ten chapters (II:1:1–10) in their entirety between October and December 1838 (*Two Democracies,* pp. 147–48).

35. TA (Beinecke), C.V.g., vol. 3, folder for II:2:4. The earlier text commencing with "The Americans have combated" begins on the fifth page and continues to the tenth of this folder. Tocqueville gave the chapter three proposed initial titles on page 5 [unnumbered]: "Of Several Particular Methods Used by the Americans to Combat Isolation and Egoism"; "How the Americans Combat the Tendency That Causes Men to Isolate Themselves through Municipal Institutions and the Spirit of Association"; and "Of the Doctrine of Utility That Democratic Liberty Causes to Be Understood." When he revised this earlier draft, he injected the word "individualism" two times in his text—in his title and in the first sentence, where he used it to replace his earlier use of "isolation." For an account of how this 1836 draft reflects Tocqueville's interest not only in the American township but also in English, Swiss, medieval Italian, and German townships that he investigated in 1835–36, see Robert T. Gannett Jr., "Bowling Ninepins in Tocqueville's Township," *American Political Science Review* 97, no. 1 (February 2003): 1–16.

36. For these vignettes, see *DA,* 419 (Muhammad and the Koran); 436 (Plutarch); 520 (Plato); 593 (Plutarch); 630 (Plutarch); 632–33 (Machiavelli).

37. *DA* (ed. Nolla), 2:264n.

38. Tocqueville to Beaumont, July 8, 1838, *OC,* VIII, pt. 1, p. 311.

39. *DA* (ed. Nolla), 2:265n, 270n, 248n.

40. I am including in this count Tocqueville's 2,300 pages of notes contained in his seventeen bulging folders in TA, box 43, "Reading notes," plus the more than 400 pages of notes compiled mainly in 1852 for his earliest studies of the Directory and Napoleon that he subsequently filed in box 44, "Sequel: the unfinished book—preparatory notes," plus the more than 1,000 pages compiled after 1856 for his sequel comprising his studies of the Revolution itself. When I refer to a "page" of Tocqueville's notes, I have in mind a single side of one of his drafting sheets. In the course of our discussion, I will use "(b)" to refer to the "(back)" side of one such page.

41. Beaumont, "Notice" to *OC* (Beaumont), V, p. 90.

42. Furet and Mélonio, "Introduction" to *OR*, 1:17–19.

43. Furet, "The Intellectual Origins," p. 117. Furet reminds us that such a policy made "even such a simple question as to whether Tocqueville read a lot or a little in his youth and during the rest of his life . . . difficult to answer in any incontestable manner."

44. Tocqueville to Hubert de Tocqueville, March 7, 1854, *OC*, XIV, p. 296.

45. Beaumont to Tocqueville, March 26, 1856, *OC*, VIII, pt. 3, p. 386.

TWO

1. Tocqueville to Nassau W. Senior, conversation of August 19, 1850, *OC*, VI, pt. 2, pp. 286–87 (*Conversations*, 1:113–14).

2. "Discours de réception 21 avril 1842," *OC*, XVI, pp. 251–69, with Tocqueville's spirited defense of liberty on pp. 266–67 and his tempered Napoleonic verdict on p. 263.

3. Françoise Mélonio, *Tocqueville and the French*, trans. Beth G. Raps (Charlottesville: University Press of Virginia, 1998), p. 86. Three months earlier, on January 18, 1842, Tocqueville had emphasized to the Chamber the need for a rejuvenated liberty as the best means to combat "demoralization" in the nation's political mores, induced by an electoral system that encouraged political representatives to be viewed and to act as venal purveyors of political favors, since the legally qualified voters in each district most often numbered fewer than five hundred. "Discussion de l'adresse: Séance du 18 janvier 1842," *OC*, III, pt. 2, pp. 197–207, with Tocqueville's opening salvo for liberty on p. 199 and his analysis of the negative effects of the present electoral laws on p. 205.

4. "Réponse de M. Molé," *OC*, XVI, pp. 270–80. Molé's defense of "this *clever, rational* despotism, as you call it" is on pp. 273–74.

5. Tocqueville to Royer-Collard, September 27, 1841, *OC*, XI, pp. 108–9 (*Selected Letters*, pp. 156–57).

6. Tocqueville to Madame Phillimore, June 20, 1852, *OC* (Beaumont), VII, p. 283. André Jardin traces the origin of Tocqueville's book to his 1842 speech and its attenuated preparatory studies in *Tocqueville: A Biography*, trans. Lydia Davis with Robert Hemenway (New York: Farrar Straus Giroux, 1988), p. 481.

7. "Discours de réception," *OC*, XVI, pp. 268–69.

8. Tocqueville to Beaumont, October 25, 1829, *OC*, VIII, pt. 1, p. 93.

9. Lionel Gossman, *Between History and Literature* (Cambridge: Harvard University Press, 1990), p. 85. Gossman's comment is made with specific reference to Augustin Thierry.

10. Tocqueville to Senior, conversation of August 25, 1850, *OC*, VI, pt. 2, p. 301 (*Conversations*, 1:137).

11. Ibid.; Tocqueville to Senior, conversation of May 2, 1857, *OC*, VI, pt. 2, p. 470 (*Conversations*, 2:176); Tocqueville to Jean-Jacques Ampère, September, 17, 1839, *OC*, XI, p. 129.

12. Jardin, *Tocqueville*, pp. 59–60.

13. Tocqueville to Senior, conversation of February 10, 1851, *OC*, VI, pt. 2, p. 346 (*Conversations*, 1:222–23); Jardin, *Tocqueville*, p. 62.

14. In 1843 Tocqueville enlisted Arthur de Gobineau's aid in compiling synopses of the German philosophers for his impending report to the Académie des sciences morales et politiques on the moral doctrines of the nineteenth century. See Gobineau's "Coup d'oeil général sur l'histoire de la morale," *OC*, IX, pp. 309–28. In 1844 he received from the Princess Belgiojoso Vico's *Science nouvelle* and read with interest her book-length introduction to it (*OC*, VII, 300–301).

15. Gossman, *Between History and Literature*, p. 36, with reference to the words of Michelet.

16. For Guizot's preeminence in the field of Restoration historiography, see Douglas Johnson, *Guizot: Aspects of French History, 1787–1874* (Toronto: University of Toronto Press, 1963), pp. 320–76, and Larry Siedentop, Introduction to Guizot, *The History of Civilization in Europe* (London: Penguin, 1997), pp. vii–xxxvii.

17. In making reference to these three cycles of Guizot's lectures, I will use the following editions: *The History of Civilization in Europe* [1828 lectures], trans. William Hazlitt, ed. with an introduction by Larry Siedentop (New York: Penguin Classics, 1997), and *Histoire de la Civilisation en France depuis la chute de l'Empire romain* [December 1828–30 lectures], 12th ed., vol. 1 (Paris: Didier, 1872) and 10th ed., vols. 2, 3, and 4 (Paris: Didier, 1868).

18. "Notes on Guizot's course on the history of civilization in France (1829–30)," *OC*, XVI, pp. 439–534. Tocqueville reviewed Beaumont's lecture notes for at least two of Guizot's classes that precede those for which we have his own notes; he indicated as well that he attended unspecified earlier lectures in Guizot's course (Tocqueville to Beaumont, March 18, 1829, *OC*, VIII, pt. 1, pp. 76–77).

19. Tocqueville to Beaumont, October 5, 1828, *OC*, VIII, pt. 1, pp. 47–71 (*Journeys*, pp. 21–41). Since Guizot's 1828 lectures circulated as part of France's vibrant underground press (*OC*, XVI, p. 441n) and were quickly published by Pichon et Didier later that year, Tocqueville could well have read them, even if he did not attend them in person.

20. Tocqueville to Beaumont, August 30, 1829, *OC*, VIII, pt. 1, p. 80.

21. For Tocqueville's use of Guizot's *Mémoires relatifs à l'histoire de France, depuis la fondation de la monarchie française jusqu'au 13e siècle*, 30 vols. (1823–35), see Tocqueville to Beaumont, September 15, 1829, *OC*, VIII, pt. 1, p. 83. In this letter, Tocqueville suggested that he owned his own volumes of the *Mémoires*.

22. Tocqueville to Beaumont, August 30, 1829, *OC*, VIII, pt. 1, p. 80.

23. As I have noted, Tocqueville's readings in history and philosophy were well developed by 1828. He thus would have integrated his coursework and readings of Guizot at this time within a frame that had been shaped and was continuing to be shaped by his readings of Montesquieu and Rousseau, with whom he showed such familiarity in his first published writings of 1835. For Montesquieu's influence on *Democracy in America,* volume 1, see Melvin Richter, "The Uses of Theory: Tocqueville's Adaptation of Montesquieu," in *Essays in Theory and History,* ed. Melvin Richter (Cambridge: Harvard University Press, 1970), 74–102. For Rousseau's influence on the *Memoir on Poverty,* see Michael Bressolette, "Tocqueville et le paupérisme: L'influence de Rousseau," *Littératures* (Annales publiées par la Faculté des lettres et sciences humaines de Toulouse) 16 (1969): 67–78.

24. Guizot, *Histoire de la civilisation en France,* 2:119.

25. Ibid., 3:109. For Tocqueville's notes for this session of January 9, 1830, see *OC,* XVI, p. 494.

26. For Guizot's introductory comments about the importance of "the moral state" to his historical system, see *Histoire de la civilisation en France,* 1:108–12. In this fourth lecture of his second cycle, he distinguished his views from those of eighteenth-century thinkers such as Montesquieu and Voltaire, who emphasized institutional and governmental factors ("the social state") as the key forces in shaping a people. For Guizot's course syllabus for his third cycle illustrating the range of components for a complete "history of civilization," see *OC,* XVI, p. 485.

27. "Notes on Guizot's Course," session of July 18, 1829, *OC,* XVI, p. 472.

28. Ibid., session of December 5, 1829, *OC,* XVI, p. 478. Tocqueville's personal observations are in italics, as determined from a careful comparison by the editor, Françoise Mélonio, with Guizot's text.

29. Ibid., pp. 481, 496–97, 501, and 533.

30. Aurelian Craiutu reaches a similar conclusion in his own assessment of Tocqueville's reading notes of Guizot: "It is important to note here that Tocqueville was more interested in Guizot's sociological *method* than the content of his lectures." See "Tocqueville and the Political Thought of the French Doctrinaires," p. 475.

31. John Stuart Mill, "Guizot's Lectures on European Civilization," *London Review* 4 (July–January 1835–36): 309, republished in *Collected Works of John Stuart Mill,* ed. John M. Robson, vol. 20, *Essays on French History and Historians* (Toronto: University of Toronto Press, 1985), p. 370.

32. "Note sur l'Inde en faisant en Novembre 1841 la lecture de l'histoire de ce pays par M. Barchou de Penhoën," *OC,* III, pt. 1, p. 511; Tocqueville to Gobineau, November 17, 1853, *OC,* IX, pp. 202–203 (*Selected Letters,* pp. 298–99); "Notes sur la Révolution française de Thiers," *OC,* XVI, pp. 537–40; Tocqueville to Senior, conversation of August 19, 1850, *OC,* VI, pt. 2, pp. 286–87 (*Conversations,* 1:112–14).

33. Tocqueville to Corcelle, May 13, 1852, *OC,* XV, pt. 2, p. 56; Tocqueville to Hubert de Tocqueville, February 23, 1857, *OC,* XIV, pp. 328–29 (*Selected Letters,* pp. 350–51).

34. Ibid., p. 329 (*Selected Letters,* p. 351).

35. Tocqueville, "1.—Sorrento, December 1850—Napoleon," *OC*, II, pt. 2, p. 301 (*OR*, 2:185).

36. Guizot, *History of Civilization in Europe*, pp. 188, 189.

37. Ibid., pp. 238, 240–41.

38. Ibid., p. 188.

39. Tocqueville to Beaumont, October 5, 1828, *OC*, VIII, pt. 1, p. 67 (*Journeys*, p. 37).

40. Ibid., p. 68 (ibid., p. 38).

41. Ibid., pp. 68–69 (ibid., pp. 38–39).

42. Ibid., p. 69 (ibid., p. 39). Furet also designates Guizot as Tocqueville's probable target, drawing our attention to the sharp "disagreement" in the views of Tocqueville and Guizot in their respective readings of English history at this time ("Intellectual Origins," p. 121). In his introduction to Guizot's 1828 lectures, Larry Siedentop overemphasizes Tocqueville's debt to Guizot, I believe, saying that his "enthusiasm for [the three cycles of lectures] knew no bounds" (Introduction to *The History of Civilization in Europe*, p. xxxi). Yes, Tocqueville was enamored by Guizot's historical method, but no, he did not subscribe to Guizot's "balance" of centralization and local liberties, as we can see in his comments here. Aurelian Craiutu similarly overstates the compatibility of the professor's and student's views on local liberties and centralization ("Tocqueville and the Political Thought of the French Doctrinaires," pp. 476, 479–83). Charles Pouthas articulates a view more consistent with Tocqueville's, I believe, when he aptly summarizes Guizot's Faustian trade-off: "all things carefully considered, [Guizot], in contrast to Augustin Thierry, sells off communal liberties at a bargain price" (*Guizot pendant la Restauration* [Paris: Librairie Plon, 1923], p. 331). See, too, Edouard Scherer's 1863 distinction between Guizot's Doctrinaire school and Tocqueville's liberal school: "The former demands order, prepared to add liberty to it thereafter; the latter proclaims liberty as tantamount to order, its condition and foundation" (cited in Mélonio, *Tocqueville and the French*, p. 120).

43. Ibid. (ibid.).

44. Guizot, *Histoire de la civilisation en France*, 4:11–12.

45. "Notes on Guizot's course," sessions of May 8 (*OC*, XVI, pp. 516–17), May 8 and 15 (pp. 520, 523), and May 29, 1830 (p. 533).

46. Ibid., session of May 29, 1830, pp. 532–33.

47. Guizot, *History of Civilization in Europe*, pp. 131–32.

48. "Notes on Guizot's course," session of May 29, 1830, *OC*, XVI, p. 533.

49. Tocqueville to Charles Stoffels, April 21, 1830, *DA* (ed. Nolla), 2:323. For a study that specifies additional levels of "Tocqueville's profound departure from Guizot's confident if conservative rationalism and progressivism," see Ralph C. Hancock, "The Modern Revolution and the Collapse of Moral Analogy: Tocqueville and Guizot," *Perspectives on Political Science* 30, no. 4 (Fall 2001): 213–17.

50. "Notes on Guizot's course," session of May 1, 1830, *OC*, XVI, pp. 513, 515.

51. *Review*, p. 161 ("État social et politique," p. 58).

52. Tocqueville to Charles Stoffels, April 21, 1830, *DA* (ed. Nolla), 2:323.

53. Tocqueville to Eugène Stoffels, October 5, 1836, *OC* (Beaumont), V, p. 436 (*Selected Letters*, p. 113).

54. *DA* (ed. Nolla), 2:248n.

55. Tocqueville to Beaumont, October 5, 1828, *OC*, VIII, pt. 3, p. 53 (*Journeys*, p. 24).

56. Tocqueville's note, "Of Centralization," appears in *DA* (ed. Nolla) 1:79–80. In it he argued that partisans of decentralization had often adopted untenable rhetorical positions, advocating, for example, separate systems of justice administered by France's seventeen separate parlements that resulted in "a political monstrosity" leading the king to consolidate "real power" in his own hands. "We have often experienced the abuse of the concept [decentralization]," he added, "without knowing the concept itself." In his note, Tocqueville demonstrated his early identification of democracy with centralization: "It is democratic governments that arrive most quickly at administrative centralization while losing their political liberty." He also demonstrated the abiding tension in his view of the aristocracy's potential contributions to local liberty: while they could serve as a prime source of resistance to administrative centralization, they posed a threat to decentralized localities owing to their "envious, haughty, exclusive" character.

57. Charles Augustin Sainte-Beuve, "Nouvelle correspondence inédite de Tocqueville," *Le Constitutionnel,* December 25, 1865, republished in *Nouveaux lundis* (Paris: Michel Lévy Frères, 1868), 10:327.

58. See Mansfield and Winthrop, Editors' Introduction to *DA,* xxxv, for this distinction in the authors' two views of despotism. Tocqueville's early draft that demonstrates the importance he attached to this contrast with Montesquieu is in TA (Beinecke), B.II.b.

59. Tocqueville to Beaumont, October 5, 1828, *OC*, VIII, pt. 1, p. 67 (*Journeys*, p. 37) [Lingard]; "Analyse de Platon," *OC*, XVI, pp. 555–57; Tocqueville to Kergorlay, September 4, 1837, *OC* XIII, pt. 1, p. 474 and to Sir George Lewis, October 6, 1856, *OC* (Beaumont), VII, pp. 407–9 [Voltaire]; Tocqueville to Corcelle, July 22, 1854, *OC,* XV, pt. 2, pp. 107–8 [Hegel]; Tocqueville to Senior, conversation of May 13, 1857, *OC,* VI, pt. 2, pp. 478–79 (*Conversations,* 2:185–86) [Martin].

60. Tocqueville to Beaumont, October 5, 1828, *OC,* VIII, pt. 1, pp. 67–68 (*Journeys,* pp. 37–38).

61. Tocqueville to Senior, conversation of May 13, 1857, *OC,* VI, pt. 2, pp. 478–79 (*Conversations,* 2:185). For Beaumont's applause for an anonymous English critic's scathing rejection on similar grounds of French historical studies—from Guizot to Thierry to Blanc to Michelet to Martin—see Beaumont to Tocqueville, March 3, 1858, *OC,* VIII, pt. 3, p. 548, with reference to "Henri Martin's *History of France,*" *Edinburgh Review* 106 (October 1857): 382–407.

62. Tocqueville to Beaumont, September 19, 1829, *OC,* VIII, pt. 1, p. 88.

63. Prosper de Barante, *Histoire des ducs de Bourgogne de la Maison de Valois, 1364–1477,* 12 vols. (Paris, 1824–26). In "The Historical and Political Thought of Prosper de Barante," in *Four Studies in French Romantic Historical Writing,* Johns Hopkins University Studies in Historical and Political Science, vol. 71, no. 2 (Baltimore: Johns Hopkins Press, 1955), p. 57, Friedrick Engel-Janosi states that "in the histories of historical writing, Prosper de

Barante, 1782–1866, lives on as the man of a preface to one book." For the continuing
interest in Barante's preface as a "particularly lucid treatment of some of the main
philosophical and rhetorical problems encountered by the new school of historians,"
see Gossman, *Between History and Literature*, pp. 117–23, and Stephen Bann, *The Clothing of
Clio* (Cambridge: Cambridge University Press, 1984), pp. 37–47.

64. Barante, *Histoire des ducs de Bourgogne*, 5th ed., 12 vols. (Paris: Delloye, 1839), 1:43.
Barante's full preface is on 1:1–88 of this edition.

65. Barante adopted Quintilian's comment as the inscription with which he
prefaced each volume of his work.

66. Gossman, *Between History and Literature*, p. 123.

67. Barante, Preface to *Histoire des ducs de Bourgogne*, 1:3.

68. Ibid., p. 41.

69. Ibid., p. 66.

70. Tocqueville to Beaumont, September 19, 1829, *OC*, VIII, pt. 1, p. 88.

71. Tocqueville to Beaumont, October 25, 1829, *OC*, VIII, pt. 1, p. 91.

72. Tocqueville to Beaumont, September 19, 1829, *OC*, VIII, pt. 1, p. 88.

73. Tocqueville to Paul Clamorgan, March 7, 1848, *OC*, X, p. 451 (*Selected Letters*, p.
204). I am using Edward T. Gargan's description of this period in *Alexis de Tocqueville: The
Critical Years, 1848–1851* (Washington, DC: Catholic University of America Press, 1955).

74. Tocqueville to Beaumont, April 22, 1848, *OC*, VIII, pt. 2, pp. 12–13 (*Selected Letters*,
p. 211).

75. G. P. Gooch, *History and Historians in the Nineteenth Century* (London: Longmans,
Green, 1952), p. 192.

76. Tocqueville, conversation with Senior of August 19, 1850, *OC*, VI, pt. 2, pp.
286–87 (*Conversations*, 1: 112–14). I have excerpted additional portions of Tocqueville's
pointed comments in my epigraph to this chapter. The *OC* deletes Tocqueville's
concluding assertion: "I hope one day to write them."

77. Ampère, "L'article nécrologique," *OC*, XI, p. 443.

78. In addition to the general plan and chapter outline referenced to this period in
OC, II, pt. 2, pp. 301–4 (*OR*, 2:185–88), I believe that Tocqueville's "Original Idea" (*OC*, II,
pt. 2, p. 29 [*OR*, 2:27]) dates from 1850–51 at Sorrento as well, even though scholars such
as Jardin (*Tocqueville: A Biography*, p. 489) and R. R. Palmer (*The Two Tocquevilles: Father and
Son* [Princeton: Princeton University Press, 1987], pp. 147, 227) have assigned it an 1856
date. The confusion stems from the full title for the note that reads: "Original Idea,
General and Primitive Sentiment of the Subject. To reread several times to put myself
back into the great path of my thoughts (1856)." This title is written on a separate
sheet of paper from the document itself, with a different pen; Beaumont indicates
that he found "this inscription on the sheet serving as envelope" (TA, box 44, folder
12). Most plausibly, Tocqueville appended this title in 1856, as he says, to his "original"
and "primitive" formulation drafted when he first sought to define his subject; he
would thus have added the title when he sifted and organized his 2,700-plus pages of
reading notes to find those that could be helpful for his sequel. Indeed, on a number
of occasions in the TA, we find such "(1856)" notations, as attached to his comments

looking back at his 1836 essay (see below, chapter 3, note 5) and the June 26, 1853 draft of his work (see below, chapter 4, note 72), and forward to proposed chapters on the Terror and the movement of the Revolution beyond the borders of France (*OC*, II, pt. 2, pp. 229 and 246).

79. Sainte-Beuve, "Nouvelle correspondence inédite," 10:326, 324.

80. Tocqueville to Kergorlay, December 15, 1850, *OC*, XIII, pt. 2, pp. 230–31 (*Selected Letters*, pp. 253–55).

81. Tocqueville to Beaumont, December 26, 1850, *OC*, VIII, pt. 2, pp. 343–44.

82. Tocqueville's interest in Montesquieu's Roman work dated from at least the time of his writing of *Democracy in America*, volume 1, where he made reference to it in two of the three direct citations to Montesquieu within his text (*DA*, 233n, 383).

83. Tocqueville to Kergorlay, December 15, 1850, *OC*, XIII, pt. 2, p. 232 (*Selected Letters*, p. 256).

84. "2. Narrate and judge at the same time . . . ," *OC*, II, pt. 2, pp. 302–4 (*OR*, 2:186–88).

85. *OC*, II, pt. 2, p. 29n, (*OR*, 2:375).

86. Thiers, Preface to *The History of the French Revolution*, trans. Frederick Shoberl (Philadelphia: Carey and Hart, 1843), p. xiii. "Perhaps the moment when actors are about to expire," Thiers said, "is the most proper for writing this history: we can collect their evidence without participating in all their passions."

87. Letter to *London Times*, published December 11, 1851, *OC*, VI, pt. 1, pp. 119–29 (*Selected Letters*, pp. 266–78).

88. Tocqueville to Beaumont, letters of January 13, February 1, February 18, February 24, March 7, April 7, April 22, and May 1, 1852, *OC*, VIII, pt. 3, pp. 11–46.

89. Tocqueville to J.-B. Roussel, December 14, 1851, *OC*, X, p. 562.

90. "2. Narrate and judge at the same time . . . ," *OC*, II, pt. 2, p. 302 (*OR*, 2:186).

91. TA, box 44, folder 29 (*OR*, 2:188).

92. For Molé's suggestion of A.-C. Thibaudeau's *Mémoires sur le Consulat*, accompanied by one of Tocqueville's vivid personal jabs, see *OC*, II, pt. 2, p. 314.

93. Richomme to Tocqueville, June 20, 1852, TA, box 44, folder 44.

94. TA, box 44, folder 52, Lafayette reading notes, addendum (a) on back side. Tocqueville here transcribed Lafayette's comments in his *Mémoires, correspondance et manuscrits publiés par sa famille*, 5 vols. (Paris: H. Fournier Aîné, Editeur, 1837–38), 5:134. These memoirs were assembled, annotated, published, and presented to Tocqueville by his friend and Lafayette's son-in-law, Corcelle (see Tocqueville to Beaumont, May 14, 1837, *OC*, VIII, pt. 1, p. 183).

95. Ibid., p. 1(b), with reference to Lafayette's passage in *Mémoires*, 4:412.

96. Tocqueville referred to Lafayette as "a contemporary" on two occasions in his chapters. See *OC*, II, pt. 2, pp. 276 and 277 (*OR*, 2:197).

97. TA, box 44, folder 29.

98. TA, box 43, folder K, subfile, "Book of B. Constant titled *De la force du gouvernement actuel*, 1796," p. 14 (*OR*, 2:223). For the passage Tocqueville referred to here, see *Constant*,

ed. Philippe Raynaud (Paris: Flammarion, 1988), pp. 57–58. Tocqueville's interest in Constant is apparent by his subsequent transfer of his notes into folder K, one of the seventeen folders of his "Reading Notes" in box 43 that he will use directly for his writing of *The Old Regime.*

99. Ibid., pp. 14–14(b) (*OR*, 2:223). The passage transcribed by Tocqueville is in *Constant*, ed. Raynaud, p. 84.

100. Ibid., p. 14(b) (*OR*, 2:223). See *Constant*, ed. Raynaud, p. 172n, for this passage.

101. Ibid. I have been unable to locate this passage in *Constant*, ed. Raynaud. I cite these passages in detail since the subject of Tocqueville's familiarity with Constant has been a matter of speculation to scholars, with George Armstrong Kelly raising the question, "Why, as seems likely, did Tocqueville not read Constant, or read him seriously?" *The Humane Comedy: Constant, Tocqueville and French Liberalism* (Cambridge: Cambridge University Press, 1992), p. 3. For other reflections on the Tocqueville-Constant relationship, see R. Pierre Marcel, *Essai politique sur Alexis de Tocqueville* (Paris: Librairies Félix Alcan et Guillaumin Réunies, 1910), pp. 180–81, and Jean-Claude Lamberti, "De Benjamin Constant à Alexis de Tocqueville," *France-Forum,* May–June 1984, pp. 19–26.

102. Tocqueville to Beaumont, June 15, 1852, *OC*, VIII, pt. 3, pp. 51–52.

103. Tocqueville to Kergorlay, July 22, 1852, *OC*, XIII, pt. 2, p. 244. In his letter to Beaumont of July 1 (*OC*, VIII, pt. 3, p. 58), Tocqueville said he had been "seriously at work" for eight days.

104. I am basing this date on Tocqueville's comments to Kergorlay on July 22 that "one or two chapters are already drafted" (ibid., p. 243). This curious formulation—"one or two chapters"—is explained when we realize, by looking at Tocqueville's manuscript, that Tocqueville was undecided whether the second chapter should stand separately or be "perhaps the continuation of the same chapter," meaning his first; Tocqueville even numbered the pages in the chapters as part of one continuous unit rather than two separate ones (TA, box 45). That the chapters are indeed completed is affirmed by Beaumont, who wrote on August 16 to say that Madame Tocqueville had written his wife "that you already have two excellent chapters completed" (*OC*, VIII, pt. 3, p. 68). I am giving the chapters an earlier date than Jardin, who says: "In June he returns to Tocqueville where he will write, from July to September, the two chapters" ("Note critique" to *OC*, II, pt. 2, p. 13).

105. Tocqueville to Beaumont, August 24, 1852, *OC*, VIII, pt. 3, p. 71.

106. *OC*, II, pt. 2, pp. 273–74 (*OR*, 2:195).

107. TA, box 45, filed in the "Rubbish of the first two chapters written at Tocqueville in 1852—end of the Republic," with reference to Jacques Mallet du Pan, *Mémoires et correspondance pour servir à l'histoire de la Révolution française,* collected and arranged by A. Sayous (Paris: J. Cherbuliez, 1851); Comte Antoine Thibaudeau, *Mémoires sur la Convention et le Directoire* (Paris: Baudouin Frères, 1824); and Joseph Fiévée, *Correspondance et relations de J. Fiévée avec Bonaparte, publiée par l'auteur* (Paris: A. Desrez, 1836).

108. Constant, *De la force,* in *Constant*, ed. Raynaud, p. 83.

109. *OC,* II, pt. 2, pp. 270–71 (*OR,* 2:192).

110. Ibid., p. 269 (*OR,* 2:191).

111. Ibid., pp. 270–71 (*OR,* 2:192–93).

112. Constant, *Des effets de la Terreur,* in *Constant,* ed. Raynaud, p. 164n.

113. *OC,* II, pt. 2, p. 271 and 271n (*OR,* 2:193). For a full treatment of the Constant-Lezay debate, plus a statement of his belief that Lezay anticipated in his work key Tocquevillian themes in *The Old Regime,* see François Furet, "Une polémique thermidorienne sur la Terreur: Autour de Benjamin Constant," *Passé Présent* 2 (1983): 44–55, with the Tocquevillian parallels noted on pp. 49–50.

114. *OC,* II, pt. 2, p. 275 (*OR,* 2:195).

115. Ibid., p. 276 (*OR,* 2:196).

116. Ibid., pp. 276–77 (*OR,* 2:197).

117. Ibid., p. 292 (*OR,* 2:208).

118. Tocqueville to Beaumont, letters of June 15, July 1, and August 24, 1852, *OC,* VIII, pt. 3, pp. 52, 58 and 71.

119. *OC,* II, pt. 2, p. 287 (*OR,* 2:204).

120. I am using "culture" here in the broad sense of "changes in belief and sensibility" defined by Roger Chartier in *The Cultural Origins of the French Revolution,* trans. Lydia G. Cochrane (Durham, NC: Duke University Press, 1991), p. 2. Tocqueville, of course, studied "political culture," as we will see throughout this book. He also studied popular culture, as reflected in his reading notes on the literary and fashion magazine *Le Mois* (*OC,* II, pt. 2, pp. 313–14 [*OR,* 2:235–37]).

121. François Furet, "Tocqueville," in *A Critical Dictionary of the French Revolution,* ed. François Furet and Mona Ozouf, trans. Arthur Goldhammer (Cambridge: Harvard University Press, 1989), p. 1022.

122. Tocqueville to Beaumont, July 16, 1852, *OC,* VIII, pt. 3, p. 62.

123. *OC,* II, pt. 2, pp. 274–76, 283 (*OR,* 2:195–96, 201).

124. Ibid., pp. 273n, 282 (*OR,* 2:194, 201).

125. Lionel Gossman describes the efforts of Augustin Thierry to achieve his own balance of what Gossman calls "syntagmatic" and "paradigmatic" ordering of historical events in *Between History and Literature,* p. 98.

126. "Original Idea," *OC,* II, pt. 2, p. 29n (*OR,* 2:375).

127. *OC,* II, pt. 2, p. 226 (*OR,* 2:216).

128. Mona Ozouf notes as well this perspicacity of the writers of the era—in whose works "all the broad interpretations of the Terror already existed *in nuce*"—in her article, "The Terror after the Terror: An Immediate History," *The French Revolution and the Creation of Modern Political Culture, 1789–1848,* vol. 4, *The Terror,* ed. Keith Michael Baker (New York: Pergamon Press, 1989), p. 4. Such thoughtful reflection in a period so close in time to the Terror, she says, causes us to reassess our own belief in the indispensability of " 'historical distance' " to our understanding of historical events.

129. Tocqueville to Beaumont, August 24, 1852, *OC,* VIII, pt. 3, p. 71.

THREE

1. Tocqueville to Pierre Freslon, September 7, 1852 (TA, unpublished [OR, 1:8]).

2. François Furet, *Interpreting the French Revolution,* trans. Elborg Forster (Cambridge: Cambridge University Press; Paris: Éditions de la Maison des Sciences de l'Homme, 1981), pp. 161–62.

3. Alexis de Tocqueville, "Political and Social Condition of France: First Article," *London and Westminster Review* 3 and 25 (April 1836): 137–69.

4. Larry Siedentop, *Tocqueville* (Oxford: Oxford University Press, 1994), p. 114.

5. Tocqueville appended this notation, dated "(1856)," to a stray sheet titled, "Article for the English review of Mill and drafts and diverse notes" (TA, box 42).

6. See above, chapter 1, p. 5.

7. Jardin, "Note Critique" to *OC,* II, pt. 2, pp. 7–26; Furet and Mélonio, "Introduction" to *OR,* 1:1–79 and 2:1–21; Lamberti, "Introduction à l'*Ancien régime*" in *Tocqueville* (three works) (Paris: Robert Laffont, 1986), pp. 895–920.

8. The essay was republished first in *Memoir, Letters, and Remains of Alexis de Tocqueville,* translated from the French by the translator of *Napoleon's Correspondence with King Joseph* 2 vols. (London, 1861; Boston: Ticknor and Fields, 1862 1:204–52), and subsequently in *OC* (Beaumont), VIII, pp. 1–54. For Tocqueville's insistence on its anonymous publication, see Tocqueville to Mill, December 5, 1835, *OC,* VI, pt. 1, p. 304.

9. Beaumont, "Preface" to *OC* (Beaumont) I, p. xxxi.

10. Sainte-Beuve, *Moniteur Universel,* December 31, 1860, republished in *Causeries de Lundi* (Paris: Garnier, 1862), 15:105n. Sainte-Beuve attributed the comment to an anonymous critic.

11. Senior, Introduction to 1836 essay, *Memoir,* 1:202.

12. *Review,* pp. 163, 160 ("État social et politique," pp. 60, 57).

13. Ibid., p. 166 (ibid., p. 62).

14. Ibid., p. 164 (ibid., p. 60).

15. Ibid., pp. 153, 156 (ibid., p. 52).

16. Tocqueville to Gallemand, August 20, 1852, *OC,* X, p. 566.

17. Tocqueville's inquiries and the documents he assembled to answer them are in TA, box 43, folder O, "Statistical studies and others done at Tocqueville," pp. 17–37 and box 43, folder A, pp. 42–46. In *OC,* II, pt. 2, pp. 293–98, Jardin published Tocqueville's formulations of his research efforts from folder O in a "Note," without the miscellaneous support documents. Jardin described these research efforts, mistakenly, I believe, as being "anterior" (p. 293) to Tocqueville's writing of his two Napoleonic chapters. Although Tocqueville's categories of financial gain were indeed all mentioned in his second 1852 chapter (*OC,* II, pt. 2, pp. 283–86), his marginal notes there show his investigations to be prospective, looking ahead to his efforts to quantify them. Since I date Tocqueville's writing of the chapters to the period of approximately June 23 through July 22, 1852, I believe he began his feudal rights research in the latter part of July and continued it until he left Normandy for Paris in early October.

18. Le Peletier d'Aunay to Tocqueville, responding to Tocqueville's letter of July 19, 1852 (TA, unpublished).

19. TA, box 43, folder O, pp. 32 and 33, published in *OC,* II, pt. 2, pp. 297, note (a), and 298. Tocqueville indicated that his conversation with Birette took place on July 28, 1852.

20. Tocqueville to Gallemand, letters of August 20 and 28, 1852, *OC,* X, pp. 566–68 and 568–70. Gallemand to Tocqueville, August 25, 1852, TA, box 43, folder A, inserted at start of file; Gallemand to Tocqueville, August 31, 1852. Both Gallemand responses to Tocqueville's letters are unpublished. Following Gallemand's advice, Tocqueville wrote to Dubosc on August 29, 1852; he did not receive a response until late November, however, after he had left Tocqueville for Paris (Dubosc to Tocqueville, November 26, 1852, filed in TA, box 42).

21. Tocqueville to Kergorlay, July 22, 1852, *OC,* XIII, pt. 2, p. 244.

22. Kergorlay to Tocqueville, August 2, 1852, *OC,* XIII, pt. 2, pp. 245–50.

23. Ibid., pp. 246–47. That Kergorlay's comment was indeed prophetic can be seen by Furet's assertion, more than 125 years later, of the continuing impossibility of compiling such "incredibly diverse . . . scattered . . . and difficult to aggregate" facts and figures. See *Interpreting the French Revolution,* p. 93.

24. TA, box 43, folder A, p. 33.

25. TA, box 43, folder O, pp. 5–7. Tocqueville indicated his satisfaction with his findings in these investigations: "What a host of useful observations furnished by a single inventory!" (p. 6[b]).

26. Tocqueville to Kergorlay, August 20, 1852, *OC,* XIII, pt. 2, p. 252. In four ensuing years of research, right up to the publication of his book, Tocqueville would never relinquish his hopes of "touching bottom" in this effort. Thus, in his *Old Regime* manuscript submitted to the printers in 1856 (TA, box 39), he drafted the following sentence for book 2, chapter 1 (*OR,* 1:116 after first paragraph): "I undertook extensive research to learn approximately the value of all feudal rights," adding the marginal note: "Very good if I can find something precise." Unable to achieve such documentation, he dropped the sentence from the final text.

27. TA, box 43, folder O, pp. 8–16.

28. Ibid, pp. 10–11, with DuParc's letter of September 27, 1852 on p. 10. An additional draft of notes on Réville's "record of properties" is in TA, box 43, folder A, p. 27.

29. This appears to be the basis for Tocqueville's conclusion in *OR,* 1:112: "I myself took infinite pains to reconstruct, as it were, the cadastre of the Old Regime . . . and I saw, on comparing property-records with our modern-day rolls, that the number of landed proprietors in those villages reached one-half and often two-thirds of the current number."

30. Tocqueville to Freslon, September 7, 1852 (TA, unpublished).

31. "Biens d'émigrés in the canton of St. Pierre-Eglise," TA, box 43, folder O, pp. 15–16. The 1824 document Tocqueville used was the "Summary of excerpts from each of the procès-verbaux of the sales of biens d'émigrés, placed in the archives of the Department of La Manche, general instructions No. 1135, 1139, 1142, 1143." Tocqueville summarized these findings in *OR,* 1:113: "But if one wishes to consult the

procès-verbaux themselves of these sales, as I have had the patience on occasion to do, one will see that most of these lands were purchased by persons who already possessed other [properties]; so that, if the property changed hands, the number of landowners increased far less than one might imagine."

32. Tocqueville to Gallemand, August 20, 1852, *OC,* X, p. 567.

33. Tocqueville to Freslon, September 7, 1852 (TA, unpublished).

34. Tocqueville to Madame de Circourt, September 18, 1852, *OC,* XVIII, p. 85.

35. TA, box 43, folder A, pp. 42–46.

36. Ibid., pp. 16–24. Tocqueville used the *Dictionnaire de droit et de pratique* (Paris, 1749) by Claude-Joseph de Ferrière.

37. Ibid., p. 42.

38. TA, box 43, folder O, p. 18. Tocqueville commented humorously on how to assess Sieyès's lower figure: "Although Sieyès was already very much a revolutionary, he was still very much a *priest.* This accounts for the fact that this evaluation, even made by him, is more often below than above the correct figure."

39. Ibid.

40. Ibid., pp. 18–18(b).

41. TA, box 43, folder A, p. 40.

42. TA, box 43, folder J, title page of reading file of Gaultier de Biauzat, dated "September 1853," pp. 41–53, with reference to J. F. Gaultier de Biauzat, *Doléances sur les surcharges que les gens du peuple supportent* (n.p., 1788).

43. For Tocqueville's conversations with Professors Walter and Oelschner in late June and July 1854, see TA, box 43, folder Q, pp. 22–38. A survey of Tocqueville's questions for his German feudal rights interlocutors exists in TA, box 42 (*OR,* 2:265–66). Tocqueville drew endnotes 7 and 8 in *The Old Regime* from these conversations.

In September, after reading *Das gesamte Württembergische Privatrecht* (1837) by August Ludwig von Reyscher, Tocqueville commented: "In reading this book, I was struck by the great analogy that existed between what happened in Würtemburg in 1836 and in France in 1788, particularly with respect to the position of the peasants and the tenure of the land" (folder Q, p. 107[b]). Tocqueville proceeded to suggest that these German books might provide "the best way" to understand the feudal situation in France in 1788, since they were written with current language and ideas, not in the "old form with old ideas" of the prerevolutionary French documents.

44. TA, box 43, folder J, reading file of Biauzat, p. 43(b).

45. Tocqueville's reading notes on Blackstone, dated "June 1853," are in TA, box 43, folder L, pp. 1–24; they are based on his reading of William Blackstone, *Commentaires sur les lois anglaises,* vols. 1, 2, and 4, trans. from English by N. M. Chompré (Paris: Firmin Didot, 1822). A summary comment, drawn from pp. 13–15 of the file and showing Tocqueville's special interests in this reading, is published in *OC,* II, pt. 2, pp. 356–59. For Tocqueville's assessment of his reading of Blackstone, see Tocqueville to Senior, July 2, 1853, *OC,* VI, pt. 2, pp. 160–61.

46. "Sujets de Prix," *Séances et Travaux de l'Académie des Sciences Morales et Politiques* 21 (January–June 1852): 507–8. The question was proposed by the Académie's Committee

of "General and Philosophical History," whose members were Guizot, Joseph Naudet, Mignet, Michelet, Thiers, and Thierry.

47. "Décisions au sujet des prix proposés pour l'année 1850," *Séances et Travaux* 18 (July–December 1850): 82–83.

48. Guizot, "Rapport sur les mémoires envoyés pour concourir au prix," presented in session of April 30, 1853, *Séances et Travaux* 25 (July–September 1853): 306–7.

49. I date Tocqueville's reading of Dareste's work to late April or May 1853, the period when Dareste received the Académie's prize. Clearly, Tocqueville began his reading after completing his own archival work of April 1853 in the Paris intendancy, as we can tell from several references he made to this archival work in his Darestian notes (TA, box 43, folder E, pp. 8[b], 21[b] and 22[b]). He completed his Darestian reading before leaving Paris for Tours at the end of May 1853, I believe, since he concluded it with a bibliographic list containing books he would bring with him to Tours, several of which he incorporated as well on another list titled "Different authors cited by the author of the principal memoir on the condition of the agricultural classes—1852," contained in TA, box 42. Tocqueville continued to use Dareste's work while at Tours, writing to Beaumont on July 1, 1853 (*OC,* VIII, pt. 3, pp. 132–33), to request six works, five of which were cited by Dareste in his work and noted by Tocqueville on a further bibliographic list in TA, box 42, that featured comments from "the author of the memoir," the shorthand he most often employed for his references to Dareste.

50. A.-E.-C. Dareste de la Chavanne, *Histoire des classes agricoles en France depuis Saint Louis jusqu'à Louis XVI* (Paris: Librairie de Gillaumin, 1853), preface, p. i. This work was the one that Dareste published after receiving the Académie's prize; although the page numbers do not match the original version of his "Mémoire" submitted to the Académie and used by Tocqueville, Dareste tells us that his published *Histoire* is "just about the same as the one I submitted to the Academy" (preface, p. ii). This 1853 published version is the one I have used for reading Dareste's "Mémoire."

51. Tocqueville dated his reading files for Le Trosne (June 1853), Quesnay (July 1853), Boncerf (November 15, 1853), and Haxthausen (October 1853) from his sojourn at Tours; in response to his request, he obtained Mirabeau's *L'ami des hommes* with Beaumont's help in July 1853 as well (see Beaumont to Tocqueville, July 2 [3], 1853, *OC,* VIII, pt. 3, p. 134). He had, of course, already read during the summer of 1852 a variety of feudal rights sources of his own, including Renauldon and de Ferrière, whom Dareste also comments on.

52. Dareste had considerable expertise in the area of France's central administration, having written an earlier treatise for which he had received the Académie's prize in 1847 and that he had published the next year as *Histoire de l'administration en France et des progrès du pouvoir royal* (Paris: Guillaumin, 1848).

53. Dareste, *Histoire,* p. 264n. Dareste's reference to Lamberville's pursuit of royal patronage was contained in a single brief footnote: "It is true that this author, Lamberville, solicited the post of inspector general of peat bogs in France." Lamberville's published work is *Discours politiques et economiques* (Paris: S. Thiboust, 1626). Tocqueville's reference to "a Mr. Lemberville [*sic*]," culminating in his query, "Who among us has not known this Lemberville?" is in *OR,* 1:159.

54. TA, box 43, folder E, p. 11(b).

55. Dareste, *Histoire*, p. 318.

56. Ibid., preface, p. ii. Since Dareste's preface was written on November 16, 1853, for his soon-to-be published *Histoire*, not for his original "Mémoire," Tocqueville would not have read this particular comment. The preface generally reflected Dareste's efforts to respond to Guizot's criticisms of April 30 by offering a view of his findings that sought to explain underlying causes.

57. Tocqueville observed: "Throughout his work, the author, it is true, seems more opposed to antifeudal passions and favorable in certain respects to the rights of seigneurs." He commented that it was surprising that the very feudal experts who had most closely studied feudal rights should have held such sympathies. See TA, box 43, Folder E, p. 18(b).

58. Dareste, *Histoire*, p. 213.

59. TA, box 43, folder E, p. 6(b). Tocqueville comments on Dareste's passage in *Histoire*, p. 119, with specific reference to two remarks by Adam Smith.

60. Dareste served as a sounding board, not an adversary, in Tocqueville's notes. On many occasions Tocqueville indicated his respect for Dareste's observations as being made "very plausibly" (p. 4[b]) or "with reason" (p. 15). Dareste, too, saw property as more mobile and feudal rights as less onerous in the eighteenth century (see, for example, *Histoire*, p. 134). He lacked, however, both Tocqueville's ability to contextualize the French feudal regime and his anger at the royal government's political shortsightedness and abuses.

61. TA, box 43, folder E, pp. 12–12(b), with reference to Dareste's passage in *Histoire*, pp. 167–68.

62. Ibid., pp. 8, 15(b)–16, and 17–17(b), with reference to Dareste's passages, *Histoire*, pp. 140, 193 and 205–8.

63. Ibid., pp. 17(b)–18, with reference to Dareste's passage, *Histoire*, p. 211.

64. Ibid., p. 8(b), with reference to Dareste's passage, *Histoire*, pp. 140–41.

65. Ibid., p. 5, with further notations by Tocqueville of the same paradox on pp. 6, 8(b), 12(b), 15(b), and 17–17(b).

66. Ibid., p. 12(b).

67. Young is identified in the first case only as "an excellent contemporary observer" (*OR*, 1:112). Tocqueville took the anonymous quote from his reading notes in TA, box 43, folder N, "Arthur Young," p. 12.

68. In its title, Tocqueville's chapter purported to assess six centuries of rural French history. None of the other sources in his feudal archive predate the eighteenth century, so he appears to have relied on the contemporary historian, Dareste, for his claims about this earlier period.

69. Dareste, *Histoire*, p. ii.

70. In his manuscript (TA, box 39), Tocqueville indicates that he takes the Péréfix anecdote from "e.9": p. 9 [8] of his Darestian reading folder, E, in a transcription referenced to Dareste, *Histoire*, p. 139.

71. Dareste, *Histoire*, p. 238, with reference to Rousseau, *The Confessions* (Penguin Classic, 1970), bk. 4, pt. 1, pp. 159–60.

72. Ibid., pp. 244–45.

73. Furet, *Interpreting the French Revolution*, p. 141; Furet and Mélonio, introduction to *OR*, 1:20–21.

74. *Recollections*, p. 87.

75. Tocqueville to Freslon, September 7, 1852 (TA, unpublished).

FOUR

1. TA, box 43, folder M, p. 15(b).

2. Tocqueville to Madame de Circourt, September 18, 1852, *OC*, XVIII, p. 85.

3. This is Ampère's description of the storm in Paris. Ampère to Madame de Tocqueville, October 14, 1852, *OC*, XI, p. 213.

4. Tocqueville to Beaumont, postscript to letter of October 10, 1853, *OC*, VIII, pt. 3, p. 156.

5. For the effects of Tocqueville's "quite serious malady," see his letter to Jared Sparks, December 11, 1852 (Harvard University archives, unpublished). Tocqueville's letter is his official response to Sparks in his capacity as president of Harvard, thanking the college for bestowing an honorary degree that June. In it he reaffirmed his deep attachment to America in general and to the great principles of "civil and political liberty" in particular, designating Harvard's [sic] college as "the principal foyer of enlightenment [*lumières*] not only in New England but on all your continent." Tocqueville wrote a separate, personal letter to Sparks on the same day (*OC*, VII, pp. 148–49).

6. Tocqueville to Beaumont, April 8, 1853, *OC*, VIII, pt. 3, p. 102 (*Selected Letters*, p. 291).

7. Tocqueville to Corcelle, November 21, 1852, *OC*, XV, pt. 2, p. 62.

8. Letters to Corcelle of December 17, 1852, and January 1, 1853, *OC*, XV, pt. 2, pp. 65 and 69.

9. Tocqueville to Reeve, March 26, 1853, *OC*, VI, pt. 1, p. 145.

10. Tocqueville to Beaumont, April 8, 1853, *OC*, VIII, pt. 3, p. 102 (*Selected Letters*, p. 291). Tocqueville's comment appears to cover a period of five months, referring back to what was most likely a November date for their last visit (see Beaumont to Tocqueville, November 7, 1852, *OC*, VIII, pt. 3, p. 78).

11. Tocqueville told Corcelle on November 21, 1852, that he had "devoured [a multitude of books] in the past month" (*OC*, XV, pt. 2, p. 64), including the letters of Madame du Deffand to Horace Walpole. On November 4, 1852, he had requested Hubert de Tocqueville's help in obtaining the travel memoirs from the early 1800s of English sea captain Basil Hall, the accounts of Nicolaï's 1781 voyage in Germany, and *Lucifer*, the German publicist's Charles Oelsner's account of his days in Paris during the Terror (Library of Clermont-Ferrand, unpublished). He does not appear to have read *Lucifer* at this time, since he requested it again in his letter to Charles Monnard of October 15, 1856 (*OC*, VII, p. 356).

12. Tocqueville to Montalembert, December 1, 1852, *OC* (Beaumont), VII, p. 294.

13. Tocqueville to Corcelle, letters of December 17, 1852, and January 1, 1853, *OC,* XV, pt. 2, pp. 67 and 71. Tocqueville told Corcelle that he found little to recommend in Nicolas's work.

14. Beaumont to Tocqueville, January 12, 1853, *OC,* VIII, pt. 3, p. 81. It is Beaumont who recapitulates what Tocqueville had praised as Macaulay's strengths.

15. Tocqueville to Corcelle, January 1, 1853, *OC,* XV, pt. 2, p. 72.

16. Tocqueville to Beaumont, March 23, 1853, *OC,* VIII, pt. 3, p. 95 (*Selected Letters,* p. 287). "I am beginning to work again very actively," he announced in this letter.

17. Tocqueville to Beaumont, April 8, 1853, *OC,* VIII, pt. 3, pp. 102–3 (*Selected Letters,* p. 291).

18. TA, box 43, folder I, p. 3, "Intendants: Immensity of their power."

19. Ibid., p. 6.

20. Ibid., p. 4. The seigneurs returned "too late," Tocqueville noted in English on p. 8.

21. Ibid., title page.

22. Charles de Grandmaison indicates this as one reason for Tocqueville's choice in his article "Séjour d'Alexis de Tocqueville en Touraine, préparation du livre sur l'ancien régime, juin 1853–avril 1854," *Le Correspondant* 114, n.s. 78 (January–March 1879): 927–28.

23. Tocqueville to Bunsen, January 2, 1853, *OC,* VII, p. 328. This line of inquiry differed from a previous search that Tocqueville inaugurated in the spring of 1852, asking for help from Gobineau and Adolphe de Circourt in determining "the origin of the new ideas in Germany in philosophy, theology, and scholarship." (Since we lack Tocqueville's letters of inquiry, I am drawing this summation from Gobineau's letter of response of April 29, 1852, *OC,* IX, p. 195.) Circourt indicated that Tocqueville's interest at that time was in "the Revolution's preparatory groundwork, which, in the second part of the eighteenth century, was on the way to realization in all of the civilized world" (Circourt to Tocqueville, May 21, 1852, *OC,* XVIII, p. 69).

24. See *OC,* VII, p. 329n, for Bunsen's recommended reading list; the editors, Françoise Mélonio and Lise Quéffelec, indicate that Tocqueville largely deferred follow-up on these readings until 1856, after publication of *The Old Regime,* when he commenced his research for its sequel.

25. Tocqueville to Bunsen, May 23, 1853, *OC,* VII, p. 333. Tocqueville was convinced, he said, "that one can view with pleasure and profit only the peoples whose language one knows."

26. Rémusat, "Burke: Sa vie et ses écrits," January 15, 1853 (part 1) and February 1, 1853 (part 2), *Revue des Deux Mondes,* 2nd ser., 23, no. 1 (January–March 1853): 209–61 and 435–90. Tocqueville's desire to peruse these particular issues of the *RDM* no doubt resulted from their presentation of the first two installments of Ampère's serialized account of his travels in America, written at Tocqueville's Norman château during his visit in July, August, and September 1852. It is also true that Tocqueville met with Rémusat on several occasions during the late fall of 1852, although it seems unlikely

that their discussions considered much of intellectual substance, since Tocqueville reported being "a bit disappointed" by their caliber (Tocqueville to Corcelle, January 1, 1853, *OC*, XV, pt. 2, p. 69).

27. Franciszek Draus recounts the role of Rémusat's article, along with Tocqueville's *The Old Regime*, in providing "a precise and detailed response" to Burke, thus compensating for the virtual absence of a serious French liberal critique of Burke in the first half of the nineteenth century. See Draus, "Burke et les Français," in *The French Revolution and the Creation of Modern Political Culture*, vol. 3, *The Transformation of Political Culture, 1789–1848*, ed. François Furet and Mona Ozouf (New York: Pergamon Press, 1989), p. 96.

28. Rémusat, "Burke: Sa vie et ses écrits," p. 455.

29. TA, box 44, folder 1. Tocqueville titled his excerpted list *"Documents on Burke,* drawn from the article of Rémusat that appeared in the *Revue des Deux Mondes* of January [*sic*] 53." On the same sheet of paper, he listed four recommended English editions of Burke's works or correspondence, gathered from an unidentified source other than Rémusat's article.

30. Rémusat recommended Mackintosh's 1791 work, *Vindiciae Gallicae,* as superior in its sensitive if idealistic defense of the Revolution to that of Thomas Paine. Tocqueville included Mackintosh's book on various subsequent lists of books to obtain, although we have no indication that he read it (TA, box 44).

31. Tocqueville read Burke, I believe, between February 1, 1853, the date of the appearance of Rémusat's article, and June 26, 1853, the date of Tocqueville's draft of a plan for his book that drew heavily on his readings of Burke (see section 2 below). I am referring here only to Tocqueville's readings of Burke's French writings; he had at least scanned statements of Burke in other contexts, such as his 1787 parliamentary comments on the "prodigious" public works of Cherbourg that Tocqueville quoted in his own 1847 article, "Notice sur Cherbourg" (reprinted in *OC*, XVI, pp. 349–93; the Burke quotation is on p. 392).

32. For Burke's speeches and public letters, Tocqueville used *The Works of the Right Honourable Edmund Burke* (London: F. C. and J. Rivington, 1815), vols. 5, 6, 7, and 8. He read his private letters in *Correspondence of the Right Honourable Edmund Burke; between the year 1744 and the Period of His Decease, in 1797,* ed. Charles William, Earl Fitzwilliam, and Lieutenant-General Sir Richard Bourke (London: Francis and John Rivington, 1844), vols. 3 and 4.

33. For a list of these passages, see Jardin's note to "Four Judgments on Burke" in *OC*, II, pt. 2, pp. 338–40n.

34. See ibid., pp. 340–42 (passages 2, 3, and 4), where Tocqueville summarized his reactions to Burke's *Reflections, An Appeal from the New to the Old Whigs,* and "Remarks on the Policy of the Allies with respect to France."

35. TA, box 43, folder M, p. 7.

36. Ibid., p. 6(b) (*Reflections on the Revolution in France* in *Works*, 5:333 [*Refléxions*, p. 237]). Where applicable, I provide in parentheses the Burkean text Tocqueville is commenting on, plus two references for it: the 1815 English edition of Burke's *Works,* used by Tocqueville, and a recent French edition, *Réflexions sur la révolution de France,*

preface by Philippe Raynaud, notes by Alfred Fierro and Georges Liébert, trans. Pierre Andler (Paris: Hachette, 1989). On two occasions I provide references to Burke's *Correspondence* in the 1844 text used by Tocqueville.

37. Ibid., pp. 6–6(b) (*Reflections on the Revolution in France, Works*, 5:303n [*Réflexions*, p. 214n]). Burke made reference here to a speech in the National Assembly by M. Rabaut Saint-Etienne.

38. Ibid., p. 12(b) ("Thoughts on French Affairs," *Works*, 5:13).

39. Ibid., p. 20 ("Letter on a Regicide Peace" (I), *Works*, 8:83 [*Réflexions*, p. 516]).

40. Ibid., p. 9 (Letter to William Weddell of January 31, 1792, *Correspondence*, 3:407).

41. Ibid., p. 12 (published in *OC*, II, 2, pp. 341–42). Tocqueville made the comment with regards to Burke's *An Appeal from the New to the Old Whigs*, but I believe it provides an apt summation of his reactions to his Burkean readings as a whole.

42. Ibid., p. 2 (*Reflections on the Revolution in France, Works*, 5:84 [*Réflexions*, p. 46]).

43. Ibid.

44. Ibid., p. 7(b) (*OC*, II, 2, p. 341).

45. Ibid., pp. 11(b)–12 (*An Appeal from the New to the Old Whigs, Works*, 6:131 [*Réflexions*, p. 416]).

46. Ibid., p. 12 (*OC*, II, pt. 2, p. 342).

47. Ibid.

48. Ibid., p. 7(b) (*OC*, II, pt. 2, pp. 340–41).

49. Ibid., p. 12 (*OC*, II, pt. 2, p. 342).

50. Ibid., p. 23 (*OC*, II, pt. 2, p. 239). Tocqueville here commented on statements of Burke in his second "Letter on a Regicide Peace" (*Works*, 8:238 [*Réflexions*, p. 590]).

51. Ibid., p. 23(b) ("Letter on a Regicide Peace" [II], *Works*, 8:255–56 [*Réflexions*, p. 599]).

52. Ibid., p. 17. Tocqueville noted Burke's 1790 view in his "Speech on the Army Estimates" (*Works*, 5:5–6 [*Réflexions*, p. 325]) and his 1793 view in his "Remarks on the Policy of the Allies" (*Works*, 7:165).

53. Ibid., p. 19(b). Burke's 1796 comments are in his first "Letter on a Regicide Peace" (*Works*, 8:82–83 [*Réflexions*, p. 516]).

54. Ibid., p. 18. For added emphasis, Tocqueville wrote "unprecedented" in English.

55. Ibid., p. 4, with reference to Burke's comments in *Reflections on the Revolution in France, Works*, 5:211 (*Réflexions*, p. 144).

56. Ibid. Tocqueville wrote "*extraordinary and unnatural*" in English.

57. Ibid., p. 15 ("Thoughts on French Affairs," *Works*, 7:54). Tocqueville recorded in his notes that the royal policy had "attracted" the nobles.

58. Ibid.

59. Ibid, p. 15(b). Tocqueville appended to this passage a pithy summation: "Signs of the Revolution indicated by Burke without being seen by him."

60. Ibid., p. 16(b) ("Remarks on the Policy of the Allies," *Works*, 7:133–34).

61. Ibid., p. 21 ("Letter on a Regicide Peace" [I], *Works*, 8:167–68 [*Réflexions*, p. 555]).

62. Tocqueville to Bunsen, May 23, 1853, *OC*, VII, p. 332.

63. Tocqueville to Freslon, June 9, 1853, *OC* (Beaumont), VI, p. 206.

64. Grandmaison, "Séjour d'Alexis de Tocqueville," pp. 928–29.

65. For Tocqueville's earlier reading of Blackstone, see Tocqueville to Senior, July 2, 1853, *OC*, VI, pt. 2, p. 160.

66. Tocqueville to Freslon, June 9, 1853, *OC* (Beaumont), VI, p. 209. Tocqueville may also have read Guillaume Le Trosne's *Administration provinciale* at this time, as indicated below in chapter 6, section 1.

67. Ibid., p. 208.

68. Ibid.

69. Tocqueville to Ampère, June 19, 1853, *OC*, XI, p. 219. Tocqueville's determination to attempt a draft at this time may have been motivated as well by Ampère's impending lengthy visit to Tours in mid-July, given the value he attached to Ampère's advice, especially with respect to the form and precision of his writing.

70. TA, box 43, folder K, subfile 5 titled, "Initial Outline." This subfile is divided into two subsections that I will refer to as "26 June 53 sketch" and "order of ideas." For the "order of ideas," see *OR*, 2:263–65.

71. This "order of ideas" was written just after the "26 June 53 sketch," I believe, even though it precedes it in the subfile.

72. TA, box 43, folder K, title page of subfile 5. Tocqueville most likely appended this title page with these comments to his drafts when he thoroughly organized his reading notes in November 1854. Two years later, in line with other "(1856)" notations for his sequel, he added a further comment to this page, drawing attention to the way his book subsequently shifted from these early formulations of it at Tours: "This whole folder is curious in that it contains the first lineaments of the book. But it applies only to the first volume. (1856)" "Saint-Cyr" is the name of the village next to Tours where Tocqueville and his wife lived.

73. "26 June 53 sketch," p. 1.

74. Ibid., p. 1(b). The text on pp. 1 and 1(b) overlaps the two pages, assuring a date of June 26, 1853 for this chapter plan. I take the proposed fourth chapter to refer to both of Tocqueville's already executed 1852 chapters, since he saw them as a single unit. I have found nothing to suggest that his interest in Napoleon or his empire, as originally stated in his Sorrento chapter plan, had diminished at this time. Since the five chapters designated here all either anticipate or describe Napoleon's ascension to power on 18 brumaire, I am inclined to view this outline as guiding a preparatory book or volume, with Tocqueville's fuller work on Napoleon still to follow. Tocqueville would indicate the general lines of this continuing Napoleonic interest in his conversation with Molé and Rémusat on April 3, 1855 (*OC*, II, pt. 2, pp. 230–32; *OR*, 2:237–38).

75. Ibid., pp. 1–1(b) for all quotations in this paragraph. As in his notes on Burke, Tocqueville wrote "*unprecedented*" in English.

76. "26 June 53 sketch," page 2. This is my numbering for this page Tocqueville left unnumbered.

77. Ibid., p. 3 (unnumbered by Tocqueville).

78. Ibid., p. 4 (unnumbered by Tocqueville).

79. Ibid., for all quotations in this paragraph.

80. TA, box 43, folder K, subfile 5 titled "Initial Outline," subsection titled "order of ideas," p. 1 (*OR*, 2:263).

81. Ibid., p. 1(b) (*OR*, 2:264). Tocqueville described his work plan in the following terms: "Research the proof of this in the works of the time: M. de Maistre, Mallet du Pan, Burke. The great enemies of the Revolution." He noted additional documents that might supplement this "feeling of horror": "They must have in the British Parliament speeches (those of Burke among others) that could render clearly this sense. Ecclesiastical documents as well."

82. Ibid., p. 2 (*OR*, 2:264).

83. Ibid. (*OR*, 2:264).

84. Ibid., p. 2(b) (*OR*, 2:264).

85. Ibid., pp. 2(b)–3 (*OR*, 2:264). Tocqueville drew a distinction between two viewpoints in considering this issue. "Seen in its final consequences," the destruction of individual property rights may have been a fundamental result of the Revolution. "But . . . if we restrict our view within the duration of the contemporary or succeeding period," such a conclusion did not apply (*OR*, 2:265).

86. Ibid., p. 3 (*OR*, 2:265).

87. Ibid., p. 2 (*OR*, 2:264).

88. Ibid., pp. 3–3(b) (*OR*, 2:265).

89. Ibid., p. 3(b) (*OR*, 2:265).

90. Ibid., p. 3(b) (*OR*, 2:265).

91. Ibid. (*OR*, 2:265). "Democratic revolutions always more violent than others," Tocqueville said. See note 106 below for the varied, often contradictory meanings that Tocqueville deployed in his "democratic" vocabulary in *The Old Regime*.

92. Ibid., 3(b) (*OR*, 2:265).

93. Ibid., p. 2(b) (*OR*, 2:264).

94. Ibid., p. 4 (*OR*, 2:265). Tocqueville had formulated this paradox in his first Napoleonic chapter of the previous summer, when he characterized the French people as "civilized among all the civilized peoples of the earth and yet, in certain respects, remaining closer to the savage state than any among them" (*OC*, II, pt. 2, p. 281 [*OR*, 2:200]).

95. Ibid. (*OR*, 2:265).

96. Tocqueville to Beaumont, July 1, 1853, *OC*, VIII, pt. 3, pp. 132–33.

97. Tocqueville to Senior, July 2, 1853, *OC*, VI, pt. 2, pp. 160–62. For Senior's subsequent report on his conversation with Macaulay, see his response to Tocqueville of August 26, 1853 (ibid., pp. 162–63).

98. Tocqueville to Corcelle, July 3, 1853, *OC*, XV, pt. 2, p. 77.

99. "Speech on the Army Estimates," *Works*, 5:5 (*Réflexions*, p. 325). I am following John Bonner and Henry Reeve, in their respective 1856 translations, in using the parliamentary recorder's transcription of Burke's speech for this quotation; I will do

the same in the remaining five Burkean quotations. Bonner and Reeve allowed readers to savor the full power of the master orator's verbal pyrotechnics in three such quotations in I:1 and I:5, although Reeve selected the wrong Burkean passage for Tocqueville's concluding quotation of I:5! See *On the State of Society in France before the Revolution of 1789; and on the Causes Which Led to That Event*, trans. Henry Reeve (London: John Murray, 1856), p. 36.

100. "Letter on a Regicide Peace" (I), *Works*, 8:82 (*Réflexions*, p. 516).

101. For Tocqueville's draft language, see TA, box 43, folder K, subfile 5 titled "Initial Outline," subsection titled "order of ideas," p. 1(b) (*OR*, 2:263).

102. In Tocqueville's 1853 "order of ideas" (TA, box 43, folder K, subfile 5, p. 3 [*OR*, 2:265]), Tocqueville had previewed the importance of Mirabeau's comment that signaled the advantages for the expansion of monarchic power produced by the Revolution's leveling tendencies: "Profound viewpoint of Mirabeau on this. The true stamp of genius. *Meémoires au Roi.*"

103. Tocqueville had developed this theme in his notes for his 1842 "Discours de réception" at the Académie française. See *OC*, XVI, p. 259n.

104. For Tocqueville's lengthy ruminations in his writing drafts on this resemblance between the propagandism of revolutions and religion, see *OR*, 1:324–27.

105. Burke's quotation is from *An Appeal from the New to the Old Whigs, Works*, 6:85 (*Réflexions*, p. 392). The full transcription by the parliamentary recorder of Burke's statement in his speech, entered by Tocqueville in his reading notes on p. 11(b) of TA, box 43, folder M, reads: "That what was done in France was a wild attempt to methodize anarchy, to perpetuate and fix disorder. That it was a foul, impious, monstrous thing, wholly out of the course of moral Nature. [Burke] undertook to prove that it was generated in treachery, fraud, falsehood, hypocrisy, and unprovoked murder."

106. Tocqueville's shifting "democratic" vocabulary in *The Old Regime* appears to preclude his denoting this process "democracy." Tocqueville uses three definitions of "democracy" in his labors in *The Old Regime:* a civil or social one, alluded to here but unnamed as such, with which we are most familiar from *Democracy in America;* a political one, best rendered in his oft-cited reading note (*OC*, II, pt. 2, pp. 198–99 [*OR*, 2:162–63]), in which "its meaning is intimately bound to the idea of political liberty," thus making it contingent upon a measure of popular participation; and a further, contradictory political one in which Tocqueville denotes a new form of egalitarian despotism that indeed precludes participation. As his work progresses, I find that Tocqueville most often employs this last definition, despite the "palpable absurdity" of its usage, deftly described in the same reading note as "an absolute government where the people take no part in public affairs but where the upper classes enjoy no privileges either and where the laws are made to favor as much material well-being as possible" (*OC*, II, pt. 2, p. 199 [*OR*, 2:163]). For Tocqueville's shifting democratic usage in *The Old Regime*, see Furet, *Interpreting*, p. 147, and Raymond Aron, *Main Currents in Sociological Thought*, trans. Richard Howard and Helen Weaver (New York: Basic Books, 1965), 1:186–87. For a valuable overview of the larger context for this discussion, see

Pierre Rosanvallon, "The History of the Word 'Democracy' in France," *Journal of Democracy* 6, no. 4 (1995): 140–54.

107. For Burke's quotation urging recovery of "the almost obliterated constitution of your ancestors," see *Reflections on the Revolution in France, Works,* 5:84 (*Réflexions,* p. 46).

108. Draus, "Burke et les Français," p. 97. A careful review of the earliest drafts of book 1 reinforce the importance of Burke in the construction of the book. Tocqueville notes "Burke" on the title page of his very first draft of I:1, dated December 2, 1853; he also prepares a sheet titled, "Different passages of Burke of which I can make use," for use in this chapter (TA, box 42).

109. Tocqueville's preoccupation with Burke's "misunderstanding" of the nobility's status is shown in various other references in his notes. In an early draft he says: "In the chapter where I demonstrate the differences between the English aristocracy and that of France misunderstood by Burke, cite the precise numbers" (TA, box 44, folder 19). In reading the *cahiers* of the Third Estate, Tocqueville finds evidence of continuing polarization between the Third and the nobles, leading him to comment: "How Burke is mistaken by false analyses" (TA, box 43, folder C, 21[b]).

110. For this passage of Burke's, see *Reflections on the Revolution in France, Works,* 5:326 (*Réflexions,* p. 233).

111. Burke's "eloquent pamphlet" is his "Remarks on the Policy of the Allies," with this passage found in *Works,* 7:133. For Tocqueville's impassioned second-person response to Burke after reading this passage, see above, p. 64.

112. In his manuscript (TA, box 39), Tocqueville debates how to present Burke's views in this passage. He first writes that Burke "did not know *[ignorait]*" the conditions created by the monarchy, but then he changes this to "poorly understood *[savait mal],*" after noting that his first formulation "is not exactly true," since it does not reflect Burke's recognition that the monarchy had "abstracted the nobility from the cultivation of provincial interest."

113. Jean-Claude Lamberti, "Introduction à *L'ancien régime,*" in *Tocqueville,* p. 898.

114. See, for example, TA, box 45, folder EE, p. 4(b). After reading in June 1857 a demand of the Third of Aix to restrict its order's ability to purchase access to the nobility, Tocqueville queried: "What would Burke have said in his comparison of the French nobility with that of England if he had read this grievance?"

FIVE

1. Tocqueville to Grandmaison, August 9, 1856, cited in Grandmaison, "Séjour d'Alexis de Tocqueville en Touraine," p. 946.

2. Tocqueville described "Les Trésorières" in letters to friends, including Ampère (June 2, 1853, *OC,* XI, p. 215) and Corcelle (June 17, 1853, *OC,* XV, pt. 2, p. 75). For his wife's winning offensive against the bedbugs, see Tocqueville to Beaumont, June 4, 1853, *OC,* VIII, pt. 3, pp. 128–29. Senior recounted day trips with Tocqueville to châteaus of the Loire in his "Conversations" of April 6, 7, 8, and 10, 1854 (*OC,* VI, pt. 2, pp. 422–29).

3. Tocqueville to Sedgwick, July 17, 1854, *OC,* VII, p. 156.

4. Tocqueville to Beaumont, December 5, 1853, *OC,* VIII, pt. 3, pp. 172–73.

5. Tocqueville's letters to Lavergne (October 31, 1853, *OC* [Beaumont], VII, p. 303), Circourt (August 13, 1853, *OC*, XVIII, p. 94), Dufaure, (August 14, 1853, *OC* [Beaumont], VII, p. 298), and Madame de Circourt (January 11, 1854, *OC*, XVIII, p. 141). For his barber's role as local informant, see Tocqueville to Corcelle, January 30, 1854, *OC*, XV, pt. 2, p. 94. Despite his boycott of French newspapers, Tocqueville did share with Beaumont a subscription to the *Kölnische Zeitung*; he also read *Galignani's Messenger*, a digest of news from England.

6. Tocqueville to Madame de Circourt, September 2, 1853, *OC*, XVIII, pp. 102–3.

7. See Grandmaison, "Séjour d'Alexis de Tocqueville," especially part 1, pp. 926–41.

8. The friends' frivolity expressed itself in an inspired exchange of poems, including one by Ampère provoked by the sight of Corcelle's trousers (Tocqueville to Corcelle, postscript, August 18 or 25, 1853, *OC*, XV, pt. 2, p. 79).

9. Tocqueville to Corcelle, September 17, 1853, *OC*, XV, pt. 2, p. 79 (*Selected Letters*, p. 293). Tocqueville writes "*treadmill*" in English, making reference to the penal walking machine observed in his American travels.

10. Tocqueville to Corcelle, January 30, 1854, *OC*, XV, pt. 2, p. 91.

11. Tocqueville to Mrs. Grote, conversation of February 18, 1854, in Senior, "Conversations," *OC*, VI, pt. 2, p. 414 (*Conversations*, 2:60).

12. Tocqueville related to Madame de Circourt his disappointment with one such evening venture, finding the memoirs of Madame la Baronne d'Oberkirch marked by "that sort of senile imbecility into which aging aristocracies tumble" (November 26, 1853, *OC*, XVIII, p. 115).

13. Tocqueville to Freslon, June 9, 1853, *OC* (Beaumont), VI, p. 207.

14. Ibid., p. 208. In a rare instance of prognostic error, Tocqueville had stated as well: "It would be a great mistake to apply myself exclusively to painting the Old Regime."

15. Tocqueville's notes on Turgot's intendancy, drawn from volumes 4, 5, and 6 of Turgot's *Oeuvres*, ed. P.-S. Dupont de Nemours, 9 vols. (Paris: A. Belin, 1811), are in TA, box 43, folder B, pp. 4–19 (published in *OC*, II, pt. 2, pp. 381–403 [*OR*, 2:304–22]). Tocqueville transcribed these notes during or after his work in the Parisian administrative archives (see references to "l'Hôtel de Ville" in folder B, pp. 31 and 38[b], published in *OC*, II, pt. 2, pp. 420, 429 [*OR*, 2:336, 344]; see reference to Turgot in folder I, p. 20[b], presumably with reference to folder B, p. 6[b], published in *OC*, II, pt. 2, p. 384 [*OR*, 2:306]).

16. In Dareste's chapter on the French central administration, for example, the author had noted: "One must read the works of Turgot during his intendancy at Limoges to understand all the vices of this royal *corvée*" (Dareste, *Histoire*, p. 244).

17. Grandmaison, "Séjour d'Alexis de Tocqueville," pp. 928–29.

18. Charles de Grandmaison, *Inventaire-sommaire des archives départementales antérieures à 1790. Indre-et-Loire. Archives civiles* (Paris: De Paul Dupont, 1867), 1:7. Grandmaison estimated on p. 25 of his introductory "Notice historique" that, even after revolutionary depredations, "the historical part of our depository still numbers more than 200,000 pieces from before the Revolution of 1789."

19. Grandmaison, "Séjour d'Alexis de Tocqueville," p. 929.

20. Ibid., p. 930.

21. Ibid., p. 931.

22. Ibid. See Pierson, *Tocqueville and Beaumont in America,* pp. 731–34, for the roles Theodore Sedgwick III and Francis Lippitt played in reviewing and notating materials for the book. Tocqueville presented Lippitt with a vast collection of American political statutes and asked him to prepare written summaries without giving him any knowledge of the purpose of this research.

23. Ibid.

24. These twenty-two subsections of notes are contained in TA, box 43, folder H, pp. 1–41 and 61–167. Tocqueville's research began with two undated files that I have designated the "undated first file" and "undated second file." We can tell from these files' sequence in folder H, which reads chronologically from back to front, that they preceded the first dated file of "5 July 53," thus suggesting a late June or early July date of compilation. At the end of 1855, Tocqueville requested from Grandmaison an overview of the intendants' archives—"a sort of résumé of matters contained within the administration of the intendant" ("Séjour d'Alexis de Tocqueville," p. 944n). Grandmaison's resulting synopsis is in TA, box 42.

25. Tocqueville to Freslon, June 9, 1853, *OC* (Beaumont), VI, p. 208.

26. The evolution of Tocqueville's interests at Tours can also be traced in the passages he subsequently selected for inclusion as endnotes in *The Old Regime.* Tocqueville transcribed the following endnotes in the following order at Tours: 27, 60, 62, 64:three concluding paragraphs ("undated first file"); 57 ("undated second file"); 41 ("5 July 53"); 70, 56 ("9 July"); 52, 36, 53 ("13 July"); 64:first paragraph, 38, 54 ("20 July"); 73, 23 ("6 August"); 25, 11, 10, 72 ("8 September"); 34 ("1 October"); 55 ("24 October"); 15, 58 ("2 November"); 19 ("30 November"); 45 ("November 53"); and 13 ("May 54").

27. TA, box 43, folder H, "undated first file," pp. 159 and 159(b). Tocqueville's note regarding the equivalent fervor for tobacco licenses will appear as endnote 27 in *The Old Regime.*

28. Ibid., "undated second file," pp. 150–150(b) and 152(b).

29. Ibid., p. 153(b).

30. For examples of such "background" research, see TA, box 43, folder H, undated file titled "Elections from the generality of Tours from 1732 to 1759: Statistics," p. 129. This file is between the files of "20 July 53" and "2 August 53."

31. According to Mrs. Grote's notes, Tocqueville believed that "the whole structure of society, in its relations with the authorised agents of supreme power, including the pressure of those secondary obligations arising out of *coutumes du pays,* is . . . little understood." Conversation with Tocqueville of February 14, 1854 in Senior, "Conversations," *OC,* VI, pt. 2, p. 408 (*Conversations,* 2:50).

32. TA, box 43, folder H, file dated "18 October 53," p. 82. Françoise Mélonio justly characterizes Tocqueville's reading at Tours as "a suspicious reading of the archive," necessary for deciphering the "art" of the Old Regime's absolutist practices (see her

article, "Tocqueville: Aux origines de la démocratie française," in *The Transformation of Political Culture*, ed. Furet and Ozouf, pp. 601–2).

33. TA, box 43, folder H, file dated "2 August 53," pp. 125, 126, and 126(b). Tocqueville concluded his comments with the following assessment of the spirit of opposition revealed in these grain strikes: "It's 1789 less the revolutionary spirit properly so called" (p. 126[b]).

34. Ibid., p. 125.

35. TA, box 43, folder H, file dated "2 November 53" titled "Subsistences," pp. 61–64. Tocqueville's renewed reading of "Subsistences," the only file he privileged with a second reading, concluded with his expression of surprise at the revolutionary mentality of the people: "The number of riots as soon as there are food shortages, the readiness with which the people—so submissive and patient in appearance—rise in revolt as soon as there is even a whiff of general excitement, is surprising" (ibid., p. 64).

36. Tocqueville to Freslon, September 23, 1853, *OC* (Beaumont), VI, p. 233 (*Selected Letters*, p. 296).

37. TA, box 43, folder H, file dated "18 October 53," pp. 77–86.

38. Ibid., file titled "Note drawn from the collection of deliberations and memoirs of the Royal Society of Agriculture of the generality of Tours, 1761," pp. 52–53 (excerpted in *OC*, II, pt. 2, pp. 355–56). Tocqueville drew on these same readings for endnotes 40 and 30 in *The Old Regime*. The latter endnote modified his initial observations, because in it he characterized even the limited conversation permitted within the societies as valuable since it helped break down class barriers.

39. Ibid., file dated "29 August 53," section titled "the government as journalist," pp. 106(b)–108. In a scathing portrayal, Tocqueville reported the full story of this debacle in *OR*, 1:140–41.

40. Ibid., file dated "1 October 53," p. 90(b).

41. Ibid., file dated "30 November 1853," pp. 1–41, with the response from four different constituencies of Angers to the King's Council's 1764 "Inquiry into City Governments" (pp. 38[4]-38[10]) subsequently incorporated as endnote 19 in *The Old Regime*.

42. Tocqueville referred to "official" and "royal" meddling in TA, box 43, folder F, pp. 10 and 16. Tocqueville's notes in folder F, transcribed in "April 54," represent a later reading of the ordinances of the kings of France, presumably deferred so as not to distort his study of the administrative machine's practical functionings by introducing considerations of its putative ones.

43. Grandmaison, "Séjour d'Alexis de Tocqueville," pp. 931–32.

44. Ibid., pp. 935–36. While granting Grandmaison's evident pleasure in Tocqueville's comment (Richard Herr refers to Tocqueville's "flatter[y]" of Grandmaison in *Tocqueville and the Old Regime* [Princeton: Princeton University Press, 1962], p. 6), I see no reason to doubt the reliability of his account. It makes sense that Tocqueville should have confirmed the direction and arranged the plan for his first volume of his book at this time, both as a response to the inherent interest and archival novelty found at Tours and as a key transitional step in redefining his topic

after his failed writing efforts in June 1853. Tocqueville would adjust his fall research with this new objective in mind, and when he did commence what would become *The Old Regime* in December, he would no longer be writing "a small chapter of thirty pages," as he had envisioned on June 9, but the full, detached book on the Old Regime that he referred to here. Given Grandmaison's report of Ampère's presence at the dinner, we can be certain that it took place at the end of August, since Tocqueville told Circourt on September 2, 1853, "Ampère left us two days ago" (*OC,* XVIII, p. 104).

My account of the timing of this crucial decision differs from that of André Jardin in his "Note critique" to *OC,* II, pt. 2, pp. 16–17, and in his *Tocqueville: A Biography,* where he discusses Tocqueville's activity at Tours on pp. 489–93. Jardin makes no mention in either work of Grandmaison's report of Tocqueville's late summer announcement; he suggests instead that Tocqueville's decision to write a separate book emerged at least four months later, while he was writing its chapters: "Thus, it is in the first months of 1854 that Tocqueville deliberately oriented himself toward a book on the end of the Old Regime and sketched its essential elements" ("Note critique" to *OC,* II, pt. 2, p. 17). For their own portrayal of the "abrupt change" in Tocqueville's plans, see Françoise Mélonio and François Furet, Introduction to *OR,* 1:8–9.

45. Tocqueville most clearly explained these plans in his letter of March 7, 1854, to his nephew Hubert. In this letter, he indicated that having established the "true and just ideas" on the Old Regime in volume 1, he would proceed in his second volume to follow the Revolution "epoch by epoch, from its beginning until the fall of the Empire." "My intention," he added, "is not to surpass two volumes" (*OC,* XIV, p. 295). Beaumont had designated Tocqueville's brother Edouard as the addressee of this important letter (*OC* [Beaumont], VI, pp. 251–53).

46. Tocqueville to Mrs. Grote, November 22, 1853, *OC* (Beaumont), VI, p. 243. Tocqueville proceeded to highlight the difficulty of his task, emphasizing that "this world that preceded the French Revolution is almost as difficult to retrieve and comprehend as the antediluvian epochs."

47. See below, chapter 6, for other sources Tocqueville read at Tours that also afforded "true and just ideas" on the prerevolutionary period.

48. For one early detour, see above, pp. 6–10. For views expressed in political writings and speeches of 1843, see *OC,* III, pt. 2, pp. 108, 171–72.

49. "Rapport fait à l'Académie des sciences morales et politiques (1846) sur le livre de M. Macarel, intitulé: *Cours de droit administratif,*" *OC,* XVI, pp. 185–98.

50. Macarel, *Cours de droit administratif professé à la Faculté de droit de Paris,* 2 vols. (Paris: G. Thorel, 1844), 1:33. For a valuable overview of these reforms by the National or Constituent Assembly, see Yann Fauchois, "Centralization," in *A Critical Dictionary of the French Revolution,* ed. François Furet and Mona Ozouf, trans. Arthur Goldhammer (Cambridge: Harvard University Press, Belknap Press, 1989), pp. 629–39. Framing his article with references to Tocqueville, Fauchois also analyzes the ongoing debate in French historiography regarding the extent of the Assembly's "decentralization."

51. Tocqueville, "Rapport sur Macarel," *OC,* XVI, p. 186.

52. Ibid., p. 188.

53. Ibid.

54. Ibid., pp. 195–96. In "Tocqueville, Napoleon and Bonapartism" in *Reconsidering,* ed. Eisenstadt, p. 138, Melvin Richter helps to clarify the backdrop to Tocqueville's argument, showing how he emphasized that a preceding "social revolution" had laid the groundwork for these radical administrative changes. Mélonio, in her introduction to *OC,* XVI, p. 26, argues that "in these years of the 1840s . . . [Tocqueville] was more sensitive to the new rationality of administrative practices than to the antiquity of their origin," adding that "the edifice seemed recent to him."

55. Ibid., p. 188.

56. Ibid., pp. 191–94.

57. Ibid., pp. 197–98. Tocqueville's aggressive critique of Macarel in his report represented a shift from that recorded in his preparatory notes for his speech. There, on his first page, he designated as one of the "qualities" of Macarel's book the fact that "M. Macarel is not an extreme centralizer. He does not possess the adoration of centralization to as high a degree as do most of his peers." Tocqueville's more nuanced critique disappeared in his final report. During his work on *The Old Regime,* Tocqueville refiled these preparatory notes among his reading notes in TA, box 43, folder A.

58. TA, box 43, folder J, p. 86(b).

59. TA, box 43, folder I, p. 6.

60. Ibid., p. 7.

61. TA, box 43, folder B, p. 11(b) (published in *OC,* II, pt. 2, p. 391).

62. TA, box 43, folder H, first undated file, p. 162(b). Tocqueville subsequently incorporated this example in endnote 64 in *The Old Regime,* including his observation from Tours that "this idea penetrated even into the penal code, so well preserved are the traditions of the Old Regime in this matter."

63. TA, box 43, folder H, file dated "2 August 1853," p. 127.

64. TA, box 43, folder H, file dated "6 August 1853," p. 124(b). In an index dated "January 55" and titled "Summary of notes on administrative justice and the immunity of public officials" (TA, box 42), Tocqueville would list more than fifty specific cases of government intrusion from folders B ("Turgot"), F ("Old French laws"), H ("Archives of Tours") and J ("France before the Revolution [miscellaneous]"). Tocqueville pursued these "filiations" in other ways too, as in his notes from an article of August 17, 1853, in *Galignani's Messenger.* There, after describing an English civil court case in which a jury awarded damages for false imprisonment to a M. Fossall against the public official who accused and imprisoned him, he marveled at the English civil law that gave citizens the right to contest "the arbitrariness of public officials." See TA, box 43, folder K, p. 77.

65. Tocqueville to Freslon, August 10, 1853, *OC* (Beaumont), VI, p. 221. In an apparent typographic error, Beaumont dated this letter "1854."

66. Ibid., p. 222. Beaumont, in his diplomatic editing of Tocqueville's *Oeuvres,* omitted Tocqueville's reference by name to the three legal scholars "in a spermaceutical state [*à l'état spermeceutique*]." I am indebted to notes provided by Françoise Mélonio for reestablishing the contempt evident in Tocqueville's full unedited phrase.

67. Ibid.

68. See, for example, "General regulations repeatedly made by the Council of State" in TA, box 43, folder H, file dated "8 September 53," p. 104(b), subsequently incorporated as endnote 25 in *The Old Regime*.

69. TA, box 43, folder I, p. 7. Tocqueville specified that this liberty was enjoyed "in all of the classes above the people."

70. TA, box 43, folder H, file dated "6 August 53," p. 117(b). Tocqueville's clearest formulation of this ambiguous relation of the judicial power to liberty occurred in his note titled "Old French Constitution: the judicial power practiced politics in a way that by nature was improper, and failed to perform what by nature it was intended to do (founding ideas)." See TA, box 43, folder K, pp. 32–34 (published in *OC*, II, pt. 2, pp. 363–65).

71. Tocqueville to Freslon, August 10, 1853, *OC* (Beaumont), VI, p. 221.

72. Tocqueville to Dufaure, January 13, 1854, *OC* (Beaumont), VII, pp. 309–10. Tocqueville's request resulted in his securing and reading a compilation of such rulings compiled by L. F. de Jouy, titled *Arrêts de règlement du Parlement de Paris* (1752) (TA, box 43, folder P, subfile titled "Ultrajudicial powers of the courts of justice," pp. 16–17).

73. TA, box 43, folder F, p. 12, with reference to François André Isambert, *Recueil général des anciennes lois françaises* (Paris: Belin-Leprieur, 1822–33), 21:113. Tocqueville would return to Isambert's collection in October 1854 to conduct a study of the "Legislative and administrative power of the courts," in which he contrasted the relative numbers of *arrêts* issued by the central government and the courts. Using Isambert's new series, volume 4, for the period January 1, 1779, through March 3, 1781, he counted 413 administrative acts of the central government, compared with only 33 administrative *arrêts* of the different courts. He concluded, however, that "there is nothing *very certain* to conclude from that, since the whim of the compiler could have inserted more of one than the other and thus reversed the true proportion" (TA, box 43, folder P, p. 9[b]).

74. Tocqueville to Hubert de Tocqueville, January 12 and February 15, 1854, *OC*, XIV, pp. 291 and 293. Tocqueville had always possessed, he told Hubert, "an invincible repugnance" to a career in administration, since "in France, the administration rarely conducts itself in the general interest of the country, but almost always in the private interest of the rulers." He also advised Hubert to maintain an objective perspective in the face of those authors of administrative law, "all of whom are *enamored* by their science, and have concluded that there is nothing more perfect in the world."

75. Tocqueville to Rivet, October 23, 1853, *OC* (Beaumont), VI, p. 235.

76. Tocqueville to Lavergne, October 31, 1853, *OC* (Beaumont), VII, p. 305.

77. See Tocqueville's drafts, up to and including his manuscript submitted to the printer in 1856, in which he titled the first four segments of this unit "Centralization in three sections" (TA, box 39, "Handwritten manuscript"). The intended cohesiveness of this grouping is evident in *The Old Regime*, where it is framed by references in the unit's first and last sentences to centralization as the Revolution's "conquest" (*OR*, 1:118) and "oeuvre" (*OR*, 1:138).

The sixth chapter of the unit (II:7) draws on a greater variety of sources for its arguments, such as statistics regarding the worker population in Paris, compiled by a M. Petiton (see TA, box 43, folder R, subfile titled "Studies furnished by several collaborators"). Tocqueville clearly saw the chapter as connected to his centralization unit, although deserving separate status, as he explained on a draft title page (TA, box 42 [*OR*, 1:355]): "I first had the idea of treating this subject . . . following centralization. But it is too important not to make it a separate chapter. Paris is perhaps, after all, the most efficient cause of the Revolution. Paris, it is true, was itself only an *effect* of which the principal cause had been centralization. It is thus natural not to speak of it until after the latter; but I must speak of it in a special chapter because the significance of Paris will be a subject to which I will continually return in the course of my book."

78. Tocqueville's argument of how the provincial assemblies contributed to the Revolution is a complex and surprising one. Far from being vehicles for a renaissance of local liberty, he argues that the assemblies preserved the royal tradition of despotic administration, since they combined, rather than separated, executive and legislative power. In continuing the French administration's tradition of despotism, they served as transitional bodies for the National Convention and, eventually, for the "Terror" (*OR*, 1:236), mentioned here for the only time in *The Old Regime*. Tocqueville suggests that he will explore this succession more fully in the second volume of his book.

79. See TA, box 43, folder I, p. 6, for Tocqueville's early formulation of this argument.

80. Tocqueville's intended focus is consistent with the thrust of an original title he considered for this section: "How the central or royal administration had laid its hands on the *pays d'états* themselves" (TA, box 42).

81. Tocqueville developed these comparisons in "August 53" in a set of notes titled, "How one rediscovers the disfigured traits of the English parish and American township in the parish of the Old Regime." TA, box 43, folder L, pp. 35–36, subsequently transferred to TA, box 42.

SIX

1. TA, box 43, folder D, p. 44 (published in *OC*, II, pt. 2, p. 373 [*OR*, 2:373]).

2. "Discours de réception 21 avril 1842," *OC*, XVI, p. 252.

3. "État social et politique," pp. 33–34.

4. "Discours de réception," *OC*, XVI, pp. 253, 255n, 254.

5. Tocqueville to Corcelle, November 23, 1852, *OC*, XV, pt. 2, pp. 64–65, with reference to *Lettres de la Marquise du Deffand à Horace Walpole*, 4 vols. (Paris: Treuttel et Würtz, 1812).

6. Tocqueville omitted any reference in his notes to vols. 2, 3, and 9 of Turgot's *Oeuvres*, ed. P.-S. Dupont de Nemours, 9 vols. (Paris: A. Belin, 1811), the volumes that contained Turgot's literary and philosophical writings, including his article in 3:309–20, "Sur les économistes."

7. TA, box 43, folder M, p. 23 (*OC*, II, pt. 2, p. 239).

8. TA, box 43, folder E, p. 24(b), with reference to Dareste, *Histoire*, pp. 270–71.

9. See above, chapter 4, p. 62.

10. In both his notes and his book, Tocqueville viewed the "economists" as interchangeable with the "physiocrats," with the two groups possessing a "common name" (*OR*, 1:209).

11. TA, box 43, folder D, pp. 24–39, with date on the file's cover page. We have no way of knowing whether Tocqueville read Le Trosne's work before or after his June 26, 1853, drafting attempts contained in his "Initial Outline." He clearly read it after his June reading of Blackstone, reminding himself on several occasions within his notes, "See my notes on Blackstone" (ibid., pp. 28, 37, and 38 [*OR*, 2:364, 369, and 370]).

12. TA, box 43, folder D, p. 24 (*OR*, 2:363). Daire's "Notice" on Le Trosne is in *Physiocrates: Quesnay, Dupont de Nemours, Mercier de la Rivière, L'Abbé Baudeau, Le Trosne, avec une introduction sur la doctrine des physiocrates*, ed. Eugène Daire (Paris: Librairie de Guillaumin, 1846), pp. 879–84.

13. TA, box 43, folder D, pp. 29(b)-30 (*OR*, 2:365), with reference to Le Trosne's comments in *De l'administration provinciale et de la réforme de l'impôt* (Basel, 1779), p. 282.

14. Ibid., pp. 30–30(b) (*OR*, 2:366).

15. Ibid., p. 30(b) (*OR*, 2:366). Tocqueville recognized the similarities between the proposals of Le Trosne and Turgot for a system of provincial assemblies, saying that "it is impossible not to see that Turgot took the ideas of Le Trosne or that Le Trosne copied the work of Turgot."

16. Ibid., pp. 31–31(b) (*OR*, 2:366).

17. Ibid., pp. 30(b)-31 (*OR*, 2:366).

18. Ibid., p. 35 (*OR*, 2:368).

19. TA, box 43, folder D, p. 46.

20. For Quesnay's personal history and political and economic beliefs, see Elizabeth Fox-Genovese, *The Origins of Physiocracy* (Ithaca, NY: Cornell University Press, 1976), especially chaps. 2 and 3, pp. 68–133.

21. TA, box 43, folder D, p. 46(b), with reference to Quesnay, *Maximes*, in *Physiocrates*, p. 81.

22. Tocqueville's notes at times cross-referenced these respective reading files. Reading Quesnay, he referred to his intendant readings: "All that I see in the administrative details [of the archives of Tours] proves to me that manufactures were favored, protected, privileged in every way under the Old Regime" (TA, box 43, folder D, p. 48[b]). Reading the intendants, he noted examples in their correspondence of "the literary and philosophical style" (see, for example, TA, box 43, folder H, file dated "24 October 53," p. 71[b]).

23. Tocqueville reiterated his heading for these readings on pp. 40–44 of TA, box 43, folder D. Jardin, ed., and Mélonio, ed., omit the repetitions of the heading from their respective versions, using it instead as a single title for the whole section (*OC*, II, pt. 2, p. 369; *OR* 2:370). In his notes on La Rivière and Baudeau, Tocqueville referred twice to Quesnay, suggesting that he already had completed his reading of him (TA, box 43, folder D, pp. 40[b] and 41 [*OC*, II, pt. 2, pp. 369, 371; *OR*, 2:370–371]).

24. TA, box 43, folder D, pp. 40, 42, 42, 41 (*OC*, II, pt. 2, pp. 369, 371, 371, 370; *OR*, 2:370–72).

25. Ibid., pp. 42–42(b) (*OC*, II, pt. 2, p. 371; *OR*, 2:372).

26. Ibid., p. 43 (*OC*, II, pt. 2, p. 372; *OR*, 2:372).

27. Ibid., p. 43(b) (*OC*, II, pt. 2, p. 372; *OR*, 2:373).

28. Ibid. (*OC*, II, pt. 2, p. 372; *OR* 2:373).

29. Ibid, p. 44 (*OC*, II, pt. 2, p. 372; *OR*, 2:373).

30. Ibid., p. 43(b) (*OC*, II, pt. 2, p. 372; *OR*, 2:373).

31. Ibid. (*OC*, II, pt. 2, pp. 372–73; *OR*, 2:373). Looking ahead to the themes of his larger work, Tocqueville suggested that "the jostling and transformation (never the destruction) of these first elements" (see epigraph to this chapter) would form "a very great part" of his future study of the Revolution.

32. Tocqueville to Beaumont, July 1, 1853, *OC*, VIII, pt. 3, p. 132. Tocqueville had put Mirabeau's *L'ami des hommes* and *La philosophie rurale* on his earlier list of books to seek at Paris or Tours (TA, box 42), adding a note by Dareste cautioning his readers as to the partiality of Mirabeau's judgments (*Histoire*, p. 138n).

33. Beaumont to Tocqueville, July 2 [3], 1853, *OC*, VIII, pt. 3, p. 134.

34. *OC*, II, pt. 2, p. 440 (*OR*, 2:359). These notes no longer exist in the TA: at Madame de Tocqueville's request, Beaumont sent them to Tocqueville's friend Louis de Loménie in October 1862 and they were never returned (see Jardin, "Note critique" to *OC*, II, pt. 2, p. 10n, for this background). Before their release, Beaumont had copied a selection of the notes, which he subsequently published in *OC* (Beaumont), VIII, pp. 149–53, and which serve as the basis for Jardin's republication in *OC*, II, pt. 2, pp. 440–44. Pages 1–23 of TA, box 43, folder D are indeed missing, suggesting that Tocqueville's reading notes on Mirabeau far exceeded Beaumont's brief excerpts, a fact confirmed by Louis de Loménie in *Les Mirabeau*, 5 vols. (Paris: E. Dentu,1889), 1:347.

35. *OC*, II, pt. 2, pp. 442–43 (*OR*, 2:360–61).

36. *OC*, II, pt. 2, p. 443 (*OR*, 2:361).

37. For an intriguing account of Mirabeau's collaboration with Quesnay on the 1758 revision of his *Mémoire concernant les états provinciaux*, subsequently incorporated as part 4 of *L'ami des hommes*, see Fox-Genovese, *Origins of Physiocracy*, chaps. 5 and 6, pp. 167–245. It was this revised version that Tocqueville read, leading him thus unwittingly to gain a literal example of Quesnay's unacknowledged influence in infusing "democratic ideas" into Mirabeau's "feudal mind."

38. *OC*, II, pt. 2, p. 443 (*OR*, 2:362).

39. Tocqueville to Corcelle, December 31, 1853, *OC*, XV, pt. 2, pp. 88–89.

40. For a helpful assessment of the physiocrats' role in conceiving a potent new role for public opinion, and of the suitability of their conception for a despotic version of the sovereign, see Ozouf, " 'Public Opinion' at the End of the Old Regime," *Journal of Modern History* 60, suppl. (September 1988): S14–S15.

41. Tocqueville to Mrs. Grote, conversation of February 13, 1854, in Senior, "Conversations," *OC*, VI, pt. 2, p. 407 (*Conversations*, 2:49).

42. TA, box 43, folder D, p. 25(b), with reference to Le Trosne, *De l'administration provinciale*, p. 117.

43. TA, box 43, folder J, p. 32, with reference to François Nicolas, comte de Mollien, *Mémoires d'un ministre du trésor public*, 3 vols. (Paris: Guillaumin, 1845), 1:5.

44. Ibid., p. 2, with reference to Jacques Necker, *Oeuvres complètes de M. Necker*, ed. A.-L. de Staël-Holstein, 15 vols. (Paris: Treuttel et Würtz, 1820–21), vol. 4, *De l'administration des finances de la France*, p. 50. Tocqueville's reading notes on Necker are undated, but his reading succeeded that of Dareste, whom he mentioned in folder J, p. 3. Looking at this same passage of Necker's, which Tocqueville would also cite in *OR*, 1:221, Keith Baker identifies seven characteristics of Necker's opinion, concluding that it serves as "a mean between despotism and extreme liberty": "Public opinion, in other words, implies acceptance of an open, public politics. But, at the same time, it suggests a politics without passions, a politics without factions, a politics without conflicts, a politics without fear. One could even say that it represents a politics without politics." *Inventing the French Revolution* (Cambridge: Cambridge University Press, 1990), pp. 193–97; quotation on p. 196. Such a version of opinion and the politics it spawns would, of course, be anathema to Tocqueville.

45. TA, box 43, folder D, p. 44 (*OC*, II, pt. 2, p. 373; *OR*, 2:373). See inscription on title page of this chapter for Tocqueville's full quotation.

46. See Tocqueville's intendants' notes of August 2, 1853 (TA, box 43, folder H, pp. 125–25[b]), discussed above in chapter 5, p. 85. See too his "Administrative investigation of the unity of weights and measures," dated "August 53" (TA, box 43, folder O, pp. 53–54, published in *OC*, II, pt. 2, pp. 373–74, as "First sign of the Revolution and its preparation"; Tocqueville filed this document dating from 1853 in what was otherwise an 1852 file).

47. Tocqueville to Freslon, September 23, 1853, *OC* (Beaumont), VI, p. 234 (*Selected Letters*, p. 296).

48. The full citation for this work is A Society of Men of Letters [*Une société de gens de lettres*], *Résumé général, ou Extrait des cahiers de pouvoirs, instructions, demandes et doléances, remis par les divers bailliages, sénéchaussées et pays d'états du royaume à leurs députés à l'assemblée des états généraux, ouverts à Versailles le 4 mai, 1789. Avec une table raisonnée des matières*, 3 vols., published by Louis-Marie Prudhomme, with a "Discours préliminaire" by Jean Rousseau (Paris: Chez l'éditeur, 1789). Prudhomme is cited as the publisher, and Rousseau as the author of the opening discourse, in some but not all editions of the *Résumé*. In some editions, the work appears in two volumes.

49. TA, box 43, folder C, subfile titled, "Work on the cahiers—done around 1836." The sketches Tocqueville inserted into the essay from his notes are in *Review*, pp. 142, 144–45, 150 ("État social et politique," pp. 39, 41, 46, 47). In the essay, he referred to Prudhomme's work by name as a "*Résumé des cahiers*" (ibid., p. 147n [ibid., p. 43n]). For the timing of Tocqueville's reading, see his note dated "January 26, 1836," with a quotation drawn from the *Résumé général*, in TA (Beinecke), C.V.a.

50. Tocqueville to Mrs. Grote, conversation of February 15, 1854, in Senior, "Conversations," *OC*, VI, pt. 2, p. 410 (*Conversations*, 2:53).

51. I base this judgment on the number of Tocqueville's "hic" interjections in TA, box 43, folder C, which is higher both absolutely and proportionately than in any other reading file.

52. We have already noted Tocqueville's fascination with the novelty of the intendants' archives, expressed to Freslon on June 9, 1853. In his foreword to Gilbert Shapiro and John Markoff's authoritative study, Charles Tilly grants Tocqueville pride of place as the originator of French historical studies of the *cahiers* (*Revolutionary Demands: A Content Analysis of the Cahiers de Doléances of 1789* [Stanford, CA: Stanford University Press, 1998], p. xxvii). Shapiro and Markoff themselves cite three contemporary analyses of the *cahiers* produced in 1789 (ibid., p. 120), all of which Tocqueville will use or plan to study in his own investigations: Prudhomme's *Résumé général*, Comte Stanislas de Clermont-Tonnerre's official *cahiers* report for the Constituent Assembly (for Tocqueville's plans in 1857 to read this report, see *OC*, II, pt. 2, p. 212n), and Samuel Dupont de Nemours's content analysis, titled *Tableau comparatif des demandes contenus dans les cahiers des trois ordres* (for Tocqueville's 1857 preliminary assessment of this work—which he located at the British Museum—as "shorter and perhaps more comprehensive than the book in three volumes that I know," see TA, box 44, folder 28).

53. The "dusty" equivalent of a *cahiers* investigation would have been a study in the National Archives of the entire collection of the more than five hundred "general" *cahiers,* uncondensed and unanthologized by the authors of the *Résumé général.*

54. TA, box 43, folder C, p. 28.

55. Ibid., title page. Tocqueville's introductory title page included as well his topic ("Analysis of 'Résumé des cahiers' "), a date ("October 53"), and advice to himself ("Reread these notes in the order in which they were made. That is to say—clergy, nobility, Third").

56. Ibid., p. 42.

57. Ibid., p. 1.

58. Ibid., pp. 20–21(b) (published in *OC,* II, pt. 2, pp. 366–67 [the concluding comment on the "section on the municipalities" is not a part of these initial remarks, since it is appended by Jardin, ed., from box 43, folder C, p. 40]; *OR,* 2:357–58). We can be certain that these thematic summaries were transcribed prospectively because Tocqueville began his corroborative notes on the bottom of the same page that contained the conclusion of his summary comments (p. 21[b]).

59. Ibid., p. 21(b).

60. Ibid., p. 22. Tocqueville took special interest in the *cahier* of the Third of Rennes, excerpted 181 times within the *Résumé général* by its authors, not just because of its ferocity but because Brittany, where it originated, would subsequently give birth to one of the Revolution's most profound and deeply rooted counterrevolutionary movements, the *chouannerie.*

61. Ibid. Tocqueville's previous transcription of this same quotation is in TA, box 43, folder C, subfile titled "Work on the cahiers—done about 1836," p. 59. His eloquent comments in his essay based on this note are in *Review,* p. 148 ("État social et politique," p. 44). The influence of Sieyès on Tocqueville's 1836 text, averred by Georges Lefebvre

("Note préliminaire" to *OC*, II, pt. 1, p. 13), Mélonio (Notes to "État social et politique," in *L'ancien régime* [Paris: GF-Flammarion, 1988], p. 399), and Furet (*Interpreting the French Revolution*, p. 134), may thus best be viewed as secondhand, filtered through the Rennes's Third's assembly and its recorded grievances, assessed by Tocqueville in the *Résumé général.*

62. Tocqueville's comments only appear to be "deductive," of course, since they are based on his former reading. George V. Taylor suggested, too strongly I believe, that Tocqueville sought only confirmation, not edification, in his *cahiers* readings: "In effect, [Tocqueville] asked each *cahier*, 'What can you contribute to my composite forecast of the Revolution?' " See his article, "Revolutionary and Nonrevolutionary Content in the *Cahiers* of 1789: An Interim Report," *French Historical Studies* 8, pt. 4 (Fall 1972): 482.

63. TA, box 43, folder C, subfile titled, "Work on the cahiers—done about 1836," pp. 59–59(b).

64. Ibid., pp. 56, 60(b), 59.

65. Ibid., final unnumbered page.

66. TA, box 43, folder C, p. 20 (*OC*, II, pt. 2, p. 366).

67. Tocqueville commented on these "rights" throughout readings in folder C. At times, as when several bailliages demanded the establishment of provincial bureaus to receive complaints during periods when the Estates-General was not meeting, he saw in such "defiance of power" a character that was "essentially anarchic" (p. 45[b]).

68. Tocqueville triggered this form of shorthand when he responded on his second page of notes to a definition of "public right" by the nobles of Alençon (*Résumé général*, 2:34): "The inalienable rights of man, the inherent principles of the social compact! These nobles were very much of their time, and to make the Revolution, they only lacked being commoners" (TA, box 43, folder C, p. 2).

69. TA, box 43, folder C, p. 45 (*OR*, 2:355). Tocqueville added a letter to his initial numbering at this point in his file to distinguish this collection of evidence of the clergy's "liberalism" and then went back and reread the whole volume of clergy grievances in order to glean liberal examples. See ibid., pp. 45–50 ([a][4]–[f][9]). When he refers to the clergy's "*democratic theories*," I take Tocqueville to be using his participatory political definition of democracy, a usage that is rare within these *cahiers* reading notes.

70. Ibid., p. 20 (*OC*, II, pt. 2, p. 366; *OR*, 2:357).

71. Ibid., p. 42, with reference to a call of the clergy of Lyon for uniform public education (*Résumé général*, 1:90).

72. Ibid., pp. 12 and 12(b), 43, 9(b), 48, 28, 13(b), and 15(b).

73. Ibid., p. 12(b).

74. Ibid., p. 48, in response to grievance cited in *Résumé général*, 1:172.

75. Ibid., p. 7(b).

76. For Tocqueville's three different usages of "democracy" in his studies for *The Old Regime*—with each corresponding to either the political, social, or despotic traits

identified here in the *cahiers*—see chapter 4, note 106, for my explanation of his definitions.

77. Ibid., pp. 44, 44(b), 47, 48(b), 49(b), 18, and 26(b)–27. In each case, Tocqueville labeled the characteristic "democratic."

78. Ibid., pp. 34(b)–35, with reference to *Résumé général,* 3:408.

79. TA, box 43, folder C, pp. 20–21(b) (*OC,* II, pt. 2, pp. 366–67; *OR,* 2, 357–58).

80. Ibid., p. 21 (*OC,* II, pt. 2, p. 367; *OR,* 2:358).

81. Gilbert Shapiro and John Markoff, *Revolutionary Demands: A Content Analysis of the Cahiers de Doléances of 1789* (Stanford, CA: Stanford University Press, 1998), pp. 29, 570.

82. The three number tables are those of the clergy (*Résumé général,* 1:335–63), the nobility (2:377–418), and the Third (3:548–96).

83. Ibid., 3:548–551.

84. A typical entry in the number table thus reads as follows: "*Accused.* Suppression of oath for defendants. (91.) 162." The table here tells us that ninety-one bailliages, in this case of the clergy, supported the suppression of oaths for the accused and that a representative sample of such a demand can be found on p. 162 of the text. *Résumé général,* 1:335.

85. TA, box 43, folder C, p. 41.

86. Ibid.

87. Tocqueville questioned, for example, the "unanimous" support for the removal of internal customs barriers, since the eastern provinces, especially Alsace, would have had strong reasons to oppose such a measure. TA, box 43, folder C, pp. 10(b)–11 and 50.

88. After reading a grievance of the Parisian nobles to abolish the confiscation of personal possessions, Tocqueville commented: "I am unable to determine if this demand was repeated by others, because the authors of the table did not judge the confiscation of possessions sufficiently important to warrant a separate listing in their table (significant)" (TA, box 43, folder C, p. 9). Later, when he had located the elusive count, he added a marginal notation to that effect, showing that he had also sought out the corresponding number count for the same demand in the table of the Third.

89. By his own count, Prudhomme had produced 1,500 revolutionary pamphlets in the two years immediately preceding the Revolution. See "Prudhomme, Louis-Marie (1752–1832)," entry by Jack Censer in *Historical Dictionary of the French Revolution, 1788–99,* ed. Samuel Scott and Barry Rothaus (Westport, CT: Greenwood Press, 1985), p. 797. Hugh Gough describes Prudhomme's involvement in the political clubs, adding that "club activity and journalism were complementary activities, both components of the political education of the nation." *The Newspaper Press in the French Revolution* (Chicago: Dorsey Press, 1988), p. 58.

90. Prudhomme provided several details of his financial status in 1789 in response to a suit that fall filed by Antoine Tournon contesting ownership of the *Révolutions de Paris.* See "Contestation between Proudhomme and M. Tournon, 3 November 1789; excerpt from a deliberation of the Committee of Police. Response of Monsieur Prudhomme, owner and editor of the 'Révolutions de Paris.'"

91. I am using here a quotation by Prudhomme from his prospectus for a subsequent proposed newspaper, the "Voyageur," in the time of the Directory. See Prudhomme, "Prospectus of 27 floréal, year 7." For a full consideration of Prudhomme's awareness of the significance of rhetoric to the developing "revolution," see Baker's signature chapter in *Inventing the French Revolution,* pp. 218–23. Baker says that "there is no better place to look [than in Prudhomme's *Révolutions de Paris*], if one wishes to follow the invention of the modern concept of revolution from the intellectual elements available under the Old Regime" (p. 218).

92. Prudhomme, "Prospectus" for *Résumé général,* May 20, 1789. This "Prospectus" appears at the front of the first volume of some, but not all, editions of the *Résumé général* of 1789.

93. Document from *"Police devoilée,"* cited in Eugène Hatin, *Histoire de la presse en France* (Paris: Poulet-Malassis et de Broise, 1860), pp. 319–20.

94. Ibid., 319.

95. Prudhomme, *Résumé général,* 1:1–2.

96. This effort to present an image of impartiality was evident in the number tables as well. For example, on the volatile issue of the nobles' demands for voting in the Estates-General, the *Résumé général* included counts of three contrasting positions. See Prudhomme, *Résumé général,* 2:418.

97. The meticulous style of the *Résumé général* prefigures a similar attention to detail noted by observers of Prudhomme's subsequent hugely successful newspaper, the *Révolutions de Paris.* Censer describes Prudhomme's newspaper's coverage of a revolutionary mutiny at Nancy on August 30–31, 1790, in terms that could well be applied to the publisher's work in the *Résumé général* of the previous year: "What principally took readers much nearer to these events, however, was the volume of copy prepared. The accounts of the background to and the actual developments at Nancy were extremely detailed. . . . Moreover, the *Révolutions de Paris* managed to refer to—and sometimes even print—competing versions of the event without introducing confusion. . . . The lion's share of the coverage was communicated in a dispassionate tone which must have seemed that of a judicious judge, not a prejudiced polemicist." *The French Press in the Age of Enlightenment* (New York: Routledge, 1994), p. 31.

98. See table A (pp. 128–29), "Predominance of Excerpts from the Twenty Most Cited *Cahiers* in Each Volume of Prudhomme's *Résumé Général* of 1789."

99. Guy Chaussinand-Nogaret, *The French Nobility in the Eighteenth Century: From Feudalism to Enlightenment,* trans. William Doyle (Cambridge: Cambridge University Press, 1985), with tables of nobles' grievances found on pp. 150–56. His count for "venal nobility to be abolished; nobility to be the reward for service" is on p. 152. Sasha R. Weitman, "Bureaucracy, Democracy and the French Revolution" (Ph.D. diss., Washington University, 1968), especially tables 6.1 (pp. 317–19), 6.2 (pp. 345–49), 6.3 (pp. 381–83), and 6.4 (pp. 402–6). His count, "For Abolition of Venality of Titles of Nobility," is in table 6.2. Weitman quantified the *cahiers* notes of Beatrice Hyslop to arrive at his figures.

100. Chaussinand-Nogaret, *French Nobility*, p. 151; Weitman, "Bureaucracy, Democracy and the French Revolution," table 6.3.

101. See *Résumé général*, 1:380, and Chaussinand-Nogaret, *French Nobility*, p. 152. For a broader comparison between the *Résumé général* and Chaussinand-Nogaret of twenty counts for selected grievances, including for both "una" and non-"una" ones, see table B, pp. 129–30.

102. Shapiro and Markoff, looking at this very issue of the two possibilities of the meaning of the "una" in Prudhomme's number counts, add their own authoritative weight to this conclusion: "In our own analyses, we do not find the level of unanimity that Prudhomme claims, in either sense." See *Revolutionary Demands*, p. 120.

103. Prudhomme, *Histoire impartiale des révolutions de France, depuis la mort de Louis XV* (Paris: Librairie de Mademoiselle Adèle Prudhomme, 1824), p. 170n.

104. François Grille, *Introduction aux mémoires sur la Révolution française, ou Tableau comparatif des mandats et pouvoirs*, 2 vols. (Paris, 1825).

105. P.-J.-B. Buchez and P.-C. Roux, *L'histoire parlementaire de la Révolution*, 40 vols. (Paris: Paulin, 1833–36), 1:322–35.

106. Stoffels's résumé of the nobles' *cahiers* is found in TA, box 43, folder R, subfile titled "Studies furnished by several collaborators." Alexis Stoffels was the son of Tocqueville's dear childhood friend Eugène Stoffels, who died in 1852. In a letter to Kergorlay at that time, Tocqueville had mourned his friend's death and worried about the family's financial status (letter of July 22, 1852, *OC*, XIII, pt. 2, p. 243). Beaumont tells us of the "tender affection" that Tocqueville subsequently bestowed on Stoffels's children, especially Alexis (*OC* [Beaumont], V, p. 467n). Hearing from the then twenty-year-old Alexis at the end of 1855 about his studies in Roman law, Tocqueville wrote to caution him that medieval monarchs used such law for their own authoritarian purposes and to encourage "greater ardor in your undertakings" (letter of January 4, 1856, *OC* [Beaumont], V, pp. 467–70). He suggested that they see each other in Paris when he arrived there in February to finish his book. It was most likely during these final few months preceding publication, when Tocqueville experienced such pressure to complete his book's endnotes, that he enlisted his godson's assistance as a "collaborator."

107. The two sections Tocqueville added are those titled "Care that must be taken of the people" and "Church and clergy" (*OR*, 1:289–90, 291). In the latter, with respect to church discipline, Tocqueville said: "Seventeen bailliages declare that the Estates-General is competent to regulate discipline." Turning to the *Résumé général*'s "Table des matières" for the nobility, and looking under "*Dogmes*," we find the basis for his count: "The Estates-General will be competent for discipline and not for dogma (17.)" (*Résumé*, 2:389).

Tocqueville's insertions of these sections, and of his other *cahiers* quantifications, can be seen in TA, box 41, subsection titled "The first and second galley proofs of notes."

108. TA, box 43, folder C, p. 41(b). Tocqueville states that the church in the Old Regime surrendered liberty in its internal affairs in return for political and financial

benefits granted by the kings, thus subscribing to the maxim, "Act servilely in order to rule."

109. Stoffels's summary of the clergy's *cahiers* is in TA, box 43, folder R, subfile labeled "Studies furnished by several collaborators." He titled his report "Of the spirit of liberty that reigns in the demands addressed to the Estates-General by the deputies of the clergy."

110. TA, box 43, folder C, pp. 51–51(b) (published in *OC,* II, pt. 2, pp. 365–66).

111. Tocqueville to Beaumont, April 24, 1856, *OC,* VIII, pt. 3, p. 394 (*Selected Letters,* p. 329).

112. Peter Gay criticizes Tocqueville's lack of specificity in this discussion, arguing that "he took the pronouncements of the physiocrats and generalized from them to thinkers who rejected most if not all physiocratic doctrines." See Gay, *Voltaire's Politics: The Poet as Realist* (New Haven: Yale University Press, 1988), p. 8n. In an 1853 note after encountering Dareste's account of the economists' reform efforts in the countryside, Tocqueville linked their school with that of the philosophes in the following terms: "The economists ended up at liberty, or at least at the destruction of ancient servitude, by considerations of the production of wealth; the great writers of the same time by general principles and political theories" (TA, box 43, folder E, p. 24(b)–25).

113. Beaumont to Tocqueville, April 22, 1856, *OC,* VIII, pt. 3, pp. 392–93; Grote to Senior, enclosed in Senior to Tocqueville, October 20, 1856, *OC,* VI, pt. 2, pp. 192–93; and Mill to Tocqueville, December 15, 1856, *OC,* VI, pt. 1, p. 350.

114. Tocqueville to Beaumont, April 24, 1856, *OC,* VIII, pt. 3, p. 395.

115. Tocqueville numbered the chapter "VI" in this first Tours draft. As indicated on a summary sheet inserted with the drafts of I:2 in TA, box 42, he planned the following chapters in this order in his first draft of book 2: I (our II:1), II (our II:2–5), III (our II:7), IV (our II:8–10), V (our II:12), VI (our III:1), VII (our III:2), VIII (our III:4) and IX (our III:3). We must remember that Tocqueville originally envisioned books 2 and 3 as a single unit, splitting them apart only in the second edition of his book, published in the fall of 1856. References to the original drafts of each of these chapters composed at Tours can be traced with these original numbers through Tocqueville's "rubbish." The chapters clearly shifted in their numbers and titles during his time at Tours (a new III [our II:6] emerged, for example), but the list provides a useful view of his early intentions. For a transcription of this list, albeit with the assignment of a different date and purpose, see *OR,* 1:71–72.

116. Tocqueville's full quotation, contained in his "rubbish" on a title page to his penultimate version of this chapter, read as follows: "Pay strict attention to the *generalities* relative to the causes of the philosophy of the eighteenth century. More profound than the definitive draft. But this latter more perceptible and pleasing to the average readers." By drawing attention to the affinity between the era's philosophy and its social equality, Tocqueville had wanted to focus more on the factors that facilitated the philosophy than on the men who professed it. This theme was well expressed in another proposed title for the chapter: "How there is in what was called the philosophy of the eighteenth century a true and permanent element

because it represents the ideas that spring naturally and necessarily from the new social state."

117. Tocqueville's antipathy to what he regarded as Voltaire's hostility to liberty was long-standing (see Tocqueville to Kergorlay, September 4, 1837, *OC*, XIII, pt. 1, p. 427), providing again an instance in which he separated praise for a writer's style or method from scorn for his failure to support liberty. In his highly selective reading of Voltaire for *The Old Regime,* most likely conducted late in his research since he filed it in folder R, Tocqueville simply gathered "extracts from several letters of Voltaire of 1770 and 71, approving the destruction of the parlements and, in general, little favorable to liberty" (TA, box 43, folder R, subfile titled "Spirit of Voltaire in political matters").

118. We can detect this shift by viewing Tocqueville's "Copy" (TA, box 40), where the first paragraph of endnote 64 initially stood alone without a title. When Tocqueville subsequently appended additional paragraphs from a different spot in the same reading file, plus a title, the endnote's focus shifted without a corresponding shift in the textual passage to which he referenced it.

119. On the cover pages of each of the three volumes of his *Résumé général,* Prudhomme introduced his work with a quotation from Virgil that signaled the ambitious nature of his enterprise: "Do not fly as agitated playthings before the fierce winds [Ne turbata volent rapidis ludibria ventis], Aeneid VI." In book 6 of the *Aeneid,* soon after first landing on the shores of Italy, Aeneas fervently prayed to Apollo, exhorting him to bless the fortunes of the Trojan people in their quest for a new homeland. He then urged Apollo's priestess, the Sibyl, to provide her unique prophetic support for this enterprise. After indicating his plans to establish a shrine in the Sibyl's honor where he would collect the records of her prophecies, he begged her to chant them in her own words and not commit them to leaves that might be dispersed by "the fierce winds."

120. Furet, *Interpreting the French Revolution,* p. 45.

121. On the cover page of his reading file of the excerpts of the clergy's *cahiers* that he read in the *Résumé général,* Tocqueville anticipated his comments in *The Old Regime,* saying: "General remark: When one assembles all of the reported abuses and all of the reforms demanded by the order of the clergy, one sees that there is enough there to bring about twenty revolutions." And after completing his readings of the nobles' grievances, he observed in a similar vein: "Same remark as that which I put on the cover of the preceding folder and for much greater reason, because here . . . there is nothing about which people do not complain, nothing that is not attacked and disparaged, called into question" (TA, box 43, folder C, cover pages).

122. For John Markoff's indication of this same shortcoming in Tocqueville's reading of the *cahiers,* see *The Abolition of Feudalism: Peasants, Lords, and Legislators in the French Revolution* (University Park: Pennsylvania State University Press, 1996), pp. 81–82.

123. Tocqueville's reading of the *cahiers* in Prudhomme's *Résumé général* supplanted contrary evidence that he had encountered in his reading of the Marquis d'Argenson's 1751 *Mémoires.* In that reading, drawing on the editor's introduction to the 1825 edition of this text, Tocqueville had noted d'Argenson's "forecast of the

Revolution" (TA, box 43, folder J, p. 22, with reference to *Journal et mémoires du marquis d'Argenson* [Paris: Baudouin Frères, 1825], p. 118). Making his own reference to d'Argenson's repeated revolutionary predictions, as well as to multiple examples of frequent political "contestation" during the prerevolutionary era, Baker recognizes the evident distortion in Tocqueville's portrait of French inexperience, saying, "This picture is surely overdrawn." See *Inventing the French Revolution*, pp. 21 and 309n. 16.

124. Chaussinand-Nogaret, *French Nobility*, pp. 157–58.

125. Ibid., p. 158. See Roger Chartier, *The Cultural Uses of Print in Early Modern France*, trans. Lydia G. Cochrane (Princeton: Princeton University Press, 1987), pp. 137–43, for a broad range of studies that support Tocqueville's assertions of the uniformity of opinion. See, too, Gilbert Shapiro, John Markoff, and Sasha R. Weitman, "Quantitative Studies of the French Revolution," *History and Theory* 12, no. 2 (1973): 187–89, and Shapiro and Markoff, *Revolutionary Demands*, p. 7 and chap. 16 ("Allies and Opponents: Nobility and Third Estate in the Spring of 1789"), pp. 296–324.

126. See, for example, Markoff, *Abolition of Feudalism*, pp. 18–20, for his summary of studies that tend to confirm Tocqueville's claim that the peasants were chiefly motivated by their concern for justice, owing to rising expectations and the functional decline of the seigneurial system, rather than by their sheer economic burden.

127. Shapiro and Markoff, *Revolutionary Demands*, pp. 351–68.

128. Tocqueville to Corcelle, September 17, 1853, *OC*, XV, pt. 2, p. 81 (*Selected Letters*, p. 294).

129. Jardin, *Tocqueville*, p. 433.

130. TA, box 43, folder J, p. 14. Tocqueville made his comment with respect to the specific problem of noble absenteeism.

131. Each figure in the table represents the number of times a particular *cahier* was excerpted in a volume of the *Résumé général*. The *cahier* of the nobility of Agen was thus presented in vol. 2 of the *Résumé* in thirty-two distinct segments, spread throughout the book. For each volume of the *Résumé*, I list the twenty *cahiers* with the highest numbers of excerpts.

132. The wording in column 1 for all but the last of these twenty grievances, plus the percentage and number of supporting *cahiers* in column 3, is drawn from Chaussinand-Nogaret, *French Nobility*, 150–56. The number counts in column 2 are from the "Table des matières" for the nobility in Prudhomme, *Résumé général*, 2:377–418, with "una" designating a "unanimous" count.

SEVEN

1. Tocqueville to Corcelle, September 17, 1853, *OC*, XV, pt. 2, p. 80 (*Selected Letters*, p. 294).

2. Roger Boesche, *The Strange Liberalism of Alexis de Tocqueville* (Ithaca, NY: Cornell University Press, 1987), pp. 21, 264–66.

3. Mélonio, *Tocqueville and the French*, pp. 137–42.

4. Tocqueville to Madame Swetchine, January 7, 1856, *OC*, XV, pt. 2, p. 268 (*Selected Letters*, p. 326).

5. Larry Siedentop, "Two Liberal Traditions," in *The Idea of Freedom,* ed. Alan Ryan (Oxford: Oxford University Press, 1979), pp. 153–74; Aurelian Craiutu, "Between Scylla and Charybdis: The 'Strange' Liberalism of the French Doctrinaires," *History of European Ideas* 24, nos. 4–5 (1998): 243–65, quotation on p. 259.

6. Isaiah Berlin, "The Thought of de Tocqueville," *History* 50, no. 169 (June 1965): 200. Berlin's comment is made in a review of Jack Lively's book, *The Social and Political Thought of Alexis de Tocqueville* (Oxford: Clarendon Press, 1962).

7. For this background, see André-Jean Tudesq, Preface to *OC*, X, pp. 18–36.

8. Jardin, *Tocqueville,* pp. 459–60.

9. Tocqueville to Corcelle, September 3, 1856, *OC*, XV, pt. 2, p. 175.

10. Tocqueville to La Rive, October 13, 1856, *OC*, VII, p. 351.

11. Tocqueville to Freslon, January 12, 1858, *OC* (Beaumont), VII, pp. 479–80.

12. Tocqueville to Corcelle, September 17, 1853, *OC*, XV, pt. 2, pp. 80–81 (*Selected Letters*, pp. 293–95). For a fuller version of Tocqueville's best statement of his pedagogical aims, see the epigraph I have used for this chapter.

13. Tocqueville to Barrot, October 26, 1853, *OC* (Beaumont), VII, p. 301.

14. Tocqueville to Beaumont, February 27, 1858, *OC*, VIII, pt. 3, p. 543 (*Selected Letters*, p. 366).

15. Kergorlay to Tocqueville, July 7, 1856, *OC*, XIII, pt. 2, p. 301.

16. Kergorlay to Tocqueville, August 22, 1856, *OC*, XIII, pt. 2, p. 305. As part of his critique, Kergorlay bracketed passages that he found to possess "something entangled"; at Tocqueville's urging, he would subsequently annotate the entire volume in this way, based on his "four or five" rereadings of the text, and submit the completed version to the author (Kergorlay to Tocqueville, September 16, 1856, *OC*, XIII, pt. 2, p. 313). Mayer indicates that Tocqueville adopted most of these revisions in the third edition of his text, published in 1857 ("Note sur l'Ordre du Texte," *OC*, II, pt. 1, p. 7).

17. Kergorlay to Tocqueville, September 1, 1856, *OC*, XIII, pt. 2, p. 311.

18. Tocqueville to Kergorlay, July 29, 1856, *OC*, XIII, pt. 2, p. 303.

19. Tocqueville to Kergorlay, August 28, 1856, *OC*, XIII, pt. 2, p. 309.

20. Tocqueville to Madame de Circourt, January 11, 1854, *OC*, XVIII, p. 142. Grandmaison reported having seen Tocqueville's collection of volumes "arranged on a narrow shelf . . . as [his] weapons of choice" ("Séjour d'Alexis de Tocqueville," p. 934).

21. Tocqueville to Corcelle, December 31, 1853, *OC*, XV, pt. 2, p. 89. A year later, Tocqueville would repeat to Corcelle his belief that Bourdaloue was a master of such carefully calibrated, unobtrusive instruction (letter of December 28, 1854, ibid., p. 130).

22. Beaumont to Senior, conversation of August 1860 in Senior, "Conversations," *OC*, VI, pt. 2, p. 502.

23. TA, box 42. I have taken all citations from Tocqueville's various drafts from this box of "Sketches and drafts." Immediately following this note, Tocqueville gave an

example of how he might employ familiar words to achieve such resonance with his readers: "Example: when I explain how the Revolution substituted a new, immense social power for the scattering of old powers, recall the destroyed powers by calling them by their names, and try, in painting the new social power, to use words that give the image of government and administration that my readers see in use every day and with which they are acquainted."

24. TA, box 42, comment affixed to Tocqueville's earliest version of I:3 dated December 15, 1853 (published in *OC*, II, pt. 2, pp. 348–49; *OR*, 1:323–24).

25. Tocqueville to Duvergier de Hauranne, September 1, 1856, *OC* (Beaumont), VI, p. 333.

26. Tocqueville's references to Mirabeau's eighth and twenty-eighth notes to the king of July 3 and September 28, 1790, were drawn from *Correspondance entre le comte de Mirabeau et le comte de La Marck, pendant les années 1789, 1790 et 1791,* published by M. Ad de Bacourt (Paris: Librairie Ve le Normant, 1851), 2:75, 197. Tocqueville used the note of July 3 in *OR*, 1:98, editing two of its phrases to tailor it to his own portrayal of liberty.

27. Tocqueville to Ampère, [January 1, 1854?], *OC*, XI, pp. 231–32.

28. Ibid., p. 232.

29. Tocqueville to Beaumont, December 28, 1853, *OC*, VIII, pt. 3, p. 177.

30. Tocqueville's decision is startling for many reasons, not the least being its direct contradiction of the advice proffered to him at Sorrento by his most trusted stylistic consultant, Kergorlay (Kergorlay to Tocqueville, January 19, 1851, *OC*, XIII, pt. 2, p. 237). Kergorlay had advised Tocqueville first to compile a "primitive canvas" of historical and narrative facts and only later, in his final definitive writing, to dispense with these facts and fill in the resulting holes by applying his own fresh meditations and observations "across all of the holes that you would thus have made in your tableau."

For Tocqueville's list of the nine initial chapters of books 2 and 3 of *The Old Regime* that he first drafted at Tours, see chapter 6, note 115.

31. Tocqueville to Beaumont, January 29, 1854, *OC*, VIII, pt. 3, p. 186.

32. Tocqueville to Hubert de Tocqueville, March 7, 1854, *OC*, XIV, pp. 294–95. I take Tocqueville's reference to "about a half volume" to indicate the compact frame of his general ideas that he was currently constructing at Tours, devoid of the wealth of corroborating facts that he knew he still would need to add.

33. "Séjour d'Alexis de Tocqueville," p. 939. In his retrospective account, Grandmaison provided his own understanding of Tocqueville's method, based on observation and conversation with the author at Tours as well as on his subsequent reading of Tocqueville's posthumously published correspondence: "He selected, linked, and set forth his ideas with great care and art, and it was only after having constructed the learned and solid framework that he turned his attention to expression and ornaments of style." Grandmaison's account provides further evidence of Tocqueville's customary discretion, since he clearly was not privy to the true nature of Tocqueville's omissions—the very facts that Grandmaison had painstakingly assisted the author to assemble!

34. Tocqueville to Ampère, May 20, 1854, *OC*, XI, p. 241.

35. Tocqueville to Kergorlay, March 23, 1854, *OC,* XIII, pt. 2, p. 283.

36. Tocqueville to Beaumont, July 16, 1854, *OC,* VIII, pt. 3, p. 224. Tocqueville added that "the political and especially the social state of this country seems to me to be exactly what I had assumed."

37. TA, box 43, folder Q, p. 4(b).

38. Tocqueville to Beaumont, October 26, 1854, *OC,* VIII, pt. 3, p. 245. For a map that situates Tocqueville's new residence, see *OC,* XIII, pt. 2, p. 371.

39. Tocqueville to Circourt, November 14, 1854, *OC,* XVIII, p. 217.

40. Tocqueville to Beaumont, October 26, 1854, *OC,* VIII, pt. 3, p. 245.

41. Tocqueville to Ampère, November 12 or 19, 1854, *OC,* XI, pp. 260–61.

42. Tocqueville would subsequently file his index at the very end of his "Reading notes" (TA, box 43), where we find it preceded by a summary sheet: "All of these notes except for the final folder R are analyzed in the great index prepared at Compiègne in 1854." The index contained no references to folder R, consisting of notes on readings conducted after its compilation, or to folder C, "Analysis of the cahiers," which Tocqueville thus appeared to have viewed less as a source for facts than as a sounding board for his analysis of them.

43. Tocqueville organized his index into eleven categories: England, Germany; Municipal and Provincial Administration, Taxes, Taille, Capitation, Public Charges; Provincial Institutions, Bourgeoisie, People; Nobility, Seigneurs, Feudal Rights; Unclassifiable; Administration, Centralization, Intendants; Bookselling, Press; Great Council, King's Council; Justice, Parliament; Church, Clergy; *Maréchaussée.*

44. These pages of excerpts are interspersed with his Compiègne chapter drafts in TA, box 42.

45. See below, note 72.

46. Tocqueville to Beaumont, March 17, 1856, *OC,* VIII, pt. 3, p. 379.

47. It is Tocqueville's newly instituted system of citations to his reading notes that provides, of course, the indispensable tool for our differentiating his Compiègne drafts from those he composed at Tours. The distinction between drafts from Tours without notations to his reading files and drafts from Compiègne that contain them is complicated on at least three occasions, however, by Tocqueville's insertion into these files of discarded sheets from his heavily annotated manuscript. We must recall as well that Tocqueville's random collection of "rubbish" is a partial one since he occasionally burned extraneous sheets for which he believed he had no further use.

48. In his Tours draft, Tocqueville's approach for this argument had been tentative and necessarily rhetorical, suffering from the forced deprivation of his facts. He began by leaving a hole for an unspecified quotation from Young: "Choose the most striking citation. Only one." He then introduced the results of his own interviews with former cultivators ("I wished myself to recover the trace of the fact so remarked by Young") and completed his case with his discovery of the "property inventories": "I researched and found in several places where it still exists a document [that] succeeded in establishing in irrefutable fashion the truth of the assertions of the voyager and substituted certainty for probability in this matter." In his Compiègne

rewrite, he replaced this tripartite account with the stream of twelve consecutive sources, assembled with the help of his index, that I noted above (see chapter 3, pp. 52–53). With his facts at his fingertips, Tocqueville was no longer forced to rely on rhetorical assertions of the truth; his facts—novel and profuse—could provide their own demonstration of it.

49. Tocqueville split his original II:2 into our current II:2–5 and his original II:4 into our current II:8–10.

50. To aid in this process, Tocqueville prepared a smaller index that he titled "Maxims or notes on the economists to have before my eyes when I finalize the definitive drafting of this chapter."

51. For III:5 and 7, Tocqueville provided a "Résumé of notes that served to make the chapters . . . very good to reread." This summary also contained notes for III:4.

52. Tocqueville to Beaumont, January 11, 1855, *OC*, VIII, pt. 3, p. 262.

53. Tocqueville to Ampère, letters of January 16 or 23, 1855, and February 17, 1855, *OC*, XI, pp. 271 and 274. For Jardin's assignment of Tocqueville's "difficulty" to these chapters, see "Note critique" to *OC*, II, pt. 2, p. 19n.

54. Tocqueville to Beaumont, August 8, 1855, *OC*, VIII, pt. 3, p. 331.

55. Tocqueville to Madame Swetchine, October 6, 1855; Tocqueville to Corcelle, November 3, 1855, *OC*, XV, pt. 2, pp. 264 and 152–53.

56. Tocqueville to Ampère, November 25, 1855, *OC*, XI, p. 302.

57. Tocqueville was working on this chapter when he wrote to Ampère on December 27, 1855 (*OC*, XI, p. 304).

58. Tocqueville's amendments to his text contained in this manuscript continued to be substantial. With reference to two chapters read aloud during Tocqueville's visit in June 1855, Beaumont commented on seeing them again in April 1856: "We knew them already but since we last saw them, you have made immense changes in them and the substance has deepened accordingly" (letter of April 17, 1856, *OC*, VIII, pt. 3, p. 388; Jardin speculates in his editorial note to this comment that the chapters in question are II:10 and 11).

59. Tocqueville's note "(1)" read: "(1) It is necessary that this enumeration be as clear, as detailed, as technical, as little formed of general expressions as possible, in order to strike the spirit more, to avoid an air of commonality, and to contrast with the general and comprehensive idea that must suddenly end it." This passage is contained in the "Rubbish of chapter VI [crossed out]/IX in which I could find much to fish out" (TA, box 42).

60. Tocqueville's role was limited, not eliminated. See above, note 48, for an example of his more informal, less authoritative presence in this first draft.

61. Tocqueville to Beaumont, letters of January 31, February 17, March 6, and March 17, 1856, *OC*, VIII, pt. 3, pp. 360, 370, 375, and 379.

62. Tocqueville proposed the system in his letter to Beaumont of February 17, 1856 (*OC*, VIII, pt. 3, pp. 370–71). He sent the first placards on March 17 and received the return of the final ones with Beaumont's letter of May 15 (ibid., pp. 379–80 and 404–5).

63. Tocqueville to Reeve, May 18, 1856, *OC,* VI, pt. 1, p. 175, slightly revising his goals expressed in a previous letter of April 23, 1856 (ibid., p. 169). Tocqueville achieved his goal almost exactly: his 1856 edition contained 110 pages of endnotes that he added to his 341 pages of text, exclusive of his preface.

64. Tocqueville may have had this proportion in mind for many months, since it would offer an explanation for his otherwise perplexing comment to Beaumont of January 11, 1855. There he had indicated that his hoped-for composition at Compiègne would constitute "a sort of entire work, which will form three-quarters of a volume" (*OC,* VIII, pt. 3, p. 262)—the approximate proportion of his final text, once the endnotes were appended.

65. Tocqueville to Reeve, May 18, 1856, *OC,* VI, pt. 1, p. 175.

66. Tocqueville to Beaumont, May 31, 1856, *OC,* VIII, pt. 3, p. 406.

67. For Tocqueville's "Copy," see TA, box 40; for his first printers' proofs, see TA, box 41, subfile titled "First galley sheet of proofs."

68. While Tocqueville indeed conducted such a comparison, it was cursory at best, since he only looked in passing at the cahiers of three bailliages—Aix, Agen, and Alençon—that were part of the larger "General Collection of *procès-verbaux,* memoirs, letters and other documents concerning the delegations to the National Assembly of 1789" that he found at the National Archives (Series B.III, vols. 1–3). For Tocqueville's notes from that review, see "Studies made at the Archives nationales (1856)," originally filed in TA, box 43, folder R and then moved to folder C. Tocqueville had announced his intention to test the reliability of the *Résumé général*'s excerpts on a sheet titled "Projects to do in arriving," contained in TA, box 44, folder 23, which described work that he planned to undertake on arrival in Paris in February 1856; there, his first priority was to investigate "cahiers of the Estates General . . . archives?" For Weitman's prescient skepticism regarding Tocqueville's claims in this matter, see "Bureaucracy, Democracy and the French Revolution," p. 272.

69. TA, box 41, subfile titled "Proofs of the preface with great additions or modifications made successively."

70. For the dating, see Tocqueville to Reeve, June 6, 1856, *OC,* VI, pt. 1, p. 181, in which he informed his English translator: "But I have not yet corrected the proofs [of the preface]." Loménie's account three years later of his severe judgment of Tocqueville's preface is contained in his article "Publicistes modernes de la France" (*Revue des Deux Mondes,* 2nd ser., 29, no. 3 [May–June 1859]: 402–28), with his critique of the first preface draft on p. 425. He presented his observations as having been advanced by "an obscure friend," who is certainly Loménie himself (see Tocqueville to Ampère, July 2, 1856 [*OC,* XI, p. 324]).

71. Tocqueville inserted in this second draft the four key paragraphs describing his own explorations of the long-concealed archives of France's Old Regime, commencing with "I have tried to see into the heart [*J'ai entrepris de pénétrer jusqu'au coeur*]" and ending with "which they never saw [*qui n'a jamais été livré à leurs regards*]." The corrections for these passages are in TA, box 41, subfile titled "Proofs of the preface with great additions or modifications made successively."

72. This claim was the only insertion Tocqueville made in his book 1 that he indexed to his reading notes. Tracing this reference of "J.30" in TA, box 39, to his appropriate reading file in TA, box 42, we see that his assertion appears to have been based on the research of Edmé de Fréminville, the eighteenth-century feudist who noted "a notable difference between the terriers of the centuries of 1400 and 1500 and those of the century of 1600" (*La pratique universelle pour la renovation des terriers et des droits seigneuriaux* [Paris: Morel et Gissey, 1746], p. 214). Perhaps uncomfortable with both his adoption of Fréminville's research and his misrepresentation of its dates, Tocqueville dropped "of the thirteenth century" from his text when he made revisions for its third edition, published in 1857 ("Variantes," *OC,* II, pt. 1, p. 326).

73. In referring to Tocqueville's "rhetoric," I am using it in the broad classical sense defined in two different contexts by Ralph Lerner in *Revolutions Revisited: Two Faces of the Politics of Enlightenment* (Chapel Hill: University of North Carolina Press, 1994), pp. xiv and 57–66, and Michael Hereth in *Alexis de Tocqueville: Threats to Freedom in Democracy,* trans. George Bogardus (Durham, NC: Duke University Press, 1986), pp. 8–9 and 91–96. Lerner describes the statesman's "use of an old art at once poetic and philosophic, seductive and hectoring, adroit and naive . . . designed to stiffen the unsteady, rouse the drowsy, and meet the enemy on his own ground" (p. 66).

74. In *Revolutions Revisited,* pp. 117–22, Lerner traces the immense presence of Tocqueville's persona, adding that the way Tocqueville "plac[es] himself between us and his subject . . . startles us as readers of histories" (p. 118).

75. Tocqueville to Beaumont, April 24, 1856, *OC,* VIII, pt. 3, p. 395.

76. Tocqueville to Kergorlay, August 28, 1856, *OC,* XIII, pt. 2, p. 309.

77. Ibid., p. 310.

78. Kergorlay to Tocqueville, September 16, 1856, *OC,* XIII, pt. 2, p. 314.

79. Kergorlay to Tocqueville, July 7, 1856, *OC,* XIII, pt. 2, p. 298. In presenting his appeal on these grounds, Tocqueville chooses to incorporate but one sentence of his much more extensive and analytical preparatory treatment found in TA, box 43, folder K, pp. 53–54 (published in *OC,* II, pt. 2, pp. 344–45; *OR,* 1:396–97). In that passage—designated by Tocqueville in his "rubbish" as "the first draft" to his argument in III:3 (TA, box 42)—he stresses that the "instinctive, irresistible, and almost involuntary love for liberty" is natural to every man, although apt to be fully experienced by only "a very small number."

80. In a marginal comment to his draft of this passage, Tocqueville expresses reservations about his depiction of the French character: "The portrait of a people is always a vague and indistinct image when one wishes to paint it as a whole. It always has more pretension than truth. A passage for *effect.* A concession to the false taste of the time" (TA, box 42, appended to title page of "Chap. X [*sic*]" [*OR,* 1:413]). Tocqueville's quarrel with the topic is with its difficulty, not with its appropriateness to the issue at hand; indeed, he speculates in his draft notes that he might have preferred to devote his entire concluding chapter to the subject of "the *French character.*"

81. Loménie, "Publicistes modernes de la France," pp. 425–26. After Tocqueville had made his revisions in his preface and conclusion, he sent them to Loménie,

accompanied by the following note: "I hasten to send you the head and the foot of my work. . . . I hope it will respond to the suggestions you made for it and will seem what you thought it should be" (ibid., p. 426).

82. Tocqueville's final additions to his text can be discerned in his proofs in TA, box 41, subfile titled "Proofs of the preface with great additions or modifications made successively." They include the two paragraphs in the preface (*OC*, 1: 85–86) commencing with "I will begin by examining them [*Je parcourrai d'abord avec eux*]" and ending with "the halo of the Revolution [*ce grand nom*]," and the seven paragraphs in *OC*, 1:244–46, commencing with "Those who, in reading this book, have carefully studied [*Ceux qui ont étudié attentivement*]" and ending with "the habits, ideas, and laws that despotism needs in order to rule [*les habitudes, les idées, les lois dont le despotisme a besoin pour régner*]."

83. Herr, *Tocqueville and the Old Regime*, pp. 91–95.

84. Sheldon Wolin, *Tocqueville between Two Worlds: The Making of a Political and Theoretical Life* (Princeton: Princeton University Press, 2001), pp. 498, 502.

85. Ibid., pp. 517, 562, 522.

86. Tocqueville to Corcelle, November 15, 1856, *OC*, XV, pt. 2, p. pp. 185–86. I have used the translation provided by Raps in Mélonio, *Tocqueville and the French*, p. 236.

87. Herr, *Tocqueville and the Old Regime*, p. 92.

88. Wolin, *Tocqueville between Two Worlds*, p. 517.

89. Tocqueville to Sarah Austin, August 29, 1856, *OC*, VI, pt. 1, p. 192.

90. Tocqueville to Kergorlay, December 15, 1850, *OC*, XIII, pt. 2, p. 232 (*Selected Letters*, p. 256).

91. Tocqueville to Kergorlay, July 28, 1853, *OC*, XIII, pt. 2, p. 256.

92. Tocqueville to Lewis, August 13, 1856, *OC* (Beaumont), VII, pp. 402–3.

93. Laurentie, *L'Union*, September 4, 1856, p. 2. In contrast to Bossuet and Montesquieu, Laurentie charged, "[Tocqueville] read and analyzed all of these administrative documents of the eighteenth century, but cites nowhere an authority."

EIGHT

1. TA, box 44, folder 27.

2. Senior to Beaumont, conversation of August 26, 1860, in Senior, "Conversations," *OC*, VI, pt. 2, p. 504.

3. For Tocqueville's aversion to philosophical discussions, see Ampère's obituary, *OC*, XI, p. 446. Beaumont told Senior that the subject of religion was "the only subject about which, during forty years of intimacy, we never spoke" (Beaumont to Senior, conversation of August 1860, *OC*, VI, pt. 2, p. 503).

4. Tocqueville to Kergorlay, July 6, 1835, *OC*, XIII, pt. 1, p. 376 (*Selected Letters*, p. 103).

5. Ampère's obituary, *OC*, XI, p. 443.

6. Tocqueville to Duvergier de Hauranne, September 1, 1856, *OC* (Beaumont), VI, p. 332.

7. Ampère's obituary, *OC,* XI, p. 447.

8. Tocqueville to Montalembert, July 10, 1856, *OC* (Beaumont) VII, p. 389.

9. TA, box 44, folder 1.

10. Tocqueville to Duvergier de Hauranne, September 1, 1856, *OC* (Beaumont) VI, p. 334. Duvergier concurred with Tocqueville's assessment in his letter of response five days later: "It is certainly highly difficult, if not impossible, to discover new facts" (Duvergier to Tocqueville, September 6, 1856, TA, box 44, folder 2).

11. Tocqueville to Beaumont, December 6, 1857, *OC,* VIII, pt. 3, p. 522.

12. TA, box 45, folder CC, p. 90 (*OC,* II, pt. 2, p. 164 [*OR,* 2:84]).

13. TA, box 45, folder EE, p. 65 (*OC,* II, pt. 2, p. 146 [*OR,* 2:104]).

14. Lynn Hunt, *Politics, Culture, and Class in the French Revolution* (Berkeley: University of California Press, 1984), pp. 22–24.

15. TA, box 45, folder CC, p. 79(b) [Rabaud] (*OC,* II, pt. 2, p. 158 [*OR,* 2:89]); ibid., p. 92(b) [Péthion] *OC,* II, pt. 2, p. 166 [*OR,* 2:85–86]).

16. TA, box 44, folder 19 (*OC,* II, pt. 2, p. 176 [*OR,* 2:163]).

17. See, in particular, Tocqueville's studies for the year 1788 contained in TA, box 45, folder CC, pp. 36–104, with a representative sample in his depiction of Rabaud on p. 31 (*OC,* II, pt. 2, p. 158 [*OR,* 2:89]).

18. "Fight of the parlements in 1787," TA, box 45, folder BB, pp. 19–30 (*OC,* II, pt. 2, pp. 80–81 [*OR* 2:392–93]); "Fight of the king with the Parlement of Paris" and "Fight of the provincial parlements," folder CC, pp. 105–37 (*OC,* II, pt. 2, pp. 81–83); folder EE, p. 58 [Sieyès] (*OC,* II, pt. 2, p. 139 [*OR,* 2:98]).

19. TA, box 44, folder 7, pp. 12, 24. For a further discussion of Tocqueville's reading of these brochures, see Harvey Mitchell, *Individual Choice and the Structures of History* (Cambridge: Cambridge University Press, 1996), pp. 239–53.

20. See above, chapter 7, note 68, for Tocqueville's cursory review a year earlier of the *cahiers* of Agen, Aix, and Alençon at the National Archives (Series B.III, vols. 1–3). In his 1857 reading, he examined these same three *cahiers* and then added those of Amiens in volumes 3 and 4 to his study.

21. TA, box 45, folder EE, pp. 7–7(b).

22. Ibid., pp. 7–8. While Tocqueville's *cahiers* readings would figure prominently in his findings for his sequel's book 1, chapter 7, it is not so clear that they contributed to his analysis of the parish *cahiers* in chapter 6. Tocqueville was certainly aware of the parish *cahiers,* having been informed by M. Delisle of their existence and potential value (TA, box 44, folder 22). But he left no notes in his archive of any particular investigation that he undertook of these parish *cahiers* that might have provoked or documented his claims that they articulated the peasants' preoccupation with their needs rather than with their rights. This absence constitutes a lacuna in our Tocquevillian *cahiers* investigations that I have been unable to fill.

23. Tocqueville to Freslon, January 12, 1858, *OC* (Beaumont), VII, p. 478.

24. We have three different versions of book 1 of Tocqueville's sequel, thanks to the extensive labors of Beaumont, Jardin, and Mélonio to decipher his rough drafts. In his initial posthumous publication, Beaumont took full advantage of his editorial

powers—and Tocqueville's chapter indexes—to remedy what he had perceived in volume 1 as his friend's deficient source documentation (*OC* [Beaumont], VIII, pp. 55–148). In 1953, Jardin replaced Beaumont's citations with lengthy transcriptions of pertinent reading notes (*OC*, II, pt. 2, pp. 31–170). In her recent rendition, Mélonio augments Jardin's transcriptions and adds her own extensive "critical apparatus" (*OR*, 2:25–113 and 375–434).

25. TA, box 44, folder 16 (*OC*, II, pt. 2, p. 195 [*OR*, 2:135–36]).

26. TA, box 45, unnumbered sheets following folder YY.

27. Tocqueville's chapter indexes are placed at the front of their respective chapter drafts in TA, box 45, section 2 ("Initial Drafted Chapters"). They range in length from an attenuated index for chapter 6 on the parish *cahiers*—containing just nine references in eight categories, none of which specifies *cahiers* readings—to expanded ones for chapters 3 and 5 that each contain over 165 headings with more than 500 references, reflecting the fact that fifteen out of the eighteen topics Tocqueville targeted for the "new classification of notes" in his "headings of ideas" referred to just these two chapters. On "Headings," p. 1(b), he noted that "it would be useless to make an index" of his Dauphiny notes, thus again suggesting that he was looking ahead to compiling the indexes. In addition to the seven chapter indexes, Tocqueville prepared a general index for the entire book 1, consisting of forty-seven references in thirty-four categories drawn from each of his research folders. He began this index with two references back to his early ruminations about the subject and style of his book contained in his "letter to Louis [Kergorlay]" of December 15, 1850. This latter index, consisting of a single sheet, can be found in TA, box 43, at the conclusion of Tocqueville's reading notes for volume 1 and just in front of his "great index" for that work.

28. Tocqueville to Kergorlay, February 27, 1858, *OC*, XIII, pt. 2, p. 332. Tocqueville repeated this statement in almost identical terms six weeks later to his other most trusted stylistic consultant, Ampère (Tocqueville to Ampère, April 11, 1858, *OC*, XI, pp. 403–4).

29. See TA, box 45, folder YY, for Tocqueville's fourteen provocative pages of "Notes taken within the folders relative to my first book and that can refer to my subsequent books."

30. Tocqueville to Ampère, February 18, 1858, *OC*, XI, p. 402.

31. Tocqueville to Mary Mottley, May 5, 1858, *OC*, XIV, p. 648.

32. TA, box 44, folder 17 (*OC*, II, pt. 2, pp. 185, 215, 217 [*OR*, 2:131, 149–50, 151]).

33. See above, chapter 6, p. 122, for the letters of Clémentine de Beaumont, Harriet Grote, and John Stuart Mill that criticized Tocqueville's slighting of the principles of 1789.

34. TA, box 44, folder 16 (*OC*, II, pt. 2, p. 195 [*OR*, 2:135–36]).

35. TA, box 44, folder 16, "Democracy—Democratic Institutions. Different Meaning of These Words—Confusion That Results from This" (*OC*, II, pt. 2, p. 199 [*OR*, 2:162–63]).

36. TA, box 44, folder 16, "Look again in the rubbish [June 1858]" (*OC*, II, pt. 2, pp. 199–200).

37. TA, box 45, folder YY, "Centralization" (*OC*, II, pt. 2, p. 200).

38. TA, box 45, folder CC, p. 78, with reference to [Condorcet], *Essai sur la constitution et les fonctions des assemblées provinciales* (n.p., 1788), 2:324. I have added the bracketed clause to highlight the full meaning of Condorcet's argument. Tocqueville also commented approvingly in his notes that Condorcet "does not wish to take away from the nobility a very high rank in society." For a helpful overview of Condorcet's brochure and of his measured defense within it of the nobility, see Baker, *Condorcet: From Natural Philosophy to Social Mathematics* (Chicago: University of Chicago Press, 1975), pp. 252–59.

39. TA, box 45, unnumbered page after folder YY, "Facts, Ideas, . . ." (*OC*, II, pt. 2, p. 137 [*OR*, 2:442]). Showing his careful cultivation of this quotation from his earlier studies, Tocqueville noted on this sheet: "See folder Q of the first volume," one of the very few instances we find of such interarchival cross-reference.

40. TA, box 44, folder 13 (*OC*, II, pt. 2, p. 336).

41. TA, box 44, folder 17 (*OC*, II, pt. 2, p. 222).

42. TA, box 45, folder CC, p. 35(b) (*OC*, II, pt. 2, p. 117).

43. Ibid., p. 39 ("Studies done at Charmonade [1857] on the year 1788").

44. TA, box 45, folder YY, "Centralization" (*OC*, II, pt. 2, p. 200).

45. Tocqueville to Kergorlay, May 16, 1858, *OC*, XIII, pt. 2, pp. 337–38 (*Selected Letters*, p. 373).

46. TA, box 45, unnumbered page after folder YY. For a discerning analysis of these same two revolutions, see Alan S. Kahan, "Tocqueville's Two Revolutions," *Journal of the History of Ideas* 46 (1985): 585–96.

47. TA, box 44, folder 16, "Chapter Plan" (*OC*, II, pt. 2, p. 195 [*OR*, 2:136]).

48. Gobineau to Tocqueville, November 29, 1856, *OC*, IX, p. 272.

49. Hunt, *Politics, Culture, and Class*, p. 3.

50. Herr, *Tocqueville and the Old Regime*, pp. 35, 43, 55, 63, 87.

51. Wolin, *Tocqueville between Two Worlds*, p. 525.

52. "Discours sur la science politique," April 3, 1852, *OC*, XVI, p. 233.

53. Tocqueville to Beaumont, May 21, 1858, *OC*, VIII, pt. 3, p. 572.

54. Tocqueville to Freslon, February 23, 1859, *OC* (Beaumont), VI, pp. 480–81. Gibbon's great originality, in Tocqueville's view, derived from his ability, even after his enormous researches, to write in a style that was "concise, vigorous, and full of life."

55. Beaumont, "Notice," *OC* (Beaumont), V, pp. 89–90.

56. Mélonio, *Tocqueville and the French*, chap. 4, pp. 112–48.

57. Ibid., pp. 202–6. See, too, Jack Censer, "The Coming of a New Interpretation of the French Revolution?" *Journal of Social History* 21 (1987): 295–309.

Works by Tocqueville

This list includes volumes of Tocqueville's works that I have referred to in my study.

Oeuvres complètes. Edited by Gustave de Beaumont. 9 vols. Paris: Michel Lévy Frères, 1864–66.

Vol. 4: *L'ancien régime et la Révolution* (1866).

Vols. 5 and 6: *Correspondance et oeuvres posthumes d'Alexis de Tocqueville* (1865–66).

Vol. 7: *Nouvelle correspondance entièrement inédite d'Alexis de Tocqueville* (1866).

Vol. 8: *Mélanges: Fragments historiques et notes sur l'ancien régime, la Révolution et l'Empire, voyages, pensées entièrement inédites* (1865).

Oeuvres complètes. Edited by J.-P. Mayer. 17 vols. in 28 pts. to date. Paris: Gallimard, 1951–.

Vol. 1, pts. 1 and 2: *De la démocratie en Amérique.* Introduction by Harold J. Laski. Preliminary note by J.-P. Mayer (1951).

Vol. 2, pt. 1: *L'ancien régime et la Révolution.* Introduction by Georges Lefebvre. Preliminary note by J.-P. Mayer (1952).

Vol. 2, pt. 2: *L'ancien régime et la Révolution. Fragments et notes inédites sur la Révolution.* Edited and annotated by André Jardin (1953).

Vol. 3, pt. 1: *Écrits et discours politiques.* Edited and annotated by André Jardin. Introduction by J.-J. Chevallier and André Jardin (1962).

Vol. 3, pt. 2: *Écrits et discours politiques.* Edited, annotated, and introduced by André Jardin (1985).

Vol. 6, pt. 1: *Correspondance anglaise: Correspondance d'Alexis de Tocqueville avec Henry Reeve et John Stuart Mill.* Edited and annotated by J.-P. Mayer and Gustave Rudler. Introduced by J.-P. Mayer (1954).

Vol. 6, pt. 2: *Correspondance anglaise: Correspondance et conversations d'Alexis de Tocqueville et Nassau William Senior.* Edited and annotated by H. Brogan and A. P. Kerr. Notes by J.-P. Mayer. Preface by Lord Roll. Introduction by H. Brogan (1991).

Vol. 7: *Correspondance étrangère d'Alexis de Tocqueville (Amérique–Europe continentale)*. Edited by Françoise Mélonio, Lise Queffélec, and Anthony Pleasance (1986).

Vol. 8, pts. 1, 2, and 3: *Correspondance d'Alexis de Tocqueville et de Gustave de Beaumont*. Edited, annotated, and introduced by André Jardin (1967).

Vol. 9: *Correspondance d'Alexis de Tocqueville et d'Arthur de Gobineau*. Edited and annotated by M. Degros. Introduced by J.-J. Chevalier (1959).

Vol. 10: *Correspondance et écrits locaux*. Edited by Lise Queffélec-Dumasy. Preface by André-Jean Tudesq (1995).

Vol. 11: *Correspondance d'Alexis de Tocqueville avec P.-P. Royer-Collard et avec J.-J. Ampère*. Edited, annotated, and introduced by André Jardin (1970).

Vol. 12: *Souvenirs*. Edited, annotated, and introduced by Luc Monnier (1968).

Vol. 13, pts. 1 and 2: *Correspondance d'Alexis de Tocqueville et de Louis de Kergorlay*. Edited by André Jardin. Introduction and notes by Jean-Alain Lesourd (1977).

Vol. 14: *Correspondance familiale*. Edited by Jean-Louis Benoît and André Jardin. Introduction by Jean-Louis Benoît (1998).

Vol. 15, pts. 1 and 2: *Correspondance d'Alexis de Tocqueville et de Francisque de Corcelle. Correspondance d'Alexis de Tocqueville et de Madame Swetchine*. Edited by Pierre Gibert (1983).

Vol. 16: *Mélanges*. Edited and annotated by Françoise Mélonio (1989).

Vol. 18: *Correspondance d'Alexis de Tocqueville avec Adolphe de Circourt et avec Madame de Circourt*. Edited by A. P. Kerr (1983).

Oeuvres. Edited under the direction of André Jardin. 2 vols. to date. Paris: Bibliothèque de la Pléiade, 1991-.

Vol. 1: *Voyages. Écrits politiques et académiques*. Edited by André Jardin with Françoise Mélonio and Lise Queffélec (1991).

Vol. 2: *De la Démocratie en Amérique I and II*. Edited by André Jardin with Jean-Claude Lamberti and James T. Schleifer (1992).

Commentaries on Tocqueville and Tocquevillian Themes

Aron, Raymond. *Main Currents in Sociological Thought*. Vol. 1. *Montesquieu, Comte, Marx, Tocqueville, the Sociologists and the Revolution of 1848*. Translated by Richard Howard and Helen Weaver. New York: Basic Books, 1965.

———. "Tocqueville retrouvé." *Tocqueville Review* 1 (Fall 1979): 8–23.

Baczko, Bronislaw. *Ending the Terror: The French Revolution after Robespierre*. Translated by Michel Petheram. Cambridge: Cambridge University Press, 1989.

Baker, Keith Michael. *Condorcet: From Natural Philosophy to Social Mathematics*. Chicago: University of Chicago Press, 1975.

———. "Enlightenment and Revolution in France: Old Problems and Renewed Approaches." *Journal of Modern History* 53 (June 1981): 281–303.

———. *Inventing the French Revolution*. Cambridge: Cambridge University Press, 1990.

Bann, Stephen. *The Clothing of Clio*. Cambridge: Cambridge University Press, 1984.

Berlin, Isaiah. "The Thought of De Tocqueville." *History* 50, no. 169 (June 1965): 199–206.

Bien, David. "Offices, Corps, and a System of State Credit: The Uses of Privilege under the Ancien Régime." In *The French Revolution and the Creation of Modern Political Culture,*

Vol. 1, *The Political Culture of the Old Regime*, ed. Keith Michael Baker, 89–114. New York: Pergamon Press, 1987.

Boesche, Roger. *The Strange Liberalism of Alexis de Tocqueville*. Ithaca, NY: Cornell University Press, 1987.

———. "Why Could Tocqueville Predict So Well?" *Political Theory* 2, no. 1 (February 1983): 79–103.

Bressolette, Michael. "Tocqueville et le paupérisme: L'influence de Rousseau." *Littératures* (Annales publiées par la Faculté des lettres et sciences humaines de Toulouse) 16 (1969): 67–78.

Brogan, Hugh. *Tocqueville*. Suffolk, UK: Chaucer Press, 1973.

———. "Tocqueville from the Heart." *Times Literary Supplement,* October 2, 1998, 40.

Censer, Jack. "The Coming of a New Interpretation of the French Revolution?" *Journal of Social History* 21 (1987): 295–309.

———. *The French Press in the Age of Enlightenment*. New York: Routledge, 1994.

———. "Prudhomme, Louis-Marie (1752–1832)." In *Historical Dictionary of the French Revolution, 1788–99,* ed. Samuel Scott and Barry Rothaus, p. 797. Westport, CT: Greenwood Press, 1985.

Chartier, Roger. *The Cultural Origins of the French Revolution*. Translated by Lydia G. Cochrane. Durham, NC: Duke University Press, 1991.

———. *The Cultural Uses of Print in Early Modern France*. Translated by Lydia G. Cochrane. Princeton: Princeton University Press, 1987.

Chaussinand-Nogaret, Guy. *The French Nobility in the Eighteenth Century: From Feudalism to Enlightenment*. Translated by William Doyle. Cambridge: Cambridge University Press, 1985.

Church, Clive. *Revolution and Red Tape: The French Ministerial Bureaucracy, 1770–1850*. Oxford: Clarendon Press, 1981.

Cosentino, Andrew J. *A Passion for Liberty: Alexis de Tocqueville on Democracy and Revolution*. With an introduction by François Furet and essays by Françoise Mélonio and James T. Schleifer. Washington, DC: Library of Congress, 1989.

Craiutu, Aurelian. "Between Scylla and Charybdis: The 'Strange' Liberalism of the French Doctrinaires." *History of European Ideas* 24, nos. 4–5 (1998): 243–65.

———. "Tocqueville and the Political Thought of the French Doctrinaires (Guizot, Royer-Collard, Rémusat)." *History of Political Thought* 20, no. 3 (Autumn 1999): 456–93.

"Democracy in the World: Tocqueville Reconsidered." *Journal of Democracy* 11, no. 1 (January 2000): 5–186.

"The Democratic Soul." *Religion and Values in Public Life* (Center for the Study of Values in Public Life at Harvard Divinity School) 6, no. 1 (Fall 1997): 1–7.

Draus, Franciszek. "Burke et les Français." In *The French Revolution and the Creation of Modern Political Culture,* vol. 3, *The Transformation of Political Culture, 1789–1848,* ed. François Furet and Mona Ozouf, 79–99. New York: Pergamon Press, 1989.

Drescher, Seymour. "Digesting the Revolution: A Tocquevillean Perspective." *World and I,* July 1989, 467–87.

———. *Dilemmas of Democracy: Tocqueville and Modernization*. Pittsburgh: University of Pittsburgh Press, 1968.

———. "More Than America: Comparison and Synthesis in *Democracy in America*." In

Reconsidering Tocqueville's "Democracy in America," ed. Abraham S. Eisenstadt, 77–93. New Brunswick, NJ: Rutgers University Press, 1988.

―――. *Tocqueville and England.* Cambridge: Harvard University Press, 1964.

―――. "Tocqueville's Two *Démocraties.*" *Journal of the History of Ideas* 25, no. 2 (1964): 201–16.

―――. " 'Why Great Revolutions Will Become Rare': Tocqueville's Most Neglected Prognosis." *Journal of Modern History* 64 (September 1992): 429–54.

―――, ed. *Tocqueville and Beaumont on Social Reform.* Translated and with an introduction by Seymour Drescher. New York: Harper and Row, 1968.

Eichtal, Eugène d'. *Alexis de Tocqueville et la démocratie libérale.* Paris: Calmann-Lévy, 1897.

Elazar, Daniel. "Tocqueville and the Cultural Basis of American Democracy." *Political Science and Politics* 32, no. 2 (June 1999): 207–10.

Engel-Janosi, Friedrick, *Four Studies in French Romantic Historical Writing.* Johns Hopkins University Studies in Historical and Political Science, vol. 71, no. 2. Baltimore: Johns Hopkins Press, 1955.

Fauchois, Yann. "Centralization." In *A Critical Dictionary of the French Revolution,* ed. François Furet and Mona Ozouf, trans. Arthur Goldhammer, 629–39. Cambridge: Harvard University Press, Belknap Press, 1989.

Fox-Genovese, Elizabeth. *The Origins of Physiocracy.* Ithaca, NY: Cornell University Press, 1976.

Frantzich, Stephen, ed. *Tocqueville in the Classroom: Exploring Democracy in America, an Educator's Resource.* www.c-span.org/classroom/lessonplans/module1.htm.

Furbank, P. N. "Tocqueville's Lament." *New York Review of Books,* April 8, 1999, 48–52.

Furet, François. "The Intellectual Origins of Tocqueville's Thought." *Tocqueville Review* 7 (1985–86): 117–29.

―――. *Interpreting the French Revolution.* Translated by Elborg Forster. Cambridge: Cambridge University Press; Paris: Éditions de la Maison des Sciences de l'Homme, 1981.

―――. *In the Workshop of History.* Translated by Jonathan Mandelbaum. Chicago: University of Chicago Press, 1984.

―――. "Naissance d'un paradigme: Tocqueville et le voyage en Amérique (1825–1831)." *Annales, E.S.C.* 39 (March–April 1984): 226–39.

―――. "Une polémique thermidorienne sur la Terreur: Autour de Benjamin Constant." *Passé Présent* 2 (1983): 44–55.

―――. *Revolutionary France, 1770–1880.* Translated by Antonia Nevill. Oxford: Blackwell, 1988.

―――. "Tocqueville." In *A Critical Dictionary of the French Revolution,* ed. François Furet and Mona Ozouf, trans. Arthur Goldhammer, 1021–32. Cambridge: Harvard University Press, Belknap Press, 1989.

―――, ed. *The Old Regime and the Revolution.* Vols. 1 and 2. With an introduction and critical apparatus by François Furet and Françoise Mélonio. Translated by Alan S. Kahan. Chicago: University of Chicago Press, 1998 and 2001.

Gannett, Robert T., Jr. "Bowling Ninepins in Tocqueville's Township." *American Political Science Review* 97, no. 1 (February 2003): 1–16.

Gargan, Edward T. *Alexis de Tocqueville: The Critical Years, 1848–1851.* Washington, DC: Catholic University of America Press, 1955.

———. *De Tocqueville.* London: Bowes and Bowes, 1965.

———. "The Formation of Tocqueville's Historical Thought." *Review of Politics* 24 (January 1962): 48–61.

———. "Tocqueville and the Problem of Historical Prognosis." *American Historical Review* 68 (1963): 332–45.

Gay, Peter. *Voltaire's Politics: The Poet as Realist.* New Haven: Yale University Press, 1988.

Glazer, Nathan. "Tocqueville and Riesman: Two Passages to Sociology." David Riesman Lecture on American Society. *Society* 37, no. 4 (May–June 2000): 26–33.

Gooch, G. P. *History and Historians in the Nineteenth Century.* London: Longmans, Green, 1952.

Gossman, Lionel. *Between History and Literature.* Cambridge: Harvard University Press, 1990.

Gough, Hugh. *The Newspaper Press in the French Revolution.* Chicago: Dorsey Press, 1988.

Grandmaison, Charles de. *Inventaire-sommaire des archives départementales antérieures à 1790. Indre-et-Loire. Archives civiles.* Paris: De Paul Dupont, 1867.

———. "Séjour d'Alexis de Tocqueville en Touraine, préparation du livre sur l'ancien régime, juin 1853–avril 1854." *Le Correspondant* 114, n.s. 78, (January–March 1879): 926–49.

Hamburger, Joseph. "Mill and Tocqueville on Liberty." *James and John Stuart Mill: Papers of the Centenary Conference,* 111–25. Toronto, 1976.

Hancock, Ralph C. "The Modern Revolution and the Collapse of oral Analogy: Tocqueville and Guizot." *Perspectives on Political Science* 30, no. 4 (Fall 2001): 213–17.

Hatin, Eugène. *Histoire de la presse en France.* Paris: Poulet-Malassis et de Broise, 1860.

"Henry Martin's *History of France.*" *Edinburgh Review* 106 (October 1857): 382–407.

Hereth, Michael. *Alexis de Tocqueville: Threats to Freedom in Democracy.* Translated by George Bogardus. Durham, NC: Duke University Press, 1986.

Herr, Richard. *Tocqueville and the Old Regime.* Princeton: Princeton University Press, 1962.

Hunt, Lynn. *Politics, Culture and Class in the French Revolution.* Berkeley: University of California Press, 1984.

Hyslop, Beatrice. *A Guide to the General Cahiers of 1789.* New York: Columbia University Press, 1936.

Jardin, André. *Tocqueville: A Biography.* Translated by Lydia Davis with Robert Hemenway. New York: Farrar Straus Giroux, 1988.

Johnson, Douglas. *Guizot: Aspects of French History, 1787–1874.* Toronto: University of Toronto Press, 1963.

Kahan, Alan S. *Aristocratic Liberalism: The Social and Political Thought of Jacob Burckhardt, John Stuart Mill and Alexis de Tocqueville.* New York: Oxford University Press, 1992.

———. "Tocqueville's Two Revolutions." *Journal of the History of Ideas* 46 (1985): 585–96.

———, trans. *The Old Regime and the Revolution.* Vols. 1 and 2. With an introduction and critical apparatus by François Furet and Françoise Mélonio. Chicago: University of Chicago Press, 1998 and 2001.

Kelly, George Armstrong. *The Humane Comedy: Constant, Tocqueville and French Liberalism.* Cambridge: Cambridge University Press, 1992.

Lamberti, Jean-Claude. "De Benjamin Constant à Alexis de Tocqueville." *France-Forum* (May–June 1984): 19–26.

———. "Introduction à *L'ancien régime.*" In *Tocqueville* (three works), 895–920. Paris: Robert Laffont, 1986.

———. *Tocqueville and the Two Democracies.* Translated by Arthur Goldhammer. With a foreword by François Bourricaud. Cambridge: Harvard University Press, 1989.

Laurentie, Pierre-Sébastien. *L'Union.* September 4, 1856.

Lawler, Peter. *The Restless Mind: Alexis de Tocqueville on the Origin and Perpetuation of Human Liberty.* Lanham, MD: Rowman and Littlefield, 1993.

Lefebvre, Georges. "À propos de Tocqueville." *Annales Historiques de la Révolution Française* 27 (October–December 1955): 313–23.

Lerner, Ralph. *Revolutions Revisited: Two Faces of the Politics of Enlightenment.* Chapel Hill: University of North Carolina Press, 1994.

Lively, Jack. *The Social and Political Thought of Alexis de Tocqueville.* Oxford: Clarendon Press, 1962.

Loménie, Louis de. "Publicistes modernes de la France." *Revue des Deux Mondes,* 2nd ser., 29, no. 3 (May–June, 1859): 402–28.

Manent, Pierre. *Tocqueville and the Nature of Democracy.* Translated by John Waggoner. Lanham, MD: Rowman and Littlefield, 1996.

Mansfield, Harvey C., ed. *Democracy in America.* Translated and with an introduction by Harvey C. Mansfield and Delba Winthrop. Chicago: University of Chicago Press, 2000.

Marcel, R. Pierre. *Essai politique sur Alexis de Tocqueville.* Paris: Librairie Félix Alcan et Guillaumin Réunies, 1910.

Markoff, John. *The Abolition of Feudalism: Peasants, Lords, and Legislators in the French Revolution.* University Park: Pennsylvania State University Press, 1996.

Markoff, John, and Gilbert Shapiro. "Consensus and Conflict at the Onset of Revolution: A Quantitative Study of France in 1789." *American Journal of Sociology* 91 (July 1985): 28–53.

Maza, Sarah. "Politics, Culture, and the Origins of the French Revolution." *Journal of Modern History* 61 (December 1989): 704–23.

Meaux, Marie-Camille-Alfred de. "*L'ancien régime et la Révolution* par Alexis de Tocqueville de l'Académie française." *Le Correspondant* 39 (November 1856): 254–82.

Mellon, Stanley. *The Political Uses of History.* Stanford, CA: Stanford University Press, 1958.

Mélonio, Françoise. "Introduction à la première *Démocratie*" and "Introduction à la seconde *Démocratie.*" In *Tocqueville* three works), 9–37 and 397–425. Paris: Robert Laffont, 1986.

———. "Tocqueville: Aux origines de la démocratie française." In *The French Revolution and the Creation of Modern Political Culture,* vol. 3, *The Transformation of Political Culture, 1789–1848,* ed. François Furet and Mona Ozouf, 595–611. New York: Pergamon Press, 1989.

———. *Tocqueville and the French.* Translated by Beth G. Raps. With a foreword by Seymour Drescher. Charlottesville: University Press of Virginia, 1998.

————, ed. *L'ancien régime et la Révolution*. Paris: GF-Flammarion, 1988.

————, ed. *The Old Regime and the Revolution*. Vols. 1 and 2. With an introduction and critical apparatus by François Furet and Françoise Mélonio. Translated by Alan S. Kahan. Chicago: University of Chicago Press, 1998 and 2001.

Mignet, François-Auguste. "Notice historique sur la vie et les travaux de M. Alexis de Tocqueville lue à la séance publique du 14 juillet 1866." In *Nouveaux éloges historiques*, 59–103. Paris: Didier, 1878.

Mill, John Stuart. "Democracy in America." *Edinburgh Review* 72, no. 145 (October 1840): 1–47.

————. "De Tocqueville on Democracy in America." *London Review* 2 (October 1835): 85–129.

————. "Guizot's Lectures on European Civilization." *London Review* 4 (July–January 1835–36): 306–36.

Mitchell, Harvey. *Individual Choice and the Structures of History*. Cambridge: Cambridge University Press, 1996.

Mitchell, Joshua. *The Fragility of Freedom: Tocqueville on Religion, Democracy and the American Future*. Chicago: University of Chicago Press, 1995.

Momigliano, Arnaldo. *The Classical Foundations of Modern Historiography*. Berkeley: University of California Press, 1990.

Nisbet, Robert. "Tocqueville's Ideal Types." In *Reconsidering Tocqueville's "Democracy in America,"* ed. Abraham S. Eisenstadt, 171–91. New Brunswick, NJ: Rutgers University Press, 1988.

Nolla, Eduardo, ed. *De la démocratie en Amérique*. 2 vols. Paris: Librairie Philosophique J. Vrin, 1990.

Orr, Linda. *Headless History: Nineteenth-Century French Historiography of the Revolution*. Ithaca, NY: Cornell University Press, 1990.

Ozouf, Mona. " 'Public Opinion' at the End of the Old Regime." *Journal of Modern History* 60, suppl. (September 1988): S1–S21.

————. "The Terror after the Terror: An Immediate History." In *The French Revolution and the Creation of Modern Political Culture, 1789–1848*, vol. 4, *The Terror*, ed. Keith Michael Baker, 3–18. New York: Pergamon Press, 1989.

Palmer, R. R., ed. and trans. *The Two Tocquevilles, Father and Son: Hervé and Alexis de Tocqueville on the Coming of the French Revolution*. Princeton: Princeton University Press, 1987.

Pappé, H. O. "Mill and Tocqueville." *Journal of the History of Ideas* 25 (April-June 1964): 217–34.

Pierson, George Wilson. "Le <second voyage> de Tocqueville en Amérique." In *Alexis de Tocqueville: Livre du centenaire, 1859–1959*, 71–85. Paris: Centre National de la Recherche Scientifique, 1960.

————. *Tocqueville and Beaumont in America*. New York: Oxford University Press, 1938. Johns Hopkins Paperbacks edition, 1996.

Pitts, Jennifer, ed. *Writings on Empire and Slavery/Alexis de Tocqueville*. Translated by Jennifer Pitts. Baltimore: Johns Hopkins University Press, 2001.

Popkin, Jeremy. "The Concept of Public Opinion in the Historiography of the French Revolution: A Critique." *Storia della Storiografia* 20 (1991): 77–92.

Pouthas, Charles-H. *Guizot pendant la Restauration.* Paris: Librairie Plon, 1923.

Rédier, Antoine. *Comme disait M. de Tocqueville.* Paris: Perrin, 1925.

Rémusat, Charles de. "L'ancien régime et la Révolution par M. Alexis de Tocqueville." *Revue des Deux Mondes,* 2nd ser., 26, no. 4 (July-August 1856): 652–70.

Richter, Melvin. "Comparative Political Analysis in Montesquieu and Tocqueville." *Comparative Politics* 1 (1969): 129–60.

———. "Tocqueville, Napoleon and Bonapartism." In *Reconsidering Tocqueville's "Democracy in America,"* ed. Abraham S. Eisenstadt, 110–45. New Brunswick, NJ: Rutgers University Press, 1988.

———. "Tocqueville on Algeria." *Review of Politics* 25, no. 3 (July 1963): 362–98.

———. "The Uses of Theory: Tocqueville's Adaptation of Montesquieu." In *Essays in Theory and History,* ed. Melvin Richter, 74–102. Cambridge: Harvard University Press, 1970.

Riesman, David. "Tocqueville as Ethnographer." *American Scholar* 30 (Spring 1961): 174–87.

Rigney, Ann. *The Rhetoric of Historical Representation: Three Narrative Histories of the French Revolution.* Cambridge: Cambridge University Press, 1990.

Rosanvallon, Pierre. "The History of the Word 'Democracy' in France." *Journal of Democracy* 6, no. 4 (1995): 140–54.

Sainte-Beuve, Charles Augustin. "Nouvelle correspondence inédite de Tocqueville." *Le Constitutionnel,* December 18 and December 25, 1865, republished in *Nouveaux Lundis,* 10:280–306 and 307–34. Paris: Michel Lévy Frères, 1868.

———. "Oeuvres et correspondance inédites de M. de Tocqueville." *Moniteur Universel,* December 31, 1860, and January 7, 1861, republished in *Causeries du Lundi* 15:93–106 and 107–121. Paris: Garnier, 1862.

Schleifer, James T. "How Many *Democracies?*" In *Liberty, Equality, Democracy,* ed. Eduardo Nolla, 193–205. New York: New York University Press, 1992.

———. *The Making of Tocqueville's Democracy in America.* Chapel Hill: University of North Carolina Press, 1980.

———. "Tocqueville as Historian: Philosophy and Methodology in the *Democracy.*" In *Reconsidering Tocqueville's "Democracy in America,"* ed. Abraham S. Eisenstadt, 147–67. New Brunswick, NJ: Rutgers University Press, 1988.

Shapiro, Gilbert, and John Markoff. *Revolutionary Demands: A Content Analysis of the Cahiers de Doléances of 1789.* Stanford, CA: Stanford University Press, 1998.

Shapiro, Gilbert, John Markoff, and Sasha R. Weitman. "Quantitative Studies of the French Revolution." *History and Theory* 12, no. 2 (1973): 163–91.

Shiner, L. E. *The Secret Mirror: Literary Form and History in Tocqueville's "Recollections."* Ithaca, NY: Cornell University Press, 1988.

Siedentop, Larry. Introduction to Guizot, *The History of Civilization in Europe.* London: Penguin, 1997.

———. *Tocqueville.* Oxford: Oxford University Press, 1994.

———. "Two Liberal Traditions." In *The Idea of Freedom: Essays in Honour of Isaiah Berlin,* ed. Alan Ryan, 153–74. Oxford: Oxford University Press, 1979.

Taylor, George V. "Revolutionary and Nonrevolutionary Content in the *Cahiers* of 1789: An Interim Report." *French Historical Studies* 8, pt. 4 (Fall 1972): 479–502.

Varouxakis, Georgios. "Guizot's Historical Works and J. S. Mill's Reception of Tocqueville." *History of Political Thought* 20, no. 2 (Summer 1999): 292–312.

Weitman, Sasha R. "Bureaucracy, Democracy and the French Revolution." Ph.D. diss., Washington University, 1968.

————. "The Sociological Thesis of Tocqueville's *The Old Regime and the Revolution.*" *Social Research* 33 (1966): 389–406.

Welch, Cheryl B. *De Tocqueville.* Oxford: Oxford University Press, 2001.

White, Hayden. *Metahistory: The Historical Imagination in Nineteenth-Century Europe.* Baltimore: Johns Hopkins University Press, 1973.

Winthrop, Delba. "Tocqueville's *Old Regime:* Political History." *Review of Politics* 43 (1981): 88–111.

————, ed. *Democracy in America.* Translated and with an introduction by Harvey C. Mansfield and Delba Winthrop. Chicago: University of Chicago Press, 2000.

Wolin, Sheldon. "Can We Still Hear Tocqueville?" *Atlantic Monthly,* August 1987, 80–83.

————. *Tocqueville between Two Worlds: The Making of a Political and Theoretical Life.* Princeton: Princeton University Press, 2001.

Zetterbaum, Marvin. *Tocqueville and the Problem of Democracy.* Stanford, CA: Stanford University Press, 1967.

Académie des sciences morales et politiques
  prize competition at, 48–49
  reports of Tocqueville at, 12, 88–90, 172n. 14
Académie de Toulouse, 101
Académie française, 80, 140
  Tocqueville's reception speech at, 15–16,
    99, 191n. 103
administrative centralization
  absence in "Initial Outline," 80, 101
  and democracy, 6, 175n. 56
  and Paris, 199n. 77
  during Revolution, 16, 72, 159
  Tocqueville's study of
    in cahiers, 110–11, 155
    in Dareste, 49–50
    for Democracy, vol. 2, 9, 10, 170nn. 30, 31
    in Guizot's lectures, 23
    in intendants' files (Paris), 59, 81–82,
      163–66 (endnotes 17, 21, 68, 75, 76)
    in intendants' files (Tours), 81–86,
      163–66 (endnotes 15, 19, 23, 27, 70, 73),
      202n. 46
    in Macarel, 88–90
    in Turgot, 82, 105, 164 (endnote 22)
  Tocqueville's treatment of
    in Democracy, vol. 1, 23–24, 88
    in 1836 essay, 24, 40–41
    in Old Regime, 93–98
  See also centralization; decentralization;
    despotism
administrative law
  Tocqueville's plan for course on, 93
  Tocqueville's study of

in Guizot's lectures, 23
in intendants' files (Paris), 91
in intendants' files (Tours), 91–93,
  164–65 (endnotes 25, 64)
in Macarel, 88–90
Tocqueville's treatment of, in Old Regime,
  95, 97
See also legists
administrative reforms of 1787–88. See Louis
  XVI
Aeneas, 124, 209n. 119
agricultural societies, Tocqueville's study
  of, 52, 54, 85, 164 (endnotes 30,
  40)
Alembert, Jean le Rond d', 7
Algeria, 58
America
  debate on civic engagement in, 161–62
  as model of liberty, 155, 164–65 (endnotes
    39, 63)
  Tocqueville's historical method for
    studies of, 4
  Tocqueville's view of township in, 9–10,
    97, 155, 164 (endnote 24), 170n. 35,
    199n. 81
L'ami des hommes (Marquis de Mirabeau), 104,
  105, 154
Ampère, Jean-Jacques, 80, 87, 186n. 26
  as stylistic consultant, 65, 136, 138, 157, 189n.
    69, 219n. 28
L'ancien moniteur, 45
An Appeal from the New to the Old Whigs (Burke),
  60, 188n. 41, 191n. 105

Archives nationales, 91, 142
  Tocqueville's study of *cahiers* collection
    at, 143, 155, 215n. 68
archives, of intendants
  Grandmaison's description of, 82, 193n. 18,
    194n. 24
  Tocqueville's study of (Paris), 58–59, 67,
    81–82, 91, 92, 95
  Tocqueville's study of (Tours), 81–87,
    91–93, 103
archives, Tocqueville's, for *Old Regime*, 10–11,
    17n. 40
Argenson, René Louis, marquis d', 209n. 123
aristocracy, Tocqueville's view of
  character of, 68, 175n. 56
  distinguished from Burke's view of, 74–75,
    192nn. 109, 114
  distinguished from Guizot's view of, 24
  English vs. French, 48, 68, 70
  See also nobility
"aristocratic" institutions, Tocqueville's
    argument for, 9, 77, 158
Aron, Raymond, 191n. 106
Assemblies of Notables (1787–88), 156
associations, civil, 1–3, 9, 158, 165 (endnote 48)
  absence of in Old Regime, 54–55, 64, 74–75,
    84, 85–86, 97

Baker, Keith, 202n. 44, 206n. 91, 209n. 123, 220n.
    38
Barante, Prosper de, 12, 17, 175n. 63
  narrative history of, 25–26
  Tocqueville's reading of, 25–27
  See also historical method
Barnave, Antoine, 154
Barrot, Odilon, 27, 133
Baudeau, Abbé Nicolas, Tocqueville's study
    of, 103–5
Beaumont, Clémentine de, 12, 122, 142, 150
Beaumont, Gustave de
  advice on citing sources, 12, 150
  as correspondent and friend, 37, 57, 58, 80,
    122, 133, 136–37, 139, 140, 143
  as editor of Tocqueville's papers, 11, 40, 135,
    151, 161, 197n. 66, 201n. 34, 218n. 24
  as source of books, 70, 81, 104
  view of French historians, 175n. 61

Belgiojoso, Princess, 172n. 14
Berlin, Isaiah, 132
Between History and Literature (Gossman), 17
Biauzat, Gaultier de, 47
Bibliothèque nationale, 82
  microfilm available at, 13
  Tocqueville's research at, 32, 142
biens d'émigrés, Tocqueville's study of, 44–45, 53,
    181n. 31
biens nationaux, in Tocqueville's questionnaire,
    44
Birette (intendant), 42
Blackstone, William, Tocqueville's study of,
    48, 65, 68, 165 (endnote 67), 182n. 45,
    200n. 11
Blanc, Louis, 24
Boesche, Roger, 131, 168n. 15
Bonaparte. *See* Louis-Napoleon Bonaparte;
    Napoleon Bonaparte
Boncerf, Pierre-François, 47, 49
Bonner, John, 190n. 99
Bossuet, Jacques-Bénigne, 217n. 93
Boulatignier, Sebastien-Joseph, 92, 105
Bourdaloue, Louis, 134–35, 211n. 21
bourgeoisie, timidity of, 23, 156, 163 (endnote
    18). *See also* Guizot, François; Third
    Estate
"bourgeois spirit," 23
Bourrienne, Louis Antoine de, 28
Bressolette, Michael, 173n. 23
Bretonneau, Pierre, 79
Brévanne (consultant for sources), 31
Brissot, Jacques Pierre, 154
brochures, revolutionary
  decentralization in, 158
  Tocqueville's study of, 153–55, 159–60
Buchez, P.-J.-B., 45, 117
Buffon, Georges Louis Leclerc, Comte de, 18
Bunsen, Charles von, 59–60
Burke, Edmund, 11–12, 13, 126, 160, 161
  described by Rémusat, 60
  influence on "Initial Outline," 66, 67, 68,
    69, 70
  Tocqueville's study of, 60–65, 67, 100, 126,
    153, 187n. 31
  Tocqueville's treatment of, in *Old Regime*,
    70–77, 136

"Burke: Sa vie et ses écrits" (Rémusat), 60

Caesar, Augustus, 97
cahiers de doléances, 12, 192nn. 109, 114
    of Amiens, 155–56
    of parishes, 218n. 22
    Prudhomme's compilation of, 114–17
        flaws in, 124–25, 128–29 (table A), 129–30
            (table B)
        of Rennes's Third Estate, 109, 128 (table A),
            203nn. 60, 61
    Tocqueville's study of
        as confirmed by modern studies, 126
        as distorted by Résumé général, 124–25
        in 1836, 107, 108–9, 202n. 49
        in 1853, 107–14
        in 1856, 215n. 68
        in 1857, 155–56, 203n. 52, 218n. 20
    Tocqueville's treatment of, in Old Regime,
        117–21, 141, 146–47
    See also Prudhomme, Louis-Marie; public
        opinion; Résumé général
capitation (head tax), Tocqueville's study of,
    54, 164 (endnotes 33, 34)
Cellini, Benvenuto, 21
Censer, Jack R., 205n. 89, 206n. 97, 220n. 57
centralization, 24, 155, 196n. 50. See also
    administrative centralization
Cervantes Saavedra, Miguel de, 7
Cessac, Jean-Gérard, Comte de, 15, 99
champarts, 43
Charles V, 26
Chartier, Roger, 179n. 120, 210n. 125
Chateaubriand, François René, Vicomte de,
    18
Chaussinand-Nogaret, Guy, 116, 126, 129–30
    (table B), 206n. 99
China, 103
chouannerie, 203n. 60
church. See clergy; religion
Cicero, 18
Circourt, Adolphe de, 186n. 23
Circourt, Madame Anastasie de, 45, 80
civilization
    and barbarism, 2, 3
    and despotism, 22
    in Dareste, 54

in Guizot's lectures, 2, 19–20, 173n. 26
Tocqueville's critique of "progress of," 22,
    23, 54, 165 (endnote 57)
Tocqueville's support for, 24
classes
    conflict of, 109, 118–19, 159
    misery of lowest, 53–54, 101
clergy
    in cahiers, 110, 120–21, 204n. 69, 207nn. 107, 108
    and liberty, 120–21
    in other sources, 163–65 (endnotes 10, 11, 12,
        45, 46, 47, 54)
    See also religion
Clermont-Tonnerre, Stanislas, Comte de,
    203n. 52
Condorcet, Marie Jean Antoine Nicolas,
    Marquis de, 154, 158, 220n. 38
Considérations sur les causes de la grandeur des Romains
    et de leur décadence (Montesquieu),
    30, 177n. 82
Constant, Benjamin, 12
    and Lezay-Marnésia, 35
    scholars' view of Tocqueville and, 178n.
        101
    Tocqueville's study of, 32–33, 35, 37, 177n. 98
    Tocqueville's treatment of, 34–35
Constituent Assembly (1789–91), 45, 88–89, 157,
    159, 160, 196n. 50
Constituent Assembly (1848), 27, 55
Consulate, 157
Convention (1792–95), 45, 199n. 78
Corcelle, Francisque de
    as correspondent and friend, 58, 70, 80, 100,
        105, 106, 126–27, 132, 133, 134, 140, 149,
        170n. 28, 177n. 94
    Tocqueville's doubts of, 127
Cordhomme, Jacques-Toussaint, 42
Cormenin, Louis Marie de la Haye, 92, 105
Correspondance (Comte de Mirabeau), 136
corvées, Tocqueville's study of, 55, 130 and
    130n (table B), 165 (endnotes 57, 58,
        59, 60, 61, 62)
cosmopolitanism, 156
"Coup d'oeil général sur l'histoire de la
    morale" (Gobineau), 172n. 14
Cours de droit administratif (Macarel), 88
Craiutu, Aurelian, 131, 168n. 16, 173n. 30, 174n. 42

culture, Tocqueville's study of, 32, 36, 159–60, 179n. 120

Daire, Eugène, 101, 103, 104
Dareste de la Chavanne, C., 12, 82
  as bibliographic source, 49, 70, 101, 104, 183n. 49, 201n. 32
  Tocqueville's study of, 48–51, 67, 100, 126–27, 183n. 49, 208n. 112
  Tocqueville's treatment of, in *Old Regime*, 54–56
  as winner of Académie prize, 48–49
  See also feudal rights
Dauphiny, 156, 219n. 27
decentralization, 196n. 50
  America as model of, 155, 170n. 35
  dangers of excess of, 24, 175n. 56
  Tocqueville's study of
    in *cahiers*, 110–11, 155
    in revolutionary brochures, 154, 158
Declaration of the Rights of Man and the Citizen (1789), 157
Deffand, Mme du, 99–100, 185n. 11
De l'administration des finances de la France (Necker), 106
De l'administration provinciale et de la réforme de l'impôt (Le Trosne), 101, 189n. 66
De la force du gouvernement actuel (Constant), 32, 33
De la monarchie prussienne sous Fréderic le Grand (Comte de Mirabeau), 158
Delisle, Léopold, on parish *cahiers*, 218n. 22
democracy
  Tocqueville's reflections in 1838 on, 7
  Tocqueville's shifting definitions of, 69, 158, 190n. 91, 191n. 106, 204nn. 69, 76, 219n. 35
Democracy in America (Tocqueville), 77, 145
  absence of fixed blueprint for, 5
  "barbarism" in, 3
  centralization in, 23–24, 88
  Drescher's view of break in, 5–6
  references to Montesquieu in, 177n. 82
  soft despotism in, 8–10, 35, 86, 96, 105
  Tocqueville's 1838 reconceptualization of, 7–10, 161

Tocqueville's historical method for, 4, 29–30
  Tocqueville's persona in, 1–2, 4
Demosthenes, 18
Des effets de la Terreur (Constant), 32, 33, 35
Des intérêts catholiques au dix-neuvième siècle (Montalembert), 58
despotism
  Burke's view of, 61
  of Caesars, 10
  of Directory, 35–36
  of European monarchs, 163 (endnote 2)
  in justice system, 90
  Montesquieu vs. Tocqueville on, 175n. 58
  of Napoleon Bonaparte, 15, 29
  as puzzle of Tocqueville's lifetime, 55
  soft or tutelary version of, 3, 6, 8–10, 23, 35, 85–86, 96–97, 105, 112, 161
Des réactions politiques (Constant), 32
Dictionnaire de droit (de Ferrière), 45
dîmes, 46, 53, 163 (endnote 10)
Directory
  Tocqueville's study of
    in Constant, 32–33
    in Lafayette, 32
  Tocqueville's treatment of, in Napoleonic chapters, 33–36
discourse. *See* language; rhetoric
Domat, Jean, 58
Draus, Franciszek, 74, 187n. 27
Drescher, Seymour, 5, 6, 40, 168n. 13, 169n. 28
Dubosc, François, 42, 181n. 20
Dufaure, Jules, 93
Duparc, Henri Charles Timoléon, Comte, 44
Dupont de Nemours, Pierre-Samuel, 104, 203n. 52
Du protestantisme et de toutes les hérésies dans leur rapport avec le socialisme (Nicolas), 58
Dupuis (alias of Prudhomme), 115
Duvergier de Hauranne, Prosper, 7, 153, 218n. 10

Economic gain. *See* peasantry
economists
  distinguished from philosophes, 208n. 112
  Tocqueville's study of, 101–6

Tocqueville's treatment of, in *Old Regime*, 122–23
1836 essay (Tocqueville), 12, 99
anonymity of, 180n. 8
audience for, 41
conceptual system of, 4
contrasts with *Old Regime*, 40–41, 47, 54
despotism in, 24, 40–41
liberty in, 41, 109
Tocqueville's study of *cahiers* for, 107, 108–9, 124, 202n. 49
Tocqueville's view of in 1856, 40
émigrés. See *biens d'émigrés*
endnotes, for *Old Regime*, 163–66
  composition of, 13, 142–43
  number of, 143, 215nn. 63, 64
  persona of archivist within, 143, 152
England, Tocqueville's study of
  feudal rights in, 48, 52
  history of (1828 letter), 19, 22, 25, 131
  local governance in, 50, 52, 103, 170n. 35
  nobility's openness in, 48, 68, 109
  old constitution in, 72–73
  progressive tax policy of, 164 (endnote 37)
  respect for rights in, 164 (endnote 39)
equality
  in *cahiers* of Amiens, 155–56
  and French Revolution, 69, 73–74, 156, 159, 165 (endnote 48)
  and liberty, 148–49
  under a master, 15 (epigram), 22, 23, 25, 36
  and philosophy, 104–5, 112, 208n. 116
  of social conditions, and democracy, 4, 5, 73–74, 104–5, 111–12, 152
Essai sur la constitution et les fonctions des assemblées provinciales (Condorcet), 158

Fauchet, Abbé Claude, 155
Fauchois, Yann, 196n. 50
February Revolution (1848), 132
feudal rights
  Tocqueville's study of
    in Dareste, 48–51
    in Fréminville, 216n. 72
    in Guizot's lectures, 19, 20
    during stay in Normandy (1852), 39 (epigram), 42–47, 163 (endnote 14)

after leaving Normandy, 47–48, 70, 81, 163–64 (endnotes 13, 41) in Renauldon, 45, 166 (endnote 77)
Tocqueville's treatment of
  in "Initial Outline," 67–68
  in *Old Regime*, 51–56, 181n. 26
Fichte, Johann Gottlieb, 18
Fielding, Henry, 18
Fiévée, Joseph, 34
Fontenelle, Bernard Le Bovier de, 7
food shortages (1772), 85, 195n. 35
foreign perspective on French Revolution
  Tocqueville's search for, 59–60
  Tocqueville's study of Burke as representative of, 61–65
  See also historical perspective
Fossall, M. (civil complainant), 197n. 64
Fox-Genovese, Elizabeth, 200n. 20, 201n. 37
France. See administrative centralization; classes; clergy; national character (French); nobility; peasantry; Old Regime; Third Estate
Fréminville, Edmé de, 216n. 72
Freslon, Pierre, 44, 45, 56, 65, 80, 81, 85, 92, 93, 101, 133, 156
Froissart, Jean, 18
Furet, François
  on feudal rights, 181n. 23
  on gestation of *Old Regime*, 37, 39, 55, 195n. 44
  on Tocqueville and Guizot, 174n. 42
  on Tocqueville and Lezay-Marnésia, 179n. 113
  on Tocqueville and Sieyès, 203n. 61
  on Tocqueville's continuity, 3
  on Tocqueville's "democratic" vocabulary, 191n. 106
  on Tocqueville's discretion, 171n. 43
  on Tocqueville's disdain for tenor of July Monarchy, 6
  on Tocqueville's view of *cahiers*, 124

Galignani's Messenger, 193n. 5, 197n. 64
Gallemand, Zacharie, 42, 44, 45
Gargan, Edward T., 27, 168n. 15
Gay, Peter, 208n. 112

German language, Tocqueville's study of, 60,
    65, 81
Germany, Tocqueville's study of
    feudal rights in, 48, 52–53, 138, 163 (endnotes
        4, 5, 6), 182n. 43
    limited venality in, 164 (endnote 42)
    local governance in, 138, 163 (endnote 3),
        170n. 35
    progress in, 165 (endnote 66)
    property ownership in, 52–53, 163
        (endnotes 7, 8), 182n. 43
    search for sources for, 59, 186n. 23
    during voyage to, 138
    Das gesamte Württembergische Privatrecht
        (Reyscher), 182n. 43
Gibbon, Edward, 161, 220n. 54
Gobineau, Arthur de, 21, 160, 172n. 14, 186n.
    23
Gossman, Lionel, 17–18, 26, 175n. 63, 179n. 125
Grandmaison, Charles de, 65, 86, 108
    on archives at Tours, 82, 193n. 18, 194n. 24
    on collaboration with Tocqueville, 82–83
    as correspondent, 98, 137
    on Tocqueville at Tours
        decision to separate *Old Regime*, 86–87
        method of composition, 212n. 33
        personal library, 211n. 20
        routine, 80
Grille, François, 117
Grote, Harriet, 59
    on conversations with Tocqueville, 81,
        106, 107, 194n. 31
    as correspondent, 87, 122
Guizot, François, 12, 17
    on administrative centralization, 23
    on commune in France, 22–23
    on feudalism, 19, 20
    on Germanic invasions, 1, 2, 19
    historical method of, 2, 19–20, 49
    as judge at Académie, 49, 182n. 46
    as minister, 27, 169–70n. 28
    philosophical history of, 20–21, 27
    as target of Tocqueville, 1–3, 11, 21–24, 35,
        56, 169n. 28
    as Tocqueville's teacher, 19–21, 27, 29, 40,
        41, 88, 126, 168n. 10
    on Third Estate, 18, 26

    on Tudors, 21–22
    See also Sorbonne, Guizot's lectures at

Hall, Captain Basil, 185n. 11
Hancock, Ralph, 174n. 49
Harvard College, 185n. 5
Haxthausen, Baron August von, 49
Hegel, Georg W. F., 18, 25
Henri IV, 54
Hereth, Michael, 216n. 73
Herr, Richard, 149, 150, 160, 195n. 44
Hervieu, Jacques-François, 42
"hic," Tocqueville's use of, 11, 50, 61, 203n.
    51
Histoire de Consulat et de l'Empire (Thiers), 28,
    29
Histoire des ducs de Bourgogne (Barante), 25, 26
L'histoire parlementaire de la Révolution (Buchez
    and Roux), 45, 207n. 105
historical method, of Restoration historians,
    17–18
historical method, Tocqueville's
    absence of fixed blueprints for, 4–5, 153
    in America, 4, 83
    assessment of sources' reliability within,
        113, 198n. 73
    blended genre of, 29–30, 136, 140
    choice of sources for, 1 (epigram), 31–32,
        153
    compartmentalization within, 31, 151–52,
        220n. 39
    conceptual blocks within, 4, 39, 69–70, 161
    configuration of components for, 4–5, 31,
        39, 157
    continuity within, 3, 157, 159
    discontinuity within, 3–4, 5, 40, 161
    emphasis on underlying causes of, 20–21,
        28, 29–30, 126, 152
    greater nuance in notes of, 63–64, 103–4,
        197n. 57
    and interlocutors, 3, 11–12, 22, 25, 57
        (epigram), 64, 101–2, 151 (epigram),
        153–54, 158, 159
    reading style within, 11, 83–84, 107–8, 125
    return to tabula rasa for, 28–31, 40, 153
    role of facts within, 1 (epigram), 20, 28, 30,
        37, 45, 140, 153

ruminations as part of, 1 (epigram), 3, 6, 7, 11, 43, 47, 55, 70, 79 (epigram), 98, 134, 152, 161, 169n. 24, 219n. 27, 220n. 39

scholars' discussions of, 168n. 15

use of oral interviews, questionnaires in, 4, 42, 44, 182n. 43

See also index; reading notes; sources; writing style

historical perspective

of Guizot, 19

of Thiers, 30, 177n. 86

Tocqueville's

at Académie française, 17

in contrast to Burke's, 63–64, 67, 68–69

memoirs as problem for, 37, 179n. 128

in "Original Idea," 30–31

as portrayed in *Old Regime*, 71, 73, 76–77

history. *See* Barante, Prosper de; Guizot, François; historical method, of Restoration historians; historical method, Tocqueville's

"History of Civilization in France" (Guizot), 2

History of England (Macaulay), 58

Hunt, Lynn, 154, 160

ideas

Tocqueville's study of

at Académie française, 16, 99

in *cahiers*, 110–12, 155–56

in Guizot's lectures, 20–21

in Le Trosne, 101–2

neglected in "Initial Outline," 100–101

in revolutionary pamphleteers, 154, 159

Tocqueville's treatment of

in 1836 essay, 99

in *Old Regime*, 122–24

See also language; "men of letters"; public opinion

index, Tocqueville's use of

for Napoleonic chapters, 34

for *Old Regime*, vol. 1, 4, 139–40, 157, 197n. 64, 213n. 42, 213n. 43, 214n. 50

for *Old Regime*, vol. 2, 156–57, 219n. 27

See also writing style

individualism, collective, 119

"individualism," Tocqueville's coining of word, 8, 9, 170nn. 30, 35

"Initial Outline" (Tocqueville, June 26, 1853), 65–70, 71–76 passim, 81, 100–101, 127, 135, 148, 200n. 11

intendants. *See* archives, of intendants

interlocutors. *See* historical method, Tocqueville's

irreligion, 62, 70, 100, 123. *See also* religion

Isambert, François André, 93, 198n. 73

Jacobins, Burke's view of, 64, 76

Jardin, André, 171n. 6, 176n. 78, 180n. 17, 195n. 44, 200n. 23, 201n. 34, 218n. 24

July Monarchy

and barbarism, 2

Tocqueville's critique of electoral system within, 171n. 3

Tocqueville's view of, 6, 10, 27, 168n. 17

Kahan, Alan, 220n. 46

Kant, Emmanuel, 18

Kelly, George Armstrong, 178n. 101

Kempis, Thomas à, 7

Kergorlay, Louis

advice to Tocqueville

on study of peasant landownership, 42–43, 45, 46

on writing style, 133–34, 211n. 16, 212n. 30

as correspondent and friend, 7, 150, 151, 157

on liberty in *Old Regime*, 148

and Sorrento letter, 28–30, 37, 150, 219n. 27

Kölnische Zeitung, 193n. 5

Koran, 7, 170n. 36

Lafayette, Marquis de, 32, 34, 37

Lamartine, Alphonse de, 24

Lamberti, Jean-Claude, 5–6, 77, 169n. 28, 170n. 34, 178n. 101

Lamberville, Charles de, 49, 183n. 53

language, Tocqueville's study of, 20, 36, 69, 154–55, 160, 164 (endnote 26), 166 (endnote 71)

Languedoc, 77, 95–96, 98, 147

La Rive, Auguste de, 132

La Rivière, Pierre-Paul Mercier de, 103, 105

Laurentie, Pierre-Sébastien, 150

Lavergne, Léonce de, 93
laws, 20–21, 34–35, 126. *See also* administrative
    law; legists
Lefebvre, Georges, 203n. 61
legists, 92
    Tocqueville's study of
        in economists, 105–6
        in Guizot's lectures, 23
        in intendants' files (Tours), 92
        in Macarel, 88–91
    Tocqueville's treatment of
        in advice to nephew, 198n. 74
        in *Democracy*, 23–24
        in 1836 essay, 24
        in *Old Regime*, 95
Le Peletier d'Aunay, Félix, 31, 32, 42
Lerner, Ralph, 216nn. 73, 74
Le Trosne, Guillaume-François, 47, 49, 100
    Tocqueville's study of, 101–2, 105, 106, 153
        timing of, 189n. 66, 200n. 11
    Tocqueville's treatment of, in *Old Regime*,
        119, 123
"Letters on a Regicide Peace" (Burke), 60, 61,
        64, 71
Lewis, Sir George, 150
Lezay-Marnésia, Adrien de, 35, 179n. 113
liberty
    absence of, as cause of Revolution, 35, 55,
        64, 69, 74, 76, 85, 86, 90, 93, 106, 111, 119,
        122, 123, 146, 148, 164 (endnote 20),
        199n. 78
    in America, 155, 170n. 35
    and aristocracy, 68, 175n. 56
    and church, 207n. 108
    crushed by Louis-Napoleon, 31, 132
    in England, 50, 170n. 35
    presence of, in Old Regime, 96, 119–21
    presence of, in Revolution, 90, 157–58
    relation between local and national, 24,
        132, 164 (endnote 31)
    as Tocqueville's chief goal, 24, 27, 68, 82,
        131–33, 148, 150, 161, 171n. 3
    Tocqueville's definition of, 15, 24, 86, 97,
        131–33, 147–48, 160–61, 165 (endnote
        50), 216n. 79
    Tocqueville's harm to, in eyes of some
        scholars, 160

Tocqueville's indexing to needs of era,
        131–33, 158
    and Tocqueville's "liberty test," 25
    vs. Barante, 27
    vs. Burke, 57 (epigram), 64, 77
    vs. Constant, 33
    vs. Dareste, 56
    vs. economists, 102–3
    vs. French historians, 24
    vs. Guizot, 24, 174n. 12
    vs. Hegel, 25
    vs. Lingard, 25
    vs. Macarel, 90
    vs. Martin, 25
    vs. Plato, 25
    vs. Voltaire, 25, 209n. 117
    Tocqueville's treatment of
        in *Democracy*, 9
        in 1836 essay, 41, 109
        in *Old Regime*, vol. 1, 95–96, 117, 119–21,
            145–50
        in *Old Regime*, vol. 2, 156, 158, 159, 161
    See also clergy; nobility
Lingard, John, 25
Lippitt, Francis, 194n. 22
Loménie, Louis de, 144, 148, 201n. 34, 215n. 70,
        216n. 81
London and Westminster Review (Mill), 107
London Times, 31
Louis XIV, 21, 88
Louis XV, 92, 102
Louis XVI, 74
    administrative reforms of (1787–88), 59, 67,
        82, 91, 95
Louis-Napoleon Bonaparte, despotism of, 4,
        27, 31, 36, 80, 97–98, 132, 133, 152

Macarel, Louis-Antoine, 12
    Tocqueville's report on *Cours de droit
        administratif*, 88–90
    Tocqueville's view of, 92, 93, 105–6
Macaulay, Thomas Babington, 48, 58, 70, 190n.
        97
Machiavelli, Niccolò, 7, 170n. 36
Mackintosh, Sir James, 60, 187n. 30
Maissemi (police informant), 115
Maistre, Joseph de, 66, 190n. 81

Malesherbes, Chrétien-Guillaume de
     Lamoignon de, 88
Mallet du Pan, Jacques, 34, 37, 66, 190n. 81
Mansfield, Harvey, 168n. 15, 175n. 58
Marcel, R. Pierre, 178n. 101
Markoff, John, 112, 130n, 207n. 102, 209n. 122,
     210n. 125, 210n. 126
Martin, Henri, 25, 175n. 61
Marxists, revolutionary interpretation of, 161
*Maximes générales du gouvernement économique d'un
     royaume agricole* (Quesnay), 102
maximum (price controls), 85
Mélonio, Françoise, 161, 197n. 66, 200n. 23, 203n.
     61
     on gestation of *Old Regime*, 186n. 24, 195n.
          44, 197n. 54, 218n. 24
     on Tocqueville's "eccentric" liberalism,
          131
     on Tocqueville's method, 168n. 15, 194n. 32
Mémoires (Mallet du Pan), 37
Mémoires au Roi (Comte de Mirabeau), 191n. 102
*Mémoires, correspondance et manuscrits publiés par sa
     famille* (Lafayette), 32, 177n. 94
Mémoires relatifs à l'histoire de France (Guizot), 19,
     25, 172n. 21
*Mémoires sur Napoléon, le Directoire, le
     Consulat, l'Empire et la Restauration*
     (Bourrienne), 28
memoirs, as sources for Tocqueville, 31–32, 34,
     37, 47. *See also* historical perspective;
     sources
"men of '89," 119, 147
"men of letters," 101–2, 122–23, 165 (endnote 63)
     naïveté of, 125
     Prudhomme's society of, 114, 202n. 48
     See also ideas; public opinion
Mézières, Laurent de, 115
Michel Lévy publishers, 142
Michelet, Jules, 24, 182n. 46
Mignet, Auguste, 24, 31, 182n. 46
Mill, John Stuart, 21, 107, 122
Mirabeau, Honoré-Gabriel Riqueti, Comte
     de, 46, 66, 72, 136, 158, 191n. 102
Mirabeau, Victor Riqueti, Marquis de, 49, 100,
     105–6, 154
     Tocqueville's study of, 104–5, 201n. 37
Mitchell, Harvey, 218n. 19

Le Mois, 179n. 120
Molé, Louis-Mathieu, Comte de, 16, 27, 31–32,
     170n. 28, 177n. 92, 189n. 74
Mollien, François Nicolas, Comte de, 106
Monnard, Charles, 185n. 11
Montaigne, Michel Equem de, 28
Montalembert, Charles de, 58, 153
Montesquieu, Charles-Louis de Secondat,
     Baron de, 173n. 26, 217n. 93
     and Tocqueville, 18, 24, 30, 173n. 23, 175n. 58
mores
     Tocqueville's statement on
          at Académie française, 16, 99
          in Chamber, 171n. 3
     Tocqueville's study of
          in *cahiers*, 110–12
          in economists, 99 (epigram), 104, 105,
               106
          in Guizot's lectures, 20–21
          in Necker, 127
          in revolutionary brochures, 154, 159
     Tocqueville's treatment of
          in Napoleonic chapters, 33–35
          in *Old Regime*, vol. 1, 117–19, 145
Morlot, Cardinal, 80
Mounier, Jean Joseph, 154
Muhammad, 7, 170n. 36

Napoleon Bonaparte, Tocqueville's view of
     at Académie française, 15–16
     on administration centralization of,
          88–90, 92
     in choice of sources for study of, 31–32
     as focus beyond *Old Regime*, vol. 1, 38, 55, 65,
          87, 157, 189n. 74, 196n. 45
     and Lafayette, 32
     in Napoleonic chapters, 33–36
     in Thiers's *Histoire de Consulat et de l'Empire*,
          28
     as topic for Tocqueville's book at
          Sorrento, 29–31
Napoleonic chapters (Tocqueville, 1852), 11,
     12, 33–37, 42, 178n. 104, 180n. 17, 190n.
     94
Napoleon III. *See* Louis-Napoleon Bonaparte
National Assembly (1789–91). *See* Constituent
     Assembly

national character (French), 32, 36, 123, 216n. 80
  Tocqueville's view of
    and "manly virtues," 121–22, 145, 148,
      156, 158
    and "French fury," 69–70, 75–76, 159
Naudet, Joseph, 182n. 46
Necker, Jacques, 47, 52–53, 119
  Tocqueville's study of, 106, 127, 202n. 44
Nicolaï (travel writer), 185n. 11
Nicolas, Jean-Jacques-Auguste, 58, 186n. 13
Night of August 4 (1789), 157
Nisbet, Robert, 168n. 15
nobility
  absenteeism of, 48, 50–51, 54, 55, 64, 165
    (endnote 52)
  and clergy, 109
  isolation of, 20
  and liberty, 110, 119–20, 158, 164 (endnote 44)
  privileges of, 164–65 (endnotes 32, 33, 34, 35,
    36, 38, 53)
  and Third, 20, 107, 109, 126
  See also aristocracy
Nolla, Eduardo, 3, 169n. 24
"Notice sur Alexis de Tocqueville"
    (Beaumont), 161

Oberkirch, Mme la Baronne d', 193n. 12
Oelschner (German professor), 182n. 43
Oelsner, Charles, 185n. 11
Oeuvres complètes (Turgot), 100
Old Regime
  absenteeism of nobility in, 48, 50–51, 54, 55,
    64, 165 (endnote 52)
  church in, 207n. 108. See also clergy
  evocations in, 84, 90, 91–92
  extant feudal rights in. See feudal rights
  failure to start gazette in, 85–86
  interaction with citizens of, 84
  liberty in, 96, 119–21
  new taxes in, 165 (endnote 51)
  overlapping administration in, 166
    (endnote 69)
  peasantry in (see peasantry)
The Old Regime and the Revolution (Tocqueville)
  archives for, 10–11
  as book on administrative law, 91
  and 1836 essay, 40–41

flaw in, 124–25
key topics in
  administrative centralization, 93–98
  Burke, 70–76
  feudal rights, 51–55
  liberty, 145–49
  opinion, 117–26
sales of, 150
several books within, 11
as success story, 161–62
target audience for, 132–33
Tocqueville's making of (chronological)
  earliest view of, 16
  "Original Idea" and plans at Sorrento
    for, 28–31
  writing of Napoleonic chapters for,
    31–38
  "Initial Outline" for, 65–70
  decision to write as separate volume,
    86–87
  first draft for (Tours), 135–38, 208n. 115
  second draft for (Compiègne), 139–40
  index for, 139
  revisions for (Tocqueville), 140–41
  construction of persona for, 141–44
  choice of title for, 142
  publication of, 153
  research for vol. 2 of, 153–56
  writing of vol. 2, book 1, of, 156
  plans for vol. 2, book 2, of, 156–59
  See also archives, Tocqueville's; historical
    method; reading notes; sources;
    writing style
"Original Idea" (Tocqueville, 1850–51), 30–31,
  176n. 78
Ozouf, Mona, 179n. 128, 201n. 40

Paine, Thomas, 187n. 30
Palmer, R. R., 176n. 78
Paris, as cause of Revolution, 94–95, 199n. 77
parish. See township
parlements, Tocqueville's study of, 92–93, 155,
  164–65 (endnotes 43, 49), 198nn. 70,
  73
Pasquier, Chancellor, 31
pays d'état. See Languedoc
peasantry

in Second Republic, 55
Tocqueville's study of
  economic gain during Revolution,
    42–47
  fury of, 46–47, 50–51, 53, 67–68, 163
    (endnote 13)
  landownership, 43–45, 52, 56, 57, 163
    (endnote 9)
  rising expectations, 46–47, 51, 101, 166
    (endnote 74)
  rural unrest, 160, 165 (endnote 64)
Tocqueville's treatment of
  in 1836 essay, 41
  in *Old Regime*, 51–55
  See also clergy; nobility; Third Estate
Penhoën, Barchou de, 21
Péréfix, 54, 184n. 70
persona, of Tocqueville
  in *Democracy*, vol. 1, 1, 4
  in *Democracy*, vol. 2, 2–3
  in *Old Regime*, 4, 13, 141–44, 146, 150, 213n. 48
  See also *The Old Regime and the Revolution*;
    writing style
Péthion, de Villeneuve, Jérôme, 154
Petiton (Tocqueville collaborator), 199n. 77
Philip the Fair (Philip IV), 23, 24, 88
Physiocrates (ed. Daire), 101, 103
physiocrats. *See* economists
Pierson, George, 168nn. 12, 15
Plato, 7, 25, 170n. 36
Plutarch, 7, 170n. 36
"Political and Social Condition of France:
    First Article" (Tocqueville). *See*
    1836 essay
Pouthas, Charles, 174n. 42
"principles of 1789," 24, 122
  as flagging device in *Old Regime*, vol. 2,
    157–58, 159
property ownership, of peasants before the
    Revolution
Tocqueville's study of
  effect of sales of *biens d'émigrés* on,
    44–45
  Kergorlay's suggested model for, 43
  questionnaire for, 44
  at Réville, 44, 181n. 28
Tocqueville's treatment of

in 1836 essay, 41
in *Old Regime*, 52–53, 56
property records (*états de section*)
  Tocqueville's study of, 42, 44, 181n. 28
  Tocqueville's treatment of, in *Old Regime*,
    181n. 29, 213n. 48
provincial assemblies, Tocqueville's study of
  during administrative reforms of 1787–88,
    59, 67, 82, 95
  in Burke, 77
  in Condorcet, 158
  in economists, 101–2
  and Terror, 199n. 78
  of Upper Guyenne, 163–65 (endnotes 16,
    26, 46)
Prudhomme, Louis-Marie, 12, 107, 125
  as owner of *Révolutions de Paris*, 205n. 90
  professed impartiality of, 115, 206nn. 96, 97
  and *Résumé général*, 114–17
  as revolutionary pamphleteer, 205n. 89
  revolutionary rhetoric of, 206n. 91
  view of self as modern-day Aeneas, 124,
    209n. 119
  See also *Résumé général*
public opinion, 13
Tocqueville's study of
  in Barante, 26
  in *cahiers*, 107–12, 155
  in Constant, 34
  in economists, 101–6
  in Le Trosne, Mollier, Necker, 106
  in revolutionary brochures, 159
Tocqueville's treatment of
  in *Democracy*, 9
  in 1836 essay, 41
  in Napoleonic chapters, 34–36
  in *Old Regime*, vol. 1, 117–26
public opinion, enlightened, 9, 108, 109, 112, 118,
    155, 159

Quéffelec, Lise, 186n. 24
Quesnay, François, 47, 49, 100, 200n. 20
  and Marquis de Mirabeau, 201n. 37
  Tocqueville's study of, 102–3, 105
Quintilian, 18, 26

Rabaut Saint-Etienne, Jean Paul, 154

Rabelais, 7
reading notes, Tocqueville's, for *Old Regime*
   on agricultural societies, 52, 54, 85, 164
      (endnotes 30, 40)
   on Baudeau, 103–5
   on Biauzat, 47
   on *biens d'émigrés*, 44–45, 53, 181n. 31
   on Blackstone, 48, 65, 68, 165 (endnote 67),
      182n. 45, 200n. 11
   on Boncerf, 47, 49
   on Burke, 60–65, 67, 100, 126, 153, 187n. 31
   on *cahiers* at Archives nationales (1856),
      215n. 68
   on *cahiers* at Archives nationales (1857),
      155–56, 203n. 52, 218n. 20
   on *cahiers* in *Résumé général* (1836), 107, 108–9,
      202n. 49
   on *cahiers* in *Résumé général* (1853), 107–14
   on Condorcet, 154, 158, 220n. 38
   on Constant, 32–33, 35, 37, 177n. 98
   on Dareste, 48–51, 67, 100, 126–27, 183n. 49,
      208n. 112
   on d'Argenson, 209n. 123
   on *Dictionnaire de droit*, 45
   on Dupont de Nemours, 104, 203n. 52
   on economists, 101–6
   on Fiévée, 34, 178n. 107
   on Fréminville, 216n. 72
   on *Galignani's Messenger*, 193n. 5, 197n. 64
   on Germany, 138, 182n. 43, 163–65 (endnotes
      1, 3–8, 42, 66)
   on Haxthausen, 49
   on intendants' files (Paris), 58–59, 67, 81–82,
      91, 92, 95, 163–66 (endnotes 17, 21, 49,
      68, 75, 76)
   on intendants' files (Tours), 81–87, 91–93,
      103, 163–66 (endnotes 10, 11, 13, 15, 19,
      23, 25, 27, 30, 34, 36, 38, 40, 41, 45, 52–58,
      60, 62, 64, 70, 72, 73)
   on Lafayette, 32, 34
   on Languedoc, 96
   on La Rivière, 103
   on Le Trosne, 47, 101–2, 105, 106, 123, 186n. 66,
      200n. 11
   on Macarel, 88–90, 197n. 57
   on Macaulay, 48
   on Mallet du Pan, 34, 37, 178n. 107

   on Mirabeau (Comte de), 66, 72, 136, 158,
      191n. 102, 220n. 39
   on Mirabeau (Marquis de), 104–5, 201n. 37
   on Mollien, 106
   on Necker, 47, 106, 127, 202n. 44
   on ordinances of kings of France, 195n. 42
   on property ownership of peasants, 42,
      43–45
   on Quesnay, 47, 102–3, 105
   on Renauldon, 45, 166 (endnote 77)
   on revolutionary brochures, 153–55, 159–60
   on revolutionary debates and Committee
      reports, 45–46
   on revolutionary decrees, 45
   on Reyscher, 182n. 43
   on seigneurial rents, 43, 164 (endnote 29)
   on Sieyès, 46, 53, 154, 155, 182n. 38
   on Thibaudeau, 34, 178n. 107
   on Turgot, 47, 82, 91, 92, 100, 105, 163–66
      (endnotes 9, 22, 29, 32, 33, 35, 48, 59,
      61, 71, 74)
   on Voltaire, 123, 209n. 117
   on Young, 47, 66, 164 (endnote 37), 184n. 67
   See also archives, Tocqueville's; historical
      method; sources
Recueil général des anciennes lois françaises
   (Isambert), 93, 198n. 73
Reeve, Henry, 7, 142–43, 190n. 99
Reflections on the Revolution in France (Burke), 60, 61
religion, 133, 151, 217n. 3
   political utility of, 165 (endnote 65)
   propagandism of, 61–62, 72, 191n. 104
   Tocqueville's study of, in *cahiers*, 110,
      120–21, 156, 204n. 69, 207nn. 107, 108
   Tocqueville's treatment of, in *Old Regime*,
      72, 120–21, 122, 147, 191n. 104
   See also clergy; irreligion
"Remarks on the Policy of the Allies"
   (Burke), 192n. 111
Rémusat, Charles, 60, 61, 186n. 26, 189n. 74
Renauldon, Joseph, 42, 45, 46, 166 (endnote 77)
Résumé général (Prudhomme)
   compiling of, 115
   complete citation for, 202n. 48
   distortion of, 116, 128–29 (table A), 129–30
      (table B)
   effect on *Old Regime* of distortion of, 124–26

epigram for, 209n. 119
fate of, 116–17
number tables of, 112–13, 120, 121
police orders to seize, 115
"Prospectus" for, 114–15
sample entry in, 205n. 84
scope of, 115–16
Shapiro and Markoff's view of, 203n. 52,
   207n. 102
Tocqueville's confidence in, 107
Tocqueville's description of, in *Old Regime*,
   143–44
Tocqueville's reading method for, 107–9,
   113–14
Tocqueville's testing of at Archives
   nationales, 215n. 68
See also *cahiers de doléances*; Prudhomme,
   Louis-Marie
"revolutionary spirit," Tocqueville's view
   of, 5, 6, 85, 103, 106, 110, 155, 156, 166
   (endnote 72), 195n. 33
Revolution of 1688 (England), 22
Revolution of 1789 (France)
   continuity of, 39, 92, 124
   discontinuity of, 39, 88–90, 124
   Tocqueville's study of, 153–59
      in Burke, 61–65
      in revolutionary decrees, Committee
         reports, debates, 45–46
   Tocqueville's view of
      fundamental causes of, 62, 69, 72–73,
         100–101
      generosity of, 149
      illusion in, 46, 67–69
      potency of, 16, 34, 63, 89–90
revolutions, religious. *See* religion
Reyscher, Ludwig von, 182n. 43
rhetoric, 160, 206n. 91, 216n. 73
   Tocqueville's use of, 77, 144, 145–49, 156, 158
   See also language
Richardson, Samuel, 18
Richomme, Charles, 32
Richter, Melvin, 173n. 23, 197n. 54
riposte, Tocqueville's use of. *See* historical
   method, and interlocutors;
   liberty, and Tocqueville's "liberty test"
Rivet, Jean-Charles, 80, 93

Robespierre, Maximilien, 18
Roederer, Pierre Louis, 154
Rome, Roman Empire
   and clergy, 121
   and Corcelle, 127
   in Guizot's lectures, 1, 19, 20
   in Montesquieu's *Considérations*, 30, 177n. 82
   Tocqueville's view of despotism in, 55, 158
   Tocqueville's view of Roman law of, 163
      (endnote 1)
Rosanvallon, Pierre, 191n. 106
Rousseau, Jean-Jacques, 18, 54, 159, 173n. 23
Roux, P. C., 45, 117

Sainte-Beuve, Charles-Augustin, 24, 28, 40
Saint-Evremond, 7
Saint Louis (French king), 54
Saint Paul, 7
Say, J.-B., 104
Schelling, Friedrich Wilhelm Joseph von, 104
Scherer, Edouard, 174n. 42
Schiller, Friedrich von, 21
Schleifer, James, 3, 168n. 16, 169n. 24, 170n. 30
Scott, Sir Walter, 18
Second Republic, Tocqueville's hopes for,
   27–28, 55
Sedgwick, Theodore, 80
Sedgwick, Theodore, III, 194n. 22
seigneurial rents, 43, 164 (endnote 29)
Senior, Minnie, 40
Senior, Nassau W.
   conversations with Beaumont, 135, 151
   conversations with Tocqueville, 28, 29,
      30
   as source for Tocqueville, 70, 81
Sévigné, Madame de, 18
Shapiro, Gilbert, 112, 130n, 207n. 102, 210n.
   125
Siedentop, Larry, 40, 131, 172n. 16, 174n. 42
Sieyès, Emmanuel Joseph, 109, 160, 203n. 61
   Tocqueville's study of, 46, 53, 154, 155, 182n.
      38
Smith, Adam, 184n. 59
Sorbonne, Guizot's lectures at, 2, 18–19, 49,
   126, 167n. 4, 172n. 19
Sorrento, Tocqueville's sojourn at, 12, 28–31,
   39, 136, 140, 150, 152

sources, Tocqueville's
　absence of citations to, in *Old Regime*, 12, 32,
　　150
　as art, in *Old Regime*, 144
　exaggeration of, in *Old Regime*, 143–44, 150,
　　216n. 72
　oral, 4, 31, 42, 182n. 43
　use of questionnaires, 43, 44, 182n. 43
　written
　　distinction between for *Old Regime*,
　　　vols. 1 and 2, 10–11, 13, 153
　　initial lists of, 31–32
　　search for novelty of, 37, 38, 82, 108, 152,
　　　153
　as voices from Old Regime, 87, 145–46
　See also archives, Tocqueville's; historical
　　method; reading notes
Souvenirs (Tocqueville), 27, 28
Sparks, Jared, 185n. 5
"Speech on the Army Estimates" (Burke), 61,
　71
Stoffels, Alexis, 120–21, 143, 207n. 106
Stoffels, Charles, 6, 23
Stoffels, Eugène, 24, 42, 151, 207n. 106

table A (*cahiers* distribution in *Résumé général*),
　116, 128–29
table B (inflated number counts in *Résumé
　général*), 116, 124, 129–30
tabula rasa, 27–31, 102, 152
taille, Tocqueville's study of, 54–55, 165
　(endnotes 55, 56)
Taylor, George V., 112, 204n. 62
Terror, the, 179n. 128
　Tocqueville's study of
　　in Constant, 32, 33, 35
　　in Mallet du Pan, 37
　　for *Old Regime*, vol. 2, 176n. 78
　Tocqueville's treatment of
　　in Napoleonic chapters, 34, 35
　　in *Old Regime*, 199n. 78
Thibaudeau, Antoine, 34, 177n. 92
Thierry, Augustin, 24, 172n. 9, 174n. 42, 179n.
　125, 182n. 46
Thiers, Adolphe, 21, 24, 27, 31, 182n. 46

historical perspective of, 30, 177n. 86
Tocqueville's view of *Histoire de Consulat et
　de l'Empire*, 28, 29, 30
Third Estate
　in Barante, 26
　in Guizot's lectures, 18, 20, 22, 26, 41
　Tocqueville's study of, in *cahiers*, 107, 109,
　　110, 111, 112, 126
　Tocqueville's treatment of
　　in 1836 essay, 107, 202n. 49
　　in *Old Regime*, vol. 1, 118–19, 121, 125
　　in *Old Regime*, vol. 2, 155, 156, 159
"Thoughts on French Affairs" (Burke), 64
Tilly, Charles, 203n. 52
Tocqueville, Alexis de
　at Académie française, 15–16
　aversion to philosophical and religious
　　topics, 151
　camaradie with friends, 80
　and compartmentalization, 151–52
　daily routine at Tours, 80–81
　decision to move to Tours, 57, 186n. 22
　as deputy, 16, 17, 27, 31, 171n. 3, 196n. 48
　desire for glory, 7, 10, 134, 150, 169n. 20
　determination to do duty, 152
　discretion, 12, 171n. 43, 212n. 33
　early readings, 18, 173n. 23
　electoral defeat (1837), 6
　as foreign minister, 27, 132
　foreign travels, 4, 5, 132, 138, 170n. 35
　as hiker, 29, 79, 152
　ill health, 47, 57–58, 79–80, 140, 185n. 5
　independence, 27
　legal training, 87–88
　and library at Tours, 134–35
　as member of conseil général of Manche,
　　132
　and romantics, 18
　as "seigneur" of Tocqueville, 43
　See also historical method; historical
　　perspective, Tocqueville's; *The Old
　　Regime and the Revolution*; persona;
　　reading notes; writing style
Tocqueville, Edouard de (brother), 80, 196n.
　45

Tocqueville, Hervé de (father), 18, 80, 153
Tocqueville, Hubert de (nephew), 12, 93, 137,
    185n. 11, 196n. 45
Tocqueville, Madame de (wife), 57, 87, 157,
    201n. 34
Tocqueville and the French (Mélonio), 161
Tocqueville and the Old Regime (Herr), 149
Tocqueville and the Two Democracies (Lamberti),
    5
Tocqueville between Two Worlds (Wolin), 149
"Tocqueville's Two *Démocraties*" (Drescher),
    5
Tocquevillian studies
    Constant-Tocqueville relationship in,
        178n. 101
    "doubles" within, 40
    "two *Democracies*" debate in, 5, 168n. 15
    view of continuity in, 3
    view of historical method in, 168n. 15
    view of Tocqueville as "deductive genius"
        in, 40
    view of Tocqueville's harm to liberty in,
        160
Tournon, Antoine, 205n. 90
township, Tocqueville's studies of, 9–10, 97,
    155, 164 (endnotes 24, 28), 170n. 35,
    199n. 81
Traité des lois (Domat), 58
Traité historique et pratique des droits seigneuriaux
    (Renauldon), 45
Tudor regime, Tocqueville's critique of,
    21–22, 55
Turgot, Anne Robert, 7, 47, 55, 70, 102
    Tocqueville's study of, 82, 91, 92, 100, 101,
        105–6, 163–65 (endnotes 9, 22, 29, 32,
        33, 35, 61, 71)
    Tocqueville's treatment of, in *Old Regime*,
        52–53, 119

Vico, Giambattista, 18, 172n. 14
violence
    as conceptual block for Tocqueville,
        69–70, 81, 159
    Tocqueville's study of, in Revolution, 51,
        69–70, 75–76, 85, 148, 159, 190n. 91

Tocqueville's study of, in revolutionary
    language, 155
    See also national character (French)
Virgil, 209n. 119
Vivien, Alexandre François, 105
Voltaire, François-Marie-Arouet, 7, 18, 173n. 26
    as model for Tocqueville's writing style,
        134
    Tocqueville's antipathy toward, 25, 122,
        123, 209n. 117

Walpole, Horace, 99–100, 185n. 11
Walter (German professor), 182n. 43
Weitman, Sasha, 116, 206n. 99, 210n. 125, 215n.
    68
Winthrop, Delba, 168n. 15, 175n. 58
Wolin, Sheldon, 149, 150, 160
Writing style, Tocqueville's, in *Old Regime*
    Beaumonts' review of, 142, 214n. 62
    composition of parts of book within
        for instruction, 96, 131 (epigram), 147,
        148
        as painting, 29, 65, 138, 149
        as woven cloth, 29, 30
    evolution of, 133–41
    Grandmaison's view of, 212n. 33
    imagery
        of archive, 18, 141–42, 143, 144, 146, 150
        of corpses, tombs, 18, 71, 75, 77, 145–46,
        148, 153
        mirroring of Burke, 71, 75, 77
        of veils, 12, 20, 71, 145–46, 150
    index, 139–40, 219n. 27
    Kergorlay's advice on, 133–34, 211n. 16, 212n.
        30
    models for
        Bourdaloue, 134–35
        Gibbon, 220n. 54
        great French masters, 134, 151
        Macaulay, 58
        Voltaire, 134
    need to be compact and precise, 134, 135,
        150, 211n. 23
    need to be "spontaneous," 134, 136
    need to find "necessary word," 135

Writing style (*continued*)
    need to integrate facts and ideas, 29,
        136–38, 139–40, 212n. 30, 213n. 48
    need to please, 134, 135, 150, 216n. 80
    persona, 141–44
    rewrites, 135, 214n. 58
    See also index; persona

Young, Arthur
    Tocqueville's study of, 47, 66, 164 (endnote
        37), 184n. 67
    Tocqueville's treatment of, in *Old Regime*,
        53, 119, 213n. 48

Zetterbaum, Marvin, 168n. 15